James H. Graff, Francis Claudius Armstrong

Perils by Sea and by Land or the Neapolitan Commander

James H. Graff, Francis Claudius Armstrong

Perils by Sea and by Land or the Neapolitan Commander

ISBN/EAN: 9783337812584

Printed in Europe, USA, Canada, Australia, Japan

Cover: Foto ©Thomas Meinert / pixelio.de

More available books at **www.hansebooks.com**

PERILS BY SEA AND BY LAND;

OR,

THE NEAPOLITAN COMMANDER.

BY

CAPT. C. F. ARMSTRONG,

AUTHOR OF "THE SAILOR HERO," "THE CRUISE OF THE DARING,"
"THE PIRATES OF THE FOAM," ETC. ETC.

————————

LONDON:

WARD, LOCK, & TYLER, 158, FLEET STREET,

AND 107, DORSET STREET, SALISBURY SQUARE.

PERILS BY SEA AND BY LAND.

CHAPTER I.

GENOA, once the stronghold of a bold untameable democracy, insolent as brave, and licentious as free, at the period of our story still held its place as a great commercial city, though its proud and haughty republic no longer existed. Time was when kingdoms were her subject provinces, and the spoils of the East served as dowries for her daughters; but in the year 18— her glory only existed in her monuments of extinguished greatness, betraying weakness under the shadow of names once so mighty.

Our story opens during the blockade of Genoa by sea and land—Massena, the most able and most amiable of Napoleon's generals, held the city with an insignificant force, in defiance of Austria, by land; whilst England's fleet, under Lord Keith, threatened the harbour and city, and blockaded the port.

Amongst the ships and vessels forming the blockade were several Neapolitan gun and mortar boats, and two fine brigs. These latter carried eighteen guns each, and were remarkable for the beauty of their construction, their great speed, and the gallantry of their commanders. One of them in particular attracted universal attention; the commander being a very young man, not more than four and twenty, who, though from his early youth in the Neapolitan service, was in reality a subject of his Britannic Majesty.

Captain De Courcy, who commanded the Vesuvius, was known to be a most especial favourite of the King and Queen of Naples, and the *protégé* of their prime minister, Acton. The Stromboli, the other Neapolitan brig, was commanded by a Sicilian, named Septimo. The two commanders were bosom friends, having served several years together in the same ship. Captain Septimo was, however, some six years Captain De Courcy's senior.

It was the month of May, and old Genoa still held out, though her defenders and her population were almost in a

B 2

state of starvation. The two gun brigs had just returned from a cruise to Servona, that town having recently surrendered. The day after their rejoining the squadron, the Vesuvius, having received instructions, got under weigh, and to the surprise of many in the fleet, who were watching her movements, stood with a fine leading breeze right into the noble harbour of Genoa. All conjectured that she was sent upon a somewhat hazardous exploit; and it was soon known that she had been ordered, if possible, to discover the exact position of the famous and audacious galley, the Prima; but, at the same time, cautioned not to incur unnecessary risk in carrying out her instructions.

The Vesuvius, to the admiration of all, accomplished her task in a most gallant and singularly fortunate manner— under a heavy fire—whilst attacked at the same time by two galleys full of men, one of which she dismasted, the other she sank—returning to her anchorage with only four men wounded.

Having reported the result of his cruise, Captain De Courcy returned to his brig, which was anchored close beside the Stromboli. In the evening he went on board that vessel to sup with his friend Septimo.

" I say, friend Hugh," said Captain Septimo to his guest, as they enjoyed their wine, "that last tack of yours was a somewhat mad act in the face of such a fire as you sustained. Any one but yourself would have been blown to pieces—and yet, strange to say, I hear you have not one man killed!"

"Not one, thank God!" returned De Courcy; "I certainly rather transgressed orders; but without that last tack, I could not positively have ascertained the exact position of that magnificent galley the admiral is so anxious to cut out ; but I am now satisfied, and so is he, that the thing is to be done. She's a perfect beauty—pulls fifty-two oars, has no end of swivels, besides two tremendous long brass guns, thirty-six pounders, so we shall have a glorious exploit to perform."

"Just the thing to please you, Hugh," returned Captain Septimo, with a shrug of his shoulders, '· you have all the chivalry of the olden time in you; Per miu fede, you do not bear the name of De Courcy, without inheriting the gallantry attached to it."

"And yet, amico," returned our hero, "how do I know that I have any real right to that name ?"

" I have several times heard you hint at something of the kind," said the Sicilian, " and as often you have promised to relate the early passages of your young life, but unfortunately something has turned up to prevent you. Now we have three or four hours to ourselves—who knows what to-morrow may bring?—and you know I am curious."

"You are right, old friend," returned Hugh De Courcy, "so here goes for a short yarn of my juvenile days; when it is spun out, you will be just as wise as myself.

"I fancy I must have been four or five years old when my recollection of persons and things awoke in me; nevertheless my memory is not very vivid respecting that period, and some scenes and events are rather obscure. One thing I remember remarkably well, and that is the house I then dwelt in—it was an immense, queer, grim old mansion—with innumerable rooms, halls, and chambers; without a particle of furniture in them, excepting in the one Dame Betty and I occupied—I never heard that the old woman had any other name. Every pane of glass in the mansion had been smashed to pieces, and daylight came in through the roof in many places. Young as I was, I gloried in rambling through those deserted, furnitureless rooms, and frequently lost myself; and when old Betty at last found me, she always commenced shaking the life out of me, and then kissing it back.

"The windows of this gloomy old mansion looked out over as wild and dreary a tract of country as can possibly be imagined, with scarcely a vestige of cultivation, excepting here and there stunted trees, all leaning the same way, showing that the prevailing wind in that district was the south-west. Within a quarter of a mile of the building was the wild and almost always storm-tossed sea—the broad Atlantic. It somehow was always blowing against the front of the old tumble-down house, and the gales did certainly make sundry strange and unearthly sounds and shrieks through the paneless windows, the holes in the walls, and the roof, and along the corridors and galleries. I used to gaze out for hours upon the troubled deep. I loved to see the strong waves with their crested heads chase each other, and with childish delight I used to clap my hands, when I beheld a tall ship drive past, with the wild billows chasing it.

"One evening, when old Betty had smoked and drunk herself into a sleepy, dreamy state, I stole away to have a ramble over the old house, for latterly she had watched me very sharply, and threatened me that some monster would carry me off. Faith, Septimo, I scarcely think I could have been carried to a much worse place; my food was none of the best, and my clothes were only fit to make a scarecrow of. Well, I stole out of the room, and because the old woman told me never to go below the second floor, down I went to the bottom—and began exploring all kinds of nooks and corners, when suddenly I was astonished by the sounds of laughter from men's voices, coming through the wall of a room I was then examining. I stopped, a little frightened, and then I heard a man with stentorian voice singing a song—the sound came from the other side of a thin plastered wall. I suppose I was rather a curious youngster, for I at once seized the remnant of a poker from an old grate, and began boring through the lath and plaster, so as to have a peephole. I worked away with might and main, till the old mortar, rotten and crumbling, gave way, and in went the poker. But, by Jove! my adventures were nearly ended then and there, for no sooner had the poker gone through, than I became early initiated into the use of gunpowder and mortar-dust, for bang went a pistol at the hole, and a voice, swearing frightfully, roared out, ' Curse your impudence, you spalpeen, whoever you are—take that for you!'—I lost the rest, for a mass of mortar and lath was dashed over my person, making me roar lustily; and, taking to my heels, I ran for my life, shouting, ' Betty! Betty! I'm kilt.'

" This proves that I was no hero in my childhood. I had just reached the stairs, with the old poker in my grasp, when a man, flourishing a cutlass, rushed out of a dark passage,—a dozen more following, shouting, and hallooing as if pursuing a fox—and seized me. I threw the poker in his face, and screaming for help to Betty—kicked like one possessed ——

" ' By the Holy Poker!' exclaimed the huge fellow, holding me up to the rest, ' it's ould Betty's pet, that young scamp Hughey. You little whelp, what brought you here a boring holes into decent people's houses, eh?—you young vagrant, I've a mind to eat you!' and faith I thought he would, for he opened a mouth of most formidable dimensions ; but just then old Betty came hobbling down stairs.

" ' Here, old lady, take your pet and tie his legs.'

" The old lady growled, caught hold of me, and shook me well, making the men laugh ; on taking me up in her arms, and saying something in Irish, she re-ascended the stairs.

" This old mansion, as I learnt afterwards, stood in the county of Kerry, and was a notorious resort for smugglers. Time rolled on, till I suppose I was about six years old, when one day the old woman suddenly entered a room in which she generally locked me up, to stop my rambling propensities. I looked up, and saw she was accompanied by a tall handsome man.

" ' There,' said old Betty, pointing to me, ' that's him ; ain't he as like as two peas, ch ? '

" The stranger came close to me, and then paused, looking earnestly into my face, whilst I gazed at him with childish curiosity.

" ' Yes, young as he is, he is like him, very like him ;' and he said these few words so kindly, and with so pleasing an expression of countenance, that I was attracted towards him, and looked up into his face, anxious that he should speak to me.

" ' Come to me, my dear little fellow,' continued the stranger, ' you do not look as if you were afraid of me—eh ? '

" ' Oh, no ! ' I replied eagerly, for a voice of kindness was new to me.

" He took me up on his knee, and kissed me, and then asked several trifling childish questions, and put in my hand some silver coins. ' Now, Hugh,' said my new friend, ' how would you like to go across that great salt water you see from the window, and in a great ship ? '

" I gazed up into his handsome face, and clapping my hands, said, ' Oh, yes, I should like to go, I am tired of the old house, and, whispering in his ear, ' and tired of old Betty.' Therein I was ungrateful, for though she was old and sometimes cross, she was my preserver ; but, as a child, I could not know that.

" ' Well, then, you shall come with me,' and again kissing me, he put me down, spoke to old Betty for some moments and then departed.

" I asked the old woman numberless questions, but she did nothing but rock herself in her chair, and murmur, ' Ochhone ! ochhone !' Poor faithful old soul, she is at rest, very long ago !

" During that night I was carried away. I must have slept very soundly, or else they gave me a sleeping potion, for when I awoke I was on board a ship and very sick, caused by the vessel rolling heavily. After three or four days the vessel came to an anchor, and the stranger, whom the men on board called Captain Acton, came and carried me into a boat launched from the ship, which was rowed into a little creek, and we landed ; the boat returned to the vessel, and Captain Acton and I walked into a town some little distance from the creek. The same night we entered a carriage and travelled for three days till we reached a great city. My kind protector took me to a large house, and told me we were in Paris, and that the people he was going to leave me with were good and kind, and would be fond of me, and that he himself would always take care of me, for the sake of my noble father.

"The persons under whose care I was placed consisted of a widow lady and her two daughters, handsome kind girls, but I did not understand a word they said. After a time I began to pick up sundry words, and before a year was out I spoke French tolerably well; and as soon as I began to understand the language I got on rapidly, so that by the time I was eight years old I could talk French as well as English, and one of the girls picked up English from me. I continually asked after Captain Acton, and they told me he was an officer in the French marine. I became very fond of the two young ladies, who were French Protestants from Languedoc, and they took great pains in instructing me to pray as they did.

"I was nine years old, when Captain Acton suddenly returned; he embraced me affectionately, and told me he was going to take me with him into Italy. I was pleased to go with him, though at the same time regretted leaving the kind friends to whom I had become attached. As Maria de Teutonville kissed me fondly, she said, in a low soft voice, 'Remember, Hugh, you are a Protestant. Your father and mother were Protestants; don't let them make you a Catholic.'

"I understood very little about the difference of creeds ; but being fond of Maria, what she had taught me made an impression, and so I said shortly, 'No fear, I will always be what you have taught me to be;' and so we parted, and we have never met since.

"We then, that is Captain Acton and myself, travelled to Marseilles, and sailed to Leghorn, and shortly after to a town called Sienna, and there he placed me in a kind of college to finish my education, where I remained five years. I was fourteen years old when my protector again came for me and took me to Naples. Captain Acton was just commencing his fortunate and extraordinary career, as the especial favourite of the Queen of Naples. I was taken on board his ship, and was engaged in many of those daring exploits that made his name so renowned. After a time I was placed in the Neapolitan navy—and soon became fondly attached to the service. Before I sailed I asked Captain Acton if I had a father or mother living, or if he was a relation of mine.

"'No relation whatever,' said he, 'but I was the firm friend of your father. Neither of your parents live. I am now in a position to push your fortune in the Neapolitan service; you have courage and talent, look forward with hope, and always consider me as a second father.'

"Now, Septimo, I have nearly spun my yarn; you know how I have prospered, thanks to Dame Fortune!"

"Eh! per Bacco," interrupted the commander of the Stromboli, "allow some credit to your daring courage in achieving exploits few, if any, would venture upon attempting."

"You are partial, amico," continued Hugh De Courcy: "however, on returning to Naples, at the age of two and twenty, I found my protector, Acton, at the summit of his extraordinary career. At this time, I suppose, he was sixty-two years old at least, and had just married a young girl—indeed, you might say a child, for to me she did not appear more than fifteen. The whole power of the Government was centred in Acton. When I proceeded to his princely mansion, he received me with his usual kindness and affection, complimented me upon my achievements, and the great good fortune that had attended my career.

"A very short time after my return to Naples I was nominated captain of a ship of war. I was presented to the King and Queen, and most graciously received, his majesty conversing freely with me for some time.

"Sir John Acton, at this time, resided in a magnificent palace, in the Roviere de Chiega. One evening, sitting with my patron in the balcony, which commanded an unrivalled view over sea and land—'I have often wished, Sir John,' I commenced, 'to ask you a few questions. You have been a generous, kind protector to me; still there is in all hearts a strong natural desire to know from whence they spring. Tell me, dear sir, who were my parents—for you have often said they were known to you—in fact, that you protected me, from the strong friendship that once existed between you and my father.

"'Very true, Hugh,' said Sir John, sipping the light wine he was drinking. 'But the fact is, you had better remain in ignorance of your father's name. This is your adopted country, you are but two and twenty, and have commenced a most successful and a splendid career—we have troublous times coming; the French Revolution is marching forward with gigantic strides—before long it will overturn half the thrones in Europe. If you live, you will achieve fame, wealth, position, therefore forget, as I do, that you are an Irishman——"

"'You!' I exclaimed, greatly surprised, 'you an Irishman!'"

"'Ah, Hugh, you look surprised; I know it is generally believed that I am a Frenchman, the son of a quack-

doctor, and born at Besançon ; but such is not the case.
The English say I am a low-born adventurer, and that
I once followed the profession of a barber, but that also
is a lie. I am, however, by birth an Irishman; my
father fled from Ireland, and was, like myself, a Roman
Catholic. On reaching France he practised as a physician, to obtain a living, having devoted some years of
his early life to the study of drugs and chemicals.
When I was about twenty years of age I went over to
Ireland, employed by the French Government as a kind
of agent; whilst there I became acquainted with your
father, who was then unmarried, of my own age, and
inspired with the same feelings respecting the grievous
wrongs our country groaned under.

" ' Your father was an enthusiast after liberty—the only
son of a nobleman whose whole energies were exerted to
crush the very breath of freedom, and to force his countrymen to bend unresistingly to the harsh laws then in existence against the Roman Catholics.

" ' Your father, I suppose from conviction, adjured the
Protestant faith, and became a Catholic. Now, it is somewhat singular.' continued Sir John, looking earnestly at me,
' that you, reared entirely in a Catholic country, should
profess the Protestant religion.'

" ' You forget,' I put in, seeing him pause, ' that often,
at a very early age, we imbibe religious opinions and impressions not easily shaken off. Now, Madame de Teutonville and her two daughters, with whom you placed me in
Paris, were French Protestants from Languedoc——'

" ' The deuce they were!' said Sir John, ' I know Captain
de Teutonville was not——'

" ' No,' I returned, ' I heard madame say he was not,
and that they made no public manifestation of their faith
whilst in Paris, owing to the disturbances at that period.
Madame and her daughters took pity upon my untaught
childhood in respect to religion—they related to me the
noble deeds of the early Vaudois, the Albigenses, and other
Protestants who suffered for their pure and simple faith.
These tales made a forcible impression on my mind, and I
vowed I would nourish the principles they taught me.
Then, singular enough, in the college in Sienna were two
English boys of my own age—one the son of a distinguished nobleman, Lord Umfreville; who was placed there
by his father, to study the Italian language in its greatest
purity—while Lord Umfreville himself proceeded on a
voyage to the Black Sea, and to explore the Caucasus.
With the Honourable Edward Umfreville I formed a sincere

friendship, and during the two years we remained together he confirmed and strengthened my early impressions.'

"'Humph! 'tis strange,' said Sir John, in a musing tone, 'your grandfather was a fierce and zealous bigot for the Protestant faith. Your father renounced his birth-right to follow the creed of his choice, and now, the grand-son returns to the faith of his grandfather of his own accord. Per Baceo! there's no ruling destinies.'

"'Rather,' I returned, 'of counteracting the will of the Almighty——'

"'But,' continued Sir John, 'I was giving you a brief sketch of your family history without mentioning names. Your grandfather's fierce resentment against your father not only caused him to disinherit him, but for fear that child of his should inherit title or property, he married, in his sixtieth year, a young lady of good family, executed some deeds, and left the whole of his estates in England and Ireland to any male progeny he might have by his second wife: in case of no heir, the estates to devolve to his younger brother. I did not return to Ireland for ten years after this, when I learnt that your father had married, and that in that short space both your parents had died, and left an only child, unprotected.'

"'Your grandfather was still living, but resided entirely on his estate in England, and had a son and heir by his second wife. I never ceased inquiring till I found you out. You know, and remember, no doubt, when I dis-covered you in an old family mansion, deserted and in ruins, in the county of Kerry, under the care of a strange old crone, but faithful and true-hearted. The house was the abode of smugglers, and the country wild and thinly inhabited. I have told you all, Hugh, that I think it necessary you should know, for a further knowledge might only tend to embitter your mind and thoughts, and perhaps make you miserable——'

"'Still,' I remarked, 'you might tell me my mother's name; she must have died young, and, alas! life could not have presented much enjoyment to her.'

"'Yes,' returned Sir John, seriously, 'such was the case. Your old nurse said, she was as fair and lovely a flower as ever bloomed and died. Your mother was a De Courcy, and of the best blood of Ireland.'

"'What!' I exclaimed, 'and did not her family stretch out their hands in pity, to her destitute and orphan child?'

"'No, bitterly exclaimed Sir John, 'not to the child of the disinherited and apostate——Ha!' he added, 'we are going too far; no more of this, Hugh; the heritage of your

fathers has passed away for ever; think only of the fame
and honour you may win here——' He paced the chamber
for some moments, and then said, ' I shall soon be a father,
Hugh. The world, no doubt, calls me an old fool, and one
fool makes many. You will see by-and-by how easy it is
to earn the name of fool.'

" Three days after this the King and Queen arrived, the
Queen making costly presents, and the King creating the
new-born child a colonel.

" Now, Septimo, you know as much about my early life
and my parents as I do myself, for I could never get a word
more from Sir John on the subject. Shortly after the above
conversation I obtained the command of the Vesuvius, and
here we are."

" Ah ! so far you have satisfied my curiosity," said Septimo, "but not a single word have you said about the
beautiful Princess of Sorento, whom all Naples gives you
for a bride."

" Then all Naples," returned Hugh de Courcy, " is in
the wrong: there's no truth in it."

" Corpo di Bacco! Hugh, you do not mean to say that
there's nothing in this rumour ? Why, I heard it positively
asserted that the King even, whose relative she is, had
given his consent to the match. Well, for my part, if I
had a beautiful princess, with an immense property ready
and willing to give me her fair hand, upon my honour, I
confess it, I never would subject myself to the villanous
smell of gunpowder again. How did you make the
acquaintance of this fascinating princess ? I was at
Gibraltar at the time. I heard some imperfect account of
some act of gallantry on your part, and gratitude on the
side of the princess, and that's all I know about the matter ;
so, as you have begun a confession, make a clean breast of
it, and tell me all about the affair. Ah! if even a little
countess would look at me, I should be in the seventh
heaven—and I am not an ill-looking fellow either."

" Very far from it, amico," returned De Courcy, laughing.

" Well, it's very surprising," sighed the commander of
the Stromboli, " here's a princess, lovely, fascinating, only
two and twenty, related to the royal family, with immense
possessions, ready to jump into your arms, and you will not
open them ; by Jove, there's something behind the scenes !"

" The Princess of Sorento is all you say," returned De
Courcy seriously, " and, moreover, most amiable, and her
character, even in the dissolute Court of Naples, unimpeachable—but she is a widow."

Oh !" exclaimed Captain Septimo, significantly. " A

widow! what then? Santa Madonna, and so because she
is a widow you scorn the peerless hand held out to you. I
have no patience with you; but I suppose there is some
difference in feeling between a man of twenty-four and one
of thirty-eight; I like widows, I see no objection to them.
I suppose you consider the brain or the heart, or wherever
those sensations, called love, lie, too full of romance and all
that kind of stuff, to see things except through a magnify-
ing glass. At your age you dream of first love, first impressions, and virgin hearts; all moonshine, and almost as
fleeting; however, let me hear how your acquaintance with
this much-talked-of and admired princess began."

"Most willingly, my dear Septimo," returned De Courcy,
"it is a very brief narrative. You remember we parted
company at Malta; you sailed for Gibraltar, whilst I
stretched over to the coast of Sicily. One morning, with
a very light wind, and the sea like a mirror, we discovered
the tops of two lofty Latine sails to windward of us, and
before two hours had passed made them out to be two
heavily armed galleys, towing a dismasted craft. Baraeco,
my first lieutenant, said he was sure, from their rig and
appearance, that they were Algerine or Tunisian rovers.

"I crowded sail on the brig, and very shortly satisfied
myself that Baracco was right. They were rovers I had
chased three months previously, and lost in a dense fog of
three days' duration. They were formidable vessels; the
largest pulled fifty oars, carried eight heavy guns, and was
said to have one hundred and fifty men on board; the
other was armed with six-pounders and numerous swivels,
with one hundred men. I felt certain the two vessels
before me were the same that I had chased. Our government was extremely anxious to capture or sink these two
corsairs, which were known to have carried off several
persons from the Sicilian coast, and plundered many villages. At this time the wind fell to a still calm, and there
we lay, whilst the rovers went steadily ahead with their
tremendous sweeps. 'By Jove, I will board them with our
boats!' I said to Baracco, and in a few minutes four boats,
full of our men, were in the water, all ready and eager for
action, and, nothing daunted by the risk we should certainly incur, we were coming up, hand over hand with
them, when they cast off the craft they were towing, which,
to my great surprise, I recognized to be the pleasure yacht
of the Prince de Trepani, a Sicilian nobleman of great
wealth, but of eccentric political opinions, and not on very
friendly terms with the court of Naples. I put half a dozen
men aboard her, to rig a jury-mast, and then continued the

chase; but, by Jove! just as we got within range, up sprang
a strong breeze from the westward, the lofty sails of the
rovers filled, and then, with their stern chasers, they gave
us a dose of grape, but luckily doing us no mischief. With
wind and oars in their favour, they laughed at us, the
breeze increasing to an eight-knot breeze, so we discon-
tinued the chase, and lay upon our oars till the Vesuvius
came up.

"The galleys had now the windward gauge of us, and
were good two leagues ahead. As soon as I got on board
the brig, I ascertained by my chart that the galleys, lie as
close as they would, could not even make the port of Borra,
on the African coast, but might run in under the land and
gain the protection of some strong battery; so, crowding
all sail, we gave chase; before sunset we had the promontory of Borra some six leagues to the westward of us, and
the two vessels keeping close together within a league of
us. Another hour of the strong breeze and the guns would
reach them, when suddenly the wind began, as is usual at
that time of the year, August, to lull, and out went the confounded oars of the rovers, and thus the whole night they
kept going away from us. 'This is too bad,' I said to
Lieutenant Baracco; 'by Jove! they will get into some bight
or other if the wind keeps light like this; if it lulled altogether, we might catch them with the boats.'

"'We shall have the breeze again with the sun,' said
Baracco, who, you know, is an old and first-rate seaman.
'If the breeze had lulled entirely, we might despair; but
when it holds on thus through the night, it's sure to blow
harder with the rising sun,' and so it did.

"About an hour after sunrise we could work our bow
chasers, and the largest galley opened fire with a long
twenty-four pound carronade, and knocked our top-gallant
yard in splinters. 'Confound the rascal's impudence!' said
I to my lieutenant, 'they are running themselves ashore,'
and true enough, by Jove! they both ran ashore, the water
as smooth as glass, under a strong fort of six heavy guns,
which commenced firing upon us the moment we came
within reach. I ran the brig in, till we had four fathoms,
and then anchored, and with a spring upon my cable I
brought my broadside to bear, and then opened a sharp
fire, both upon the galleys and the fort.

"The smallest galley was totally dismasted at our first
broadside; but as I glanced with my glass over the deck of
the larger, I was horrified at perceiving, clustered upon her
poop deck, a number of females in white robes, waving
white scarfs and shawls in a frantic manner. In an instant

I ordered the firing to cease, for I guessed at once that these females had no doubt been guests on board the Prince De Trepani's yacht when captured. I saw also that the corsairs were crowding into their boats, and escaping ashore; so, manning our boats, and desiring my men to be careful how they fired in the direction of the poop, we pulled up alongside, under a smart cannonade, and boarded; Lieutenant Baracco at the same time silencing the battery.

" After a very fierce struggle (for the corsairs fought savagely, having a large amount of specie aboard the larger galley), I made my way to the poop, where I caught a glimpse of a tall swarthy follower of Mahomet, with a dozen others, forcing the shrieking females over the side into the boats. Escaping the shot of the corsair's pistol, I cut him down, and took the female from his grasp, and in five minutes more we drove the remainder of the crew over the side, cursing and uttering tremendous imprecations. Hundreds of country people from a small town, within a mile of the spot, had poured down, and several mounted Arabs were galloping furiously along shore, discharging their guns at us, and even riding into the sea, to gain a nearer shot, but, firing one of the brass cannons loaded with grape, we sent them flying in all directions.

"The lady I had released was Clarina De Oluzza, Princess de Sorento; there were nine other ladies, two slightly wounded by splinters, whilst the robes of the young and horrified princess were pierced in many places by musket-balls. Fastened to the deck, we found the Prince de Trepani, the owner of the yacht, and seven other gentlemen, three of whom were severely wounded ——one, I am sorry to say, a Cavalier Albato, died on the passage to Naples.

" However, to shorten my story, for it gets late, after a good deal of labour we got the larger galley off, and sank the smaller by a broadside. The princess and her companions I lodged in the Vesuvius, the prince and the cavaliers in the galley, and before night I made sail for Naples. So now you know all about my meeting with the princess."

" Stay, my friend; in the name of the saints, don't finish your story in that kind of way!" said Captain Septimo, anxiously. " Corpo di Bacco! I have fifty questions to ask; you put me in mind of the story-tellers of Stamboli; the rascals always stop at the most interesting part, till they hand round their turbans to be filled with copecs."

"By Jove, you are complimentary, Septimo!" returned

our hero, laughing heartily, " but what's your first question ? "

" Why, of course," returned Captain Septimo, " I want to know what brought the Princess de Sorento and the Prince of Trepani into the hands of the Tunisian corsairs ? "

" Oh ! that question is very easily answered. The Princess of Sorento has a favourite residence at Terracena. The prince, it seems, invited her and a large party of ladies and gentlemen to a *fête* aboard his magnificent yacht; which in a tremendous thunderstorm was forced off the coast, and a white squall afterwards dismasted her, and thus she and her living freight became a prize to the rover, who intended carrying them into Tunis, had I not fortunately turned up."

" Well," demanded the Neapolitan, " what did the princess say to you when she recovered her voice—can't you describe her to me ? Who was her first husband ? how came he to die ? and, besides——"

" Bastanza, amico," laughed De Courcy. " I'm off. Catch me spinning you yarns of princesses or widows. You are as insatiable of news as a lady's-maid. Addio !— to-morrow we shall have other work besides spinning yarns."

CHAPTER II.

As the morning sun shone bright over land and sea, the commanders of the various ships, forming the blockade of old Genoa, beheld the signal flying from the masthead of the admiral's ship, for all commanders and captains to assemble on board. This signal was promptly obeyed.

During this assembly of officers, it was finally determined by the admiral that an attempt should be made to cut out the famous galley, called the Prima. Captain Beaver was appointed to lead the expedition, consisting of ten boats, one of which was to be commanded by Captain Hugh De Courcy—one hundred officers and men composed the attacking force. It turned out a remarkably dark night, as the boats for the expedition assembled round the Minotaur. Captain Beaver led in the cutter. Our hero followed, in his own boat, with a picked crew; the vessel's launch followed; all expected to approach the Prima galley unperceived, but a gunboat stationed between the piers espied them, and opened fire. This gave a spur to exertion. The Minotaur's boat and that of our hero were first alongside the noble galley ; here an unexpected and formidable obstruction presented itself. The gunwale of the galley projected three or more feet upwards, from the side of the hull, and the assailants discovered that the Prima's gunwale was strengthened by a strong barricade, along the summit of which the enemy had mounted some blunderbusses and wall pieces. Besides these uncomfortable obstacles, the great oars or sweeps were locked ready for use, with the handles screwed to the thwarts. On board the Prima there was a crew of two hundred and fifty fighting men, and besides being chain-moored to the mole, she was also guarded by numerous batteries. But what will not the ardour of British seamen surmount? Our hero was the first who boarded, amidships on the starboard side, and immediately after a midshipman and a boat's crew belonging to the Hacrleim rushed over the side, whilst a number of seamen came climbing up the mizzen on the quarter. Our hero, cutlass in hand, made towards the poop, where a considerable number of French soldiers had assembled. A fierce struggle ensued. Captain Beaver and a Lieutenant Gibson, with a cheer, rushed to the assistance of De Courcy and his lieutenant, who, with about ten men, were driving the French soldiers on the poop, over the side. With Captain Beaver's assistance the French were finally driven overboard to the mole, where they kept up a rambling fire; the numerous galley-slaves shouted and jumped for joy, at what they conceived their deliverance, singing out, "God bless the King of Gibraltar!" The chains still held the galley, and the men sent to free her from them suffered so severely from the attacks of the French ashore, that De Courcy, with a few of his men, sprang upon the mole, and drove them before him a good distance along the pier, when a discharge of grape from a battery above them killed one or two of the Neapolitans, and a piece of splinter from a mooring post struck our hero down, and a party of French soldiers rushed over him, and on towards the galley, forming a large body at the mole-head, round which the galley, then freed from her chains, had to pass.

When De Courcy recovered sufficiently to understand his situation he found himself lying amongst half a dozen dead French soldiers. By the firing from the mole-head, and the tremendous discharges of shot, and shell, and musketry, he judged that the galley was then on her way out—and that to rejoin her was out of the question; without a moment's hesitation, he divested himself of his uniform, coat, and boots, and stripping a dead French soldier of his long grey coat, and shoes, and gaiters, put them on, and groping

c

about, found a hat and a musket, of which he took possession; and then, as well as he could, in the darkness, looked about him, but the galley was out of sight—the firing had ceased. The tramp of the soldiers returning, their officers cursing and swearing furiously at the loss of the Prima, induced De Courcy to lean back against a parapet wall, intending to fall into the ranks as they passed, and get inside the town ; his perfect knowledge of French rendering it quite easy for him to personate a Frenchman, provided no very critical examination took place as to what regiment he belonged to, for it was too dark to distinguish marks or numbers on his accoutrements : he managed extremely well to drop in to the rear. The men were furious, and kept cursing the English the whole way along the mole, till they reached the great iron gates which led into the city. There, a large body of fresh troops were preparing to proceed along the mole, but the officer in command, after a volley of oaths, said there was nothing to do, for the cursed Anglais had carried off the galley : they might, however, bring in the dead and wounded, but that was all that was to be done. By the light of several torches, De Courcy perceived by his accoutrements that he belonged to the forty-fifth regiment of foot. Watching his opportunity, he slipped out through the inner gate, and continuing along the sea-wall, descended a flight of steps, and then entered the city, by the Porte del Mare, without being questioned. It was now past two o'clock in the morning, it would be light in little more than two hours, so, continuing along the sea-wall, on the other side of which are the arcades, where the great mass of braziers, tinkers, and smiths carry on their noisy trades, even to the present day, he entered a low arch, and sat down on a bench, to think what next was to be done. He knew the city of Genoa quite well, for, when a lieutenant, he had anchored in the port, in the Santa Catarina Frigate, and remained three months there, becoming acquainted with many of the young nobility and most influential signors. Amongst those from whom he had received much kindness was Signor Garetti, a great friend at one time of Sir John Acton's, from whom he brought letters of introduction, and received every attention and many invitations to the signor's mansion, and passed many cheerful hours in the society of his two amiable daughters.

Well aware that the Genoese detested the French, and longed for the British to gain possession of the town, he resolved, as soon as the people were up, to proceed to the mansion of the Signor Garetti. If he still resided in Genoa.

he might, with his assistance, procure a boat and get back to his ship.

There was little life or activity about the inhabitants of Genoa, for they were experiencing all the horrors of famine. We suppose it is conformable to the usages of war, though it is very repugnant to those of humanity, to create such a state of misery. At all events Lord Keith was resolved to starve the French out. As the day broke, scattered parties of the half-famished population began to move about; business there was none, save and except the work the French themselves required, and which they forced the Genoese artisans to perform, whether they liked it or not.

Leaving his musket in the vault, De Courcy passed out into the street, regarded by the gaunt-looking people whom he encountered with intense surprise. For a moment he could not think why; but recollected that his fine open healthy countenance, and his strong powerful frame showed the very perfection of good living, so very different from the half-starved soldiers of General Massena. De Courcy smiled when he thought of this, and how awkward it would be to encounter any soldiers belonging to the regiment of the man whose garments he then had on; he quickened his pace, crossed the Piazza Annunziata, and walked rapidly up the Strada Balbi, till he reached the well-remembered portals of the Signor Garetti's mansion.

It was yet very early, and as was the custom in Genoa, the great gates in front of the mansion were wide open, admitting any one into a very large, lofty hall, round which were several out-offices, besides the porter's domicile. Entering the hall, he looked around him; but at that hour it was quite deserted—not even the porter was visible. De Courcy sat down on one of the seats, and fell into deep thought.

He sat for a considerable time, not wishing to disturb the inmates of the mansion at so early an hour. After a while the noise of a key turning a lock startled him; so, jumping up, he placed himself behind a pillar, and remained silent. The door slowly opened, and a male domestic held it so; three females, attired in the graceful costume of Genoa, with the long veils descending over the person from the head to the feet, passed out into the hall, and there paused, for from the street came the audible sound of the marching of soldiers. The three females conversed in a low voice, whilst the domestic advanced cautiously towards the great gates and peeped out.

De Courcy remained perfectly still, gazing on the graceful figures of the females; the tramp of feet passed on, and after a few moments all sounds ceased. One of the females

c 2

then said, "They have passed down the street, cara, so send the servant-man on before us, and we can follow;" the other two turned round and desired the domestic to precede them.

It is a very strange thing, but it does occur, and more frequently than people imagine, let sober matter-of-fact people think or say what they please, but there are some countenances, seen for the first time, that make an extraordinary impression upon us, not afterwards easily, if ever, erased. As Captain De Courcy gazed out from behind the pillar, and his eyes rested upon the features disclosed by the drawing back of the long veil worn by the female that came forth from the mansion, he experienced an indescribable feeling—one, however, of exquisite pleasure. The face of the young girl—she could not be more than seventeen—was very lovely, but it was only a momentary glance he obtained, for the veil was again drawn over the sweet features that so fascinated him, and the three females passed out into the street. Hugh De Courcy could not resist the inclination to look out and see which way they were going; and even to follow them came into his head. But they had scarcely gone a hundred yards from the great gate, and proceeded down the street leading to the church of the Annunziata, when they were met by some fifty or sixty of the very lowest orders of Genoese, driven to fury and exasperation by the privations they had endured during the siege, who, with drawn knives, were driving about a dozen French soldiers, carrying baskets of some kind of provisions to their barracks, across the street. The three females endeavoured to return; two were thrown down, the third fled up the street.

The soldiers dropped their hampers and drew their swords, and fiercely attacked their pursuers, heedless of the prostrate females; but in a moment De Courcy was on the spot striking the men out of his way. One of the girls had regained her feet, our hero lifted the other in his arms; her veil was on one side, and again he beheld that beautiful face; she was quite sensible, and clung to him in great terror. By this time the mob had increased, and a scene of frightful confusion ensued. Our hero's uniform confounded him with the soldiers, and he found himself fiercely attacked with one female in his arms, the other holding the skirt of his long grey coat: the soldiers also, reinforced, used their swords without scruple.

"Tonnerre de Dieu!" exclaimed a French soldier, as our hero was forcing his way through the mob, "throw down the girl and help us."

Hugh De Courey had no other weapon than his own strong arm, with which he was making rapid way through the crowd, when two ruffians, apparently butchers, with drawn knives, made a rush at him, shouting, "Cospeto! stick your knife in him;" but suddenly seizing a huge mallet from the hand of a man beside him, De Courcy struck down both men, one after the other, and exerting his strength he cleared the mob, rushed up the street and entered the portal of the Signor Garetti's mansion, with the half-fainting girl in his arms, and the other following close behind. Bugles were sounding, drums beating, and soldiers flocking into the street from all quarters; but as Hugh De Courcy entered the great hall of the merchant's house, half a dozen domestics rushed out and closed the gates.

De Courcy placed the half-fainting girl on a stone bench, whilst the other maiden called on the domestics to run out into the street and see what had become of her sister Terese.

"Ah, Madonna! I ought not to have deserted her." Then, turning to the fair girl seated on the bench, trembling with agitation and alarm, she asked, anxiously, "Are you hurt—dearest, are you hurt?"

"No, dear, I am not at all injured, thanks to this generous soldier," and the fair girl looked up, with almost startled amazement, into the handsome and flushed features of De Courcy—who had lost his hat, whilst his long grey coat, having been torn open, displayed his uniform, striped with gold lace. The young maiden paused, bewildered, for she at once perceived that her deliverer was no common soldier.

"I am rejoiced, signora," said De Courcy, "to hear you say you are unhurt, for in truth you were rudely borne to the ground by those furious rioters."

"Ah! here is my father," cried the other maiden, quite bewildered, as she caught a glimpse of our hero's features. As she stood thus puzzled, her memory recalled the person of a certain Lieutenant De Courcy to her mind. The Signor Garetti, a gentlemanly-looking person, hastily advanced, and at that moment the domestic returned with the missing young lady, to the great joy of her sister.

Signor Garetti anxiously inquired what had occurred; as he did so our hero turned round, looking him in the face, and making a sign of silence, for the signor recognized him at once, notwithstanding his soldier's coat, and was starting forward with an exclamation; but, checked by De Courcy's sign, and recollecting how matters stood—for he

was quite aware that De Courey commanded a man-of-war
brig during the siege—he sent the females into the mansion,
and then took our hero into a private room, where he
shook him cordially by the hand, requesting to know by
what extraordinary ehanee he came to be in Genoa, in the
disguise of a Freneh soldier."

Whilst our hero was engaged in explanation, the three
young maidens proceeded into the baek saloon, whieh eom-
manded a view of the harbour, where the Signor Garetti's
spouse was anxiously awaiting their appearanee.

"What on earth is all this eommotion about?" ex-
elaimed the mother of the two girls to her daughters;
"and you, my dear Mary, are you eertain you are not
hurt?"

"Not in the least, dear madam," replied the young girl
ealled Mary.

"How in the saints' name did it all happen?" demanded
the Signora Garetti.

"My dear mother," said the eldest girl, "we prevailed
on Mary Wharton to accompany us to the Annunziata this
morning early to hear a military mass, ordered by General
Massena, to eneourage his half-starved soldiers, by offering
up prayers for the sueeess of the Freneh arms; we were to
have been admitted into a private ehapel, and intended to
have seen the whole eeremony without being seen ourselves. But a horrid crowd of rioters threw Mary and myself down, and but for the gallant gentleman that eaught
up Mary like an infant, and thrust through the frightful
seene, knoeking several of the rioters down, we should
have been trampled to death."

"Why, they told me your deliverer was a Freneh
soldier!"

"Ah, madre mia!" said the eldest daughter, "I reeol-
leeted him at onee, but I was so bewildered; and even
now I am afraid to let his name be known."

"Who ean he be?" asked Mary Wharton and Madame
Garetti in the same breath.

"Why, Lieutenant De Courey, who was here three years
ago, in the Neapolitan frigate Santa Catarina."

"Lieutenant De Courey! the handsome Englishman in
the Neapolitan navy," said the mother, in great astonishment. "Impossible! you know we heard that he eom-
mands a splendid brig, and is with the English fleet outside."

"Nevertheless, dear mother, our deliverer is the same
gallant sailor who turned the heads of half the fair maidens
in Genoa three or more years ago. I knew him at onee.

Is he not very handsome, Mary?" continued Bianca Garetti; "he looked with exceeding admiration on your beautiful face; besides, he is a countryman of yours."

Mary Wharton blushed, but with a sweet smile said, " I know I owe him perhaps a life, and rejoice that he escaped so well, for at one time I shuddered when two terrible-looking men rushed on him with their frightful knives."

" But what can possibly bring Captain De Courcy into Genoa, and in disguise?" said the Signora Garetti, "that's the mystery."

" Soon solved," said her husband, entering the room at that moment, and overhearing the words ; and seating himself, he gave them the explanation he had received from our hero.

"Now, girls, you must keep this affair to yourselves, for if he were known to be here, or in this city, he would suffer a long imprisonment."

"Oh, father," said the eldest girl, "I guessed who he was the moment I looked into his eyes."

"Ah! by St. Nicholas," said the merchant, "you had better not look too often into his eyes—by St. Peter, I think him one of the handsomest and finest fellows in Italy! Luckily, I am nearly six feet myself, so I have left him to dress in a suit of my clothes, and, speaking Italian and French like the natives of both countries, he will escape detection till I manage to get him on board his own ship, or till the city surrenders ; and the sooner that desired event takes place the better; for, by all the saints, bad meat at two dollars a pound, and three dollars apiece for starved fowls, is both expensive and bad living; but now, girls, go, change your dresses, it's time for breakfast, such as it is."

CHAPTER III.

THREE weeks passed over rapidly, and to De Courcy agreeably. Those three weeks had a decided influence on his after career; for, in Mary Wharton he beheld a combination of fascinations irresistible to a person of his temperament and disposition. There was a purity and innocence in her manners and conversation so widely different from the gay Court beauties he had been in the habit of associating with in Naples and Palermo, that it struck him forcibly. Notwithstanding that most of his life had been spent in foreign lands, Hugh De Courcy was still an Englishman at heart; strange to say, also, his tastes and habits were English. He had often before been captivated by beauty of face and grace of manner, but the effect had not been lasting; he was, therefore, quite free from any engagement of the heart, when accident thus threw him into the society of, and daily intercourse with, Miss Mary Wharton.

This pure-minded and elegant girl was the niece of a wealthy English baronet, whose early life had been passed in great mercantile speculations, in which he amassed an immense fortune. Sir Charles Wharton was connected by marriage with Signor Garetti, and thinking his niece looked delicate, had sent her out to spend a year or so with this amiable family.

Hugh De Courcy discovered that at length he loved, and, with all the natural ardour of his temper and disposition, he gave way to the new and overpowering sensation. Still, in the midst of this new phase of his existence, he did not forget his duty; the Signor Garetti had as yet found it impossible to smuggle him out of the city, or get him on board his brig. Lord Keith was resolved to starve out the French garrison; therefore very little contention between his fleet and the city took place. A few days after taking up his residence in the Genoese merchant's mansion, our hero was greatly disgusted and shocked on hearing from his host the result of the cutting out of the Prima galley. It appeared that the numerous galley-slaves on board that vessel had, in the joy of their hearts at their supposed deliverance from slavery, exerted themselves vigorously at the oar to run the galley out, and by their exertions the Prima was undoubtedly captured. It was daylight when she was brought under the stern of the admiral's ship, the Minotaur. This beautiful specimen of the early ships of war of that class excited universal admiration, so graceful and elegant was her build and fittings. She was above one hundred and sixty feet long, and twenty-two broad; in her hold she had thirty brass swivels, intended to be mounted upon her forecastle and poop. The wretched slaves, released from their chains, delusively looked forward to their final freedom, but, to their infinite horror, Lord Keith ordered them to be sent back, although he must have known that the miserable men would at all events be again re-chained. Two hundred and fifty, therefore, were sent back; fifty more, with better luck, escaped in the British ship Expedition, which was blown off the coast by a violent storm.

" What have they done with the unfortunate wretches ?" demanded De Courcy; "truly it was a breach of faith when we released them we promised, if they exerted themselves to free the galley, which they did, to set them at liberty."

"I grieve to say," said the Signor Garetti, sadly, "the French general ordered the ill-fated beings to be shot; they are to be butchered this day in the great square of Aqua Verde."

"Good heavens!" exclaimed De Courcy, in indignant disgust, "how horrible! two hundred and fifty human beings slaughtered in cold blood!—can no effort be made by the inhabitants to save them?"

"No, my dear sir; and, moreover, not a soul will express even a regret at their certainly unmerited fate."

"My Lord Keith's conscience will trouble him some of these days, when he hears of their fate," said our hero.

The Signor Garetti shrugged his shoulders, with an expression as much as to say he very much doubted it.

"I have at length arranged," said the signor, "for your escape out of this city to-night. Captain De Courcy, it will be attended with some danger; but I know you care little for peril."

"No," returned our hero thoughtfully; he was thinking of Mary Wharton; "but I trust, signor, you will incur no risk."

"Oh, none whatever; the two men who will take you off in their small fishing-boat you must keep with you till the French capitulate, and it will not be long ere it takes place; we are fairly starved out. Yesterday, no money could purchase enough provision for one family's consumption for two days, and what was to be had was only the leavings of the French commanders."

"Signor Garetti," said Captain De Courcy, "I shall always remember your kindness and hospitality."

"Per Baeco," interrupted the Genoese, smiling, and laying his hand with much kindness of manner, on the young man's shoulders, "say nothing about hospitality; by St. Nicholas, you have had poor fare; but, by-and-by, I trust, when Massena thinks fit to retire, and you gain possession of the city, we shall have the pleasure of seeing you again; there's an abundance of provisions to be had, but they cannot get them to us, the blockade is so strict."

During the evening Captain De Courcy and Mary Wharton were for a short time alone together. It was the first of June, and the weather exceedingly warm, the chief saloons in the Garetti Palace were, as was usual with all the mansions in the Strada Balbi, on the south side of the street, at the back: for the windows commanded magnificent views over the wide harbour, the land projecting to the west and south-west with its gigantic lighthouse on its rocky extremity, whilst to the eastward the view is terminated by the bold promontory of Portofinno. With a good glass all the vessels of the blockading squadron could be clearly distinguished, and one day our hero had pointed out to Mary Wharton the Vesuvius standing in under a cloud of canvas, and exchanging shots with some of the French gunboats within the harbour. They sat together gazing out on the sparkling waters of the port. They were to separate that night, perhaps for ever; for who can count on human life? There was a shade of seriousness on the expression of Mary Wharton's lovely features as she sat, with her book upon her lap, and her eyes resting on the deep blue sea before her. Had Mary's heart remained unscathed, or did it feel anything beyond the merely worldly interest we all show for each other during short periods of social intercourse? Such was not the ease with Mary Wharton. It was not her nature; for warm, loving, and confiding was her young heart. She could not be blind to the evident admiration, so delicately, yet so ardently expressed, by the eyes, the tone, the words of Hugh De Courcy. The heart and the feelings spoke in all he said and did, and Mary, young as she was, could not remain ignorant of our hero's sentiments towards her. The manner in which they first met had also its effect; woman's heart is grateful; De Courcy, she knew, had risked his life for her, still Mary's heart was not yet won: so the fair girl thought, but love creeps into the citadel by very insidious and mysterious ways.

Hugh De Courcy was not the first captive to the charms and fascinations of Mary Wharton; before the French took possession of Genoa the beautiful English girl excited much admiration amongst the gay nobles and gentry of Genoa. The merchant possessed a very handsome mansion in the beautiful district of Sestri de Ponente, and there the family of the Signor Garetti spent the summer months. Adjoining the merchant's mansion was the splendid palace and grounds of the gay Count de Spinola, who became a constant visitor at the Signor Garetti's mansion, and, like all Italians in love, he became passionately enamoured of the English guest.

The Genoese merchant knew little of the count's disposition, temper, or habits. He was young, accomplished, and handsome; had travelled a good deal, was wealthy, and a prodigious favourite with the Genoese ladies. At heart, the Count de Spinola was a libertine, and totally unprincipled and vicious, but with sufficient tact to hide his imperfections. The Signor Garetti therefore did not consider the count a bad match in any respect for his beautiful relative and guest. The Count de Spinola was aware that Mary Wharton was the niece and heiress of an English baronet; but, so far as money was concerned, having a princely fortune himself, he cared little. He had a certain pride of birth, for he was of ancient descent; he therefore was satisfied on that score ; and as to winning Mary's love, he never doubted his ability to do so. He was not, however, aware that there was a certain mystery attached to the birth and parentage of Mary Wharton; neither did the Signor Garetti think it requisite to mention anything about it, for, the truth was, he was mystified himself. When the count spoke to him concerning his wish to gain the young girl's love, the worthy merchant informed him that Mary was completely her own mistress. " As far as her heart is concerned, gain that first," said the signor, good-humouredly, " it will be easy to arrange other matters afterwards."

The count was vain enough to think that the easiest part of the affair, but he soon found that he had greatly overrated his powers of persuasion and fascination, for Mary Wharton did not admire either the person or the manners of the gay count. The Genoese nobleman was piqued, but disguised his disappointment, secretly avowing that Mary should be his. Then came the army of Massena, and all parties were forced to remain within the walls of Genoa.

Our readers will, we trust, pardon this digression, absolutely necessary for the clear elucidation of what has to come.

We will now return to the saloon where we left fair Mary Wharton and Captain De Courcy gazing out on the beautiful scene before the windows of the merchant's palace. After a few common-place observations, our hero looked into the calm, serious features of Mary; and, in his low, persuasive voice, said, " I am looking, Miss Wharton, on the fair scene before us, perhaps for the last time, for who can say what the morrow will bring in a sailor's life ? "

" Why, Captain De Courcy," returned Mary, " colour the picture with so sombre a shade ; a sailor lives in hope, does he not ? " and she raised her beautiful eyes to his. There was so much kindness and sweetness in the look of those dark, lustrous, hazel eyes, that Hugh De Courcy was almost tempted to throw himself at her feet and declare his passionate love and devotion for her. That something of the kind would have occurred there is no doubt ; but the door of the saloon opened suddenly, and a gentleman rather richly dressed, with an affectation of the Spanish

style, still partly adopted in Italy at that period, entered
the room. Close after the stranger came the eldest daughter
of the Signor Garetti; and as our hero looked into her
features, he fancied that she appeared disturbed. Mary
Wharton no sooner beheld the stranger than her cheek
flushed, and then the colour receded, leaving her rather
paler than before. The gentleman advanced into the saloon,
with an easy, graceful, nonchalant air, but paused, evidently
greatly surprised, as De Courcy raised his tall, graceful
figure from his seat, with the intention of retiring, as he
did not wish to attract attention from strangers. Our hero
had noticed the change of colour in Mary Wharton's
cheek, and he felt a sensation at his heart he could not
well define.

"May I be favoured, Miss Wharton," said the Count
de Spinola—for he it was—"with an introduction to this
gentleman, who is a perfect stranger to me? I thought I
was well acquainted with all the visitors who have the
entrée of the Signor Garetti's mansion."

Before Mary or Bianca Garetti could reply, Captain De
Courcy, looking the count full in the face, said, calmly,
"It may not be agreeable to me, signor, to be intro-
duced."

"Then, signor, you do not know who I am!" returned
the count, haughtily.

"If you were the Grand Duke of Tuscany, or the Dey
of Algiers," returned our hero, with a smile, "it would
make no difference with me," and, with a bow to the ladies,
De Courcy left the saloon.

"Insolence!" passionately exclaimed the count, turning
to Mary Wharton, and gazing at her with a flushed cheek;
"this insolence shall not pass unnoticed. Pray, who is this
stranger?"

"My lord!" exclaimed Mary Wharton, her cheek now
vying with the rose, "this scene is unaccountable; the
visitors of the Signor Garetti have a right to expect
courtesy at least. I wish you good evening!" and as Mary
was hastening away, Bianca having followed our hero out
of the room, the count stepped before the indignant girl,
saying, in a penitential voice, "I pray you pardon me,
signora: do not impute to me the entire blame of this
really foolish interchange of words. Surely you will
admit that there was nothing very extraordinary in requesting an introduction to a gentleman I beheld enjoying
a *tête-à-tête* with one I adore?"

"This is too bad!" exclaimed Mary Wharton, scarcely
able to restrain her tears; "be satisfied, count, that I will

never permit a repetition of this insult;" and, snatching her robe from the hand of the count, who strove to detain her, she instantly left the saloon.

CHAPTER IV

CAPTAIN DE COURCY, uneasy and indignant, quitted the saloon, but was at once joined in the next chamber by the Signora Bianca.

" This is very unfortunate, Captain De Courcy," said the good-natured Bianca, in a soothing tone, " I did all I could to stop the count from entering the room, but he seemed strangely enough to be determined upon it."

" Pardon me, fair Bianca," said our hero, " having given you any uneasiness. Knowing that I might bring your good father into trouble by betraying who I was, induced me to submit to the insolence of this signor. Pray, who is he? he must be very intimate with Miss Wharton to accost her so cavalierly."

" Indeed, Captain De Courcy, he is not," said the Genoese maiden warmly, " dear Mary cannot bear him."

" Had I known that," interrupted our hero, with a glow of pleasure on his cheek, " I should have felt greatly inclined to have put him out of the window."

Bianca smiled at the sudden change of De Courcy's manner and the pleased expression of his features, and then informed him who the stranger was, and his being a near neighbour of theirs when at their residence at Sestri. She did not deny the fact of the Count of Spinola being greatly enamoured of Miss Wharton ; but she insisted on it, that Mary, so far from giving him encouragement, did all she could to shun his society

" Where has he been these few weeks? for this is the first time I have seen him visit here since my arrival," asked our hero.

" We have not seen him these three or four weeks," replied Bianca; " we heard he was confined to his palazzo by indisposition; we were therefore quite surprised when we saw him walking up stairs. Knowing, if he saw you, he would wonder who you possibly could be, I tried to stop him; but, in a laughing and bantering kind of way, he walked on, saying he would take the Signora Wharton by surprise."

Whilst Bianca was speaking they heard a man's foot pass the door and descend the stairs humming a canzonette in a careless easy tone.

"I will go look for Mary now," said Bianca; "she has got rid of her troublesome visitor."

When the family assembled at the evening meal, Captain De Courcy thought Mary's sweet face looked anxious. The Signor Garetti said,—

"I am sorry to hear of the strange conduct of the Count of Spinola; I cannot account for it, for I thought you were a stranger to him; still he had no excuse for acting as he did, and he seriously offended Miss Wharton afterwards."

"Did he?" hastily exclaimed the Neapolitan commander, "then by my—" he paused, for he saw that Mary's eyes were fixed upon him with a very serious expression; there was a sadness in the look also that affected him, and he said, "It was all very silly, but you cannot expects wise heads on young shoulders; time will teach us to have better control over our tempers. Perhaps the count had no meaning, after all, in his words."

"I do not know that, my young friend," said the Signor Garetti, rather seriously, "I was coming home, with the express intention of persuading you to forego your somewhat hazardous design of getting on board your ship to-night—for I am perfectly satisfied, from what I heard to-day, that General Massena intends to evacuate the city in a few days. The French are making secret preparations for a retreat, and therefore you had better wait for that event, rather than run the risk of escaping to-night."

"I should be too happy to stay," said De Courcy, with a rapid glance at Mary's serious face, " but I should like to regain my ship before the capitulation takes place. You can understand why? As to the risk, there's peril in every action of a sailor's life; it is the charm that leads to glory so often—but, indeed, there is little to be incurred, once we clear the wall of the city."

"Oh!" said the Signor Garetti, "we can get you out safe enough from the private landing-place of the Doria Palace. The danger is from the guard-boats that row about the harbour all night, and the gunboats that keep under weigh; and since the affair of the Prima, double vigilance is used. Do you know that General Massena has almost half his army incapable of marching, so severe has been the privation they have suffered?"

The time for our hero's departure drew nigh—he was to leave about an hour before midnight; the two men and their small boat were to wait for him under the wall of the Doria garden, the Signor Garetti, for a considerable bribe, having procured the key of the passage leading to the water's edge, from the gardener.

De Courcy did not again find an opportunity of speaking to Mary Wharton alone, but at the usual hour of retiring to rest he took an affectionate leave of the whole family : they bade him farewell, the two girls, who really felt almost the affection of sisters for him, said the kindest things possible, Bianca repeating, "We are only saying good-bye, Captain De Courcy, for a few days, for I am sure we shall have the British flag flying over the walls of old Genoa before a week is over."

"I trust so, signora," said De Courcy, and then taking the hand held out to him by Mary Wharton, he pressed it respectfully to his lips; if the words were few that he uttered, before so many persons, they were impressive ones, and Mary felt her heart beat quicker; he gazed for a moment earnestly into that beautiful, truthful face, that neither sought nor wished to disguise the pure feelings of her heart; a volume of words could not have expressed more than that look—for it said as plainly as speech, that his whole heart was hers, and as he gently let go the small hand, there was a tear in Mary's eyes.

Wrapped in long mantles, the Signor Garetti and Captain De Courcy left the merchant's mansion, the great bell of the Annunziata tolled the hour before midnight, as they proceeded up the Strada Balbi, and across the Piazza Aqua Verde. To get to the Palace Doria, it was necessary to pass through the inner gate of the city, which was strongly guarded; without this gate, the city still extended along the borders of the port, with many magnificent mansions—amongst them the great Palazzo Doria,—or rather fortress, for such it resembles even at the present day, and extended along the margin of the port, having, at the time of our tale, and even now, extensive and beautiful gardens stretched out before it. Along the foot of the gardens ran the sea-defences and ramparts. After sunset, this gate was closed against all ingress or egress, without a special pass from the officer whose duty it was to guard this important post.

The Signor Garetti had obtained a permission, for himself and friend, to pass the gate, any time before midnight. Many Genoese merchants and signors had these permissions, their mansions being outside this gate, which goes by the name of Porta di San Tomaso—the outer gate of all, defended by drawbridge and portcullis, is the Porta della Lanterna.

Garetti and our hero advanced towards the gate, and

entering the side-arch, not the main entrance, they passed
the sentinel, and came into the presence of the warder.
As they did so, a party of soldiers marched out from the
guard-room, and took up their position, with their loaded
muskets, their butts resting on the ground, completely
barring the narrow entrance.

The French officer took the paper, one of his men
holding a large lantern, and looking it over, said, " I am
sorry, Signor Garetti, but since this order was written I
have received instructions to arrest your companion, whoever he may be; the order is from General Massena
himself; but you, signor, are perfectly at liberty to proceed
through the gate, or retrace your steps."

Garetti looked confounded, and started back, gazing
bewildered at our hero, and the guard blocking the entrance
to the arch.

" Well, sir officer," said Captain De Courcy, stepping
forward, " since such is your order, you have nothing to do
but to execute it, for by arresting this gentleman's companion, you of course mean me. I do not dream of the
folly of resistance, therefore am ready to follow you, and
now, Signor Garetti, I must wish you good night;" and our
hero held out his hand. The worthy merchant, who had
evinced great esteem for his English guest, looked grieved
to the heart, as he warmly pressed De Courcy's hand;
whilst the French officer, holding up the light, surveyed
the tall and striking figure of our hero with great surprise,
and no little admiration.

" This gentleman," said the French officer, pointing to
Captain De Courcy, " shall receive no discourtesy, he shall
sleep in one of my servant's rooms till I receive the
general's orders to-morrow."

As there was nothing more to be said, and certainly
nothing to be done, but summon up a stock of patience,
the friends separated, the Signor Garetti returning to his
own house, whilst our hero followed Captain Sloftet up a
flight of stairs, into a small square chamber, with a pallet,
a table, and two chairs, a window, strongly grated, and
crossed with iron.

" I am sorry," said Captain Sloftet, who was a very
civil kind of personage, " that I cannot offer you anything
in the way of refreshment, since, monsieur, we ourselves
only get enough to feed four honest hearty men a day.
Parbleu ! we have to feed twenty-four upon it. Cursed
state of things this."

" Bad enough indeed, monsieur," returned our hero,

looking at the parched, starved face of the Frenchman, "but it cannot last much longer, I should think."

"Parbleu! not unless we eat one another; but, monsieur, to look at you, you cannot have suffered much by the smallness of your rations."

"Some persons," said our hero, with a smile, "require but a small amount of food."

"Diable! returned the Frenchman, "it's impossible you could keep up those good looks upon our rations, at all events. I know that some of the wealthy merchants here, by immense sacrifices, have managed to live tolerably well; but you are a curiosity in Genoa, I should say, for vigorous health and good looks."

"Do you know, monsieur," questioned De Courcy, "the cause of my strange arrest to-night?"

"No, on my honour I do not," said Captain Sloftet, frankly, "but you, surely, have some idea yourself?"

"Yes, I may surmise," returned our hero thoughtfully.

The Frenchman then withdrew, and almost immediately after he heard the heavy foot of a sentry without his door, keeping guard.

As there was no use in tormenting himself with conjectures respecting his arrest, which, somehow, he connected with the visit of the Count of Spinola to the mansion of the Signor Garetti, De Courcy threw himself on the pallet, partly undressed, and very soon fell fast asleep.

In the morning Captain Sloftet very civilly provided our hero with the requisites for a rough toilet and a remarkably spare breakfast. Our hero acknowledged to himself that a month of that sort of diet would materially affect any constitution, for it was barely sufficient to keep body and soul together. Early in the day he heard the tramp of a large body of cavalry, as if passing through the gate, and almost immediately after Captain Sloftet entered the room.

"General Massena," said the French officer, "on his way to the Porta della Santerna, has halted here; he desires to see you at once—pray follow me."

Captain De Courcy did so. They descended the stairs, and, passing through a group of slovenly-dressed officers, all cavalry men, lounging about a large, scantily furnished chamber, Captain Sloftet opened a door and ushered our hero into another and much smaller chamber, but well lighted, and looking into the square of Aqua Verde.

General Massena, or, as Napoleon styled him, the Favoured Child of Victory, was at this period about thirty-eight years old. This great general showed his

D

consummate skill in holding Genoa against the Austrians
without the walls, and the British squadron, under Lord
Keith, blockading the port; for so vast were the fortifica-
tions of Genoa, that it would have taken twenty-thousand
men to garrison the walls, and he had not half that force.
He was a tall, handsome man, with very pleasing features;
he has been accused of cruelty, and it was a cruel act,
certainly, the putting the galley-slaves to death; but it was
a far greater cruelty the sending them back, once freed.
However, General Massena was capable of great kindness
and generosity, and was dearly loved by those he commanded.   He was conversing with an Italian officer, in a
very brilliant uniform, who turned round as our hero
entered the room.   Both the Italian and De Courcy started
as they recognized each other; the former for a moment
looked confused, but, immediately recovering himself, said,
"I am surprised—how is this, Captain De Courcy, you a
prisoner here?"

"Yes, your highness," returned our hero, "it's the
fortune of war."

" What, prince!" exclaimed General Massena, gazing
with considerable curiosity at his prisoner, " is this gentleman the Captain De Courcy who commands the Vesuvius, and who was supposed either killed or drowned in
the cutting out of the Prima galley?"

"Most assuredly it is," said the Prince of ——, the
same our hero had released from the corsairs, " for I have
had the pleasure of seeing him several times at the court
of Naples, and can testify to his undoubted courage,
gallantry, and skill as a sailor; and to him also I owe my
escape from slavery."

" Well, this is very strange," said General Massena; "I
have had several communications from Lord Keith repect-
ing this officer; he was thought to be a prisoner at first, but
I assured his lordship no such person was taken the night
of the attack upon the Prima; I should never dream
of detaining a gallant gentleman a prisoner when offered a
fair exchange.   But why I think this strange, prince, is,
that yesterday I received an anonymous letter, stating that
if I would order the arrest of a person in company of the
Signor Garetti, who would attempt to pass through the
Porta del San Tomaso, at the time of eleven that same
night, I should capture a prisoner of importance, who was
residing in the city as a spy."

A flush of passionate indignation covered the cheek of
Hugh De Courcy as he heard those words.

" I should very much like, general," said our hero, " to
have my hand on that false villain's throat; it would be
the last lie that his foul mouth should utter."

" I believe you, mon Dieu!—in truth, Captain De Courcy,
your grasp would not be a pleasant one. Our throats, in
this city, at present, would ill bear compression. But make
yourself easy, Monsieur le Capitaine ; I do not intend, now
I know who is my prisoner, to take advantage of this
anonymous writer's piece of information ; you are at
liberty to return on board your ship. My Lord Keith
will, on his part, release Captain Patrizio Galleani, the
commander of the Prima galley. Now, pray explain
how you came to be in Genoa ? "

" You are very generous, General Massena," said our
hero, rejoicing at the fortunate termination of his captivity ; and continuing, he freely stated the particulars,
trusting that the Signor Garetti's hospitality to him would
not be the cause of his incurring the general's displeasure.

" Not at all, I assure you, Captain De Courcy ; I have
been greatly indebted to Signor Garetti's profuse liberality
in providing for my individual comfort. There is not a
better man in Genoa. You can now, Monsieur De Courcy,
repair to the signor's mansion. In an hour or two I shall return from the visit of inspection to the Porta della Santerna.
Orders shall then be given for a boat, with a flag of truce,
to be manned, to take you on board your admiral's ship."

Hugh De Courcy returned General Massena suitable
thanks for his generous intentions.

" Brave men know one another by instinct," said the
general with a smile, and, holding out his hand, which
our hero pressed warmly, Massena went on his visit of
inspection.

The Prince de ———, before his departure, said, very
kindly, as he squeezed De Courcy's hand, " I have not
forgotten the service you rendered me and the Princess of
Salerno in releasing us from the corsairs ; but I am now a
banished man, and my estates confiscated. My political
opinions displeased my cousin Ferdinand, and he proceeded to harsh measures. I could never forget the cruel
murder of my aged uncle, Prince Caraccedi ; I therefore
embraced the cause of liberty. So our careers, Captain
De Courcy, are different ; but nevertheless, your gallantry
and courage I have not forgotten, and the time may come
when fortune will be on my side. I now bid you farewell ;
but if ever in my power, I shall remember you."

Hugh De Courcy bowed, and the prince departed.

Captain Sloftet entered the room.

"I rejoice, Captain De Courcy, at your restoration to liberty; believe me, I never like to see a brave man incarcerated."

"You are very kind, captain," returned our hero, and after thanking him for his attention, he left the gate-house, and proceeded leisurely along the Place di Aqua Verde, and thence into Strada Balbi. Pursuing his way in a very thoughtful mood, he entered the mansion of Signor Garetti, to the infinite amazement of the porter and other domestics of the establishment, and ascended to the saloon; the Signor Garetti was from home, having gone into the city.

On entering the saloon, he perceived that it was only tenanted by fair Mary Wharton, who had her back to the door; and so deeply buried in thought was the maiden that she did not even raise her eyes at the sound of De Courcy's step. He slightly coughed, which caused her to look round. The moment she beheld our hero she uttered an exclamation of uncontrolled joy, whilst a bright colour came to her before pale cheek. It was impossible to mistake the expression of her eyes, even if he had not caught the words she uttered in her surprise. The next moment De Courcy was by her side, one fair trembling hand in his, and giving way to the full and overpowering feelings that occupied heart and soul, our hero breathed forth his vows of love, of life-long devotion and fidelity.

Mary Wharton scarcely breathed; she had betrayed, to a certain extent, her own feelings in the joy of her heart at seeing him safe and free, when she fully expected that he was pining in captivity. It was not a surprise to her to hear that Captain De Courcy loved her; her heart told her that before his departure; but she scarcely could be said to know the extent of her own affections till the Signor Garetti returned to his mansion, and it became known that Captain De Courcy had been arrested by order of Massena, and that a long captivity might be the consequence. Mary passed a restless night; she confessed to herself that she was more than interested in the fate of De Courcy, and thus, when giving way to his impetuous feelings, and his glowing ardent words fell upon her ear, she felt so over-powered and conscious of the state of her heart that she made no effort to disguise her feelings; and thus, loving and beloved, the enraptured De Courcy drew the trembling girl gently towards him, impressing upon her lips the first kiss of true, pure, and devoted love. What, then, was the world to Hugh De Courcy? Nought—his arms encircled his world; he thought of no other, cared for no other: but even from dreams of love and present hopes of a blissful future, one which no shadow was to pass, we are suddenly roused into dull realities, and forced, despite our fairy visions, to look upon this world as it really is—a world of trial, privation, and alas! of suffering. Not only to the poor, but the honest hard-working artisan and daily labourer; for out of that great and mighty class, that supply the aristocracy with wealth, the foundation of power, how few can sit down, even at an advanced age, and say, " Blessed rest is now to be our portion, our reward for years of toil and suffering."

Our lovers were roused from their day-dreams of the future by the entrance of the Signor Garetti and a French officer, in uniform. Mary Wharton immediately retired, and the Signor Garetti, after congratulating our hero upon his release, and being permitted to return to his ship, introduced Captain Caubert as the officer appointed to accompany him on board the Minotaur, and effect the proposed exchange of prisoners, the captain of the Prima for Captain De Courcy.

Having taken leave of the Signor Garetti's family, who showed much attention, affection, and kindness in their manner, and a word and look with Mary, understood by both, our hero left the mansion, and in half an hour more was pulling away in a six-oared gig, with a flag of truce hanging over her stern, for the admiral's ship.

CHAPTER V.

COUNT ADRIAN SPINOLA, whom we introduced to the notice of our readers in the preceding pages, was a young nobleman of considerable wealth, with a name conspicuous in the annals of the Genoese Republic. Left his own master at an early age, he travelled into Germany and France, and without imbibing revolutionary principles in the latter country, he contrived, nevertheless, to not only indulge in all the vices of the period, but adopt the very worst as models for his future adoption. The beauty, grace, and fascinations of Mary Wharton created a powerful impression on his impetuous nature; he never dreamed of opposition, he considered his personal appearance, wealth, and high position too attractive and too desirable to be scorned or despised by any maiden, no matter how high her position. But Mary Wharton was, nevertheless, indifferent to all his attractions, personal and otherwise. This roused the worst feelings of his nature, and Adrian Spinola vowed he would yet attain his object; if he could not win her willing consent, she should, under any circumstances, be his.

His first business was to ascertain if there was a rival in
the case; she was too young when she left England to
have surrendered her heart, too young even to know what
love was; he had all her movements watched, but no rival
was discovered, till at length the spy in his pay, one of the
Signor Garetti's female domesties, brought him word that
there was a young man lately come in a mysterious manner
into the domestic circle of the Signor Garetti, that this
young signor was remarkably handsome, and that she felt
satisfied he was not only a lover of Mary Wharton's, but
was sure he was from England, for she overheard them
both speaking a strange language, which was neither
Italian nor French, and must be English.

This information roused the hateful passions of Adrian
Spinola into action. If he could not possess Mary Wharton as a wife, he swore none other should. But how an
Englishman could get into Genoa puzzled him, and he
determined to judge for himself; and receiving communication from his spy, he contrived to surprise, as our readers
already are aware, the two young people together.

Adrian Spinola, though only two or three years older
than Captain De Courcy, was yet a keen discerner of
character; he had been educated in a different school
from his English rival. One glance was sufficient for
him to judge how matters stood between the lovers. His
next object was to ascertain who De Courcy could possibly
be; he was no native of Genoa, he was satisfied of that. So
he set another agent to work to help out his diabolical plan.
Assassination was not to be thought of under French rule,
for, to do them justice, they rooted out from the city and
adjoining territory, during their occupation, hundreds, if
not thousands, of those wretches who lived almost openly,
in Genoa and its dependencies, and found full employment
in their detestable trade, for before the French Revolution
no city could have existed in a more corrupt or vitiated
state than that of Genoa.

The Count of Spinola's spies found out that the Signor
Garetti was extremely anxious to get the stranger domiciled
in his mansion, without the walls, and finally they discovered that he had obtained a pass for himself and another
gentleman to leave the city by the inner gate of San
Tomaso, before twelve o'clock that night.

Satisfied that the stranger was an Englishman, Adrian
Spinola wrote the anonymous letter to General Massena
that caused our hero's arrest. But the following day the
count learned that his plan had failed, and that the person
he insinuated in his letter to be a spy, was no other than

the gallant Captain of the Neapolitan brig, an Englishman of the name of De Courcy. This added infinitely to his vexation, for he soon learned the chivalrous, gallant character De Courcy bore, and how very unlikely that an attachment once formed, between him and Mary Wharton, could ever be broken. He felt relieved, however, that they were for the present separated; but even in this his pleasure was of short duration, for four days afterwards General Massena, finding it impossible to hold the city longer, agreed to certain terms of capitulation, and finally consented to evacuate the town of Genoa, and retire with his troops to Nice. General Massena expressed his unmitigated contempt for Austria, and in one of his conferences he observed to Lord Keith, " If ever, my lord, France and England understand each other, they will govern the world." *

General D'Ott, after three days' occupation of Genoa with his Austrian troops, also quitted, leaving the British ships alone in possession of the place.

Captain De Courcy's return to his ship was a joyful event to his officers and crew. Lord Keith and many of the principal officers of the British ships heartily congratulated him on his safety; they had feared some untimely accident had occurred to him on the night of the cutting out of the Prima.

The blockade of Genoa being over, our hero found himself, to a certain extent, his own master; he was no longer under Lord Keith's orders; Captain Septimo had sailed with the news to Naples, De Courcy entered the port of Genoa with the Vesuvius, and anchored off the Doria Palace, and at once landed and proceeded to the mansion of the Signor Garetti.

The half-starved inhabitants of Genoa were evincing the utmost joy at their deliverance from their misery, and provisions of all kinds poured in through the east and west gates, and in numerous vessels from the various towns along the east coast.

On reaching the mansion of the Signor Garetti, De Courcy was received by the Signor and all his family with unmistakeable pleasure, and in the eyes of Mary he read an expression of pure joy that filled his heart with rapture.

" We are going to-morrow," said the Signor Garetti, " to our country mansion at Sestri. I have sent servants, and all things necessary to make the girls happy after the state of suffering they have all endured these last three months. We shall be so delighted to see you there, and

* Victoires et Conquêtes.

shall have an apartment expressly fitted up for you;—
besides," continued the Signor Garetti, taking him aside,
"our dear Mary has spoken to me upon the subject of
your declared attachment to her, as you wished her to do,
and I much desire to have a long conversation with you on
the subject of your mutual happiness. It is requisite that
you should know how the dear girl is situated, and at the
same time, recollect, she is but a guest with us, her uncle
is her guardian; however, we shall have time enough to
talk of all this, and believe me, as far as I have been able
to judge, her choice is one that will, I am convinced, be
approved of by her uncle."

Captain De Courcy could not be otherwise than pleased
by the words and kind manner of the Signor Garetti;
nevertheless the conversation for the first time recalled the
sailor to the recollection of his real position. They made
him for the first time reflect that Mary Wharton was the
niece of an English baronet of good family and great
wealth—as the Signor Garetti informed him—and possessed a considerable fortune at her own disposal; her
guardian and relative therefore had an undoubted right to
expect for his niece's husband a gentleman of birth, education, and position in society. At first De Courcy felt perplexed; he had not even a right to the name he bore—all
he knew was, that it was his mother's. He had a reputation, it is true, in the Neapolitan navy, for skill, courage,
and honour; of fortune he possessed but little. These
thoughts did not arise to his mind in the first raptures of
successful love—to adore Mary, and to be loved by her, was
all he thought of, and this ardently-desired object attained,
he considered himself the happiest of human beings—
but now worldly thoughts were thrust upon him, and for the
first time he trembled to think there might arise obstacles
to their union unthought of before. "But," said our hero,
half aloud, and in a triumphant tone, "possessed of Mary's
love, I defy the world." The world is a very large object
to oppose, and alas! very often, despite our best endeavours,
defies us.

Captain De Courcy, to the infinite delight of Mary and
the fair sisters Garetti, proposed to take the whole family
to Sestri, in the Vesuvius. It would be a delightful
sail. Mary was passionately fond of the sea, but as yet
she had had no opportunity of viewing the delightful
scenery of the Rivieri de Ponenti; and the delight of
being in her lover's beautiful ship, in which he had performed so many gallant exploits, filled her innocent heart
with pleasure.

On the day appointed, the Vesuvius was dressed in her gayest attire; all damaged or injured sails removed, and new ones hoisted in their place; her decks were as white and as polished as holy-stone and manual labour could make them. The handsome gig of the Vesuvius, the thwarts covered with flags, conveyed the Signora Garetti, her two daughters, and Mary Wharton on board the Neapolitan brig, her crew attired after the English fashion, with the name of the Vesuvius embroidered in red on their white knit shirts, and in gold letters on their round hats. Every rope was coiled in its place; in a circle, every brass pin highly polished, and the guns looking as innocent as guns can look. The Neapolitan flag floated over the stern, not a sail was set, and so beautiful were they furled to the yards that they appeared scarcely of the bulk of a lady's kerchief. Having prepared the ladies for the report, a gun was fired, and, like magic, the tall tapering masts were covered from heel to truck with a cloud of snow-white canvas, and the brig bending gracefully to the delightful Tramontana, then blowing freshly out of the harbour, glided swiftly from her moorings, out into the glorious sparkling sea, lying in all its beauty before the palaces and walls of Genoa.

"Oh, how lovely!" exclaimed Mary Wharton, to Captain De Courcy, as she gazed upon the scene they were leaving.

"Yes, dear Mary," said our hero, looking into those soft expressive eyes, "it is a beautiful and striking scene, and well may old Genoa be proud of what her sons have done, if we revert to the time of its early founders, who raised their magnificent city upon a sterile and barren strip of land, and by their valour and industry made her "Queen of the Sea," she covered with her argosies. It is from the sea, Genoa is seen to the utmost advantage.

They were rounding the mole Nuovo—on the rock above it rises the gigantic Faro. De Courcy called all their attention to the magnificent view the city presented seen from this spot; her stately palaces rising from the sea, which, like the ranges of an amphitheatre, imparts an indefinable charm to this queenly city. On rounding the Faro, and bracing the yards, sharp on a wind, the brig lay along the shore of that magnificent suburb, San Pietro de Arena, where every house is a stately palace. The sea, with the breeze off the shore, was like a sparkling, rippling lake, undisturbed by the slightest swell, and yet with the refreshing, delightful Tramontana, the Vesuvius, glided through the water at the rate of eight knots an hour.

The whole line of that enchanting coast, from Genoa to

the Cape de Noli to the west, and Porto Finno to the east, lay before the eyes of the delighted party on board the brig. The lofty hill backing the city of Genoa now appeared in full view, its sloping sides gay with suburban palaces, and gardens one mass of bloom of the red oleander ; here and there it was fringed with the oak woods and olives, forming, altogether, a glorious back-ground to the noble city.

On glided the Vesuvius over the rippling sea, the gay and happy party on board, seated beneath a snow-white canopy, enjoying the delicious freshness of the breeze ; and the maidens, in their graceful costume—so simple yet so elegant—making the quarter-deck of the war vessel look like Cleopatra's galley.

The Signora Garetti being by birth an Englishwoman, and her husband engaged in great commercial transactions with England, had brought up both her daughters to admire everything English : whilst they both spoke the language as fluently as the language of their fatherland.

"Now confess," said the elder daughter, to De Courcy, pointing to the lovely scenery lying to the rear of the beautiful little town of Pagia, which they were fast approaching, " Now confess, Captain de Courcy, much as you must love your native land, that this line of coast exceeds in beauty and variety anything you have ever seen along the shores of Britain."

" I may fairly confess that, fair lady," said our hero, " for you must know that I never beheld a mile of England's coast in my life."

The whole party looked surprised ; even Mary raised her eyes to his face with an inquiring look, whilst Madame Garetti said, " Is that possible—then you never were in the British navy ?"

" Never," said our hero ; " neither have I ever set foot upon the shores of Britain."

Until now De Courcy had never spoken of himself to any of the Garetti family ; they were aware that he was a British-born subject, but they supposed he had originally served under the flag of England, and afterwards, like many others, accepted higher command in the Neapolitan navy. There were many English officers in the service of the King of Sardinia, and therefore it did not cause any surprise at seeing him in the service of the Neapolitan king. But his disclaiming all knowledge of England created great astonishment.

" I see," said De Courcy, with a smile, to Madame Garetti, " that you are surprised. One of these days I will tell you my history ; " and he looked at Mary Wharton with a somewhat serious expression, which, however, he immediately changed into one of solicitude, as he thought he saw Mary's sweet face becoming thoughtful. But, directing her attention to the shore, he inquired which of the palaces, scattered over the beautiful hills of Sestri, was the Garetti mansion. Mary Wharton pointed it out: it was on the sea-shore, the gardens and pleasure-grounds rising in terraces up the gently sloping sides of the hills.

" That lofty and stately palace adjoining ours," said the Signora Garetti, " is the Count Spinola's. I cannot think," she added, " what can have become of him: since the evacuation by the French we have not caught sight of him ; he used to be a very constant visitor, especially when we resided at Sestri."

Madame Garetti and her daughters walked about conversing with Lieutenant Barracco—a tall handsome, though no longer young man; he was at this time near thirty-five, and had served twenty years, and though a skilful officer, was as yet but a first lieutenant. There were times when our hero felt almost ashamed to hold a commission above one he thought equally brave and skilful as himself. So he considered, but Captain De Courcy did not do himself justice ; for his gallantry and daring courage fairly gained him the command he enjoyed.

" I cannot but think," said De Courcy, in a low voice, to Mary, " that this same Count de Spinola had something to do with my arrest at the gate of San Tomaso."

" Oh! I hope not, Hugh," said Mary anxiously ; " he surely could not be so base ; besides, what could lead him to suppose that you were a person subject to arrest ; he could not know that you were an Englishman."

" And yet somebody, dear Mary," returned our hero thoughtfully, " must have been aware of it—for the French Captain who commanded the guard at the gate of San Tomaso, told me, before I left, that I had been arrested owing to an anonymous communication sent to General Massena."

Mary looked unhappy, saying, " I shall never feel at ease in the count's company again, with this idea in my head, but I expect Mrs. Arbuthnot will arrive shortly, and then we shall leave immediately for England."

" Till this war is ended, dear Mary, there will be great risk in your making the voyage to England, for the whole of Italy, and part of Germany, is so overrun with the armies of France and Austria, that a passage through those countries will be hazardous."

" Perhaps," said Mary, "we may obtain a passage to

England in some British man-of-war, through the interest
of the Signor Garetti; or my uncle may have arranged
with Mrs. Arbuthnot the manner in which we are to
proceed."

"Would to Heaven it was in my power to offer you this
vessel, dear Mary! I can resign my command."

"My dear Hugh," said Mary Wharton, looking up with
confident affection into her lover's features, "much as I
should feel the safety your presence would ensure us, I
would not exact such a sacrifice on any account. You
love your profession, and your beautiful ship; honour
requires you to continue your command at least as long as
this war lasts. Let us have patience and confidence, dear
Hugh; we are both young, and hope and true affection will
enable us to bear an unavoidable absence.

"You are right, Mary," said Hugh De Courcy, with a
look of devoted affection, "I have much to say to you, but
this is not the time. We are approaching the shore, so I
must see to anchoring;" and pressing the little hand that
rested on his arm, he turned to give some directions to his
lieutenant.

In a few minutes, the brig was at anchor within half a
mile of the shore, and in less than a quarter of an hour the
whole party were pulled ashore in the gig. They found
the Signor Garetti waiting for them.

CHAPTER VI.

SOME weeks after the Garetti family had settled down in
tranquil enjoyment in their country mansion, in Sestri, the
Signor Garetti and Captain De Courcy, who had just returned from a cruise to Leghorn, with the Neapolitan
squadron of gunboats, sat in the summer pavilion, built on
a terrace facing the sea. The weather was extremely hot,
but a pleasant and refreshing west wind came in through
the open windows, projecting verandahs shading the sun's
rays from the saloon, a magnificent jet of water was thrown
up from a marble bason in the garden beneath the window,
which, falling in a graceful mushroom form in a wide circle,
ran in rivulets through the flower beds, imparting a delightful
freshness to the scorched plants, as well as affording a
pleasing sound of falling water to the ear.

After some trifling observations about the weather, the
Signor Garetti said, "I have wished-for this opportunity,
my dear sir, to impart to you information it is necessary
you should hear, respecting my beloved charge, Mary,
before writing to her uncle, Sir Charles Wharton, who, I

am sure, must be extremely anxious, owing to the troubled state of Italy, and knowing that the French forces had possession of Genoa."

"I am equally anxious," said De Courcy, "to communicate to you and Sir Charles Wharton my actual position; you, my dear sir, know nothing of me, save the rank I hold in the Neapolitan service—but of my private history you know nothing. I have told all to Mary, and to her loving and generous nature there appears no obstacles; but her guardian may think differently. As to anything relating to Mary's position or fortune, they can never make any difference to me; I seek neither fortune nor station, her love is all I covet. I have put aside a sum of some ten or twelve thousand pounds, the fruits of certain prizes, the ransom of some wealthy Tunisian captives, and gifts from his Majesty of Naples. I am also assured of the command of a remarkably fine frigate, just ready for launching; and if fortune still favours me, and my life is spared, I may fairly hope to obtain a position worthy of Miss Wharton's station in society."

"I am quite satisfied, Captain De Courcy," said the signor, "that the main point, with Mary's uncle, will be her happiness, and proof that the object of her choice is calculated, by character and disposition, to make her so. I know a great deal of Sir Charles Wharton, and am connected with him by marriage, and intimately acquainted with his disposition and character, and can therefore positively say, that fortune will have little, if anything, to do with his acceptance of your proposals. But now listen, till I tell you a melancholy and somewhat strange history. It will fully explain our dear Mary's position and other matters also.

"Some nineteen or twenty years ago, Sir Charles Wharton arrived in this city from England—he was, at this period, about eight and twenty; I had been married about two years, and my daughter Bianca was nearly nine months old. Sir Charles was a handsome man, of aristocratic birth and manners; nevertheless, he was engaged in great mercantile speculations, and was one of the partners of a very wealthy firm. This was the first time we had met, but for four years previously we had constantly corresponded. At this period my lamented sister Elese was living, and about two and twenty. She was considered very handsome; at all events, I know, a more amiable disposition never existed. We all became intimately acquainted with Sir Charles Wharton, who intended passing the winter months in Genoa. An attachment ensued between my sister Elese and the baronet, and long before the winter was over they became devoted to each other, and Sir Charles made proposals to me for the hand of my sister, which were joyfully accepted; and no obstacle lying in the way of their union, the month of May in the following spring was fixed upon for their marriage.

"In the month of March, we were all residing in this mansion—a happier family it was impossible to see. Alas! how little can human happiness be depended on—what trivial circumstances often-times change the whole tenour of our lives! An event at this time occurred that for many a day wrecked the peace of mind of the kind-hearted baronet, and, no doubt, will tinge the whole of his life—but I was going to say, we all determined to spend a week in Genoa, to witness some interesting religious ceremonies ordered by the Pope to take place as a thanksgiving.

"My wife and Elese drove to Genoa in the carriage, whilst Sir Charles and I rode on horseback; the children (Terese was then born) and their nurses were to follow the next day, for the weather was boisterous, and the waters of the Polchevera were high; alas! we ought not to have gone at all on that day, for during the night it had rained tremendously. The torrent of the Polchevera, which you know, as we passed through it yesterday, had not sufficient water to reach our horses' knees; this stream, or rather torrent, is subject to the most sudden and violent changes; having its rise amid the mountains of the Boghette range, it becomes, after storms, summer and winter, so enormously swollen, that no passage can be attempted across it, till it falls; its bed, at this moment dry, might after a thunderstorm be a sheet of foaming flood, more than a mile in breadth. On reaching the borders of the stream we found it much more swollen than we imagined; the long, lofty, and narrow bridge, spanning its water, stood like an island in the middle of the stream. Whilst we hesitated, and were, in point of fact, about to give up our expedition, a Signor Lupati, a gentleman I knew, and who resided in San Pietro de Arena, rode up, saying, 'You need not be afraid, the passage over the bridge is quite easy and safe,' he consequently rode on, and as the main body of the torrent always runs under the numerous arches of the long bridge, he easily rode through the water, over the road, and gained the bridge. This induced us to follow, especially as the females said they were not at all afraid.

"We rode over and the carriage followed, and had just gained the steep ascent of the bridge, when a roar like thunder was heard, and the next instant the torrent of the

Polchevera came thundering down the valley with a wall of foam, and with the speed of the race-horse. To turn the carriage was out of the question, as the bridge was but barely the width of the vehicle; it was built by the Durazzo family.

"'Drive on, drive on,' said the unfortunate Signor Lupati, spurring his horse into the stream, on the other side of the bridge, thinking to cross before the wall of waters reached the spot. Vain hope : scarcely four yards from the bridge, when the foaming stream struck against the arches, making it rock to the foundation, and terrifying the horses to such a degree, that we took the ladies from the carriage. The unfortunate Signor Lupati, horse and man, were overwhelmed, and submerged, and were never more seen, the torrent rushing into the Mediterranean with a fury terrific to look at, opposing itself to the heavy swell then running in, and in the shock—casting its foam forty feet into the air.

" We were all dreadfully shocked at witnessing this terrible calamity: such events were not, however, of rare recurrence, for not a season passes but many lives are sacrificed to the sudden fury of this dreaded torrent. But knowing the unfortunate gentleman, and witnessing his melancholy fate, rendered it infinitely more shocking, and knowing also that no human power could give the slightest assistance.

" Our situation was extremely critical. I was not exactly afraid that the time-honoured bridge would give way, though it rocked like a ship at sea, but the waters kept rising, and the rain was beginning to fall heavily ; the carriage was a light open vehicle, and afforded no shelter ; the horses were violent and unruly, and there appeared no chance of escaping from the bridge perhaps for twenty-four hours. In this dilemma, we observed the people on the west shore dragging up from the beach one of their light fishing boats, and then, lifting it, they carried it a considerable distance up the stream. On the west side of the bridge, the torrent, though it runs violently, still runs over no obstacles, so that two men, launching the boat higher up, and having a long warp attached, safely guided the boat up to the parapet of the bridge. It was a long large boat, capable of holding us all, and the people having the warp ashore had it in their power to haul us to land ; the horses, afterwards, were to be fastened to the boat and made to swim ashore.

" My wife and sister were not frightened ; the thoughts of remaining all night exposed to the inclemency of the weather terrified them much more than the passage in the boat.

"Into the boat we got, that is, my wife and sister, Sir Charles and myself; the three servants were to come the next trip with the horses.

"The man who held the rope—for to use oars was out of the question—then let the boat float across the stream towards the west shore, not attempting to resist the fierce current; but when just within ten yards of the shore, a huge boulder, hurled down the stream by the first violence of the torrent, struck the boat violently, and the shock and heel-over threw Elese out; my wife would have met the same fate, but I had my hand round her waist, and hold of the gunnel of the boat at the same time. The moment Elese touched the water, a wild shriek escaping her lips, Sir Charles threw himself out of the boat and grasped her garments; he was no swimmer, but he resolved to perish with her if he could not save her; fortunately they were near the bank, and a shoal jetting out before them, Sir Charles contrived to keep his legs and hold my poor sister till the fishermen, running into the water, threw ropes over them and dragged them on shore in a half-drowned state. A fever of a severe kind followed this untoward accident to my sister, from which she recovered in some degree, though her constitution seemed to have received a shock, which did not exactly show itself then, further than by a somewhat tormenting cough.

"In the month of May, however, Sir Charles and Elese were married, and thinking change of scene and air would remove her cough and weakness, they went and passed a few months at Nice, then Aqui, and returned to Genoa, preparatory to embarking for England; for Sir Charles had received letters requiring his presence in that country. But Lady Wharton was not able to undertake the voyage; she expected to become a mother in a few months, and the physicians consulted were decidedly against her attempting the voyage. Sir Charles would have purchased a handsome villa on the coast for her, but I insisted on her residing at our mansion in Sestri till her husband's return; and the love she bore to my amiable wife made such a residence, in some slight measure, compensate for the baronet's absence.

" I was, at this time, embarked in a very lucrative commerce, in which Sir Charles had a share; my sister, as our family resided almost entirely in Genoa, had this house to herself.

"Whilst residing with Sir Charles Wharton at Aqui,

Lady Wharton took into her service a young female of great personal attractions, excellent education, and very superior manners for her station. She called herself Magdalene Caracci, said she was of a good family, but that reduced circumstances had forced her to seek service. Though she had no testimony of character to show, but offered herself unsupported, so much was my sister prepossessed by her appearance and her story, that she at once took her as her own especial attendant; and, indeed, we all, when we saw her, were ready to congratulate Elese upon the acquisition she had secured. My sister treated her more as a companion than an attendant. She kept quite aloof from all the other domestics, chiefly remained in her mistress's room, reading to her during her periods of weakness and illness, so that Lady Wharton became greatly attached to her.

" Lady Wharton expected to be confined in the month of December; she preferred the event taking place in Sestri, though I wished her to remove to Genoa. Sir Charles was expected to arrive the first week in the month.

" One night, the last day of November, I was roused in the dead of night, by the arrival of a messenger from Sestri. My sister, he said, was taken alarmingly ill, and he had been sent for me and the family physican; the doctor had been summoned first, and had left for Sestri at once. My wife was greatly alarmed. I dressed hurriedly, mounted a horse, and rode off for Sestri, leaving her to follow in the morning. Alas! I never saw my sister again in life. A child was born, but the mother did not live even to bless it. I cannot dwell upon this terribly, fearful scene. Poor Elese was retiring to rest apparently as well as usual, when a terrible fit of coughing brought on spasms, and just as the doctor arrived and received the poor babe, she drew her last breath.

" The physician declared that the child had reached its time, and was a fine, full-grown female infant.

" I was deeply affected at this event: I loved my sister tenderly; a nurse for the poor little thing was procured, but it was obliged to be reared by hand. Magdalene Caracci implored, with tears in her eyes, to be permitted to take charge of it, which, of course, was willingly assented to, for until Sir Charles's return we could not interfere with the attendant selected by his unfortunate wife. Not, indeed, that any of my family objected to Magdalene Caracci, all we ever saw of her was unimpeachable; she was certainly silent and reserved, the domestics called her proud and haughty, and above her situation;

E

but she had always appeared attentive and devoted to Lady Wharton.

"Now comes the mysterious part of my story," continued the Signor Garetti. "We received a letter from Sir Charles, stating that he would be with us shortly, *viâ* Hamburg, as affairs relative to his brother compelled him to take that route. He felt deeply anxious about his wife, and trusted he should, without fail, be with her before Christmas—his letter to her, alas! I will not speak of it—it was full of the fondest affection.

"Three days after receiving those letters, Magdalene Caracci and the child disappeared.

"The baby, its nurse, and herself slept in the same chamber in this mansion. That morning, not hearing any stir in the room at a rather late hour, the other domestics knocked at the door, but no answer was returned; finally the door was opened, and, to the amazement of those who entered, the nurse was found buried in so profound a sleep, that they could not awake her—she had been dosed with opium; but Magdalene Caracci and the child were gone. I was summoned immediately; this fresh misfortune completely bewildered and paralyzed me; I sent, however, to Genoa for an active officer of the police, and set him and his agents upon this Magdalene Caracci's track, for it was very evident that she had left the house during the night, by a back door leading into the garden; but there ended all trace, and no efforts on the part of the police officer could gain the slightest intelligence of her or the child. On the 18th of December, Sir Charles Wharton arrived, looking heart-broken and miserable: he had received my letters in Turin, which had acquainted him with the deplorable loss of his wife; but now, as he eagerly asked for his child, I had to inflict a fresh and terrible blow. He was completely prostrated; but after a few days of crushed spirits he revived, and prepared to take the most energetic means to discover his child; he himself went to Aqui to make inquiries concerning this Magdalene Caracci, but in vain; he then wrote to the British Consul at Naples, to search if such a person could be found there answering to the name and description of Magdalene, but was again baffled.

"One evening we were sitting together, Sir Charles Wharton's spirits completely prostrate, his mind shattered, and his health visibly affected. I used every argument I could think of to cheer him, for I did not yet despair of finding his little lost one. I remarked to him, 'There must be some object in this abduction of the child. This

Magdalene Caracci, in my opinion, has, from her first entrance into your service, been playing some deep game; but for what object I cannot imagine. The love of gold could have no part in her schemes.'

"'Benedetto,' said Sir Charles, with a sigh, 'I have offered £1,000 for the restoration of my child, as you know, in all the continental papers; and if money was her object, she might at any time have absconded with my beloved Elese's jewels, worth more than that. When she disappeared with the child, she took nothing in the world with her, even left unclaimed the handsome salary Elese engaged to give her. She never received a portion of it: always said, 'Let it be in your hands, madame, I do not require it; for everything is found me that I can desire.' In my opinion, she was a woman of a higher rank in life than we supposed her, though she endeavoured to hide her knowledge and manners as much as she could; depend upon it, her name is not Magdalene Caracci.'

"I assented to this, because I had long thought the name a feigned one.

"'I wished,' continued Sir Charles, 'before my departure for England, to speak to you upon the subject of my brother James: you know I was uneasy before I left, respecting him and his affairs, and on my journey here I crossed from London to Hamburg on purpose to judge for myself. On reaching Hamburg, I learned that my brother had dissolved partnership with the mercantile house of Fripps, Holden, & Co., but that their accounts were still unsettled. My sister-in-law was on the point of being confined, and lived in a country house about half a league from Hamburgh, but that my brother himself was in Italy. All this I heard from an old friend, who had been for many years settled in Hamburg. He appeared to wish to say more, but seemed to hesitate. Now, you must know, my brother and I, from the period of our first separating to try our different fortunes, corresponded only at long intervals. James Wharton was a remarkably handsome man, and fond of a life of pleasure and excitement. I feared, at first, he had embraced a career he was not adapted for, but after a year or two he wrote me word that he liked his adopted profession, that it gave him opportunities of seeing a good deal of the world, that he had travelled all through Italy and Germany on mercantile business; therefore it was just the life he liked, and he was sure to prosper.

"'Three or four years after this I was told my brother had married a Miss Co_lan, daughter of a rich British merchant, now dead, and had received £15,000 fortune with her ; in fact, he wrote to tell me so, and I congratulated him, and wished him every prosperity.

" 'Finding my old friend in Hamburg hesitating, and yet, apparently, wishing to tell me something, I pressed him hard ; and then he told me that my brother and his wife lived most unhappily, that there were reports that he had married an Italian lady in Italy, of great beauty, others said he was this Italian beauty's *cavaliere servante*, but it was very well known that they travelled through Italy together ; that this, reaching his wife's ears, rendered her life miserable.

" 'This account annoyed me, and fretted me exceedingly. I did not believe that he could be so base as to marry two women, but thought it not unlikely that he was unfaithful to his marriage vow. I set out to visit my sister-in-law, but arrived just an hour after her confinement. She was extremely ill, and quite incapable of seeing any one for several days, so, inquiring where I might be likely to find my brother, and being told he was in Milan, I left Hamburgh. Deeply anxious to reach Genoa, I travelled rapidly to Milan, and inquired at a certain bank for my brother's residence ; he had been in Milan, but was gone on to Venice. By making inquiries and employing a very clever cicerone, I discovered that my brother had left Milan in a travelling chariot by post, and that a lady and female attendant accompanied him. Thus the report I heard at Hamburg was confirmed. I felt exceedingly shocked and distressed, but anxious to rejoin my beloved and, alas! now deeply-lamented Elese, I hurried on here, little imagining the awful calamity it was God's will to afflict me with.

" 'I shall return at once to England,' continued Sir Charles, ' but I wish you to discover, if you can, by writing to Venice to your correspondent there, who this female with my brother is. I intend, according to what I hear, to offer his unfortunate and deserted wife an asylum in England for herself and child.'

" I promised my brother-in-law to do all I could, in this affair, and some days afterwards he left for England, leaving agents and directions, and offering ample rewards for any discovery of his lost child. I also never ceased in my inquiries. Rather more than three years passed over, nothing satisfactory turning up about the lost child or Magdalene Caracci. At one time I thought I had got a trace, but was deceived. All I could learn concerning James Wharton was, that he had visited Padua and Venice, with a very beautiful woman, travelling with him

as his wife, that they lived in great luxury, but saw no
company, and that they quitted Venice for Rome and
Naples. As I said, rather more than three years passed
over, when I received a letter from Sir Charles, dated
Como, in which he merely said, 'My unfortunate brother
and his wife are both dead, from malignant fever, they have
left a fine little girl, nearly four years old; I refrain from
particulars till I see you.'

" Ten days afterwards the baronet arrived, with a nurse
and the little girl his niece.

" We were all exceedingly rejoiced to see this kind-
hearted, generous relation, and the lovely little girl, his
niece. Sir Charles was in very low spirits; he had suffered
a great deal, the death of his brother and his wife had
deeply affected him. My two little girls were in raptures
with little Mary, and my wife insisted on having the care
of her."

CHAPTER VII,

" After some days, when Sir Charles had a little recovered
himself, he took an opportunity of speaking to me in
private.

" 'I wish,' commenced the baronet, with a sigh, 'to
leave little Mary with you for a year or two—I shall not
return to England for more than that space of time; but
first let me tell you the strange and unaccountable events
that preceded and followed my misguided brother's death,
events which have strangely perplexed and bewildered my
mind, and raised hopes in my breast I dread to indulge.

" ' In the first place, then,' continued the baronet, ' you
must know that Mary is not my niece.'

" ' Not your niece ! ' I exclaimed, in the greatest astonishment.

" ' No,' he returned, and then, with a sigh, added, ' I
must tell you everything, so that you may understand all,
and thus be able to advise and consult with me upon this
mysterious affair.

" ' About five weeks ago, I received a letter from the
friend I mentioned to you that I had in Hamburg.

" ' He merely said, ' I regret to have to tell you that your
brother is dangerously ill in Milan, not expected to live;
Mrs. Wharton, notwithstanding the cruel treatment she has
received, has left Hamburg to nurse him.'

" ' I instantly departed from England, and travelling
through Germany and Switzerland reached Milan, and

looking for the address sent me by my Hamburg friend, I anxiously proceeded to the mansion denoted.

" 'It was in the Corso di Porta Romano. But my brother, by the advice of his physician, had left Milan and taken a villa on the borders of the Lake of Como; the lady of the mansion looked a very obliging person, so I begged her to give me some information concerning my brother.

" 'Your brother,' said the landlady; 'indeed, yes.' 'How long has he been ill?' I inquired.

" 'Oh, a considerable time, signor; he was taken ill of the malignant fever of the marshes at Buffalora, which was raging terribly some months ago: but he was not very bad when he and his lady arrived here, but it came on much worse, from neglect and too high living, and then assumed a very severe form.' 'How long ago, signora, is it since Mrs. Wharton came here?' 'Oh, three months ago, signor.'

" 'This satisfied me that the female with him could not be his wife. 'Pardon me,' said I, risking a question, ' Was his wife an English woman?'

" 'The Signora Betio, the owner of the mansion, looked surprised at me, saying, 'Do you not know that your brother's wife is an Italian, and a very beautiful woman, and most fascinating; and that they have a lovely little girl, about three years old, or more, perhaps?'

" 'I said I had not seen my brother for some years, and thanking the landlady, and procuring the directions from her where to find my brother's residence near Como, I left Milan, greatly disgusted and annoyed, and wondering what had become of my brother's lawful and unfortunate wife.

" 'On reaching Como, late that evening, I inquired of the landlord of the inn how far it was to the Villa Baradella.

" 'Oh, you can reach the villa, signor,' said the land-lord, 'in a boat, in less than an hour, by crossing the lake, but by land it will occupy you nearly four hours.'

" 'I engaged a boat, therefore, for the next morning, and with a very anxious mind I left the quay about nine o'clock, in a boat with an awning, and pulled by four men. It was very hot, but at any other time I should have been in raptures with this enchanting lake—its pellucid waters and its gorgeous scenery—but my mind was so pre-occupied that I saw none of the beauties around me.

" 'The Villa Baradella was on the very shore of the lake, nearly opposite to the villa of Pliny the Elder. I landed under a handsome pavilion, and as I ascended the steps to the terrace, a servant came from the house to meet me. I guessed, from the man's countenance, that my brother must be very bad indeed; therefore, I inquired how the Signor Wharton was, with a feeling that the answer would be distressing.

" ' There is no hope, signor,' returned the domestic, in Italian, ' even that he will live through the day.'

" ' I am the Signor Wharton's brother,' said I. While speaking I observed a tall female figure in a mantle, with a long veil over the head, reaching nearly to the feet, leave the house through a saloon window, that opened to the ground, leading by the hand a beautiful little girl, between three and four years old; they passed on, the female without looking towards me, entered the pavilion built over the waters of the lake. ' The Signor Wharton's child, I suppose?' said I to the man, as he preceded me into the house.

" ' Si, signor.'

" ' And the lady?' I continued,

" ' The child's governess, signor,' returned the man.

" ' Is Mrs. Wharton here?' I demanded, as the domestic showed me into the saloon.

" ' Yes, signor, but she has caught the fever, and is quite insensible. I will send the doctor to you, signor, for you had better not enter the sick chamber.'

" ' I have no fear,' I replied, ' and my duty and affection require my presence in my brother's chamber; but I will see the doctor first, as it might agitate my brother to see me suddenly.'

" ' The man bowed, and left the room. I paced the chamber, shocked and grieved; my brother dying; his wife, whether the Italian or his lawful wife, I could not say, also in danger.

" ' Presently the door opened, and a very gentlemanly signor entered the room, and introduced himself as the physician.

" ' I am sorry, signor,' said he, when I made him aware who I was, for the domestic did not do so, ' I am sorry I can give you no earthly hope; indeed, the Signor Wharton can scarcely live out the day, perhaps not an hour.'

" ' Good God!' I exclaimed, ' this is terrible. Is he sensible?'

" ' At times, signor; very short intervals of quiet; the spasms are fearful.'

" ' How long has Mrs. Wharton been attacked?' I questioned.

" ' She was ill and weak when she arrived here, signor.

" 'Ah,' said I to myself, ' then this poor lady is his true wife ; ten to one but this governess is his Italian mistress.'

" 'The doctor continued : 'I wished in her weak state to prevent her entering the room, but she insisted on seeing her husband. When I informed your brother she had arrived, he seemed greatly shocked, and in the midst of a terrible attack of spasms, implored me not to let her in. ' She will catch this fever and die,' he said ; and then as he recovered a little, he added, ' Tell the governess to keep with the child in the pavilion, and on no account to come near the house.'

" 'He had scarcely concluded speaking, before his affectionate and unfortunate wife rushed into the room, and threw herself almost in hysterics on the bed, taking his hand in hers, and weeping bitterly.

" 'Your brother fainted ; I had Mrs. Wharton carried to another chamber, and the next morning she was in a high fever, and is now insensible ; still she may recover.'

" 'And the governess ? ' I inquired, with some hesitation. ·does she visit my brother's chamber?' I knew not whether the doctor guessed or knew the real state of the case or not, but he looked me seriously in the face, as he said, ' Nothing can exceed the attention of the signora; night and day she is unceasing in her attention to both Mr. and Mrs. Wharton.'

" ' Is Mrs. Wharton conscious of her attention?' I questioned.

" 'No, signor, returned the physician, ' she lies in a perfectly dreaming, quiet state; suffers no pain.' .;

" 'I then requested the doctor to prepare my brother for my presence, and he left the room. In five minutes more I was summoned to the sick chamber.

" 'With a feeling of awe and deep regret that thus we were to meet after years of separation, and that this meeting was, alas ! to be only the prelude to a final separation, I entered the room.

" 'The chamber was lofty and large ; the rays of light through the two great windows being subdued and softened by a projecting verandah and venetian blinds ; scarcely an article of furniture was allowed in the room ; it was kept as cool and airy as possible. My eyes first rested on the simple couch on which reclined my unfortunate brother ; he lay on his back, his face rigid, pale, and haggard ; the eyes closed, the broad massive forehead white as snow, to which his thick clustering dark hair, worn long, showed in strange contrast.

" 'I paused close by the bed, almost choking with

emotion, the tears stealing down my cheeks like burning drops, for I saw at once that the destroyer's hand hovered over his noble brow.

" ' I could scarcely believe I beheld James Wharton, one of the handsomest men of his day, and then but eight and twenty.

" ' Presently he opened his eyes, and they rested on me ; he shook—the very couch shook with the emotion he seemed to feel. ' Charles,' said he, in a low, trembling voice, motioning with his hand for the doctor to leave us ; and then, as I seized his wasted hand and pressed it to my lips, though he struggled to take it away, he continued, ' Charles, do you come to forgive me? I have deeply wronged you '—and he groaned bitterly.

" ' Not me, James,' said I, with deep emotion, ' not me ;—but do not give way to such intense suffering ; think of your wife and child.'

" ' Child! ' he repeated, with a terrible start, and turning half round,—' I have no child,—oh God, God ! ' he exclaimed, ' thou art just; his features altered fearfully, as he grasped my hand, as I stood shocked and amazed at his words. ' Hear me,' said he, ' life is ebbing fast—fast. The child in this house is '—the noise of a door opening caused him to pause and raise his eyes towards the sound —I did the same, and was startled at viewing a tall female, covered from head to foot in a long veil; it was the same figure I had seen with the child. I could not see a single feature, but she at once turned round and closed the side door by which she had entered the room, and disappeared ; a cry of agony escaped my brother's lips ; he was in a terrible fit of spasms ; I rung the bell with violence, and the physician entered the room hurriedly, and approaching the bed, said, ' Ah, I thought so, the excitement has hastened the event, he is dead.'

" ' I was bewildered, confounded, ' Good God ! ' I exclaimed, ' dead,' and I gazed at my brother's face, which lay as it were in a haze. But the will of God was accomplished, I had no longer a brother.

" ' Stunned by this sudden blow—I call it sudden, because it was not so immediately expected—and the words he had uttered, my mind became excited to an extraordinary degree. My brother had denied his child : he must, thought I, as I returned to another room, have been wandering in his mind : there could be no meaning in the words, ' I have no child here.'

" ' After a short time, the doctor came into the saloon, he

sat down. 'There is no chance, I fear,' said he, 'of Mrs. Wharton living, she has altered much in a few hours.'

" 'This is very terrible,' I replied, 'husband and wife the same day.' 'I do not say she will die to day,' continued the doctor, 'but I mean all chance of recovery is gone. Will you come and see her? she is in no pain, and looks serene and quiet, though much wasted, and her eyes are constantly closed.'

" 'I proceeded to the chamber, where my sister-in-law lay; two female attendants were in the room, one a middle-aged Englishwoman, highly respectable, who had come with Mrs. Wharton from Hamburg. I had never before seen my sister-in-law, and with a painful feeling of curiosity and much emotion I let my eyes rest upon her face. It was a very interesting one, though pale as death and terribly wasted; but in health she must have been handsome: for the features were perfect, and the long tresses of her rich brown hair fine as silk. She had a high, beautiful forehead, and her brows finely arched.

" 'She lay perfectly still, breathing like an infant, Mrs. Hudson, her attendant, every now and then moistening her lips; but it was, alas! very evident that she was wasting away most rapidly.

" 'With a sigh, I retired from the chamber, requesting my sister-in-law's attendant would give me five minutes of her time.

" 'The servants had placed refreshments on the table, but I required none; my mind was too miserable and my thoughts too overpowered to think of food.

" 'Presently Mrs. Hudson entered the room. She looked very distressed and much moved; she had lived with her mistress long before her marriage; ' and to see her thus cut off—sacrificing herself for an ingrate;'—she checked herself and sat down, the tears running over her cheeks.

" 'I am aware, Mrs. Hudson,' I commenced, ' of the cause of my sister-in-law's unhappiness; but we will not speak of that now; we are no longer *his* judges; but whose is the little girl I saw here with the governess?'

" 'Governess!' repeated Mrs. Hudson, in a tone of bitter scorn; 'but it is not my business—I beg pardon, Mr. Wharton; but surely you don't mean your own blessed little niece, the sweetest child that ever breathed—though they have taught it their own language.'

" 'Ah,' said I, mentally, 'I thought so; my brother's mind was wandering when he disowned his child. Then how comes the child, Mrs. Hudson, to speak Italian, and not English; its mother, surely, taught it her own language?'

"'Bless me, sir, the child was taken from my poor mistress when it was scarcely ten months old; and Mr. Wharton has had it reared somewhere in this country ever since. We never saw the dear child till we came here, ten days ago: my mistress could scarcely believe it was her own child, at first: it's not like her, certainly, sir, except in the eyes—more like its father; and indeed it's very like you.'

"'Could you bring me the child, Mrs. Hudson; I long to see my little niece?'

"'Certainly, sir; one of the women shall go to the pavilion for it, for it sleeps there with madame.' Mrs. Hudson pronounced the word madame with a toss of her head and a most contemptuous look.

"'All this is very strange, and indeed mysterious,' I soliloquized, as Mrs. Hudson left the room. 'There is evidently some mystery about the child.' I remembered that Mrs. Wharton was confined about three and a half years ago, whilst I was in Hamburg. What could induce my brother to take his child from his neglected wife, and cause it to be reared by his mistress? Altogether, the affair was obscure and mysterious. My position also was a peculiar one. What was I to do with this Italian woman? As I paced the room backwards and forwards, I observed that it grew extremely dusk, and, lifting the venetian blinds, I found the sun was near setting, and that a thunder-storm was gathering over the lake.

"'Mrs. Hudson soon returned with the little girl. It was in sooth a lovely child. I felt a strange sensation creep over me, as I gazed into its large and wonderfully beautiful dark eyes. The little girl looked earnestly into my face and shook back her little curls; the perspiration ran from my forehead. I thought her the living model of Elese, Was it fancy that acted so powerfully upon me? but you yourself, Benedetto, remarked the likeness—indeed, you all remarked it the moment you saw the child.

"'Bless me, she is very like you, sir;' said Mrs. Hudson, 'though it has its mother's eyes too.'

"'Then Mrs. Wharton's eyes are dark?' said I.

"'Oh, yes, sir, large and quite black; beautiful eyes she had; and the baby had its mother's eyes when it first saw the light; and we remembered it from the eyes more than anything else.'

"'Then the child, no doubt, is my niece,' said I thoughtfully.

" 'Lord bless us, sir,' said Mrs. Hudson, 'whose else ? I hope you did not think it was madame's.'

" 'I started at Mrs. Hudson's words, and again a confusion of ideas crowded into my brain. The dear child kept earnestly regarding me; she seemed pleased with my fondness. I kissed and petted her, and spoke to her in Italian, and she answered me very sweetly. Mrs. Hudson evidently did not understand Italian, so I said, What is your name, my love?'

" 'Mary,' said the child, 'Mary Magdalene.' Good God! how I started at the name. I felt all my blood rush to my head.

" 'Mrs. Hudson heard the name, for she immediately said the child was christened Mary, and had no such heathenish name as Magdalene.

" 'Magdalene was a common Italian name : but a chord was touched that vibrated through my whole frame 'And where, Mary, dear, is your mamma, now?'

" 'The child looked seriously into my face, saying, ' My mamma is in the pavilion.'

" 'Mrs. Hudson, though not understanding Italian, still caught the word mamma.

" 'Oh, sir, the poor child has been taught to call madame, mamma; but, please God, she will learn differently, now, and also to speak her poor mother's language.'

" 'Kissing the dear child, I let Mrs. Hudson take her away, whilst I remained in profound thought.

" 'The doctor had crossed the lake to Como, but would be back, he said, very early in the morning. There was nothing he could do for Mrs. Wharton; the fever had passed off. She was dying from exhaustion ; it was impossible to get her to take nourishment.

" ' I took a glass of wine and a biscuit, and retired to a room prepared for me, facing the lake. The night was intensely hot; and now and then a flash of lightning gleamed over the dark waters, illumining the scene without for a brief moment.

" 'I felt no desire for sleep, and kept pacing the room, with the windows wide open ; there was not a breath of air, but the storm was heaving—and about midnight it burst over the lake, with a grandeur and power terrible to hear, but sublime to look upon. The storm-gust rushed across the lake, and the lightning seemed to rest upon its waters, so prolonged and repeated were the flashes, whilst the waves were driven like snow-drifts into the air. The opposite shore was lit up clear as noon-day, as far as distinctiveness of outline went; whilst the deep blue of the lightning tinged the whole scene, as if viewed through one of Claude Lorraine's glasses.

" ' But those lake storms are of short duration. A deluge of rain fell, the wind instantly lulled, the thunder rolled away in the distance, and before an hour had elapsed the moon burst forth through the masses of cloud, and threw a flood of quiet, silvery light over the still uneasy waters of the lake, though they were rapidly recovering the calm, mirror-like surface. A delicious coolness came over the before-heated atmosphere, that revived my spirits wonderfully. Still I could not sleep. So, sitting down by the window, I gazed out over the wide waters spread before me.

" ' Even disturbed and troubled as I was, I could not view the scene before me unmoved. The great masses of thunder-cloud were still hanging over the high land, behind the quaint tower of the Baradella ; flashes of lightning still gleamed over the lake ; the instant after, contrasted by the bright moon's rays, and then again a mass of dark silver-edged cloud passed over the luminary, and all became involved in shadow. It was now nearly three o'clock in the morning. I threw off my coat, determined to lie down for an hour or two ; when, in a brilliant gleam of moonlight, I beheld a small boat, pulled by one man, come out from the deep shadow cast over the waters by the pavilion ; and, to my great surprise, I beheld a female, wrapped in a dark mantle, seated in the stern sheets.

" ' Surprised at seeing a boat with a female coming out from the landing-place of the villa, at that hour, I kept my eyes fixed upon it, and as the full moon was at this moment shining as bright as day, the boatman's face was clearly visible ; I could tell every feature ; he was a young man. The boat had to pass across my window ; I let the venetian blind fall, but still gazed steadily through its folds upon the female, for somehow I fancied it was the Italian the child called mother. She had the hood of her mantle drawn partly over the head, but as the man pulled out from the shore, she turned, and, pushing back the hood, gazed earnestly up at the mansion. I fell back, with an exclamation of profound amazement. Merciful heavens ! am I sleeping or waking, I mentally exclaimed ; I felt I became pale as death. Tearing aside the blinds, I gazed out with an intense eagerness, but all was dark, and involved in gloom ; a vast mass of cloud covered the whole vault above, but a vivid flash of lightning, for an instant, gleamed over the waters. I could see the boat, the man

pulling vigorously across the lake. I shouted aloud in my
excitement, 'Magdalene, Magdalene Caracci, in the name
of God, return,' I paused and listened, all was so still that
the sound of the man's oars in the rollocks, fell distinctly
on the ear. I was bewildered. Was I the slave of my
own heated brain, disturbed by recent events and want of
repose? The perspiration streamed from my forehead, for
I could have sworn, that when the female turned her face
towards the villa, and I gazed down upon that pale beautiful face. I could have staked my existence that I beheld
the remarkable features of the mysterious Magdalene
Caracci. Hastily putting on my garments, I hurried down
stairs; there was no stir in the house, the chamber occupied
by the dying Mrs. Wharton being in another wing of the
villa.

" ' I entered the saloon. and throwing open the window,
jumped out on the terrace—I scarcely knew what I did. I
thought only of Magdalene Caracci. I was satisfied it was
her. I ran to the little quay, where I had landed some
hours back, and where I had observed a small pleasure-
boat, about fourteen feet long; it was still there, fastened
by a chain, but no oars. I looked about me, and seeing a
shed close by, I went there, and I found oars and sails.
Taking a pair of oars, I leaped into the boat, thinking of
only one thing—the pursuit of Magdalene Caracci. I cast
off the chain, and seizing the oars, pulled off, with all my
strength, in the direction I considered the boat was
gone.

" ' I stood up first to see if I could discover any traces,
but the heavens were again dense, and another thunder
storm was sailing over the lake; still I pulled on for the
opposite shore. I can pull a good oar, few Oxford men
that cannot, and I was a strong man. In twenty minutes,
as I stood up to look before me, a blinding flash of lightning burst out from the cloud overhead, and the peal of
thunder that followed was so astounding, so appalling, that
I fell back upon the bench, for an instant bewildered; the
crash of all man's engines of war, discharged at the same
moment, was child's folly to the stunning rattle of heaven's
own artillery. Flash after flash, and peal after peal
followed, and then came the roar of the storm's gust right
down the lake, sporting with the water and tossing it into
the air. One oar was torn from my hands, so lightning
like was the blast in its rapidity; the boat spun round, and
heeled over till she half filled, and then dashed on before
the wild gale, like a scared sea-bird.

" ' I could do nothing but steer the boat, with one of the

oars I still grasped, dead before the gale. You know what lake storms are, terrible and brief; they expend their fury in a few moments, but often times, with certain winds, these storms follow one another with uncommon rapidity and continue for hours.

" ' In ten minutes I was driven ashore, close to the walls of a magnificent villa residence. I gave the boat a pull up, for there is little disturbance of the water on the lake of Como; and then I turned along the shore, thinking the boat I was in pursuit of must, of course, have been also driven on land; but I was at once stopped by the terrace walls of a mansion, that projected considerably into the deep waters of the lake. Daylight was rapidly advancing, the storm's gust had passed on, and the sky was breaking again into masses.

" ' I returned to the boat, the wind had totally ceased; so, with my one oar, I pushed out once more, and sculled past the walls of the villa. This villa I afterwards learned was the most splendid on the lake, and called the villa Odaleschi. The shore here rose into a lofty wooded hill; a splendid waterfall tumbling over a succession of vast rocks, and falling into the lake, with considerable violence and uproar.

" ' I could see no sign of a small boat anywhere, though daylight rendered every object distinct; but coming down the lake were several picturesque boats, with their striped awnings and lofty, narrow sails of different colours; they were market-boats from the villages, to Como.

" ' I now began to think how my strange absence would amaze all at the villa. I had been so absorbed in the idea that I was pursuing Magdalene Caracci, the stealer of my child, and that this child was again found in the little girl I was induced to believe my niece, that I forgot everything else. Scull back across the lake, which was full two miles broad at this part, I could not, for I was tired and exhausted; to pursue my search after Magdalene was also out of the question; when the sight of a floating piece of wood attracted my attention. It was the oar I had lost; I picked it up, quite pleased, for I was fatigued with the exertion of sculling across; and in less than a quarter of an hour I was back under the walls of the pavilion. It was then nearly six o'clock, but I did not see any one up about the place; I fastened the boat, went in again through the window, and was proceeding to my chamber, when I encountered one of the female domestics.

" ' She seemed surprised at seeing me up. I inquired how Mrs. Wharton was; she said in the same state.

"'I begged her to go to the pavilion, where the child and her governess slept, to see if the latter were there.

"'The woman looked astonished, repeating the word 'there.' 'Oh, yes, signor, she is there. She and the child and one of the female domestics have slept there ever since the Signora Wharton arrived.'

"'I doubt, nevertheless,' I replied, 'if she is there now;' for, in my own mind, I set down the governess and Magdalene Caracci as one and the same person.

"'The woman looked incredulous, but said she would see. I saw her cross the terrace and proceed to the pavilion, and I heard her knocking at the door. Presently she came running back, looking frightened; and, seeing me at the window, she said,—

"'You are right, signor, the signora is not there; the child is fast asleep; the servant slept in another room, and did not hear a stir in the night.'

"'I knew such was the case,' I replied; 'I saw her cross the lake in a small boat, pulled by one man, about two o'clock this morning.'

"'Madonna! signor, can that be possible?' said the girl; 'I must go and tell the child's English nurse, for the little girl will be frightened.'

"'I should, my dear friend,' continued Sir Charles, 'prolong my story to a most tiresome length, were I to tell you minutely all that occurred during the next ten days. I must therefore be more brief.

"'My unfortunate sister-in-law died the third day, without recovering the power of speech, but, nevertheless, regained the use of her senses. She understood what was said to her by Mrs. Hudson; and when she was told I was in the mansion, she evinced intense eagerness to communicate with me. I sat by her bedside, holding one of her poor wasted hands; but she, some hours before she died, made signs that she wished to write something.

"'A sheet of paper was given her, and a pencil; and, with a trembling hand, supported by her faithful attendant, she wrote, 'Oh, be a father to my child!' and then, though on the point of fainting, she added,—

"'The child is mine; call her Mary, and no other name; God bless her!' and then she fainted. In three hours she was dead.

"'The amazement of all the household at the disappearance of the Signora Magdalene—they knew her by no other name, for they were all hired at Como—was very great indeed. She took nothing with her, neither did she leave any letter, paper, or document, whereby I could trace her. I paid several fishermen to pull along the shores of the lake to try and trace the fugitive. Strange to say, a small boat was found, about two miles below the villa Odaleschi, with a pair of oars; but the boat turned out to belong to a gentleman's villa within half-a-mile of us, and was supposed to have broken from its moorings. We could hear of no one missing in the vicinity; therefore, though I felt satisfied that the boat was the same I pursued, still we could not trace the boatman or his companion.

"'My mind was completely bewildered. Mrs. Hudson persisted there could be no mistake about the child; the mother, also, on her death-bed, declared the little girl to be hers. What could I say or do? but let the child be whose it may, I vowed to love it as a father—for I still, against all these bewildering circumstances, believe that Mary is my child,—the child of my lamented and dearly-loved Elese. From my own troubled state of mind I was forced to rouse myself, to perform the last sad duties to my unfortunate brother and his spouse. I had them both interred in the strange antique church of San Fedale, in Como.

"'On paying certain sums to the clergy, and going through some prescribed forms, I also employed the sbiri of Como to institute some inquiries after Magdalene Caracci; but they failed, though I doubt much whether they exerted themselves.

"'I was greatly surprised to find neither papers nor letters of any consequence amongst my brother's effects. A couple of hundred pounds was all his desk contained. Having paid all the servants, and settled with the owner of the villa for a twelve-month's rent, I left the place, with Mrs. Hudson and the dear child, who began, very quickly, to evince an affection for me.

"'After staying a few days at Milan, and a few more at Turin, I came on here; and now, Benidetto, what think you of my narrative? Do you think Mary is my child or my niece?'"

CHAPTER VIII.

"I had listened very attentively," continued [the Signor Garetti, "to Sir Charles Wharton's narrative, every word of which was impressed upon my memory, and I felt satisfied, putting all the circumstances together, that this Magdalene Caracci had forced herself into the service of Lady Wharton for the express purpose of stealing her child.

F

" The motive for this action was not so easy to discover ;
but I also felt convinced, mystified as the poor child's
birth was, that, nevertheless, she was Sir Charles
Wharton's child, and not his niece ; and I told him so.
" He was rejoiced. ' I shall always feel myself her father,'
said the baronet, ' and will act the father to her ; still I do
not think, for many reasons, that it will do, without some
proof, to produce her to the world as my daughter, after
the death-bed declaration of my lamented sister-in-law.

" ' There is still a dark cloud enveloping the whole affair ;
for what became of Mrs. Wharton's child if Mary is my
daughter?' However, Captain de Courcy, not to weary
you with further arguments on this subject, which will not
in the least enlighten you, or clear away the mystery,
Sir Charles a week afterwards departed for Hamburg, to
wind up his brother's affairs ; how he settled them I cannot
inform you ; he remains silent upon that subject, merely
stating to me that he had closed the account.

" You now know our dear Mary's history ; not a single
incident through the lapse of years has occurred to throw
a light upon the past.   Mrs. Hudson, Mary's affectionate
nurse, died two years ago, in England, protesting to the
last that Mary was, unquestionably, Sir Charles Wharton's
own lawful niece.   I have nothing more to add; what
think you of this certainly singular narrative ? "

" That it is perplexing and mysterious, certainly," said
Captain de Courcy, "but it only renders my love and
devotion to the dear girl ten-fold greater.   I suppose she
is fully acquainted with her own history? "

" Yes," returned the Genoese ; " Sir Charles, about two
years ago, related to her all the circumstances I have just
detailed to you.   At first Mary's affectionate heart felt
shocked ; she had forgotten all the early part of her life ;
and, reared with tender care in England, she had soon
ceased to speak the Italian language as her natural tongue,
though she still retained her perfect knowledge of it.   But,
as I remarked, it greatly grieved her affectionate heart, and
indeed preyed upon her mind, and probably injured her
health ; which induced the baronet to send her out to
spend the winter with us, hoping that change of air and
scene, with the society of her early companions, would
relieve her mind, and dissipate her sad thoughts ; and, I
feel rejoiced to say, she has quite recovered.   Now let me
congratulate you, my dear young friend, on having gained
as pure and loving a heart as ever beat in a maiden's
bosom."

" I trust that a life of devotion," said De Courcy, " if

it pleases God that our union takes place, will prove my appreciation of her beauty and her amiability. You will be surprised, my dear sir, to hear that to a certain extent there is a strong resemblance in our history, for I am myself very imperfectly informed as to my real birth. Sir John Acton took me under his protection, when in Ireland; he discovered me in an old mansion under the care of an aged dependent; he told me I was the son of a beloved friend, and that he would educate, protect, and provide for me. I was educated in the college of Sienna, and afterwards placed, by Sir John, in the Neapolitan navy. He has never enlightened me further on the subject of my birth, but has promised to do so on my return from this expedition, if it pleases God to spare me."

"You surprise me," said the Signor Garetti; "I would certainly insist on Sir John being explicit with you respecting your birth and family, before you unite your destiny with Mary Wharton. It would be absolutely necessary that you should know your real name."

"I have come to that determination,' replied our hero, "for I would never dream of giving my beloved Mary a name I had no title to."

"Of course you will have to visit England," said the Genoese, "and see Sir Charles personally."

"Such is my intention," replied our hero; "but as there are some rumours of peace between England and France, I could not, with honour, resign my present command, till satisfied on that point. I intend sailing for Naples in a few days, so as, if possible, to return before Mary leaves for England."

During the following day the family of the Signor Garetti were surprised by a visit from the Count of Spinola. Captain de Courcy was in Genoa, attending to some concerns respecting the Neapolitan flotilla, just returned from Elba.

The Count expressed great regret that Captain de Courcy was absent, as he said he came with the intention of apologizing for the apparent rudeness of his manner on meeting him at the Signor Garetti's mansion, in Genoa; he felt great regret, and acknowledged he spoke inconsiderately, and finally begged the Signor Garetti to make his apology to him.

The Count spoke with such apparent sincerity, and appeared so amiable in his manner, and quiet in his deportment, that even Mary lost the feeling of apprehension she had at first experienced on seeing him. The Count took his leave, hoping that the friendly terms on which he had formerly visited at the Signor Garetti's mansion would still continue, as he had come to pass some time at his palace, in Sestri.

The Signor Garetti, who knew nothing whatever of the private character of the Count, and who had always felt flattered by his acquaintance, was pleased at his present manner, and resolved to exert himself to make the two young men friends.

The next day, Captain de Courcy returned to Sestri. Mary at once mentioned the visit of the Count, and declared that though at first rather displeased at it, after remembering her lover's suspicions against him, he spoke so frankly, and was so respectful and unobtrusive, that her reserve soon wore off.

" Well, dearest," said De Courcy, " I bear no malice to the Count; indeed I may have been mistaken, and perhaps hasty in imputing to him a circumstance he assuredly might have nothing to do with. A man can do no more than apologize; therefore, if I meet the Count as a guest at the Signor Garetti's, I will greet him in as friendly a manner as he can desire.

The rivals met on the following day, and so exceedingly well did the Count play his cards, and so agreeable did he make himself, that De Courcy became quite friendly with him, visited his magnificent palace, and inspected his superb collection of paintings and statues, by the first masters in Italy, the past and existing.

Hugh de Courcy was of a generous, forgiving nature, naturally lively and fond of society, and was in general as much courted in the circle he mixed in as any young man of high rank in the Neapolitan court. He was neither suspicious nor jealous, by nature, but certainly passionate, hasty, and fiery, if deceived and wronged where he placed confidence.

Lieutenant Baracco, of the Vesuvius, who visited at the Signor Garetti's, made himself very agreeable to the young ladies, and became an especial favourite of the Count de Spinola.

Captain de Courcy had, as we observed before, a great esteem for his lieutenant, whom he always considered a neglected officer, and who was ten years older than himself. In his conduct to his superior officer, Baracco was always respectful, and extremely diligent in his duty.

One evening, about a fortnight after the renewal of the Count de Spinola's visits to the Garetti's mansion, Captain de Courcy and Lieutenant Baracco left Sestri, and embarked in their gig, to proceed on board the Vesuvius. They were to sail in a day or two for Naples.

On reaching the brig, Lieutenant Baracco, who appeared extremely gloomy and thoughtful, was rallied by Captain de Courcy on his apparent seriousness.

" It pains me, Captain de Courcy," said the lieutenant, in a low and sad tone, " to be the person to dispel the dream of happiness under which you seem so blessed."

Hugh de Courcy started, and turning round, said, with a flushed cheek, " What can you mean, Baracco ? "

" Will you listen to me with patience, Captain de Courcy ; you know my attachment to you ? " asked the lieutenant, in an earnest tone.

Our hero stood bewildered ; a thousand ideas and thoughts rushed through his brain. He, however, replied,—

" Come into the cabin ; I will listen to you there, though I cannot, for my life, imagine what you mean."

They descended into the cabin ; the sun was setting, and but a faint light entered the saloon of the brig, for the awnings were still overhead, and the curtains drawn across the windows to exclude the blaze of a July sun.

De Courcy threw himself into a seat, and passed his hand over his heated brow, for, besides the sultriness of the weather, he felt excited, flushed, uneasy.

Ordering the steward to bring him some water, he requested his lieutenant to let him understand what he meant by his strange words.

" It is an unpleasant and painful thing for even the dearest friend to do ; and yet I feel it my duty to warn you," said the lieutenant, with some hesitation of manner.

" You are deceived, Captain de Courcy—cruelly deceived."

" By whom ? " exclaimed our hero, almost fiercely ; his hot blood boiling at the word deceived.

" By the Count de Spinola, and by her——" Hugh de Courcy started to his feet ; his first intention was to seize his lieutenant by the throat ; for he guessed what he meant, and the heat-drops of agony rolled down his forehead ; but, sinking back into his seat, he forced himself into calmness, saying,—

" Pardon me, Baracco, I am hasty ; say what you have to tell ; you act from friendship, and, right or wrong, your motives are disinterested. Pray go on."

Lieutenant Baracco remained a moment silent ; the expression of his features could not well be seen, but his voice was low and hesitating, as he said, " Will you come with me this night to the Signor Garetti's mansion; to the pavilion on the sea-beach, at the hour of ten, and judge for yourself? I will not say another word; if, afterwards, you ask me any questions, I will answer them; more I will not say now." And he rose to his feet, and prepared to leave the cabin.

Hugh de Courcy hesitated one moment; his blood was on fire; but he then said, " Be it so; order the four-oared gig to be ready in an hour; we can reach the beach by that time easily."

" You had better go on shore at the rock above Pazia. You can land there without attracting observation," observed the lieutenant.

" Very good," answered De Courcy, calmly, as far as the sound of his voice went; but had any one placed their fingers on his pulse, they would have started with dismay.

Lieutenant Baracco left the cabin. Captain de Courcy swallowed a goblet of wine, and then paced the saloon with hurried and agitated steps. We shall not attempt to lay before our readers his thoughts; they were past delineating.

" The boat is ready, sir," said Captain de Courcy's coxswain. Our hero started, and felt as if a red-hot iron had penetrated his brain; but, taking up his sword, which he had thrown upon the table, he buckled it on, and left the cabin.

The twilight of the south had disappeared; there was no moon, but the deep blue firmament above was spangled with its millions of bright worlds.

The Vesuvius lay under the shelter of the west mole, beneath, as it were, the lofty beacon that then threw its light across forty miles of sea.

There was not a breath of air to disturb the still calm waters of the harbour. The tall tapering spars of the man-of-war brig appeared to tower to the sky, and her ropes looked, at a short distance, like silken threads.

Captain de Courcy and his lieutenant entered the gig; the men gave way, and the light craft shot through the still waters like an arrow.

CHAPTER IX.

AFTER rounding the Lanterna, the boat containing our hero pulled in from the projecting rock for the strand of San Pietro de Arena; the distance thence to Pazia being only six miles. In something more than an hour, the keel grated upon the shingly beach, in a kind of sheltered bight, under a range of lofty rock, projecting about sixty yards into the sea from the beach, affording an easy landing when the westerly winds blew in a surf upon the shore. Great alterations have taken place all along that exquisitely beautiful coast during the last fourteen years, but its main features are the same.

Captain de Courcy sprang ashore; so did Lieutenant Baracco, telling the men to await their return. Our hero walked on with a rapid step; he did not exchange one word with his lieutenant till they came within sight of the pavilion, built upon a terrace, within a short distance of the sea-beach, and about two hundred yards from the mansion of Signor Garetti. De Courcy paused; they were then standing under the outer wall of the gardens of the Spinola palace, which we have already stated adjoined those of the Signor Garetti. There was a door in this wall leading out on to the beach.

"It yet wants twenty minutes to the time," said Lieutenant Baracco, striking a repeater; "place yourself beneath the wall of the pavilion, within the recess of the porch; be · silent, and observe what happens. I will return to the boat and await you."

De Courcy made no reply, but walked on till he came beneath the pavilion; he then looked up and beheld a faint light.

This very unusual circumstance caused him to start, and he felt his heart beat wildly. He, however, placed himself in the deep niche of the gate that led into the Signor Garetti's gardens. He could see still the window of the pavilion, and, as he gazed up at it, many a bitter thought rushed through his brain—one minute seriously regretting the mean part he was acting; the next, angry with himself for permitting any human being to throw a shade of suspicion on the purity of Mary Wharton, and execrating his own madness for listening to the scorpion suggestions of jealousy. Suddenly he beheld the blind before the window move; it was raised, and then a strong light was thrown upon a human head, that for an instant was protruded, drawn back, and then the blind let down. All the blood in De Courcy's body seemed to rush to his brain—he had seen the face of Mary Wharton. He felt tempted to scale the walls and enter the pavilion; but, just then, looking along the strand, in the imperfect light, he beheld a dark figure emerge from the door in the wall of Count Spinola's garden. The figure stood still several moments, and then advanced towards the pavilion.

Instantly giving way to his fiery nature, without waiting to observe further, De Courcy left the porch, and advanced rapidly to meet the figure. They encountered half way, and Captain de Courcy at once recognized the Count de Spinola. The latter started back a pace or two, saying, in a hesitating voice,—

"You, Captain de Courcy, here?"

"Yes, Sir Count, I am here!" returned the commander of the Vesuvius. "You little expected me, no doubt, to interfere with your assignations."

"By what right, Captain de Courcy," said the young nobleman, haughtily, "are you become a spy upon my actions? I may, with just reason, ask you, and with a better face, why I found you here at this unusual hour?"

"This is evasion, Count," fiercely interrupted De Courcy; "I know your intentions; you have basely deceived me; you knew I——"

"Sir!" equally fiercely retorted the Count, "I know or care nothing about what you know. Before you came here, I was the accepted lover of Miss Wharton."

"That is a false lie, Count de Spinola!" exclaimed De Courcy, "and you shall answer to me with your life for your falsehood. How you have contrived to corrupt the heart of Miss Wharton, I know not; but I have now evidence both of her weakness and your perfidy."

"All is fair in love, as well as in war," mockingly laughed the Count; "the gallant Captain de Courcy is not always the conqueror."

"Enough of this," retorted our hero, conquering his passion; "draw, sir, and let us end this recrimination of words!"

".Per Bacco, willingly, Captain de Courcy, but pray retire a little just round the corner of yon wall; it will prevent the fair lady in yonder pavilion being disturbed."

De Courcy clenched his hand. With difficulty he refrained from striking the Genoese to the ground; but he walked on, followed by the Count, till they turned the corner of the long wall, when suddenly three men, disguised, rushed out from a recess, and threw themselves, with drawn stilettos, upon De Courcy, who had not even unsheathed his sword.

Perfectly self-collected whenever danger assailed him, De Courcy at once grew calm, and, receiving the blow of the nearest assassin on his left arm, which was wounded, he felled the villain with his right hand, by a blow in the throat, instantly springing back; as he did so, the sword of the Count de Spinola passed through his coat, inflicting a wound of little consequence in his side. The blow was struck from behind. But De Courcy had now his sword drawn, and, striking the nearest ruffian across the face with the edge, he rushed upon the Count, who was a skilful swordsman; and who, base and bad as he was, possessed courage; but Hugh de Courcy beat down his guard, and ran him through with such force that the thrust bore him to the ground. As De Courcy released his sword, he received the blow of a stiletto from behind, which sank deep in his left shoulder; he staggered, but, still undismayed and boiling with rage, he drove his sword through the villain who had struck him, laying him beside the senseless body of the Count. The remaining two men fled, leaping over a low wall, and disappearing among the groves of orange and citron, bordering the Count's grounds.

De Courcy made no attempt to pursue; disgusted, sick at heart, and weak with loss of blood, he stood for a moment gazing upon the two inanimate bodies at his feet. He then kicked off the mask from the dead assassin's face, but the features were strange to him; he put his hand on the Count's heart,—he was not dead.

A moment he hesitated, and wiped away the perspiration that streamed from his forehead, and then walked on towards his boat, becoming weaker and weaker from the loss of blood.

It was nearly three-quarters of a mile to the boat, which he reached totally exhausted. The men were lying list-lessly on the thwarts. Lieutenant Baracco was absent, but the next moment he came running along the beach.

De Courcy could only just throw himself upon the stern sheets, where he fainted, from the loss of blood and over-exertion. When he opened his eyes, which he did from the application of the sea-water to his temples, he perceived the boat going rapidly through the water; one of the men, his coxswain, an Englishman of the name of Benson, an old man-of-war's man, who was much attached to his person, was supporting his head, with great anxiety expressed in his features; whilst Lieutenant Baracco was binding up, with strips of linen, the worst wound he had received, that in the left shoulder. His entire garments were satu-rated with blood.

" Good God!" exclaimed the lieutenant, in a low voice, " what has occurred? How have you received these wounds?"

Seeing his men, who were greatly attached to him, look-ing terrified and anxious, De Courcy made an effort, and raised himself, saying,—

" Give way, my lads, there is no danger in a few flesh wounds ; that villain has paid with his life, most likely, for his treacherous attempt upon mine. But pull on board as quickly as possible."

The light boat flew through the waters, and in an incredibly short time she rounded the Faro : and, doubling the west mole, shot up alongside the Vesuvius. De Courcy, excepting the excessive weakness from loss of blood and the stiffness of his left shoulder and arm, did not suffer much pain ; with the assistance of his lieutenant he got on board; his officers and crew evinced intense surprise ou seeing and hearing that he was wounded. On gaining his cabin his surgeon was immediately in attendance and dressed his wounds, none of which he declared were dangerous ; but he wished his patient to at once lie down ; but this he would not do. Having taken a restorative draught, he seated himself to write a letter to the Signor Garetti, which occupied him half an hour; he then requested Lieutenant Baracco's attendance. When the lieutenant entered the cabin our hero was leaning back, exceedingly pale, and looking exhausted. "You will get the brig, Signor Baracco, under weigh with the dawn, but hail a shore-boat, and let this letter be left at the mansion of the Signor Garetti. If the wind permits, when clear of the harbour, take a direct course for Naples, and I pray you keep to yourself the events of this night. Some other time I will speak to you on this subject ; at present I am too much exhausted."

The next morning the brig was under weigh: the officers and crew were very anxious in their inquiries of the surgeon, who assured them that Captain de Courcy was only weak from loss of blood, and in three or four days he would be again on his legs.

The fourth day Captain de Courcy, to the infinite joy of his officers and crew, came upon deck ; his face was very pale, and the expression of his handsome features sad and serious. He looked also care-worn and haggard, as if mind, more than body, had suffered ; during those four days he had not opened his lips to Lieutenant Baracco on the subject of his attempted assassination ; merely asking questions relative to the position of the brig. On gaining the deck he looked around him : a young midshipman, a fine handsome lad, about fifteen, the son of a Sicilian gentleman of good family, but small fortune, who was a great favourite with Captain de Courcy, was standing near, and touching his cap, said, looking anxiously into his commander's face,—

" I trust, sir, you are better; you look as if you had suffered much."

" Thank you, Stefano," replied De Courcy, putting his hand, kindly, on the lad's shoulder, " I should be well enough in body, but the mind will not let the body get strength. What craft is that away to the south-west? Her very lofty spars betoken a vessel of war."

" We only observed her, sir, some few minutes ago; she came out from the port of Cagliari."

Captain de Courcy took a glass from the hands of Stefano Pamfili. The Vesuvius was about two leagues from the east coast of Sardinia; contrary winds, light and variable, had driven the brig within sight of that island, along whose coast she kept working to windward.

" That is an English frigate," observed our hero; " she is working to windward like ourselves." After walking the deck for half an hour Captain de Courcy descended to the cabin, requesting the first lieutenant to favour him with his company for a short period.

From the time of leaving Genoa, our hero had observed that Lieutenant Baracco maintained a gloomy abstracted silence to all on board the brig; he seemed to the other officers and crew to perform his duties like an automaton, never speaking a word beyond the sentences required for working the ship. The attempted assassination of their commander remained a constant subject of conversation amongst the petty officers and crew; but, of course, no kind of conjecture or surmise came near the mark.

Lieutenant Baracco descended to the cabin, and found his commander stretched on a sofa. He was still weak and languid, though his wounds were healing rapidly.

" You may think it strange, amico," said our hero, kindly, to his lieutenant, as he sat down, with a very serious expression of countenance, " that as yet I have never spoken to you upon the subject of my attempted assassination at Sestri."

" It is a subject, Captain de Courcy," returned the lieutenant, " painful and distressing, I know, to you; and to me equally so, because I am bound by my sacred word not to reveal to you the very thing you must be most anxious to ascertain. I am myself exceedingly bewildered respecting the manner in which you were wounded, for you must suppose, if I considered you incurred any risk of life that night, I should not have quitted you. Your return, desperately wounded, and almost bleeding to death, confounded and distressed me. Yet, knowing how little I could relieve your curiosity, I refrained from attempting to satisfy my own."

" Well," observed our hero, with a sigh, " you may let
me hear all you are at liberty to disclose ; I will then inform you of what occurred after you left me. Alas ! that
night has blasted the happiness of a life."

" You are too young, Captain de Courcy, to feel this
terrible calamity long ; change of scene, and a strong determination to drown memory, will do wonders."

De Courcy's lips trembled with emotion, but he made no
remark.

Finding that his commander remained silent, Lieutenant
Baracco continued, "It is somewhat difficult to give you
any important information, without infringing on my oath ;
however, you shall hear my statement; pardon me, at
the same time, if I probe a wound yet fresh : it is unavoidable.

" Aware of your attachment to Miss Wharton, and of
her, as I considered, sincere affection for you, Captain de
Courcy, I was amazed at being told, in confidence, that it
was deplorable to see you so grossly deceived. I was
startled, and demanded an explanation. ' Give me your
oath not to betray me,' said my informant, ' and I will
save your commander from becoming a dupe.'

" I refused to believe in such treachery, but still, anxious
to be of service to you, I took an oath to remain silent as
to the name of my informant. I was then told that, long
before your acquaintance with Miss Wharton, the Count
de Spinola had become deeply enamoured of her, and that
the Signor Garetti was flattered and pleased at the circumstance ; for the young Count was handsome, wealthy, of
high descent ; and, moreover, a countryman of his. My
informant solemnly declared that Miss Wharton was also
seriously attached to the young Count, and while residing
in Sestri they were constantly walking and rambling
through the pleasure grounds together." Lieutenant
Baracco paused, for De Courcy stretched out his hand,
and, taking a glass of water, drank it; his lips appeared
parched, and his cheeks deadly pale, but he waved his
hand, and the Neapolitan continued.

" Just before the family were forced to return within the
walls of Genoa, by the advance of the Austrians to invest
the city, the Count de Spinola and Miss Wharton had a
serious quarrel or misunderstanding ; from what cause I
cannot say, but Miss Wharton was heard to say that all
intercourse between them should cease.

" It was some time after this that you took up your abode
in the mansion of the Signor Garetti : previously, Miss
Wharton had received a letter from the Count, begging

pardon, and earnestly imploring forgiveness. That letter was returned.

" Whether Miss Wharton really intended to forget the Count, or she began to feel an interest in your attentions, who can say?

" On the evacuation of Genoa by the French, and afterwards by the Austrians, the Garetti family, as you know, went to reside at Sestri. You then became the accepted lover of Miss Wharton; and then the Count de Spinola renewed his visits to the Signor Garetti's house : and finally, as my informant swore, the Count regained his power over the heart of Miss Wharton.

"I declared this to be impossible. 'Well, then,' said my informant, 'I will afford Captain de Courcy an opportunity of judging of the faithlessness of his mistress. This very night Miss Wharton gives an interview to the Count, in the pavilion at the bottom of the garden. Miss Wharton wishes the Count to throw himself on the generosity of Captain de Courcy, confess all to him, and trust to his noble nature to forgive them both.'

"'And do you assert this to be a fact?' said I, indignantly.

"'Tell your commander to be under the pavilion wall, at ten o'clock to-night, and he will see the Count seeking an interview with Miss Wharton; let him then judge for himself; only tell him to keep his temper, and listen patiently to the Count, who, after all, is not near so much to blame as Miss Wharton.' You know, Captain de Courcy," continued the lieutenant, " how I gave you the information. I thought, if you did meet the Count, he would cordially explain ; if the whole account was false, that you would surely discover it. Your return, wounded, and declaring that your[1] life had been attempted by assassins, has surprised me, and caused me intense grief; for the more I think over the circumstances of the case the more I am satisfied that I acted wrong in listening to what I did, and afterwards in telling you of it."

" No," said Hugh de Courcy, bitterly ; " no: such treachery on the part of the Count deserved the fate he has met. Whether he is alive or dead I cannot say— I think the latter ; but before I banish this subject for ever from my mind and thoughts, I will tell you what occurred after I separated from you under the wall of the Signor Garetti's residence."

Having narrated to his lieutenant his meeting with the Count, his language, and finally the dastardly attempt to take his life, our hero continued,—" It is therefore very evident that the Count, some way or other, obtained information of my intended visit to the pavilion, and had hired assassins to be ready to take my life. This part of the affair is exceedingly mysterious, for it was nearly nine o'clock when you proposed the expedition to me; and how he could know or calculate upon my coming is most extraordinary, and has caused me many an hour of painful and perplexing thought."

"The attempt to assassinate you," said Baracco, "is certainly a most extraordinary occurrence; the Count, according to what you say, was surprised to meet you, and yet had assassins posted to take your life."

"Yes," observed De Courcy, with a sigh; "there is something in the whole affair perplexing and contradictory; and I cannot but think your informant has been playing a deep and deceitful part."

"No," said the lieutenant, speaking in rather a hurried and eager tone; "you would not think that if you knew who it was. Do you doubt, then," he anxiously added, "the infidelity of—Miss Wharton?"

"No," exclaimed De Courcy, bitterly, "that I do not; her presence in the pavilion at that hour, her looking out, evidently for the Count, who was coming to the pavilion, the words of the Count himself, and one or two circumstances not heeded at the time, are convincing proofs that one I could have worshipped as an angel was, after all, a woman. But here let the subject end; from me you will never hear a word more; and I beg, as a favour, that you never mention it. When I reach Naples, I will exert all my interest, in certain quarters, to get you what you undoubtedly deserve; that is, the command of this brig, with the rank of captain. The Serena frigate is launched, and I am to have the command as soon as she is ready for sea. All I have to request of you is, that not a word of what has passed be breathed abroad; it is not likely it will travel otherwise to Naples; for, in my opinion, Genoa will be in the hands of the French in a very short time. The latest news I heard was, that Bonaparte had crossed the Alps, with a powerful army, entered the city of Milan, and proclaimed, afresh, the Cisalpine Republic."

CHAPTER X.

LEAVING our hero to pursue his voyage to Naples, where great changes were about to take place, we return to the mansion of Signor Garetti, on the very day that Captain de Courcy bade farewell to his esteemed friends, to proceed on board the Vesuvius, intending to sail in a couple of days for Naples, in order to be back before Mrs. Arbuthnot arrived to take Mary to England.

Miss Wharton, after the departure of her lover, became unusually depressed—depressed in a manner she could not account for: her sanguine heart could not discover any very great obstacles in the way of her union with the first and only choice of her heart. Hugh de Courcy was aware of her early history; she, also, had become acquainted with his; and this knowledge only strengthened their attachment.

The fair girl had brought from England with her, as a personal attendant, a young and very pretty maiden, belonging to a respectable family, and who mixed but seldom with the other domestics of the establishment. Her name was Phœbe Manners.

The eldest daughter of Signor Garetti had also a favourite attendant, but of a very different stamp indeed from the English girl. She was a Milanese by birth, remarkably handsome in face and person; vain to excess, artful and designing, with an inordinate love of money for so young a girl. Julietta had the art to hide from her mistress's eyes her faults. She had exquisite taste in dress, and was also a most useful person as a young ladies'attendant. To this girl the Count de Spinola owed all the information he had received concerning what took place in the Signor Garetti's mansion.

After the departure of Captain de Courcy, Julietta remarked to the elder Signora Garetti, while attending on her toilette, "I am sure that the Signora Wharton suffers a great deal from the heat of the weather; she looks so languid and depressed."

"So would you, Julietta, if you had lost your lover: it may be several months before Miss Wharton sees Captain de Courcy again."

"Why, I thought, Signora, he was coming back immediately from Naples."

"Yes, if he can, Julietta; but he is not quite his own master; he may be ordered elsewhere: this is a time of war, and the sea is covered with the enemy's cruisers and ships of war; besides which, poor Mary may have to leave for England shortly: therefore it is possible that many a long day may intervene before they again meet."

"Well," said Julietta, in a serious tone, "love is a very curious thing—no accounting for likings and dislikings:

for my part, I would never give my love to a sailor, who has so many chances against his life."

" But, my good girl, we have no power over our affections; we lose our hearts when we least expect it."

" Ah, Madonna Signora," returned the waiting maid, "that's true ; but don't you think it curious that the Signora Wharton did not love the handsome Count de Spinola, and he so madly in love with her ? I am sure if this Captain de Courcy had not come here she would in time have loved him."

" Well, I think it is very possible he might have gained her affections," replied Bianca Garetti, thoughtfully : " the Count is a very agreeable, handsome man, and of high family, and wealthy ; and it would have been delightful to have had dear Mary always near us: but, bless me, Julietta, open that side window : these rooms are insufferably hot."

" Why do you not sleep in the pavilion chambers this summer, signora ? " remarked Julietta, " they are so cool and delightful, with the sea so close; it is so pleasant to hear the ripples on the beach. Those apartments have been ready this week."

" Well, indeed, Julietta, you are quite right, I always intended to sleep there in July; but we will go there to-night. I am sure Mary will rejoice at the change ; for those great trees stop the air from the sea. So get everything we require there for to-night."

The pavilion mentioned by Julietta was a very tasteful and beautiful building, erected upon a lofty terrace, directly on the sea-beach, only fifty yards from the clear, bright water.

It consisted of a magnificent saloon ; the upper rooms, four in number, being expressly fitted up as sleeping chambers during the hot months.

With the earliest summer heat all the carpets, window-curtains, and draperies of all sorts, vanish out of the Italian summer mansions; even the soft-cushioned seats are removed, and light cane sofas used instead. The windows of the pavilion reached to the floor ; and the heat was excluded by venetian blinds and projecting verandahs, so that, in fact, the great heats of an Italian climate are less felt by the natives, than is an unusually hot month with us in England.

Mary Wharton was pleased with the intended change ; for she really suffered from heat ; and she also loved to hear the gentle ripple of the sea on the fine beach beneath the windows.

That night the three girls, with their own attendants, proceeded to sleep in the pavilion, but sat some time in the saloon, enjoying the delicious view.

The Signora Garetti retired a short time before Mary, who was interested in reading, now and then lifting the verandahs to look out upon the calm and scarcely rippling waters. Having finished her book, Mary, about half-past ten by her watch, prepared to retire. Lifting the blinds, she inhaled the sea-breeze, and then proceeded to her chamber above, where she found her maid looking out of the window.

"Do you know, Miss Mary," observed Phœbe, letting the venetian blinds drop, "I heard a footstep beneath the window on the shingle ; and, on peeping through the blinds, I am certain I saw the tall figure of a man walking rapidly along the strand ? "

" A fisherman, perhaps," said Mary, going to the window and gazing out along the beach. " You are quite right, Phœbe," she continued; " see, there are two figures at a distance, close by the Count de Spinola's garden wall." Phœbe looked ; but the distance, and obscure light, rendered the figures mere dark outlines.

" Well, Miss Mary, I do not think that fishermen go about the sands at this time. It is more likely to be the Count de Spinola's own man, Guisseppe Spino, going in, after having had a gossip with Julietta."

" I see them going round the wall," rejoined her mistress ; " so we need not trouble about them."

Shortly after Mary retired to rest ; but very early in the morning she was roused by Phœbe rushing into the room, exclaiming, in a terrified tone, " Oh, Miss Wharton, how horrid ! What a frightful crime was committed last night ! Oh ! if we had only known——"

But before Phœbe could say more, the two sisters, half-dressed, with cheeks pale as death, came into the room.

" What on earth is the matter ? " exclaimed Mary Wharton, looking as pale as themselves. " What has occurred ? "

" We have only heard vague particulars, dear," said the eldest of the sisters ; " but one thing is certain, the Count de Spinola was, this morning, found lying on the strand— they say, mortally wounded—run through the body ; and the body of another man, masked, was lying dead beside him."

" Good heavens ! " returned Mary, clasping her hands, and looking terrified, whilst strange thoughts flitted

G

through her brain. "But how did you hear this, Bianca?"

"Madonna! the whole household knew it at daylight this morning. My father, as chief magistrate of Sestri, has gone to the count's mansion, to investigate this horrible transaction. A fisherman of Pazia, who, it seems, beheld the whole affair, gave the alarm first."

"Oh, Miss Wharton," exclaimed Phœbe, "I am sure the figures of those men we saw last night must have been the unfortunate count and the assassin!"

"But what could bring the Count," responded Mary, looking more frightened than before—"what could bring the Count under these windows?"

"Oh, it is a horrid affair, Madonna!" exclaimed the Signora Garetti; "but, Phœbe, where is Julietta? I have not seen her this morning."

"Dear me!" said Phœbe, with a start; "I missed her when I woke this morning!"

For the two girls slept in the same room.

"Pray go up to the house, Phœbe, where I am sure she is," said Bianca Garetti; "and tell my mother we shall be up directly to breakfast."

"This is very dreadful, as well as mysterious, Bianca," observed Mary, finishing her toilette hurriedly; "you said there was a dead body beside that of the unfortunate Count, who, I trust in God, is not fatally hurt! Did you hear who the dead man is?"

"No, indeed," replied Bianca; "the gardener it was who first brought the intelligence here; but let us go to the house."

In a very terrified and uneasy frame of mind, Mary Wharton followed the sisters through the garden; just before they reached the mansion they beheld Julietta coming towards them down a side-walk. She looked so exceedingly pale, that all perceived it.

"Why, where on earth have you been so early, Julietta?" exclaimed her mistress; "you are looking pale and frightened."

"Blessed Mary! signora," returned Julietta; "so would you, also, if you had heard all I did from old Tomaso,— he knows all the fisherman told the Signor Garetti; and he says the English captain who comes here killed the unfortunate Count, and that he must have been nearly killed himself."

A faint exclamation called the attention of the two sisters to Mary Wharton, who was a step or two behind. She had heard the girl's words, and sank down on a seat, with a sickening sensation stealing over her. The sisters anxiously sat down beside her, so shocked and startled, that they did not see the look of malice and satisfaction which passed over the features of Julietta.

" Dear Mary," said Bianca, " do not give way to alarm ; Julietta was very wrong to speak as she did; besides, she may be quite wrong."

" No, indeed, signora," returned Julietta, in a cold tone, and with a steady look into the pale face of Miss Wharton, " I am not wrong. I beg pardon for frightening the signora ; I did not think at the time. This is such a horrid affair—the poor Count left for dead in such a barbarous manner."

Mary rose from her seat, looking distressed and shocked ; but she said firmly, as she took Bianca's arm, " I feel quite satisfied, if Captain de Courcy had anything to do in this melancholy affair, that he acted honourably and fairly ; it appears much more likely that his life was attempted, and that——"

" Oh, Madonna," sharply interrupted Julietta, " what business had this English captain on shore at that hour of the night, lurking under the walls of this garden? "

" Julietta," exclaimed Bianca, pausing in astonishment, and looking the girl steadily in the face, " you are forgetting yourself, and have spoken in an exceedingly improper manner."

" Well, signora, if you think so," returned the girl, " I am quite ready to quit your service ; I always speak what I think, when it is the truth."

" I shall take you at your word, then," replied Bianca, angrily; " after such language—language quite uncalled for, and besides somewhat singular, and which leads one to suppose——"

" Oh, the saints be praised ! " interrupted the girl, quickly; " you are welcome to suppose what you please. I am, thank God, no slave ! " And, turning round, she walked on rapidly towards the house.

" Well, I never heard such language, and so much impertinence before, from any one," said the younger sister; " surely, after such conduct, Bianca, you will not allow her to stay an hour in the house."

" There is something in this beyond mere words," remarked Bianca, thoughtfully.

" She was audacious, and her eyes sparkled with passion ; she shall leave instantly. But, dear Mary, do not grieve so," added the young lady, affectionately.

"You may depend on my father learning all the particulars of this certainly sad affair."

"I am greatly amazed," replied Mary, " at Captain de Courcy's being on shore, and in this vicinity, at such an hour, and must believe there is some false statement in the affair."

" We shall soon hear," said the two girls, as they all entered the house, meeting Madame Garetti in the hall, just on the point of seeking them. She at once perceived that Mary had heard the intelligence, for she saw that she looked pale, and had a troubled expression on her features.

Kissing her affectionately, for she was fondly attached to her, the Signora Garetti said all she could to console her; giving it as her opinion that she would hear a very different version of the affair when her husband returned from the Count's abode.

Mary felt very sad during breakfast; the idea that Captain de Courcy was dangerously wounded haunted her mind. The strange impertinence of Julietta also surprised and fretted her.

The Signora Garetti, when she heard of Julietta's conduct, was highly indignant, and at once approved of Bianca's intention of dismissing her. " It is very strange, my love," continued that lady; " but, latterly, I have observed something very peculiar about Julietta; a prying, anxious curiosity concerning all matters occurring around us; and an inquisitiveness out of character in her position. She also dresses beyond her situation."

"Indeed, I mentioned that to her the other day," said Bianca, " and I thought, at the time, she answered me rather abruptly; however, she shall leave this day."

As Bianca spoke, they perceived, through the window, the Signor Garetti advancing up the avenue towards the breakfast room. " Ah! here is my father," continued Bianca, anxiously; and in a few minutes that gentleman entered the room, looking extremely troubled; but he at once approached Mary, and pressing her hand affectionately, said, "I see you have been making yourself uneasy, my dear Mary. This is a sad affair, certainly; moreover, rather unaccountable ; and, until we hear from, or see, Captain de Courcy, it must remain so."

"But," observed Mary, in a low, hesitating voice, "we heard that Captain de Courcy, as well as the Count de Spinola, was seriously wounded. By your saying 'till we hear from Captain de Courcy, we must be still in doubt,' It is, then, evident that he *was* engaged in an encounter with assassins last night."

" I will tell you all I have heard, Mary," returned the Signor, sitting down; " it is better than permitting the mind to torture itself with imaginary evils."

"But is the Count de Spinola mortally wounded?" anxiously asked the Signora Garetti.

" He is dangerously wounded, but there are hopes of his life, the surgeon says;" replied her husband. "But let me relate the particulars of this singular occurrence.

" The only witness that I could procure this morning was the half-witted poor fellow who goes about the shore during the nights, watching the fishermen's boats. The men club together and support him: he goes by the name of Gatto. It was he who gave the alarm to some fishermen of Pazia; and they followed him and found the body of the Count de Spinola lying insensible, with a terrible sword thrust through the body (the Signor Garetti's hearers shuddered); lying near him was the dead body of a man, with a mask over his face. This man, I have every reason to believe, is one of those curses of our city, a paid bravo, or rather, assassin: his body is not yet recognized; but no doubt it will be before to-morrow. Several of the gentlemen of Sestri and Pazia were present at my examination of the half-witted man, Gatto.

" It appears he was lying, last night, half asleep, half awake, in the cave in the rock at Pazia; he often lies there; and last night, about ten or eleven, he heard a boat's keel grate on the sand and shingle, to the eastward of the rock; he crept out, and had a look on the beach, and saw a boat, with six or seven men in it; two of them jumped on shore; they were in uniform, he says, and they passed close under where he was. They were speaking in Italian, for he heard the shortest of the two say, ' About a mile from here.' It was not dark, and as they came close he recognized easily the tallest stranger to be the English captain who resided at our house (for De Courcy, more than once, gave this poor fellow some silver when he met him on the beach). He then lay down again, keeping his eyes upon those in the boat, and took it into his head to go and see what the two officers were about; but, as he walked along the rocks, he presently saw one coming back; and just at the Count's garden wall, he saw this person stop and speak to a figure, in a mantle, and then come towards him. Gatto says he slunk into the rocks, and the stranger passed on.

" You must not imagine," continued the Signor Garetti, " that I got this account from Gatto as I give it you—far from it; it was gathered from his rambling, unconnected discourse; and with some difficulty and some coaxing.

"Gatto says that he remained in a crevice of the rocks, watching to see if the tall captain would come back; and presently he saw two men turn the round of the wall, and then three men rushed out from the shadow, and a fight commenced between the tall captain and the other four figures. Of this he was positive; he was not, he says, fifteen yards from them; and he saw the tall captain run his sword through one who attacked him from behind, and then kill another; the other two then sprang over the wall and disappeared. He was so terrified that he lay crumpled up like a ball, his teeth chattering; and then he beheld the tall captain—as he called the commander of the Vesuvius—come along the sands. He crept after him; frightened out of his wits at staying near the dead bodies. He saw him enter the boat and pull out to sea : and then he ran, as fast as he could, to the nearest fishermen's cottages, and told them what he had seen ; but they were as frightened as Gatto, and not one would stir till daylight; and then four of them went together, and found, to their horror, the Count and the dead man. They gave the alarm at the palazzo, and a man, on horseback, went directly for a surgeon.

"I took down the depositions of Gatto and the fisher-man," continued Signor Garetti, "and despatched a messenger to Genoa, with a note for Captain de Courcy; he has, however, not yet returned, but I expect him in less than an hour.

"So now, my dear Mary, you have all the information I can give you, till my messenger returns."

The young girl had listened to Signor Garetti's narrative with intense eagerness ; she readily perceived that the Signor tried to hide from her the fact of Captain de Courcy's being severely wounded; for the gardener had declared that Gatto said that the captain was hardly able to reach his boat; added to this, she was perplexed with the idea of Captain de Courcy's being on shore, and near the pavilion, at that hour of the night, and his meeting with the Count de Spinola.

Whilst the whole family were making various remarks upon the subject, a domestic entered the room, with a letter, saying, "Antonio has returned, signor, from Genoa; he could not deliver your letter, for Captain de Courcy's ship had left the harbour with the dawn."

Mary felt a strange misgiving creep over her, as the man continued, "This letter was left for you, signor, at your palazzo; one of the harbour pilots received it from an officer of the Vesuvius, with directions to leave it in the Strada Balbi."

"This is from Captain de Courcy," said the Signor Garetti, looking serious, despite his endeavours, and, breaking the seal, he read it through, frequently changing colour, then letting it drop upon the table, with the exclamation of,—"St. Nicholas! this is startling. There is a traitor and slanderer somewhere. By all the saints, De Courcy has acted rashly!"

An exclamation of surprise and pain from Mary announced to the kind-hearted Genoese that he had said more than he intended.

"What does Captain de Courcy say?" inquired Madame Garetti, anxiously. "Why has he put to sea? he was not to leave till after to-morrow; surely he has not sailed for Naples."

Her husband looked extremely uncomfortable: he scarcely knew what to do. Our hero's letter was evidently written under the exasperation of a moment of disappointed love;—the feeling taking full possession of his mind, that Miss Wharton had sported with his passionate devotion to her: and that, in point of fact, she had never loved him; this cruelty lacerated his proud, but noble heart, almost to frenzy. He explained the attempt upon his life, but spoke of it with contempt; he begged the Signor Garetti to accept his warmest thanks and gratitude, for the kindness he had shown towards him; and ended by saying he trusted that Miss Wharton—if she grieved over the fate of the Count de Spinola—would at all events do him the justice in believing that he would never have sought to take his life, had he not treacherously endeavoured to stab him in the back, whilst his miserable hired assassins attacked him in front. This is the outline of a letter that probed our hero to the quick to write.

After some moments of thought, Signor Garetti rose from his seat, and, taking Mary Wharton by the hand, said, with the affection of a fond relative, "Come with me to the library, Mary dear, and let us have a few minutes' conversation; you know I would act for you, and give you the same advice I would my own daughters—to leave you in the state of uncertainty that you are would be worse, infinitely worse, than to let you know all. Truth can hardly be expected to adapt herself to the crooked policy and wily sinuosities of worldly affairs; for truth, like light, travels only in straight lines—still, truth is best, always."

Mary Wharton, with a sigh, rose from her seat; with

difficulty she refrained from shedding tears, so great was the depression she felt; but, summoning all her natural fortitude to her aid, she followed the signor into his library.

Placing a chair for the fair and gentle girl, who looked so resigned and patient, though well aware she was about to receive a most sudden and unexpected blow to her future happiness, the Signor Garetti sat down beside her.

"You know, my dear girl, that your happiness and your interests are very dear to me; for I consider you are, in point of fact, the child of my lamented and much-loved sister; therefore you may safely depend upon my not asking you to act derogatory to your maiden purity of thought or action. Aware how you and Captain de Courcy are situated, awaiting only your father's—I call him father, though the world calls him uncle—consent to your union, I feel acutely the strange situation you are both placed in, by the treacherous and infamous duplicity of the Count de Spinola; nevertheless, to understand this you must read this letter of Captain de Courcy. I will make no comment —read it carefully—conquer your emotion; and, before I say what I think, let me hear your sentiments. Remember, your lover has been sorely tried; if he has shown weakness, and given way to passion, remember the provocation; therefore read his letter, conquering your own feelings and emotion as much as possible."

CHAPTER XI.

We believe it is Koslay who says, "Stability in love is otherwise called 'faith;' where faith is between the parties there may be jealousy—but where perfect love exists there can be none;" admitting that where jealousy is there is love too.

Now Mary Wharton's love for Hugh de Courcy was as near to perfect love as any denizen of this earth can pretend to feel; her own nature was so pure and confiding, that she could not bring herself to believe that any cause, not even the evidence of sight, ought to have had any effect upon the mind of her lover.

She therefore read De Courcy's letter through, trembling with emotion, and with a violent exertion preventing the tears from flowing down her cheeks. She was very pale as she finished it, and, laying it down on the table, she looked up into the serious countenance of the Genoese.

"I did not expect," she said, calmly, "that Captain de

Courcy's proud nature would, or could, be led to place the slightest faith in the vile insinuations of a detestable slanderer; I should have thought he would have scorned, or struck to the earth," she proudly added, her pale cheek flushing, and her beautiful eyes sparkling with indignation, "the man who dared to breathe such a slander on the woman he professed to love with implicit faith."

"Ah, my God!" she continued, clasping her hands, and her emotion conquering her assumed firmness, "the whole world should not have made me believe him untrue. No, God forgive me!" and she hid her face in her hands, "no; I would not have listened to an angel's whisper against his faith and love.

"But, dear Mary," interrupted the Signor Garetti, "is perfection in man to be found on this earth? Man's faith can never be put in competition with that of women. We are slaves to passion; in love we are blind—worse than blind; we are either fool or madman. That De Courcy has exhibited a weakness, both in listening to a slanderer and in seeking information by a wrong method, I do not deny. His impetuous nature must have been artfully acted upon; and we are, after all, imperfectly informed, as you have read. He was decoyed on shore; led beneath the pavilion; singular to say, he sees you look forth, and the next moment beholds the Count de Spinola approaching the pavilion; the Count meets him, and then falsely declares you were lovers before you saw De Courcy; grossly insults him; insidiously draws him into a situation where he is attacked—both by himself, and by, till then, concealed assassins; severely wounded, and smarting under your supposed duplicity to him—weak from loss of blood, he writes this letter, under a terrible delusion; and yet, Mary, on my soul I do not believe there exists a nobler heart than that which beats within the breast of Hugh de Courcy."

"I thought so once," returned Mary, in her low, sweet voice, "but he was untried. In deception faith dies; happiness is more credulous than misfortune—so at least I have read; this event has not weakened my love for De Courcy; but it has weakened my faith in his stability. I must, however, implore you to take no steps whatever in this affair; De Courcy has acted rashly and weakly. He has suffered; and, oh! if you only knew," and her voice trembled, "how my heart suffers for him; but no, explanation must not come from me."

"My sweet, kind-hearted Mary," said the Signor, with much emotion, "how is poor Hugh to be undeceived?"

"His own heart will undeceive him," replied Mary. "When his passion cools; when he comes to reason calmly upon the insidious information he received from some designing traitor, he will detect falsehood in every word the villain, whoever he is, poured into his ears; and how he poisoned his own happiness, and, alas! wrecked mine, by giving way to passion; and, depend on it, when once he discovers his own weakness, he has too noble a heart not to seek forgiveness of one who, alas! at one time, thought him—what no mortal is—perfection."

Signor Garetti remained thoughtful; he had a kind, generous heart; but he was a man of the world; he had no romance in his disposition; he looked upon human feelings with the eye of a mere mortal. He was also an Italian, and therefore not quite equal to judge the feelings of a pure English heart in an affair of love.

Jealousy, the bane of an Italian's existence, the engine capable of moving him to the commission of frightful deeds, he looked upon only as a positive ingredient in all love affairs, and therefore the Genoese thought that a fair explanation of the circumstances, from Mary to her lover, would set all right; but Miss Wharton thought differently, and consequently the Signor gave way to her wishes, and made up his mind to let things take their own course, consoling himself with the old adage—the course of true love never runs smooth.

As the news of the Count de Spinola's dangerous situation, and the cause of it, got abroad, it led to surmises and insinuations; the genuine Italian took the Count's part. Powerful love countenanced assassination, and no one thought the worse of Count de Spinola, whose recovery was long doubtful.

Before a fortnight had expired, the state of affairs in Italy, and the triumphant successes of Bonaparte, filled all minds with forebodings for the future. The Genoese felt satisfied that France would again seize upon Genoa. Whilst in this state of uncertainty, Sir Charles Wharton and Mrs. Arbuthnot arrived in a British corvette from England. Mary's joy was great. Suffering under the cruel causes that had separated her from her lover, this arrival of persons she dearly loved banished for a time the deep despondency that she had permitted to prey upon her mind.

She requested the Signor Garetti and his family not to mention to Sir Charles any of the circumstances of her acquaintance with Captain de Courcy. It appeared to her that they had separated for ever; she began to despond, and therefore wished the whole buried in oblivion.

Sir Charles thought she looked somewhat pale and delicate, but Mary assured him it was only the remains of what they had all suffered during the siege of Genoa.

" I do not intend to delay here," said Sir Charles to his niece ; " I left England purposely to take you home in the same ship I came out in. . The Captain brought important despatches for Lord Keith, and returns immediately; and so good an opportunity must not not be lost. The French, under Massena, will advance upon this city, and you must not be exposed to a second incarceration within the walls of Genoa."

That evening Sir Charles Wharton had a long conference with the Signor Garetti : we will detail their conversation to our readers, as it is necessary to the future understanding of our story.

" So you have dissolved partnership, and given up all further mercantile speculations, Sir Charles ? " observed the Signor Garetti.

" I have, my dear friend, and finally wound up our partnership of years. I have amassed more wealth than either Mary or myself require ; and I must make others happy with the riches God has been pleased to place in my hands. After a residence of some months in England, I propose going, with Mary and Mrs. Arbuthnot, to pass a year or two in Sicily ; if, in the meantime, the former does not barter away her priceless heart to some fortunate pretender for it. I shall never object to any choice she makes ; for, depend upon it, she is not to be won by either a handsome person, or title, or wealth. She will only surrender her heart for sterling merit; therefore I always feel confident and secure of her future happiness. But, as I before said, I purpose going to Sicily ; all the rest of the continent is involved in war and upset with the revolutionary armies of France. I have also another reason ; I am almost persuaded that Magdalene Caracci is a Sicilian by birth, and may be traced, by a residence in that country of some months. But I have now to communicate to you intelligence I would not commit to paper, or trust in letters."

The Signor Garetti expressed himself anxious to hear any particulars relating to the mystery attending their dear Mary ; that for his part he had totally failed in gaining any trace of Magdalene Caracci.

" You shall now learn, amico," said Sir Charles, " some circumstances, none but my dearest friend and relative should hear : for it involves the honour of my unfortunate brother James.

"I wrote you word, on my return to England, after visiting Hamburg, that I had settled all my brother's affairs, and closed the account of the firm in which he was a partner.

"Imagine my surprise, dear friend, when, in handing me over documents to peruse, and vouchers of all sorts, Mr. Frip, the head partner of the firm, produced two bonds, each for £14,000, purporting to be money advanced me by my brother James, to carry out some speculations I had in hand. I felt my blood chill, for, at a glance, I saw these bonds were forgeries."

"St. Nicholas!" uttered the Genoese, "can this be possible?"

"Such was the case," replied Sir Charles; "in a moment I checked my surprise, and acknowledged my signature, and that I was indebted for the money to the firm. 'The interest is paid to the week before your lamented brother's death,' said Mr. Frip, 'but, pardon me,' he added, 'you of course secured the most part of this large sum, £24,000, remitted by your brother to Milan, just five weeks before his death?'"

"I was thunderstruck," continued Sir Charles, "for the last forged bond was dated only a month or so before he died. Fortunately I conquered my emotion, and, God pardon me! a few falsehoods saved my brother's name and my own from ignominy. I thus discovered that my unfortunate brother's profuse extravagance was backed up by forged bonds and acceptances of mine, which the firm of Frip held as unquestionable security, and my brother raised the amount on them. I found, when all was settled, that he himself was deficient, notwithstanding the two bonds of £28,000, which I acknowledged, in a sum of £9,000, which, with the two recently accepted bills in my name, in all amounted to a sum of nearly £40,000. How he spent this very large sum is a mystery. If he had lived three months longer all must have been discovered, for the affairs of the firm of Frip and Co. were involved, and they were about to call in the monies due to them on the securities they held.

"Thus, I should have been applied to for the £28,000. I at once settled all my brother's liabilities, without remark; though I clearly perceived that Mr. Frip was exceedingly surprised that so wealthy a man as myself should be paying such heavy interest for a sum I could have settled at any time; but of course he hazarded no remark.

"I was myself completely bewildered : here was a sum

of £14,000 remitted to a bank in Milan, and placed to my brother's credit, just five weeks previous to his death. Where was that sum? for, as I told you before, I found but £200 in his desk, after death. Thus, reckoning his wife's fortune, £1,500, and the £6,000 of his own, and the lucrative result of his mercantile dealings with the firm of Frip, during the first four years, he must have spent in that time a fortune amounting to nearly £80,000. This appeared incredible.

" I wrote to the bank at Milan, merely requesting to know if my brother, Mr. James Wharton, had drawn the entire sum of £14,000, remitted them on such and such a date, for his use.

" I received an answer to this before I left Hamburg. Messrs. Parodi and Ghilini, the bankers, stated in reply, that Mr. James Wharton had drawn the entire sum himself, on the 17th of May, 178—, £600 in cash, the remainder in letters of credit upon the banking houses of Becarelli and Gambara, of Naples, and Valloti and Co., of Palermo.

" There was matter for thought; it was very evident to me that, dreading discovery, my brother was preparing for flight.

" I made no further inquiries there, though I determined to do so on my return to England; now the question is— what became of those letters of credit for this large sum, £13,000. It struck me at once that this Magdalene Caracci had obtained the amount, and that she and my misguided brother planned the stealing of my child to screen themselves from my resentment, with the idea of having me in their power—and then compromise matters by the restoration of my child. My unexpected appearance at Como, and his death, frustrated all her plans, no doubt; and she fled and left the child behind, as no longer useful in carrying out the original project. You will say this is a somewhat chimerical and romantic method of clearing up the past; but in truth, dear friend, I did not arrive at this elucidation of the mystery till after months, and I may say years, of perplexing thoughts and conjectures. Now what say you to my solution of the difficulty?"

The Signor Garetti had listened attentively to Sir Charles Wharton's statements. He certainly thought there was a degree of probability in his conjectures concerning Magdalene Caracci, but there was also a great deal remaining concealed behind, quite impossible to explain. What had become of Mrs. Wharton's child was a question that

bewildered him ; in fact, at times, he himself wavered with
respect to Mary's parents—for Mrs. Wharton appeared so
positive that she was her child. If Magdalene Caracci
were still alive, what object could she have in leaving Sir
Charles Wharton in the dark respecting Mary; when she
might feel satisfied that he would sacrifice a large sum—
nay, half his fortune—to be thoroughly satisfied that Mary
was his child.

The Signor Garetti expressed these thoughts to Sir
Charles, who listened to them attentively. " There is a
great deal of reason, my dear friend," said the baronet, "in
what you say. But, somehow or other, I have taken it
into my head, that by a residence in Palermo and its
vicinity, for some time, I may be able to hear something of
this Magdalene Caracci. Italy is so completely convulsed
and distracted by warfare, that there is no possibility of
gaining the slightest intelligence of private individuals.
Naples is again in the hands of King Ferdinand ; Cardinal
Ruffo having driven out the Republicans ; so that I may
be able to prosecute inquiries there."

After a good deal of conversation on the same subject,
but which led to nothing, the baronet prevailed on the
Signor Garetti to let his youngest daughter, Térese, proceed
with Mary and him to England, and thence to Palermo.

Mary had proposed this to Térese, to whom she was
greatly attached ; and Térese was enchanted with the idea
of visiting the country that gave her mother birth. The
Pallas corvette, commanded by Captain Goodwin, was
to sail in three days, so that all the family were exceedingly busy, preparing for Térese's journey.

Meanwhile the Count de Spinola was slowly recovering ;
and rumour of the approach of the French created great
excitement to the people of Genoa.

This rumour expedited the movements of not only Sir
Charles Wharton, but also of the English men-of-war in
the harbour.

A most tender and affectionate parting ensued between
Mary Wharton and the members of the Garetti family.
The Pallas was ready for sea, and a message from her
captain hurried our heroine in her leave-taking.

With a heavy heart, though she exerted herself to hide
the depression she felt from all eyes, save those of her
affectionate companion and beloved friend Térese, Mary
Wharton, with tears in her eyes, bade farewell to those so
tenderly loved. It was with exceeding pain that the
Signor Garetti and his amiable spouse saw their cherished
guest and relative depart, and with the painful knowledge

in their own hearts that she left the land of the south with
an exceedingly heavy heart; though trusting that hope
would soon revive in the mind of one so young, but who
had been so rudely and so suddenly deprived of the felicity
she so confidently looked forward to.

The Pallas, a very handsome and fast-sailing corvette,
left the port of Genoa an hour before sunset. She had a
fine breeze from the eastward, to fill her lofty canvas, and
rapidly she glided forth through the still waters of the port.

Mary, leaning on the arm of Térese Garetti, stood upon
the deck of the corvette, gazing back with uncontrollable
emotion upon the gorgeous scene she was leaving, perhaps
for ever. The last rays of the setting sun fell full upon
old Genoa, covering her with its golden tints. The sky, a
blaze of crimson, sea and land all blended together in one
gorgeous hue. Mary vividly remembered the last time she
gazed upon the same scene, when her lover was beside
her ; she stood upon the quarter-deck of his noble ship,
proud of his love and devotion to her—proud of his gallant
exploits—and looking to the future with hope and confidence ; and now the contrast was painful to a degree.
Térese felt the arm that rested on hers tremble, she looked
up with affection and pity in her glance, into her friend's
face ; Mary's eyes were dim with tears.

CHAPTER XII.

CATO says, " An angry man opens his mouth and shuts up
his eyes."

Captain De Courcy was an angry man when he sat
down and wrote the letter to which we have alluded to the
Signor Garetti. He took no time for reflection ; he acted
on the spur of the moment, whilst smarting under the
cruellest disappointment a man can endure—the supposed
faithlessness of the woman he adores.

Hugh de Courcy was also smarting under the pain of
three severe wounds, and exasperated at the cowardly
attack made upon his life; therefore no wonder he wrote
under the influence of passion, which distorted and magnified everything.

A prostration of strength for some days left him time for
thought and reflection ; and just as the Vesuvius came
within sight of the beautiful bay of Naples, he began to
think that there was a vast amount of mystification in what
Lieutenant Baracco had related to him.

During the voyage from Genoa to Naples, he had also

observed that his Lieutenant was gloomy, abstracted, and exceedingly reserved.

It was not the character or nature of Hugh De Courcy to give heed or listen to insidious representations. His passionate love for Mary Wharton, and the terrible agony he experienced when he heard of her duplicity, and that from the lips of a man he esteemed and believed, overpowered his judgment; and he yielded to act an espionage upon his mistress, that on cool reflection he despised himself for giving way to. He was still, however, convinced that Mary Wharton intended to see the Count de Spinola in the pavilion that night—the evidence of the concerted meeting was so palpable; but he was puzzled beyond measure by the attempt upon his life, which was a clearly premeditated affair. He did not blame himself for breaking off his engagement with Mary Wharton, only for the method in which he did dissolve their intercourse, and for his abrupt departure.

There were moments, also, when he believed that he had acted under a delusion : the character of Miss Wharton appeared so open and confiding, her nature so pure and innocent, and her affection for him so chaste, devoted, and trusting, that he worked himself into a frenzy when he looked back, and thought of those sweet and happy hours he had spent by her side : and was it thus all his dreams of felicity in his union with her were dashed to the ground and gone for ever?

Sick at heart, and disgusted with the world, as even youth will be when suffering under disappointment and crushed hopes, Captain De Courcy came to an anchor in the harbour of Naples.

The Court of Naples, under its imbecile king and its licentious queen, were enjoying, in frivolity and pleasure, one of those short intervals of freedom from French rule, that Naples so often experienced during all the years of Bonaparte's power.

What with confiscation and execution, the unfortunate Neapolitan nobles and gentry were considerably reduced in numbers and fortune. Thanks to Lady Hamilton and Lord Nelson, most persons adverse to Ferdinand the Fourth's rule were exterminated ; the insurgents butchered ; princes hanged ; and even women—for example, the celebrated Madame Fonsica—condemned to end her days by the hangman's knot; treaties were broken ; faiths and oaths disregarded ; and now, the weak king, led by his licentious queen, returned to Naples, to enjoy themselves, previous to their second flight from their capital. Ferdinand the Fourth

is not represented even by his own subjects as cruel, but
Lady Hamilton and his ministers did with him as they
pleased; and cruel and disgraceful were the acts committed
at that period. Some of the Neapolitan prisoners, sent to
Lord Nelson's captains, and confined in prison-ships,
moored in the midst of British men-of-war, complained
bitterly of their cruel treatment: for twenty-four days they
were left unprovided with everything necessary to existence : they had only bread to eat, putrid water, or wine
mingled with salt water, to drink, and bare planks to lie
upon—their houses had been pillaged, and the greater part
of their relations and friends imprisoned and massacred,
so that they could not expect assistance from them. Pity
that the noble hero of Trafalgar and a hundred fights besides, with more glory attached to his name than ever fell
to the lot of man, should sully his fair fame and truly
gallant and heroic character, by permitting himself to be
blinded by the attraction of a woman dead to feeling or
shame.

Captain De Courcy was still somewhat weak when he
anchored before Naples; but he had despatches for the
Neapolitan Government; so he proceeded at once ashore,
and learning that Sir John Acton was at his mansion on
the Chiaga, he proceeded there without any delay.

Sir John received his protégé with great cordiality,
feeling in reality a strong affection for him.

"Ah, you are welcome back, Hugh," said Queen Caroline's favourite, for he was still prime minister of the Government of Ferdinand the Fourth; "but you are looking poorly :
have you been wounded?"

"Not in the service of his majesty, certainly," returned
Captain De Courcy, "but by the stilettos of a cowardly set
of miscreants."

"I heard nothing of that from Captain Septimo,"
remarked Sir John; "he told me you behaved most gallantly in the affair of the Prima galley, and that you were
left for dead on the mole, but that you contrived to escape
being made a prisoner. I heard all that; however, you
shall tell me your adventures this evening.

"You see we have got possession of Naples again; and,
to make up for lost time, our gay Neapolitans are as lively
and volatile as ever. By the by, now is your time to take
fortune at her beck; your beautiful Princess of Sorento is
here—more lovely and captivating than ever, and has been
anxiously asking where you were, and when you were
expected to return. Lady Acton told me, in confidence,
you have only to ask and be accepted. Why, zounds! you

look very grave. Hugh," added Sir John; "not lost your
heart, I hope, to any of the fair daughters of Genoa?—I
know they are very bewitching."

Hugh De Courey, with a slight increase of colour, said,
" As far as the daughters of Genoa are concerned, Sir John,
I am heart-whole; but where is Septimo—gone to join the
British ships?"

" You will be expected to sail for England in your new
ship," continued Sir John, "and a most magnificent craft
she is. She is ready for sea; and I expect in a few days
that the despatches and orders you will have to take will
be ready. This is only a temporary success, depend upon
it; the French will return with an overwhelming force,
and Ferdinand will have to fly, and perhaps abdicate the
throne."

" What, with the British fleet in the Mediterranean?"
exclaimed De Courcy, surprised.

" Ah," replied Sir John, "have you not heard of the
famous battle of Marengo? Buonaparte has defeated
General Melas, slain near five thousand of his tooops,
nearly eight thousand wounded, taken nine thousand prisoners, and secured thirty pieces of cannon; and with,
comparatively speaking, a very small loss to the French.
Thus France has gained possession of twelve important
fortresses—Genoa included. I suppose, when you left,
Lord Keith was still there?"

" He was." returned our hero, greatly surprised; "I
heard that this wonderful man, Buonaparte—for, unquestionably, he is a great and marvellous genius—had, in an
extraordinary manner, crossed the Alps; but it was supposed that his army was exhausted and powerless."

" Faith, Hugh, it does not look like it, by this battle of
Marengo. However, Lord Nelson has sailed for England
indisposed, leaving the blockading squadron off Malta in
charge of Captain Troubridge, of the Culloden. You will
have to leave despatches with the admiral of the fleet there,
but not lose time. Your duty in England will depend on
our ambassador; but we shall have time enough to talk of
this. You must attend the fête to-morrow, and thank his
majesty for your new appointment."

" What fête, Sir John?" demanded Hugh De Courcy,
whose thoughts were at that moment elsewhere.

" Why, this new fête of Santa Maria Predi Grotto. The
King and Queen, and all the nobility, will be there, and in
the evening there will be a presentation at the Villa Reale;
this you, of course, must attend."

After some further conversation on affairs relating to the

Neapolitan naval service, and which it is not necessary to trouble our readers with, our hero left Sir John's mansion to visit his new ship.

Captain De Courcy had many acquaintances, and some friends, in Naples; for, in times past, he had been a universal favourite with the gay and pleasure-seeking Neapolitans; but now he had neither spirits nor inclination for society. He longed to be once more at sea; the idea of visiting England occupied his mind; he thought of Miss Wharton, and sighed to think that the delicious dream of his union with her was dissipated for ever; he was also determined to press Sir John Acton to declare to him the name of his father, and give him any further particulars concerning his family in his power.

The Neapolitan frigate Serena excited his utmost admiration; he thought her the handsomest vessel he ever beheld : though only intended for thirty-two guns, she was fully as large, and had as great capabilities, as a French forty-gun frigate. She was nearly ready for sea; at all events, four or five days would complete her full equipment, and render her fit for war service.

After dinner, Sir John, Lady Acton, and our hero were left together; her ladyship still looked almost a child, though considerably improved in manner and conversation, and talked a great deal to Captain De Courcy concerning the fair widow, the Princess of Sorento. "You are a most especial favourite, Captain De Courcy," said Lady Acton, "but I am beginning to think you are not quite master of your own heart, or you could never resist the charms of the beautiful Clarina ; all our cavalieros are in despair at her insensibility."

"In truth, your ladyship," replied De Courcy, "the princess would be throwing away her affections on me; for I confess to you, though smarting under a cruel disappointment, I am too recent a sufferer from the blind god's malevolence to venture again to lose myself in a fresh entanglement."

"Come, now, I insist on it, Captain De Courcy," said Lady Acton, eagerly, "that you tell me all the particulars of the affair. You have been in love, and the lady has jilted you?"

Hugh De Courcy coloured to the temples.

"Now, do you know," continued her ladyship, "it's a good sign to see you blush; it shows you are not hackneyed in love affairs, like our Neapolitan cavalieros, who throw off a fair one and take another, with as much ease as you would a glove; but, upon my word, she must be a fastidious

H 2

and bold girl to cast away the love of the gallant and much-admired commander of the Vesuvius."

"As you two are proceeding to talk of love affairs," remarked Sir John, "I will just take a nap; your tale will act as a narcotic. I shall hear an indistinct kind of buzz rather pleasing than otherwise. So now, Hugh, you may begin;" and the prime minister of Queen Caroline stretched himself on a sofa, with the intention of enjoying a siesta after dinner.

Captain De Courcy would much rather that her ladyship had retired and left him with Sir John, whom he anxiously wished to question concerning his parents; besides, he had no wish that Lady Acton should become his confidante in his unfortunate love adventure, as he considered it. But there was no getting off; and, in fact, he had, child as she appeared, good reason to esteem Lady Acton, who had always evinced the greatest interest in his affairs and promotion, and, indeed, did more for him in talking to the Queen concerning him than he was aware of. He therefore determined to tell her candidly the whole tale; and he did so.

"By Jove, Hugh," suddenly exclaimed Sir John, jumping up, "you have kept me awake instead of putting me to sleep. It appears, now, that you have lost your ladye love, and killed her lover. If I was in your place I would marry the Princess of Sorento in a week, and send a polite invitation to this curious English girl, who, in my opinion, was making a fool both of you and the ill-starred Count of Spinola. I always understood that you give very ugly sword-thrusts. What do you say, my lady?"

"Why, that I think quite differently from you both," answered Lady Acton, seriously.

"The deuce you do!" cried Sir John; "the thing is quite plain!"

"No," replied her ladyship, "I think it is very obscure; the only thing I see clear in it is, that the Count of Spinola really intended to assassinate Captain De Courcy, and that he merited the punishment he met. But I do not see that a lady should be accused of unfaithfulness because she happened to look out of a pavilion window precisely at the moment this count was walking along the beach."

"But, zounds! cara," said Sir John, "did not his friend Baracco tell him it was a concerted meeting?"

"Well," said Lady Acton, quietly, "why should he have believed his friend? He should have seen his mistress, and have heard her justification or her confession of wronging him. For my part, I think the person who told Lieutenant

Baracco this story of this beautiful girl's unfaithfulness was a traitor and a spy of this Count of Spinola."

Captain De Courcy started; his cheek felt burning. "Good heavens!" he exclaimed, mentally, "have I thrown away a treasure on suspicion?"

"I see," continued Lady Acton, "you are staggered, Captain De Courcy; like all men in love, you were blinded by jealousy and rage. Don't shake your head, for I do believe an Englishman can be just as jealous as an Italian."

"With this little difference, carissima," remarked Sir John, with a laugh, "that he refrains from sticking a knife between his rival's ribs, which you will allow is an unpleasant operation."

"Ah," observed her ladyship, "your climate, Sir John, is not so hot as ours; neither is your love."

"Faith, I do not know that," returned the prime minister, "I mean our love for your bewitching sex. Now, there's Hugh has settled this worthy count's affairs in this world, and some other worthy with him; if that's not showing love I do not know what is."

"But, Sir John," put in Captain De Courcy, "I did not kill the count from jealousy or disappointed love. He tried to take my life, and I defended myself."

"Precisely the same thing to the count," returned Sir John.

"Well, Captain De Courcy," said Lady Acton, "I tell you what I would do. I would insist on Lieutenant Baracco's telling me who was his informant."

"But your ladyship forgets," said Sir John, "Baracco has sworn not to tell; so they may quarrel, and then Hugh will run him through the body. No, no, my advice is the best; forget the fair lady, and marry the princess. You will see her looking glorious in her beauty to-morrow, for she accompanies the Queen to the fête, and you will have a long chat with her at the Villa Reale in the evening; that's the sensible way of doing business."

But our hero thought otherwise; he bestowed no thought at all upon the princess, but a great deal upon what Lady Acton had said.

Her ladyship having retired shortly after, De Courcy, in the course of conversation, said, "I very much wish, Sir John, as I am going to England, to know who was in reality my father; you have told me that I bear my mother's name, to which I have no right. Now, my father's, if I am justly entitled to bear it, I should like to give a wife, if ever I take one."

"Well, it's a very natural feeling," said Sir John; "but

I am afraid to explain the past to you now, for an event has occurred (it happened years ago, but did not come to my ears till recently), which places you in a peculiar and unpleasant situation, if you persist in claiming your name. Your rights, as far as I understand, are irrevocably lost."

"As to any rights of property," said Hugh De Courcy, "I do not care about them; I have enough for my wants; but I burn with an intense desire to know my father's name."

Sir John remained buried in thought some moments, and then said, looking into De Courcy's anxious countenance—

"If I tell you, Hugh, will you quit the Neapolitan service?"

"No, certainly not; not while the war lasts, and his majesty honours me with the command of his ship; no, I should be an ingrate to do so."

Sir John again seemed in profound thought; suddenly he said, rubbing his hands, and with a smile on his countenance, "I have it. You will doubtless sail for Malta and England in four or five days. In the first place, as you earnestly wish it, I will get Baracco the command of the Vesuvius. The day before you sail, I will put a sealed packet into your hands; it will explain all about your birth to you, your father's name, and the rights of which your grandfather deprived you, and the means of clearly proving your birth; but only on this condition—that you give me your honour not to break the seal of that packet, unless you are on the point of leading a lady to the altar to be your wife; or, that any one should dispute your right to the name of De Courcy. Should either of those two contingencies occur, you may break the seal. There, now, do not dispute my purpose; I consult your happiness—I do, upon my honour."

"I am under too many obligations to you, Sir John," returned Hugh De Courcy, "to dispute your wishes; let it be as you say."

"Very good," answered the prime minister, squeezing our hero's hand affectionately; "we are in very troublous times. The horizon is dark over the fortunes of this kingdom, indeed over all Italy. The revolution marches forward with gigantic strides, and thrones totter like nine-pins. Napoleon throws the ball; we can see no end to his ambition or his power; to-morrow, however, be prepared to accompany me to this fête; you must see the King, and thank him for your new appointment."

CHAPTER XIII.

T,IE Fête of Predi Grotto attracted all the votaries of pleasure and piety from all parts of the kingdom of Naples to the city. Crowding the streets were to be seen women from Ischia and Procida, in their rich and almost Grecian costumes, than which nothing can exceed the gracefulness and richness, consisting of a long petticoat of bright-coloured satin, crimson border and caftan, edged with gold, golden ornaments for the hair, and richly embroidered slippers. The sun glistens on the quantity of golden ornaments which peep forth amid gay-coloured ribbons, massive gold ear-rings and neck-chains, all set off to great advantage by the certainly Oriental style of beauty of these islanders. Groups of Neapolitan country people, in their picturesque attire, monks and soldiers, civilians, and a few, very few, cavaliers, crowded every spot during this day of joyous festivity.

The whole extent of the Riviera is crowded with newly erected booths; one of the luxuries to be had within is the well-known snail broth, and slices of bread and jam, thickly plastered with stewed snails—Heaven save the mark!

Near the Cap de Monte, at the extremity of the Toledo, and just as you enter Ponte de Salute, several immensely long tables are laid out, and during the hours of the night incessant banqueting goes on; gaily coloured flags float in the breeze on every side, and the ear is saluted with song and joyous laughter wherever it turns; in sooth, the Nea-politan is a laughter-loving, indolent, careless, maccaroni-eating biped; and nature, kind nature, supplies him with almost every luxury with remarkably little toil. At this period, the street had a goodly sprinkling of soldiers, in rather a handsome uniform.

We do not know whether it was Ferdinand the First, or his successor, who, when asked to change the uniform of his troops, and pad their breasts, to protect them from sword-cuts, replied,—

"Ha! clothe the troops as you will, but as for pad-ding, Saint Maria! it would make them very hot; and besides, I should get padding for their backs, not their breasts."

From the Chiaga, until the procession reached the church of Predi Grotto, the whole distance was lined with troops.

The Neapolitans, at that day, and much later still,

affected the Spanish style of costume, the ladies especially ; the ladies of the court all wore dresses of bright blue satin, embroidered with gold, and long white veils, wrought in gold, and fastened in the hair by jewelled diadems.

The royal carriage was drawn by eight horses, not driven, but led by royal domestics, clad in gorgeous liveries ; running footmen, in white and pale blue silk, ran alongside the carriage with lighted brands, the tips decorated with tufts of feathers. After the royal carriage, came the persons of most rank—ministers, &c.

In one of the royal carriages was the Princess of Sorento and four other ladies ; she was magnificently dressed, and dazzled the beholders more by her beauty and grace than even her diamonds and rich dress. Captain De Courcy was in the prime minister's carriage with Lady Acton, and as the princess's carriage passed, as part of the royal cortége, the princess recognized our hero, and, with a flush on her beautiful cheek, which was very evident to a keen observer like Lady Acton, she saluted him most familiarly and graciously. De Courcy lifted his hat from his head and bowed, as the carriage passed slowly on, and then Lady Acton's carriage joined the long train of equipages that filled up the Chiaga.

" Upon my word, Captain De Courcy, you are a favoured individual ; what a sweet smile you received ; but is she not lovely ?—and only twenty ! "

" She is very beautiful indeed, Lady Acton," said our hero, suppressing a sigh, for he thought of another whom he thought equally beautiful, and with a far sweeter and gentler expression of countenance.

The Princess of Sorento appeared perfectly sensible of her beauty, and proud of her rank ; Mary Wharton, just the very contrary.

" And can it be possible," mentally thought De Courcy, even amid the blaze of beauty and the gay scene that sur-rounded him—" can it be possible that I have wronged Mary. and that——but no, it cannot be, and I am making myself ten times more miserable."

Having reached the Chapel of Predi Grotto, the Royal family alighted, and in succession the cortége that accom-panied them, and entered the chapel, which was—except-ing where the King and Queen and the royal party sat—crowded to suffocation.

After the service the party returned to Naples in the same order, amid the firing of cannon from the forts and the shipping in the roads.

Sir John Acton and our hero followed the royal carriage to the Villa Reale, and shortly afterwards had an audience of the King. Ferdinand the First was at this period in his fiftieth year; though accounted an imbecile and weak king, he was nevertheless much liked by his people, for he was good-natured and extremely familiar in his manner to all ranks.

Our hero was received most graciously, kissed his majesty's hand, and returned suitable thanks for his appointment to the Serena frigate. As he was recently from Genoa, his majesty asked many questions concerning the siege, talked of Lord Keith's services, but spoke with enthusiasm of Lord Nelson, whom he styled the first naval commander in the world. Whilst passing encomiums on the English admiral, the Queen, with several ladies, and amongst them the Princess of Sorento, entered the saloon.

Queen Caroline could never have been accounted a handsome woman; she was both masculine in person and in mind. It is said that Lady Hamilton once boxed her ears or gave her a slap in the face; all that we can say to this is, that her ladyship was extremely rude, and bold withal.

Captain De Courcy was a favourite with the Neapolitan Queen, who was much more accessible and familiar with her court, and preserved much less etiquette than existed in any other court in Europe.*

Having kissed the Queen's hand, her majesty remarked, " that he looked not so well as when last in Naples," and graciously inquired, "if he had suffered from any wounds during the siege of Genoa."

"No, your majesty; I was fortunate to escape."

" Well, that's very strange," said the Queen, turning to the Princess of Sorento, who had approached whilst the King and his minister were earnestly conversing at a window.

"I thought, princess," continued the Queen, "you said this morning that Captain De Courcy had been seriously wounded, and confined to his cabin during the voyage from Genoa here? "

Clarina Obruzza, Princess of Sorento, with a very peculiar smile, looking our hero in the face, said, "And was not that the case, Signor Capitano?"

Thus appealed to, and before the Queen, Hugh De Courcy could only say, "I would not dream, your majesty,

* All writers agree that the Neapolitan Court was the most dissolute in Europe, and that a licence and freedom existed altogether without parallel.

of contradicting so fair an accuser; I did suffer, your majesty, from a wound or two, but not received in your gracious majesty's service."

"Ah, now I can guess," said the Queen, who was very fond of all amorous stories and affairs of gallantry; so at least historians say. "Some love affair, no doubt. Captain De Courcy found his time pass pleasantly enough amongst the fair dames of Genoa; and that city, I am told, is not the safest in the world for gallants getting entangled in the meshes of Cupid."

"I can assure your majesty," said our hero, "with a flush on his cheek, catching a very arch smile on the features of the princess, "that the wounds I received were in self-defence, and——"

Our hero hesitated, for he instantly recollected that if he said any more he would involve himself in a worse entanglement; but, before the Queen could request him to continue, he was fortunately relieved by the King hastily approaching, with Sir John Acton. De Courcy and the ladies immediately fell back, whilst his majesty and Sir John engaged the Queen in earnest conversation.

"Now, confess, Captain de Courcy," said the princess, gently tapping our hero on the arm with her fan, without which no Neapolitan female stirs—"now confess; his majesty has just saved you from getting into, what shall I call it—a dilemma?"

"And why, fair lady," said Hugh De Courcy, "should you suppose I was in a dilemma? Really I begin to think that molehills are magnified into mountains here in Naples."

"Oh, then you admit, most gallant captain, that there is or was a molehill. I am afraid that you found the hearts of the fair maidens of Genoa made of more impenetrable materials than our Neapolitan belles—was not that the case?"

"Upon my word, princess," returned our hero, vexed at finding his Genoese adventure, though distorted, apparently so well known in Naples, "upon my word, princess, some one seems to have taken considerable pains to circulate a very distorted account of a very simple affair, and one I should think of so common an occurrence as little likely to excite the curiosity of an Italian."

"Oh, but you forget," said the princess, with a very bewitching smile, "that though the circumstance of a cavaliero being the sport of a fair lady's caprice is nothing uncommon, yet, happening to the gay and gallant Captain de Courcy, who has hitherto been so irresistible amongst my fair compatriots, it has created such a sensation, that really since we heard of your adventure, we have all been dying with curiosity to know the real truth of the case. So now, do confess, and relieve, at least, my curiosity;" and the beautiful eyes of Clarina Obruzza were fixed upon his, with such a beseeching and captivating expression, that our hero confessed to himself that the princess was very beautiful, and a very dangerous person for a lover smarting under disappointment to encounter; especially as he well knew that the princess had a decided partiality for him, not only from gratitude, but from personal inclination. What our hero said or related concerning his adventures in Genoa we know not, but we know that they retired to one of the windows of the magnificent saloon, which enjoyed a glorious view of the bay, and remained some time in earnest conversation, the other ladies chatting in another, whilst the Queen and King engaged Sir John Acton in serious conversation.

This ended, his majesty and Sir John left the saloon, and the Queen approached the window where the princess and Captain De Courcy were conversing.

"There is a service for you to perform, Captain De Courcy," said the Queen, "before you sail for England, that will, I make no doubt, be agreeable to you. His majesty has determined to remove with the court to Palermo, and he has selected the "Serena" frigate to be got ready for our reception. You will hear the reason for this somewhat sudden move from Sir John."

"Your majesty confers upon me a most gracious mark of favour," cried De Courcy, certainly gratified by the royal intention; "and I shall, at once, see that everything be ready for your majesties' embarkation."

"It appears," continued the Queen, "that his majesty was inclined to bestow the command of the Vesuvius upon Lieutenant Baracco, but your lieutenant has petitioned for the post of first lieutenant of the Serena, preferring to be under your control, to commanding the brig; his majesty, therefore, granted his request, thinking, of course, you would be pleased to have all your former officers from your old ship commissioned to your new."

Though somewhat surprised at this proceeding of Lieutenant Baracco, Captain De Courcy at once said, "he felt highly pleased at his majesty's gracious condescension; that he had a great partiality for his officers, and rejoiced to have them again under his command."

"I am happy," added Queen Caroline, in a low voice, and with a very meaning look, "to see you and our charm-

ing cousin such friends. You are one of fortune's favourites, Captain De Courcy;" and the Queen tapped his
shoulder with her fan, smiling most facetiously; "I need
not say, · take fortune when she smiles.'"

Hugh De Courcy coloured to the temples, but bowed
low; and then, with a few words addressed to the princess,
who, after the Queen's departure, called his attention to
her, he retired, with abundant motives for serious reflection.

CHAPTER XIV

IT was night—all Naples was illuminated; the Toledo, the
Chiaga, were a blaze of every variety of coloured lamps;
the ships in the harbour were brilliantly lighted up; the
land was covered with the gay, pleasure-seeking Neapolitans. The lovely bay was alive with boats, also filled with
a gay throng. There was a ball at the Villa Reale, and
festivities of all kinds in mansions of the petty nobles, in
the houses of the citizens; the very lazzaroni, ragged,
half-naked, were eating and drinking, and making love;
for, after all, the lazzaroni of Naples are a very important
part of its population—whether for sedition, riot and
plunder, or defending their beautiful city; for, positively,
during the French invasion, the lazzaroni were the only
fighting subjects of his majesty of the Two Sicilies.

It was the night of the Festa di Santa Maria Predi
Grotto; Napoli was, as we stated, in a delirium of pleasure.
It appeared impossible that any one not stretched upon a
death couch should think of anything but enjoyment. The
moon, that useful luminary to all romance writers, stood
high in the heavens, silvering with her light the smoke of
Vesuvius; from the open windows of the villas, lights
gleamed out, putting the mild moonbeams, that shone so
pleasantly upon the vine-covered verandahs, to the blush,
that artificial light should be preferred to her chaste illumi-
nation. The broad-leafed palm-tree nestled in the soft
breath of the night breeze. All was lovely; and yet amid
the luxuries of nature, and the luxuries of art, man was
restless still.

We must beg our readers to follow with us the footsteps of
a man of the middle height, wrapped, even on such a night,
when the breeze would not have ruffled an infant's curls,
in an immense dark mantle, and his head covered with a
slouched beaver, the mantle held close up to his face, leaving only a pair of dark eyes visible. This sombre, and
certainly not pleasure-seeking stranger, passed at a quick
pace through the well-lighted thoroughfares, and avoiding

all intercourse or word with the gay revellers, plunged into one of the numerous narrow dirty streets at the back of the Toledo, and traversing two or three of these deserted thoroughfares, dived beneath a low dark arch, and paused before a doorway; but a very faint light entered this arched passage. The stranger, groping over the door, found the handle of a bell; for though this house was in an obscure part of the city, it nevertheless, some years back, was a house of no mean appearance. The lapse of years had rendered this quarter of the city no longer a desirable one; the wealthy civilians that owned the houses moved elsewhere, and the houses became the abodes of the poorer class.

Presently a slide in the door was pushed back, and a man's face, and that not a very prepossessing one, showed itself at the aperture; the light of a lamp he held in his hand flashing in the eyes of the stranger.

"Your number?" said the man at the slide, in a gruff voice.

"Five hundred and one," returned the stranger without.

"Benissimo!" returned he within, and back went the slide; heavy bolts were drawn, the key turned in the lock, and the door opened: but there was no light, all was dark within the door.

"What number here?" inquired the same voice.

"One less," returned the stranger.

"Benissimo!" again exclaimed the man who had opened the door; and suddenly shifting a dark lantern, the passage or hall became illuminated.

The man who let the stranger in was attired in the every-day costume of a Neapolitan citizen of the lower class; having bolted and locked the entrance door, he led the way, without a word, along the passage, till he came to another door, against which he knocked five distinct blows one after the other; and then, after a slight pause, a single blow, and the door fell back. There was no one to be seen; but the muffled stranger beheld a staircase lighted by a solitary lamp. He walked on, and mounted the stairs; his guide remaining behind, and the door closing of itself. On gaining the top of the flight of stairs, he reached a landing-place. Seated on a chair, with a table beside it, was a man dressed in a mantle with a mask on his face; and on the table were a brace of pistols, and a sabre; and near them an open book, with pen and ink beside it.

The man in the mask took up a pistol, and, cocking it,

as the stranger gained the landing-place, pointed it at him, saying, " Write your number! " pointing with his pistol to the book.

The stranger, without showing any surprise, took the pen, dipped it in the ink, and wrote under several other numbers on the same page, " 500 " and " one "—the five hundred in figures, the one in letters.

" Benissimo! " cried the man in the mask, laying down the pistol.

The stranger passed into an antechamber, lighted by a lamp; a long table in the middle, covered with mantles— the stranger took off his, and threw it amongst them. Beneath the mantle, the stranger's attire appeared that of a naval officer in the Neapolitan service, and, light flashing on his features, revealed those of Guiseppe Baracco, first lieutenant of the new frigate " Serena."

The sound of voices, from an inner room, fell at times plainly on the ear, as Lieutenant Baracco approached a door, and, throwing it open, entered without any hesitation of manner, a long and lofty saloon. It was but indifferently lighted by two brass lamps, that stood on a long table in the middle of the saloon, covered with a green faded cloth. Along this table were seated about twenty individuals ; at the head of the table sat a well-dressed, handsome man, of about six or eight-and-thirty; at the foot, leaning his elbows on the table, and his head resting on his clasped hands, sat no less a personage than one of the common lazzaroni of Naples, half naked, bare-footed, and bare-legged, with his long matted hair hanging down to his shoulders: his breast, sunburnt to the colour of mahogany, and hairy as a camel's back, was quite bare : there he sat, eyeing the other well-dressed personages on each side of him, with a quiet composed look; he did not even turn his head as the lieutenant entered the saloon.

The other personages looked up, and one, near the head of the table, made room for the new comer beside him.

The table, we forgot to mention, was covered with letters, and papers, and writing materials; but neither wine, nor food of any kind, was to be seen.

The persons assembled in this room were members of a secret society termed " Caracciolo." Their object was to re-establish democracy, combined with a detestable system of socialism, precisely similar to a society at this moment existing in France, called the " Marianne."

This society was to be supported by anarchy and blood-

shed. Its confederates were bound by the most solemn
vows of fidelity and secresy. All relations in life were to
be sacrificed to its interests.

Those who belonged to this society were, of course,
rank revolutionists, and of the same party that drew
within its net the unfortunate Prince Caraccioli. They
first sought the restoration of the Parthenopean Republic
—this was their first object; the next, the destruction of
the royal family and the high nobles, and the massacre of
every Austrian in Italy. This last resolution we can
scarcely blame an Italian for entertaining, so execrable
and so horrible has been the power of Austria; so treacherous and detestable her rule.

The murder of Jean Debry, Benneci, and Robergiot, by
order of the Emperor of Austria (Francis), just previous
to this meeting, had roused and increased the feeling
existing against Austria and kingly rule—for amongst the
members of this secret society were two Frenchmen,
cousins of Jean Debry. This barbarous murder of three
French gentlemen, who were in a manner sacred under
the character of ambassadors as we said, excited feelings
of vengeance; they were assassinated by Austrian hussars,
after leaving Rastadt.

This foul deed excited the indignation of Europe, for all
their papers were seized. Austria, as usual, made a miserable attempt at justification, saying that the assassination
was committed by the hussars themselves; that they had
only orders to seize the papers. But, in point of fact,
these papers were as sacred as the persons of the assassinated.

Another member of this secret society was a Frenchman
of the name of Goudoc; he was a nephew of the Monsieur
Goudoc whose wife, a very beautiful Englishwoman, was
purposely placed in the way of the King of Naples, so that
her charms might alienate Ferdinand from his Queen.
But the Queen discovered the plot, and forthwith banished
Monsieur and Madame Goudoc.

An intense hatred to Ferdinand's Queen Caroline existed
in the breasts of all the confederates, and a determination
to destroy the latter, by any means, universally prevailed
amongst the members, which at this time consisted of five
hundred and one—Guiseppe Baracco being the very last
member admitted and sworn.

They had several places of meeting, and pretty much the
same forms were used for obtaining admittance. Any spy,
thinking to obtain an entrance into the chamber of conference, by accidentally acquiring the knowledge of a

number, was sure to be detected, from the simple precautions adopted. If a spy contrived to pass the first door by
giving the right number to the man who answered the bell,
he would be sure to fall a victim: for more than a dozen
armed men were located in a chamber adjoining the hall,
listening to the answer of the conspirator, who remained in
darkness. Again on the stairs, the man with the pistol
would instantly shoot the person who wrote the presented
number altogether in figures; whilst each night of meeting
the rules were changed, and the whole 500 carefully made
acquainted with the change, for sometimes only six or eight
might attend, sometimes a hundred—then again, every
member was known personally one to the other. This was
essential.

The lazzaroni sitting at the foot of the table was a
remarkable personage in his way: he was a modern Mas-
saniello, but only in one signification—his great power over
his tribe; his name was Marco Campobello, his aim was
liberty and equality, and he represented two thousand of
his caste, ready when wanted to use their knives upon the
aristocracy of Naples.

Our readers may rationally inquire what was Lieutenant
Baracco's inducement in joining this desperate and dangerous society of democrats of the worst sort?

Disappointed hopes in the first place; hatred to the
Government; and double hatred to Hugh De Courcy,

Guiseppe Baracco was of an old impoverished Calabrian
family; his father, a noble, but degraded, whose title and
property were abolished and confiscated, and himself
banished for high treason; he died in France, supported
by his wife, who was a Neapolitan lady of good family, and
who, through the interest of her own family, was permitted to retain a very small estate in the vicinity of
Castellamare, provided she refrained from following her
husband into exile.

She therefore remained in Naples, and at an early age
placed her son in the navy, hoping that his services, as he
advanced in years, would neutralize the treason of his
father. She died, however, shortly after her husband, and
at the time when young Baracco was third lieutenant of a
frigate in which Hugh De Courcy was a midshipman.

Even as a midshipman, De Courcy distinguished himself,
and in boarding a French ship, from which Baracco was
driven back slightly wounded, the young midshipman, by
his courage and his gallantry (the captain and two
lieutenants being carried below, desperately wounded), so
encouraged the men, about to strike their colours, that they

followed him again upon the Frenchman's deck, and after a terrible conflict, forced them to strike their flag.

This splendid action, and the taking of a ship of superior force, when the the Captain and two first lieutenants were desperately wounded, and the third lieutenant beaten back, created the liveliest feeling of enthusiasm for the young midshipman, the protégé of the Queen's minister, Acton, in the Neapolitan court. The King made him at once (a most unusual proceeding, though he had passed his time), second lieutenant of the Marie Caroline, the name of the frigate, the previous lieutenant having died of his wounds. Now, by right, Guiseppe Baracco was entitled to this step, but the name ho bore was against him—his father's treason was not forgotten.

This laid the foundation of all the errors of Guiseppe Baracco's after-life; from that hour he nourished an intense hatred to young De Courcy, which he so disguised as to cause our hero to regard him as a sincere friend.

When De Courcy obtained the command of the Vesuvius, he never ceased his exertions till he got Sir John Acton to appoint Baracco his first lieutenant; nevertheless, Guiseppe Baracco secretly vowed that one day or another he would remove Hugh De Courcy from his path. Before quitting Naples for Genoa, Baracco joined the society of the Caraccioli, so they styled themselves, "as avengers of that certainly cruelly murdered prince."

At the siege of Genoa, when left behind on the quay, in the attack upon the Prima galley, Baracco was the most eager in spreading the report that his captain was shot dead whilst fighting on the mole, and consequently he assumed the command of the brig : he did not believe this to be the fact himself, but he hoped it, and thought he might succeed to the command on the return of the brig to Naples. But it was soon ascertained by the fleet that De Courcy's body was not amongst the dead, neither was he a prisoner. This surprised all; and Baracco began to have hopes that he was positively drowned, and his body washed out to sea.

But from this pleasing dream he was awakened by a boat from the enemy with a flag of truce. This was the message from Massena, that Captain De Courcy was alive and well, and that an exchange of prisoners would be agreed to.

Thus vanished Lieutenant Barocco's dream of retaining the command of the Vesuvius. After the surrender of Genoa, Lieutenant Baracco enjoyed with his commander the hospitality of the Signor Garetti. He very soon per-

I

ceived the state of affairs between Mary Wharton and his
commander; and also he perceived that the Count de
Spinola was a disappointed lover. Baracco and Spinola
were both Italians; Hugh De Courcy an Englishman.
Baracco easily insinuated himself into the confidence of
the count: two men of similar tastes and habits—for
Baracco in secret was a bad and vicious man—soon came
to understand one another; and, finally, Baracco became
the confidant of the count, and the two not only plotted
Hugh De Courcy's separation from Mary Wharton, but
Baracco even agreed to lure him ashore, under a false
pretence of his mistress's infidelity, whilst Spinola placed
hired assassins in ambush to take his life; the Signora
Garetti's attendant, Juliette, being their agent in this
affair, and cunningly devising the plot to deceive De
Courcy.

Even if the scheme failed in convincing him of his
mistress's infidelity, his life would be sacrificed by the
assassins' daggers. It was an Italian's refinement of
revenge, to probe his rival's heart first, by proving to him
that another was preferred by his ladye love to himself,
and then complete the treachery by slaying him; but in
the most important point they failed, for De Courcy nearly
slew the count, and killed one of the assassins.

Lieutenant Baracco, though furious at the failure of his
dastardly treachery in its most important point, consoled
himself with the reflection that he had crushed our hero's
happiness, apparently for ever. The order to weigh anchor
and sail to Naples at once released him from all fear of
a discovery which at first terrified him.

On reaching Naples, the very first thing Baracco did
was to write an anonymous letter to the Princess of
Sorento, stating all that had occurred in Genoa, but disguising the name and country of Mary Wharton; merely
saying "that De Courcy had become passionately enamoured of a lady in Genoa, who had jilted him, and that,
in his rage, he had slain the lady's real lover, and narrowly escaped assassination from bravos, hired by the slain
lover's relations, or perhaps the lady herself."

This information was conveyed to the princess for the
express purpose of poisoning her mind against De Courcy;
for it was very well known in the gay world of Naples that
the fair princess was quite inclined to bestow herself and
fortune upon her deliverer from captivity, and that even the
King and Queen consented to this union, so great a favourite
was the commander of the Vesuvius. This information
certainly piqued the princess, and, to mortify De Courcy, she

spread the report among the ladies of the court, and even told the Queen: but the consort of Ferdinand only laughed, saying, "I do not believe a word of this story. Captain De Courcy is not at all a likely man to love, and sue for a lady's love, and be rejected. I will find the truth out."

Lest our readers may think we deal very lightly with Queen Caroline of Naples and her court, we will quote a French writer's opinion of the Queen, her court, and the Neapolitans in general, at this period.

He first declares the court of Naples pre-eminent for depravity and profligacy, the ruling spirit of it being the Queen, the sister of the hapless Marie Antoinette, but possessed of none of her virtues. He then continues as follows :—

"Quant au peuple, les vices les plus honteux forment la base de son caractère, des mœurs et des usages, grossièreté, paresse, dissimulation, mutinerie, ferocité, lâcheté de moindre danger, nulle foi, nulle probité, la debauche la plus infame, &c. &c.

"La plus grande liberté règne dans cette comté et cette ville, et les femmes y sont moins réservées que partout ailleurs."

We now return, after this brief explanation of the past, to the chamber where the secret society of the "Caraccioli" were assembled on the night of the Festa di Santa Maria di Predi Grotto.

CHAPTER XV

THE individual seated at the head of the long table, at which were collected the members of the secret society of Caraccioli, had been formerly a colonel in the Neapolitan army, and had served under General Mack, a name of calamitous celebrity. When this general marched upon Rome with the Neapolitan army, accompanied by the King, Colonel Frugoni commanded one of the regiments of cavalry; but in the first engagement with Championet, the revolutionary general, he and his whole regiment turned their backs and fled; and, though General Mack was partly successful, and entered Rome, he and his whole army were forced to scamper back to Naples as fast as the light-heeled Neapolitans could run. Colonel Frugoni was disgraced and dismissed the army, though he offered to prove that it was his men who fled, and that he followed to bring them back; but as he did not rejoin the army afterwards the excuse was not allowed. However, as the whole army in their turn fled, with the King at their head, he had the consolation of knowing he was not the only coward in the King's service.

When the King and his court took refuge on board Lord
Nelson's ships, and Naples was triumphantly entered by the
French, Charles Innocent Frugoni joyfully embraced the
republican party and remained in Naples, whilst Cardinal
Ruffo drove out the French and restored Naples to the King.
The ci-devant colonel pretended to join the royalists, but
secretly he was one of the democratic conspirators.

Colonel Frugoni was a bad, vicious, unprincipled man, and
a coward—nevertheless, he was elected one of the ten chiefs
of the conspirators, who were now only waiting for the
approach of the French army from Northern Italy to com-
mence a revolution in Naples, and seize upon the royal
family.

Charles Frugoni, as soon as Lieutenant Baracco had taken
his seat, said to him, " This is joyful news we have received;
Napoleon Buonaparte has passed the Alps, and gained a famous
victory at Marengo. This battle," continued Frugoni, " will
lead to the conquest of all Italy. The Austrian general,
Melais, has retired behind the Mincio and surrendered to
France all the fortresses he had subdued; so, in fact, Napoleon
remains master of Piedmont, Lombardy, and Liguria. Besides
this, he has insisted on every Austrian prince being rooted out
of Italy, and has assigned Tuscany to the Prince of Parma."

" This is news indeed," said Lieutenant Baracco; " and now
I can account for this sudden resolve of King Ferdinand and
his court to proceed to Palermo."

" What !" exclaimed several of the persons seated at the
table ; " is it the King's intention to quit Naples ?"

" When did you hear that, Signor Boracco ?" demanded the
president, Frugoni.

" Not three hours ago," returned Lieutenant Baracco, " and
from one who had it from the Queen's lips—from Captain De
Courcy, who has been recently appointed to the Serena, in
which frigate the court embarks."

" It is too bad," exclaimed several voices, " to see foreign
minions in the highest posts in the kingdom ; that minion and
paramour of the Queen, Acton, governs the state as he wills,
and now gives the command of our finest frigate to this boy,
Captain De Courcy, no doubt his own son."

" That post ought to have been yours, Signor Baracco ; "
said the president; " what an opportunity it would have
afforded for entrapping the whole royal family !"

" Could not the officers under this Englishman be bought? "
asked a conspirator.

" No," said Lieutenant Baracco, bitterly ; " they and all the
men, late of the Vesuvius, are devoted to him: his mad valour
has gained him the admiration of a parcel of sycophants."

" By St. Januarius!" said a loud harsh voice, from the bottom of the table, "if this maladetto Englishman stands in our way, why not remove him? By all the saints, one would imagine that there was not a knife to be found in Naples, or a hand to use it."

It was Campobello, the lazzaroni, who spoke, and the conspirators gave a murmur of applause.

" Campobello is quite right," said Frugoni; " he must be removed; he must not have the command of the Serena to take the King to Palermo; if he is removed the command would devolve on you, Baracco."

"Say but the word," cried Campobello, " and before this time to-morrow he will cease to exist."

The president spoke in a low tone to Lieutenant Baracco for a few minutes, and then said aloud, " We will put this proposal of Campobello to the vote."

There were twenty-one persons present, who all voted without hesitation for the assassination of Hugh De Courcy, and the amount to be paid the vile perpetrators of the act if they succeeded. The lazzaroni laughed at the idea of failure, with two thousand knives at his command.

" The first thing to be done," said the president, " is to send a trusty messenger to the commanders of the two French frigates off Civita Vecchia. If they put to sea at once and lie off the coast, they can, if you, Baracco, command the Serena, capture her, together with Ferdinand and the Queen. Then hoist the tricolour, and, backed by Campobello's comrades, the city will be ours. The fort will surrender on the first summons, for the revolution once proclaimed, there are thousands ready to shout ' Down with Ferdinand the imbecile!' "

After some further conversation, relative to their own private views, and the expectations of the conspirators, they separated, quitting the mansion one by one, and dispersing to their different homes.

The night of the Festa di Santa Maria Predi Grotto drew to its close—the revellers had retired as the grey light of morning struggled with the fading lustre of the illuminations; the sober citizens sought their couches—the lazzaroni theirs; from one year's end to the other, winter or summer, storm or calm, it was all the same—their couch was the stone steps of a palazzo, the portico of a church, beneath colonnades, or the lee side of a stone wall; they slept not on feather-beds, or upon down, but they lived, married, reared up children; never worked; never troubled about the morrow; never even concerned themselves what became of their bodies, when the grim destroyer claimed them in the end. An hour before sunrise

Naples slumbered ; an hour after sunrise the streets were again alive.

Hugh De Courcy had spent most of the night at the Villa Reale. Must we confess the truth, a great part of the time beside the beautiful Princess of Sorento—one of the most dangerous women amongst the Queen's favourites, for beauty and fascination of manner.

Clarina Obruzza, Princess of Sorento, was passionately attached to the handsome Englishman, as the Neapolitan ladies called Hugh De Courcy.

The Queen, at first, though De Courcy was an especial favourite with her, and even more so with the King, was somewhat opposed to the idea of the princess bestowing—not her affections, but her hand and fortune upon one who was then styled a mere adventurer, gifted with, certainly, a singularly handsome person, most aristocratic manners, unquestionable courage, and extraordinary gallantry. Still for a princess, allied by blood with the royal house of Ferdinand of Naples, to bestow herself upon an unknown foreigner, let him have earned ever so great a character for gallantry and remarkable exploits, was rather a bold step. Yet, after a long conference with her minister, Sir John Acton, the Queen had said to the princess, "It is possible the King may consent."

This occurred before De Courcy's departure to the siege of Genoa, when, we must admit, that being heart-whole, after releasing the princess from captivity, he had for a time yielded to the fascinations of the dangerous and truly amiable widow. Still he made no declaration of love, but being very young, and somewhat susceptible, and mixing in so profligate a court, where the Queen set the example of licentiousness and familiar intercourse, he was led away by his own spirits and the beautiful Clarina's fascinations.

Clarina Obruzza, formerly Clarina de Crotono, was the only daughter and heiress of the Marchese de Crotono, a cousin to King Ferdinand. Before her father's death she was betrothed to the immensely wealthy Prince of Sorento, who owned large estates in Italy and Sicily.

Clarina was fifteen when she gave her hand to the prince, who was exactly fifty-six ; not a very likely period of life for a gentleman to captivate so young and so lovely a girl as Clarina.

But marriages were not generally contracted for love amongst the nobility of Italy ; on the contrary, love generally had little to do with articles of marriage.

Young ladies dreamed and thought of love afterwards ; but to do Clarina justice, she was a virtuous wife, whilst that character lasted. The prince was a kind, good man, and a fine cavalier for his years, and he was a fond husband ; but he died three or four years after his marriage, leaving his young widow the entire of his noble property; as she was very young, he left her and his estates under the care of the King, till she should reach her twenty-second year, when she would become her own mistress.

It may be supposed that so young and beautiful a widow, connected with the royal family, and mistress of a princely fortune, at once became an object of immense attraction.

But Clarina Obruzza, Princess of Sorento, was firmly re-solved that the next time she entered the marriage state she would select a husband for herself, and marry for love and love alone.

The King and Queen were anxious that the princess should, being connected with the royal blood of the King of the Two Sicilies, make a suitable match—and not one derogatory to her rank and station. So that when she had passed eighteen months of widowhood, the former proposed to her for a husband the Duke of ——, a nobleman possessing vast estates in Calabria, and one of the very highest of the Neapolitan nobles.

The young widow declined the proposal with a profound reverence, and, on Queen Caroline questioning her closely as to her reasons for refusing so high a suitor, replied, with a smile,—

" Madame, I prefer descending the ladder to mounting. My late husband, whom I lament—for he was a good, kind, and a scrupulously honourable man, above suspicion—was fifty-six when I married him ; the Duke of —— is acknowledged to be sixty-three; so your majesty, if you will permit me, I prefer descending, and would rather prefer a husband who has as yet only counted six or seven-and-twenty of the steps of the ladder of life."

" How ridiculous you are, Clarina! " answered the Queen. " Marry the duke ; you can have as many lovers, and suit yourself as to age, as you like. Look at the Countess de —— ; she is only seventeen. She married the old Count de ——, who is sixty-eight, and bedridden. She has as many lovers as there are days in the month. Did you ever see a happier woman ? "

Clarina laughed, saying, " Happiness, your majesty, is diffi-cult to define. She that sips of many pleasures, drinks of none. I must find one heart that corresponds with mine ; till that occurs, I remain Clarina Obruzza."

" You are romantic, princess," retorted the Queen ; " I dare say some of these days you will repent your decision, and having wasted your youth in seeking for an imaginary deity."

Clarina first saw De Courcy at a court ball, when she was struck with his noble figure, handsome features, and much more fascinated by his agreeable, off-hand manner; but De Courcy was a sailor, and he shortly after went to sea, and the fair Clarina lost all remembrance of him in the gaieties of the gayest of courts.

It was impossible to live and mingle in such a circle as surrounded Queen Caroline without in some measure being contaminated by its influences.

Clarina loved pleasure, she began to be flattered by the homage paid to her beauty, and permitted herself to be surrounded by gay cavalieros, who called themselves her slaves, who swore by her eyes, wrote sonnets on the beauty of her hands and feet, &c.

Clarina began to waver, and Queen Caroline to see that a few months' more gaiety would bring the young princess to her way of thinking, when the event occurred already related, that again introduced De Courcy to her notice, and in a dangerous guise to a heart already prepossessed in his favour.

She had heard of his gallantry and his exploits amongst the corsairs of Barbary. She then beheld them. She witnessed his courage and his power, when he released her from the hands of the piratical rovers; and from that hour she secretly resolved, if she could not have De Courcy's love, none other should have hers.

It may appear strange that a young and lovely woman, almost a girl, with rank, wealth, and certainly an unblemished reputation, should find any great difficulty in winning a young and dashing sailor's heart, and this same sailor a mere dependent and protégé of the Queen's minister.

Most persons would imagine that Hugh De Courcy would have been dazzled, overpowered by the attentions and evident partiality of the beautiful Clarina, and would eagerly have followed up his good fortune; for already the partiality of the princess had raised up against him a host of enemies— some really dangerous; his position and rapid advancement being already looked upon with exceeding envy. The elevation of so young a man, and a foreigner, created murmurs against the Queen and her minister's partiality, but they were unjust: his youth De Courcy could not help, but his honours he deserved; for there was not an officer, in the Neapolitan service at all events, that could compete with him for brilliant services and real knowledge of his profession.

De Courcy certainly did not love the Princess Clarina; but admired her, and, when near, was fascinated by her powers of pleasing, for the princess had a charming, if not a powerful voice, was highly accomplished, and, there is no doubt, would have made any man she really loved, and who loved her in return, a most amiable and charming wife.

But strange to say, De Courcy, reared as he had been in foreign lands, frequenting and enjoying foreign society, was singularly English in his ideas and feelings : he was also somewhat romantic ; and though aware that the beautiful Clarina had married a man nearly old enough to be her grand-father, merely performing a contract entered into by her parents, without her heart being concerned in the affair in the slightest degree, yet there was something in her being a widow distasteful to the young sailor. Besides, he was quite aware of her having been reared in, and habituated to, the customs and society of a most corrupt and licentious court ; and he could scarcely bring himself to believe that her mind could remain pure and uncontaminated.

Thus, he refrained from allowing his heart to become captive to the princess's fascinations ; when suddenly he was ordered to Genoa, in the Vesuvius, to join Lord Keith's fleet.

On his return, when smarting under disappointed love, he again fell within the attractions of the princess. We know not how things might have turned out had not events inter-fered.

On the night of the Festa di Santa Maria Predi Grotto, Hugh De Courcy left the royal palace at a later hour than Sir John and Lady Acton ; taking his mantle from an attendant, he threw it over his shoulders, and proceeded to seek the hotel where he had resided from the period of his return to Naples.

The principal thoroughfares and the vicinity of the royal palace only were illuminated ; the other streets had no light except that derived from the full moon.

Our hero's hotel was the Villa di Roma, to reach which he had to proceed along the quay, which was still crowded ; every ten or twelve yards, stalls and booths met his eye, roasting and broiling perpetually going on ; water melons, in hundreds, exposed for sale ; vendors of maize were offering the golden ears to the numerous crowd of passers-by ; oysters were handed about, with the wine of the country, to hundreds seated on the wooden benches before the stalls ; whilst guitar players and singers were merry with their melodies, for the chances of a small coin. At times the ear was stunned with cries of " Aqua gelata," a drink the Neapolitans are very fond of, with a little aniseed mixed up with it—for ice is ever grateful in their warm climate.

The young man passed along, quite unconscious that he was followed by a tall figure, in the ragged costume of the lazzaroni, and that this man spoke to more than a dozen of his tribe that he passed on the way. Presently, as De Courcy turned into a street less frequented, and which led by a short cut to his hotel, a crowd of lazzaroni men, women, and girls, came, hand and hand, singing a Bacchanalian song, from a side street, and quite encircled our hero before he could avoid them. As this was often done during festivals, when the lazzaroni became half intoxicated with wine, and they chanced to stumble on a cavaliero by himself, in order to extort some small coin, Captain De Courcy stood still, and put his hand into his pocket to draw out some silver; in doing so his mantle fell back, displaying his court uniform; just then the circle became gradually less, as they danced round him, the women and girls singing in chorus, when a wild shriek—one evidently of terror—from behind him, caused him to turn rapidly round. The movement saved his life—for the blow of a long poniard-shaped knife, aimed at his back by a strong hand, glanced along his vest, tearing it open, and, inflicting a mere scratch, came out again at his side. The hand that held the knife attempted to withdraw it, whilst several of the men made a rush at De Courcy, drawing their knives and cursing fiercely; but our hero, with a sudden wrench, tore himself away from the ruffian holding the knife, and, springing to one side, drew his sword. With wild shrieks and shouts the whole crew rushed, pell mell, up the street, one of the villains, as he fled, aiming a fierce blow at a young girl— one of the lazzaroni, by her scanty dress—and felled her to the ground, bleeding from mouth and nose.

The noise and confusion of this scene brought many persons to the spot; but De Courcy drawing out the knife that had so narrowly escaped taking his life, stooped down and raised the girl, whose shriek, he judged, had saved his life.

" What is the matter? what has happened?" cried a multitude of voices; at the same time the speakers gathering round our hero, whose mantle had fallen to the ground, displaying his naval uniform to the crowd.

" Get some water," he exclaimed to some women, gaily dressed, who crowded near. " This poor girl is hurt."

" Ah, St. Janarius !" said the women, " it's only a lazzaroni ragazza." " She'll come to of herself, Signor Capitano," echoed several voices ; " they are used to blows !" " But what has happened to you, signor?" inquired some of the men.

Hugh De Courcy seized a vendor of " aqua gelata," and emptying his cooling beverage into a can, notwithstanding the grimaces of the owner—who was, however, appeased with a coin four times the value of his entire evening's speculation— proceeded to wash the blood from the female's face, which was a remarkably beautiful one, though pale, and the eyes closed, and the complexion dark. But she came rapidly to herself, and then one of the bystanders called out— " Eh, per Bacco ! it's the daughter of the fierce Campobello, the lazzaroni : come away, neighbours, if you don't want a knife in your ribs. St. Janarius ! he's a dangerous customer." In two minutes, De Courcy was alone with the girl, who could not be more than sixteen. She was clad in a very short, bright red petticoat; her well-formed foot and leg quite bare. A chemisette and a thin tattered scarf formed her entire clothing.

" Ah, Santa Maria! where am I ? " she exclaimed, in a very sweet voice, looking wildly about her : then, seeing De Courcy, she sprang to her feet, and with the rag of a scarf she wiped away the blood that still flowed from her nostrils.

" Do not stay here, signor," she hurriedly said, in pure Italian ; " you will not be alive another ten minutes."

" Oh, do not be alarmed about me," said our hero, kindly ; " I have my eyes about me, and my good sword in my hand : I should think little of a dozen such assassins : but did not you utter the shriek that saved my life ? "

" Yes, signor," answered the girl, shuddering : " you saved my life once, and I have saved yours now. May the saints still preserve you ! But go hence." And, suddenly turning round, she darted off down the road with the swiftness of a fawn.

" Ah, by Jove ! that's strange," cried De Courcy, half aloud : " I remember now." And picking up his mantle, he hastened to his hotel, keeping the knife that had so nearly cut the thread of his existence.

CHAPTER XVI.

Hugh De Courcy, having gained his chamber in the Hotel Villa Roma, threw off his coat and examined the cut he had received. It was trifling ; a little water and a piece of sticking plaister was all it required. But, thought our hero, it was a most providential escape. His next exclamation was, " To whom do I owe this pleasant remembrance ?" and he took up the knife to examine it. It was a most formidable weapon : the blade, a keen double-edged steel, about ten inches long and two broad, firmly embedded in a rough handle of horn. On this horn was a smooth part, and rudely cut on it were the letters "A. C."

" No doubt," thought De Courcy, " they stand for Antonio Campobello, the turbulent lazzaroni of the Campo Formio.

I have heard of this worthy. But why he should seek to assassinate me is somewhat singular, for the lazzaroni are certainly not the professional assassins of this good city of Naples. Then this girl, who saved my life by her wild shriek, is his daughter. Could it be her father that struck her down by so brutal a blow? For her sake I must let the ruffian escape the clutches of the law; yet, I would like to know the instigator of this vile act."

Hugh de Courcy, though he had no recollection whatever of the girl's features, remembered well the circumstance of saving a young girl's life, a short time before he proceeded to the bombardment of Genoa.

Walking along the mole head, after leaving his gig, which returned to the Vesuvius, then lying at anchor in the bay, he was attracted by screams from the sea, and, looking in the direction of the sound, he perceived three persons struggling in the water; two of whom contrived to get on the bottom of a small boat, which had been capsized by a sudden squall. Throwing off his upper garments, he plunged in, and reaching the spot, caught a young girl by the hair, just as she was sinking, and kept her up till some boats pulled out to their rescue. The girl was insensible, but De Courcy was too humane to leave her—she was of the poorer class—to the care of the boatmen, and had her carried on shore. The man and woman who clung to the boat claimed the girl as their niece; she was carried to a small locanda, near the quay, and a surgeon sent for, and she was then well tended, and recovered. Leaving a small sum of money for the girl's use, he proceeded to his hotel to change his own garments. From that hour he never thought more of the accident.

He now wondered how this girl, who spoke such pure Italian, could have remembered him; and he resolved to try and see her again—nay, even to have a conference with the very ruffian who had attempted his life, supposing it was the lazzaroni Campobello.

But we know not what to-morrow may bring forth. The following day brought other circumstances into play, that entirely drove from his mind the attempt upon his life the night before.

He had scarcely finished his breakfast the next morning, when a domestic from Sir John Acton summoned him to his guardian's presence.

In five minutes our hero was on his way to the mansion of the prime minister.

Sir John was pacing the chamber with an uneasy expression of countenance.

" So," said the minister, pausing in his walk, and looking

our hero kindly in the face—" so your life was attempted last night in the Stradi del Monti ? Thank God, the ruffian failed!" and he held out his hand and seized that of De Courcy with considerable emotion.

"How on earth did you know that, dear sir? said De Courcy, feeling much the kind manner of his protector.

"I should be badly served, Hugh," answered Sir John, "if I remained ignorant of such occurrences; but sit down, I want to talk to you, for in half an hour you must start on board, and have the frigate in readiness to receive the King and Queen by sunset."

"By sunset!" repeated De Courcy; "that's short notice."

"Don't be alarmed, they have been on board since daylight; but I would not allow you to be disturbed. Now listen to me. Your friend Baracco is a traitor."

The young man started to his feet, his face flushed, and his thoughts flew back to Genoa and Mary Wharton, like an electric shock, whilst he repeated,—

"Baracco a traitor! Good God! A traitor to whom? "

"To his King and country," replied Sir John. "Listen: I have been aware for a long time that a society existed in this city calling themselves Caraccioli — avengers, they first styled themselves, of that ill-starred prince; but, in fact, a society of bloodthirsty democrats, whose whole aim is to overthrow the Government, massacre the royal family, and of course, all the King's ministers; let in the French, and, in the confusion, seize all they can. Their majesties intend leaving Naples for Palermo this evening, and during the absence of the court, I am to take measures for the arrest of all the conspirators."

"But how is it possible," exclaimed De Courcy, "that Guiseppe Baracco is a conspirator? A man I placed such confidence in, and in whose friendship I trusted. What could be his inducement to turn traitor to his King? "

"I, of course, cannot explain to you all his motives; but I surmise a few. I know he has been a discontented man ever since you superseded him; and also when he failed in boarding the Pluton. He afterwards applied for the restoration of his father's forfeited estates, and was refused; in fact, he has been a marked man ever since he espoused the cause of Prince Caraccioli, on Count Thurn's ship, on board which that unfortunate prince was hung."

"Thank God," said Hugh De Courcy, with a flush on his cheek, "I was absent then with the Russian fleet, bombarding Ancona, or my service in the Neapolitan navy had expired."

"Hush, hush, Hugh!" interrupted Sir John, looking considerably disturbed; "don't talk of that—it's past. The prince was a doomed man. No human power could have saved him."

"Except Lady Hamilton," answered De Courcy, bitterly, "and she would not be seen till the poor old man was strung up like a felon; and then she walked the quarter-deck to behold his agony."

"Hugh De Courcy," said Sir John Acton, sternly, "why this to me? You know I gave you my sacred word that I exerted myself to the utmost; but when two women, with unlimited power over those who could have controlled his fate, were resolved he should die—and like a dog—he died. But no more of this—I cannot bear it; and take care, Hugh, how you express your sentiments upon this subject to others; it is too recent to be forgotten.

"Now to resume our previous discourse with respect to Baracco. I am quite satisfied of his being a traitor. You cannot doubt my system; for one of the very principal members of the secret society of the Caraccioli is my paid agent; he was present last night at a meeting held in an old uninhabited mansion, formerly belonging to Caraccioli, in the Stradi di Ova. There were twenty-one members present, and Baracco was one; and that turbulent democrat and furious revolutionist, the lazzaroni Campobello, another; this rascal can raise near three thousand men in a moment. There are five hundred and one influential members; and the ramifications are extensive; those insurgents who escaped from the forts are still in the city, though hundreds have been executed. Now, the worst of it is, that there are hundreds of sailors in our ships who adored Caraccioli, and who were furious at his death. Baracco and his agents are keeping up this feeling. I fear there are many such spirits in your frigate. Now the first thing you must do, when you get on board, is to arrest Baracco."

"You give me a terrible task," said De Courcy, with considerable emotion; "I esteemed Baracco, and he seemed sincere in his friendship to me."

Sir John Acton looked our hero, for some moments, in the face, with a very thoughtful expression.

"I see," said he, after a pause, "that I must be candid. For the sake of your future fortune and advancement I thought to remain silent; but, after all, perhaps, the straight path is the best. He that deals with an Italian must use deception; but I now deal with my own countryman;" and, opening a desk, Sir John took forth three pieces of a torn letter, and, joining them together, laid them on the table; and then, looking up into the features of the surprised De Courcy, he said, "Read."

There were but six lines, and some words were lost. The writing was in Italian. De Courcy read them, staggered back, his face flushed with passion, and, striking his forehead with force, he exclaimed,—

"My God! what a madman I have been!"

"Adieu," muttered Sir John, in a very low voice, "to all the hopes of a match with the Princess of Sorento."

The words De Courcy read were as follows:—

—————————"Juliette has promised to have the Signora Wharton in the Pavilion to-night. Chance may assist us; at all events ————————— him ashore, and depend on me, for ———————— and his troubling you or me —————— —————— say 10 o'clock.

"Spinola."

"Well!" remarked Sir John, "you can scarcely have any scruples in arresting this precious friend of yours now?"

De Courcy's heart heaved with intense emotion. He was still pale; but, in a low calm voice, he asked, "This letter, then, was written to Guiseppe Baracco?"

"It was," said Sir John.

"May I ask how it possibly came into your hands?"

"Certainly; the events of last night have determined me no longer to procrastinate. Your life is never safe, whilst this friend of yours is at liberty."

"What!" said De Courcy; "was last night's attempt on my life owing to Baracco?"

"Unquestionably owing to him," answered Sir John. "It was observed at the meeting of the Caraccioli, last night, that you were in the way; that if Baracco had the command of the frigate, which he would if you were removed, the King and royal family would be in the power of the conspirators.

"That pleasant gentleman, Campobello, the lazzaroni, laughed, and good-naturedly engaged to remove you, before twelve hours were over—this was agreed to unanimously, so that you need not feel flattered by the feeling that exists among the Caraccioli for yourself.

"As soon as my agent got free, he sought an interview with me: I was at the Villa Reale—so did not see him till my return; I was startled, for the plot was well conceived; but I was doubly anxious about your life, as I felt quite satisfied that that rascal Campobello would follow up his intention. I despatched a messenger to you at the palace; you had left, and my messenger hurried towards your hotel, and arrived on the spot when your life was attempted. just at the time you were assisting some lazzaroni girl who was hurt; he soon learned the circumstances from the bystanders, and knowing that you were safe for the night, he hurried back to tell me."

"I am sure, Sir John," exclaimed De Courcy, with much emotion, "you have been a father to me, and I can never show or express to you sufficiently my gratitude."

"And yet," replied the minister, with a smile, "by Jove, you will not marry the Princess of Sorento, all I can say to you."

"Not now," said De Courcy, with a very serious and disturbed countenance; "but, I pray you, tell me how you obtained that torn letter?—and then I will go on board and arrest this most treacherous and false villain, Baracco."

"You must do it carefully and quietly," remarked Sir John; "no intelligence of his arrest must reach the city; let no one in the frigate communicate with boats or the shore. You have all your officers and crew of the Vesuvius on board, but you have also nearly two hundred, and perhaps more, strangers to you in the frigate. You will have the royal guard with you, and the marines."

"I have not the slightest fear of the seamen," said De Courcy. The Vesuvius, now commanded by Captain Gramani, with two gunboats and three armed zibees, is now in harbour, and will, of course, accompany his majesty to Palermo. The Thetis frigate, and the two brigs with her, will in a few days be here, and also Septimo.".

"Yes, I am aware they are all expected," observed Sir John; and then he added, more seriously, "I fear the power of revolutionary France will crush us in the end; but let me tell you how I obtained that letter, and then you may depart. Lady Acton accompanies the Queen, as well as the Princess of Sorento, and all the ladies of the court, so you will have enough to do; but, as I said, now for the finder of this letter, which I deliver to you; you may want it, for—your vindication with a certain fair one."

Hugh De Courcy eagerly took the letter, and put it carefully in his pocket-book.

"You have a young midshipman now on board the frigate, formerly of the Vesuvius, to whom you are very partial."

"Ha!" cried De Courcy; "young Stefana Pamfilé—a brave and kind-hearted youth. It was through him, then, Sir John?"

"Yes," returned the minister, "it was—his father was a great friend of mine, and served me here on my first arrival. The boy will tell you all himself; it's no use wasting time now. So hasten to your ship; all the arrangements for their majesties' passage to the mole, and proceeding on board, will be arranged; but recollect my orders concerning Baracco, arrest him quietly, no bustle or noise—arrest him on your own responsibility. On arriving at Palermo, hand him over to the authorities there. I will arrange for that; but the King is to know nothing of the affair; should he remark Baracco's absence, say he is ill; and now farewell! You will sail for Malta, and England, as soon as you have landed their Majesties, and the special envoy joins you. You will have all your despatches this evening, and—the packet we spoke off. I shall see you again on board."

CHAPTER XVII.

In a very thoughtful mood Captain De Courcy returned to his hotel, and ordered his personal attendant, a young Englishman, who had served him faithfully for three or four years previously, but who did not accompany him to the siege of Genoa, to pack up and get on board as soon as possible. Having given these directions, he proceeded towards the mole.

Amidst the reflections that crowded the brain of De Courcy was one predominant and absorbing—the thought that the beautiful Mary was perfectly guiltless of the weakness he had so rashly and cruelly accused her of. Bitterly he now bewailed his credulity, and the passionate haste with which he had judged her, and the rash impetuosity he had displayed in quitting Genoa.

Would his still fondly-adored Mary forgive him? was the next thought. Would they ever meet again? After such cruel desertion, perhaps she considered their intercourse for ever at an end; how face her, how approach her, after such unjustifiable treatment; again (he coloured to the temples), when he recollected how weakly and thoughtlessly he had acted ever since his return to Naples: to drown thought, to drive away the image of one who daily and nightly haunted his thoughts and dreams, he had, in a manner, yielded to the fascinations of the Princess Clarina; and though he had spoken no word of love to her, or the slightest approach to love, he had appeared more than pleased and flattered by her attention; he knew he was jealously and eagerly watched by many a Neapolitan noble and cavalero when near the princess, and perhaps the beautiful Clarina herself might be deceived by his conduct; he did not deny to himself but that in time he would have probably returned her affection, provided he had remained convinced of Mary Wharton's desertion of him; but now the case was reversed, Mary was pure as an angel in his mind, and he the reverse. Gentle, and we hope fair, reader, excuse us that we cannot. consistent

K

with truth, make our hero a perfect character. Was there ever a man perfect, alas! or woman either? though the latter approach much nearer to perfection than ever man can boast of doing.

Hugh was only four and twenty, and though brave, generous, and noble-minded, was a slave to impulse, and, at times, to passion; the consequence was, that many of his good qualities were occasionally marred by those two failings.

As he proceeded to the mole, the disagreeable duty he had to perform gave him some uneasiness; after years of intercourse with one whom he was accustomed to esteem as a friend, it was painful to a degree to have this delusion dissipated; but ten times more so, to find that not only was his friendship a farce, but that, in fact, he had been bestowing his affection on an assassin and a traitor.

As he turned round a corner of the government stores, previous to reaching the mole, a young female darted out from an arch, and for an instant stood before him; it was the Lazzaroni girl who had saved his life the night before.

"Ah, ragazza!" exclaimed De Courcy, in a kind tone, and taking out his purse, which he intended for her, but the girl impatiently put back his hands and shook her head, with an anxious disturbed look, saying, "I do not want money, signor. Listen!" she gazed down the long blank wall, and along the store-houses; there was no one near at the moment, and then she hurriedly said,—

"There are fifty men on board your ship who have sworn to take your life; they were all entered on Wednesday and Thursday last. Santa Maria, I am watched!" and, turning round, she darted in under the low arch and disappeared.

De Courcy, rather startled, looked round, but saw no one; the place looked deserted, for the stores belonged to the government, were out of use at that time, and opposite them was a long blank wall. He had taken that way purposely as a nearer road, the sentinel on duty letting him pass, being in uniform. The girl at first surprised·him; but the intelligence she imparted was startling; it was not that he feared for his life—he was accustomed to brave death, and was naturally and morally incapable of fear; but it proved to him the dangerous inroad the revolutionary spirit had made amongst the Neapolitans, and also that the intentions of the society of Caraccioli were really deadly. He at once surmised that the Lazzaroni girl had contrived to gain this intelligence by overhearing some secret conference of her father with some of his comrades, and out of gratitude had warned him.

Hugh De Courcy was quite aware that the complement of men wanted for the new frigate had been made up from merchant vessels and fishing crafts, a large bounty being offered; for though the Neapolitan frigates were remarkably beautiful crafts, as to build, rigging, and equipment, their crews, except in two or three instances, were notoriously defective, and scarcely ever under thorough control.

Baracco had entered one hundred men into the ship's books during the week. Now if the Lazzaroni girl spoke the truth, and De Courcy placed uncommon faith in her warning, the fifty intended assassins were amongst those hundred.

This was certainly a critical state of things; the King and his court would be on board before sunset; the preparations along the mole were proceeding rapidly. So hurrying along, De Courcy entered his six-oared gig, which was waiting for him at the extremity of the mole, steered by the young midshipman Stefano Pamfilé.

The frigate was at anchor, about half a mile out from the mole head; it was a beautiful day, the heat tempered by a brisk west wind, that just rippled the surface of the bay, and filled the sails of the numerous craft that covered its waters.

No boats can be more picturesque than the fishing-boats of the bay and islands of Naples; their bright colours, lofty peaked prows, their taut latine sails, and the gaudy, though scant attire of the fishermen themselves, make the picture a pleasing and varied one; and when we add to it the noble vessels of war that then graced the bay, all dressed and decorated in honour of their Majesties' embarkation, we greatly enhance the beauties and grandeur of the scene. Captain De Courcy made no remark concerning the torn letter given him by Sir John, to young Stefano Pamfilé, he reserved that for another time; he had a trying and intensely disagreeable duty to perform, and it engrossed all his thoughts.

He looked up with pride—the pride of a sailor—at the noble frigate he was commander of; her beautiful proportions, her lofty spars, her square yards, her sails so symmetrically furled. She was covered from truck to deck with flags and streamers; splendid awnings shaded her carpeted quarter-deck. and bouquets of the choicest flowers were hung in fanciful festoons in every place.

Just previous to approaching the side of the frigate, Captain de Courcy perceived Lieutenant Baracco pacing the quarter-deck, with a telescope under his arm.

The young commander pressed his lips hard, for it pained him to see the man he had once esteemed about to be arrested as a traitor, and most likely to receive the doom of one, and that shortly.

If the crime of conspiring against his life had been the only one Baracco had been guilty of, De Courcy would have cared little about the meeting that was now to take place; but he had wounded him in a far more sensitive part—he had,

K 2

by falsehood and base treachery, perhaps, deprived him of what was dearer to him infinitely than life.

There was little time, however, for reflection, for the gig dashed up to the vessel, the sides were manned as usual, the officers standing ready to receive their commander. Captain De Courcy, before he ascended the ladder, said, in a low voice, to the young midshipman,—

"When you see me descend to the cabin with Lieutenant Baracco, desire Lieutenant Burtoni, with two of his marines, to remain within call; let them station themselves by the cabin-door."

The midshipman looked a little startled, but, touching his cap, bowed, saying, "Very well, sir."

De Courcy reached the quarter-deck, and as Lieutenant Baracco, in his usual manner, came forward to receive his commander, said, with considerable calmness, and almost, as he thought, in his usual manner, "Pray, follow me to the cabin, Mr. Baracco."

Do as he would, it was scarcely in human power so completely to master his feelings that no symptoms of what was passing in De Courcy's mind should be perceptible to the person he addressed.

The Lieutenant paused, his cheeks grew deadly pale, as his eyes met those of De Courcy, but the latter descended to the cabin without another word or look; and he stood for a moment rooted to the deck. No one had heard the words addressed by the captain to him; instantly, collecting his scattered thoughts, he rapidly crossed the deck, and looking over the side, perceived the six-oared gig waiting.

Turning to the third lieutenant, who was standing near the gangway, he said, "I must be quick; by St. Nicholas, we have little time to lose!" then rapidly descending the side, and jumping into the boat, he exclaimed, "Pull away, my lads; I must reach the mole in less than ten minutes."

"Ay, ay, sir," returned the men, again seizing their oars, and the light boat shot from the side like a meteor.

No one looked surprised at this sudden movement of the first lieutenant, for they thought he was acting in obedience to the orders of their commander. The boat had measured half the distance to the mole, as young Stefano Pamfilé came up from the main deck, with Lieutenant Burtoni and two marines, and walked on towards the quarter-deck. At the same moment, Captain de Courcy, wondering what kept Lieutenant Baracco, re-ascended upon deck.

"Where is Lieutenant Baracco?" he demanded, addressing his second lieutenant.

"Just pulled ashore, sir," returned the officer, looking rather puzzled, "in your gig; did not——"

Hugh De Courcy looked for an instant confounded; with a hasty stride he gained the frigate's side, looked over the bulwarks, and at a glance saw pursuit was hopeless. Young Pamfilé stood pale and puzzled; whilst the officer of marines and his two men remained gazing round them, with surprise and curiosity discernible in their countenances.

Captain De Courcy was chagrined; he had not, then, disguised his countenance, and Baracco must have feared discovery; but there was no time to lose, or much mischief might ensue.

"You may retire and dismiss your men, Lieutenant Burtoni," said De Courcy to the marine officer, and then, with a motion of his hand, he requested the attendance of the confounded and bewildered young midshipman.

Leaving all the officers of the frigate considerably mystified, Captain De Courcy again entered the cabin, took pen and paper, and hastily wrote a few lines, which he folded and directed to Sir John Acton. He then looked up, and seeing young Pamfilé standing before him, appearing very miserable, said, kindly,—

"You have committed no error, my dear Stefano; it was impossible to foresee this *contretemps*. We must remedy it as well and as soon as we can; hasten on shore with this note. See Sir John Acton if possible, and bring me back an answer; lose not a moment."

In two minutes the young midshipman was rowing swiftly towards the mole, in a four-oared gig.

It was necessary to make some kind of explanation to his officers, as there was a great deal to be done, therefore summoning the second lieutenant, an officer of tried courage and considerable experience, De Courcy said,—

"You must act as first lieutenant, Signor Vasari, for the present, and I shall exert myself, and use my interest in getting this temporary command confirmed."

The lieutenant's face flushed with surprise and a feeling of gratification. Still he did not like to venture a question, and waited for his commander to solve the mystery; but Captain De Courcy did not intend to give any further explanation till he heard from the Prime Minister, merely concluding,—

"I wish you to get the ship's books, and note down for me the names of all the men who were entered on last Wednesday and Thursday, and let me know the number. You must be quick."

"I will return with the list in less than ten minutes."

"Ha," said De Courcy, taking the list when brought, and running his eye over it, "sixty-four men and two boys on those two days. What kind of men are they?" he demanded. "Merchant sailors, fishermen, or what?"

" There's a mixture of all sorts, sir," said the lieutenant, " but the most part of them have served in the king's ships. Several of them were formerly in the Minerva, and a dozen or more served under the unfortunate Prince Caraceioli. I fancy there are a few insurgents amongst them ; but you know, sir," added the lieutenant, " they were pardoned on the surrender of Castel Nova."

" Well, I tell you what you must do, Signor Vasari. Divide those men, so as to put not more than ten together in any one mess, and place those particularly, and mind, secretly, under the surveillance of a quarter-master, and let them be carefully watched; when we get to Palermo I will be more explicit." He then went up on deck, looking very thoughtful.

In less than half-an-hour both boats came back. The midshipman brought a note from Sir John; De Courcy opened it. It contained but the following few lines :—

" Dear Hugh,

" Your friend had his wits about him ; perhaps it's as well as it is ; I will remedy the mischance ; however, make your second lieutenant first, and so on ; and let young Pamfilé be acting third lieutenant; he has served his time, and is a good lad. Say nothing about Baraeeo ; let your officers and crew think what they please. You will, of course, be expected o steer the royal barge—six o'clock is the time fixed,

" Yours affectionately,

" J. ACTON."

It may be supposed that the advance of rank in the different officers created the most intense surprise, but also, equal gratification ; as to young Pamfilé, he was in eestasies.

Amongst the crew the most profound wonder was evinced at the strange, mysterious desertion of the first lieutenant: and there were many amongst them who looked exceedingly blank, and no little startled, especially when they found the way they were separated into messes.

We are not going to detain our readers with a minute description of the embarkation of their Neapolitan Majesties; they having no doubt witnessed, and, if not witnessed, at all events read of the embarkation of our own gracious Queen. There was the usual amount of powder expended on shore and afloat ; flags and banners waved; the mole was carpeted ; bands of music ; arches of evergreens and choice flowers ; countless boats filled with a delighted crowd; land and sea alive with eager gazers ; shouts of " Viva il Re Ferdinande ! Viva il Regina !" and thousands of other equally loyal vociferations.

Who would have thought, to have witnessed their Majesties' embarkation, that their beloved Napoli contained a few thousand subjects who would willingly have sacrificed the whole party.

Yet, generally speaking, Ferdinand was well liked; but the fierce and dangerous doctrines of the French Revolution had sown its seeds, and they had taken root; it required years to exterminate them; and, like weeds, they are struggling for existence still.

A tremendous roar of artillery burst from the Castle of San Elmo, then from Castel dell Ovo, then from the Minerva. Then a burst of flame rushed from the frigate's side, then the Vesuvius roared in reply, then the gun-boats, then the zebees, and then, as if in mockery, the private endeavours of patriotic individuals to waste powder, followed; and amidst the whole rose shouts, roars of artillery, screams from the Lazzaroni, waving of kerchiefs and scarfs, and tossing of hats.

The frigate, with her royal freight, was under weigh, covered with a cloud of snow-white canvas, now for the first time spread towards the breeze. She glided majestically out into the bay, followed by the other war vessel in harbour.

On board the frigate were the King and Queen, Lady Acton, the Duke and Duchesse de Almario, Prince Montefalcone, the Princess of Sorento, and a few ladies, their attendants.

The remainder of their Majesties' suite followed in the Vesuvius.

Sir John had taken an affectionate leave of his *protégé*, told him he need not be uneasy respecting the singular escape of Lieutenant Baracco, for that he was sure to be arrested by his agents, before twenty-four hours were over, gave him the promised packet, which contained full particulars of his birth, &c., and bade him farewell.

"You will have a difficult card to play," said Sir John, at parting, "for I assure you the Princess fully expects that you will lay yourself and fortune at her feet; and I know that the King is prepared to create you a Count, on your marriage with the Princess. You would take your title from one of the Princess's fiefs in Sicily."

De Courcy made no reply, though he felt exceedingly distressed, but in his present situation, with his royal master requiring every instant his attendance, there was no time for thought.

The Queen was exceedingly gracious, complimented our hero highly upon his arrangements, the beauty of the ship and the admirable order and exquisite neatness maintained throughout the whole vessel, every part of which both King and Queen visited and inspected.

Numerous were the questions our hero had to answer, not only from their Majesties, but from Lady Acton, and the Princess Clarina, who attended the Queen over the ship.

King Ferdinand, as usual, was extremely affable to the various officers, and even the crew; to many of whom he spoke. His Majesty, not knowing Lieutenant Baracco personally, might probably have mistaken the first Lieutenant for that officer, for during his passage over the ship he did not once mention the absent officer's name.

"With this wind, Captain De Courcy," observed his Majesty, returning to the quarter-deck, just as the sun dipped beneath the wave, presenting to view one of those glorious sunsets seen only in southern climes, "how many hours will our passage to Palermo occupy?"

"Scarcely more, your Majesty, than twenty-four hours; by to-morrow's sunset, I trust your Majesty will have landed."

They were then passing the Islands of Procida and Ischia.

The awnings were removed, and the full splendour of this unrivalled scene was viewed by the Royal party with unmingled delight, till the short twilight of the south involved the enchanting landscape in misty obscurity.

CHAPTER XVIII.

CAPTAIN DE COURCY paced the quarter-deck of the Serena, immersed in thought; it was ten o'clock, their Majesties were below with their attendants at supper; the water was singularly smooth, for the wind was at north, and the frigate was steering south and by west.

A most careful watch was preserved throughout the entire ship. It was a glorious night, though the moon had not yet risen, and the deep blue firmament above was studded with its myriads of worlds.

The sea appeared like a sheet of fire, encircling the ship, from the uncommon phosphoric state of the element. As our hero looked astern he could just get a sight of the white sails of the Vesuvius, but she was far astern—the Serena sailed superbly.

He was standing gazing back at his late favourite, and his thoughts fixed upon the time when he had stood beside fair Miss Wharton on the quarter-deck, thinking no greater felicity could fall to the lot of mortal man than Mary's love, and he felt sure that love was his. Where was Mary then? was his next thought. Was he remembered or forgotten?

"On what, or on whom, are Captain De Courcy's thoughts fixed now?" said a soft pleasing voice beside him, and a gentle tap of a fan caused him to start like a guilty thing, as he turned round and recognized Clarina Obruzza and another lady, on whose arm she was leaning.

"A sailor's thoughts, fair lady," replied the young captain, "are mostly centred upon his floating home."

"He thinks, sometimes, it is to be hoped," observed the princess gaily, "upon his lady-love; was there ever a sailor without a guiding star to cheer him on his lonely course? But what a lovely night! the heat below was so oppressive, that with my fair friend here I have intruded on your solitude."

"Say not intruded, princess," replied De Courcy, "for seldom or ever is a sailor's life so charmingly broken in upon as now——"

"Still, I should think," replied the princess, gazing up with wonder at the towering masts, and their broad spread of snow-white canvas, "there must be, at times, a charm in a sailor's life; the consciousness of his power in controlling such a beautiful vessel, of mastering storms and tempests; and then the change into a scene like this, so calm, so lovely—there is such room for thought; his must be a barren mind indeed that can behold a night like this, upon the wide ocean, with heaven's bright vault above, and this rippling sea beneath, that cannot find food for thought and deep reflection, and wonder and awe of Him who created both."

Clarina Obruzza spoke as she thought, and her voice was soft and persuasive.

"You say truly, princess," returned our hero; "nowhere, probably, is there a greater field for thought than on the boundless sea."

"For my part," observed the princess's companion, with a very strong inclination to yawn, "I think the sea is just about the very last place in the world for thought. except, indeed, one train of thought, and that is the calculation of how soon we may get to the dear land again. It may do very well for lovers, provided they are not sea-sick, which I assure you, Clarina, I am very much inclined to be; and the only thought that occupies my mind is the very unromantic one of getting to my couch, and praying to the Madonna to shorten our voyage."

"Ah! duchesse," returned Clarina, laughing, "I forget; you are no lover of the sea, so I will not tax your good nature any longer."

"Indeed, my dear," said the Duchesse De Almanio, a young and very charming woman, and whose husband was nearly four score, "I do not think I shall improve the sensations I experience, in the least, by going below; the air is reviving, but as you and Captain De Courcy appeared to be getting into a remarkably poetical and romantic mood, and as I am a plain matter-of-fact kind of personage, I wished to bring you back to the world we live in, and that, at present, is confined to this little ship. Now suppose we were to fall in with a French ship, with the horrid tricolor flying from its mast I suppose, what would you do, Captain De Courcy, with his sacred majesty on board, to say nothing of our precious selves?"

"Run away, duchesse," replied our hero, laughing.
"Ah, it's very well to say run away," remarked the duchesse,
"but ships cannot always run away."

"In that case, your grace, we must get his majesty's permission to fight; but I can assure you, we shall not be
reduced to either alternative, for there are no French ships
nearer than Civita Vecchia, and I think, without boasting,
that the Serena would have nothing to fear from them;
either in running or fighting."

"By-the-bye," said the princess, "I have not seen your
friend and shipmate, Baracco; has he remained on shore, or
been advanced? for I think I heard you say he was appointed first lieutenant of the Serena. I do not forget your
gallant friend's services when in the Vesuvius."

"You gave him and all the crew substantial proof of that,
princess," said our hero, "but Lieutenant Baracco has other
objects in view; he remained on shore, and will not, I
believe, again serve in his majesty's navy."

"I am sure you must regret the loss of an old comrade,"
answered Clarina, pacing the deck with our hero; the
Duchesse De Almanio sitting down beside two or three
ladies, who came up from below, the heat being oppressive.
The moon had then risen, and a strange lurid glare was diffused
over the whole atmosphere, the breeze suddenly dying away.

As the princess spoke, the loud flap of the sails against
the masts attracted her intention. "Dear me, Captain De
Courcy," she exclaimed, pausing in her walk, "how suddenly
the wind has ceased, and what a strange light the moon
gives! Is this a common effect at sea?"

"There is a great deal of electricity in the air," observed
De Courcy, "and the heat has been great, until yesterday's
breeze lessened it. I should not wonder but that, as the
moon goes down, we shall have a change, probably thunder,
which will cool the air."

"I hope not," cried the princess, "for though I am not
afraid of thunder-storms they affect my nerves and head."

"Then I sincerely trust," said our hero, "that we may
escape such a visitation."

One of the officers coming up, requesting a word with his
commander, interrupted the conversation, and shortly afterwards the princess and all the party retired below.

There was now not a breath of air, and the heat became
intensely oppressive. Captain De Courcy would not leave
the deck during the night; and as the moon declined, vast
masses of clouds rose up in the south-west quarter, and in a
magical manner the whole heavens became like a huge pall;
and still not a breath of wind disturbed the surface of the
water—whilst the heat continued increasing.

" Get our light canvas furled," cried our hero, to Lieutenant Vasari, " we shall have a heavy thunder-storm before daylight."

" I have no doubt but that it will be violent," replied the lieutenant ; " this heat, and the previous state of the atmosphere, puts me in mind of the tremendous storm and eruption of Mount Etna, four years back ; which, though it lasted but four hours, strewed the coast of Naples with wrecks."

" It's tremendously dark," observed our hero, " and, by the low moaning sound aloft, it will not be long before the storm breaks. Send the hands up and furl all, and let the topgallant masts be struck ; with our present freight we cannot be too cautious."

Captain De Courcy had scarcely uttered the words, before a burst of flame issued from the heavens over them, so blinding from its intense vividness, that the eyes of all involuntarily closed ; the crash that followed seemed to shake the ship to its very centre, a tremendous motion was felt over the whole vessel, several of the king's attendants hurried up to know, by desire of their Majesties, if the ship had struck. But the gallant frigate was untouched ; her crew were roused, and every inch of canvas was securely furled ; for those acquainted with the Mediterranean are well aware of the terrific force of the first storm-gusts, and the uncertainty of their direction.

Flash after flash, followed by peals of thunder, so prolonged and so deafening, that many of the officers and crew stood bewildered ; and still the ocean slept, its surface appearing, during the vivid glow of the lightning, like a mighty mirror of polished steel ; and then was heard a roar aloft, even more fearful than that of the heaven's artillery ; the clouds to the south-west were rent asunder, like magic, and the storm-king rode forth on his fiery steed.

Each officer was at his post, and crew at theirs, to be ready to set the storm stay-sails the moment the gale should settle in one fixed point. There was not one drop of rain : at length, with a roar of might, the tempest struck the sea, within a hundred yards of the frigate, driving before it one sheet of foam : a second, and it reached the ship, striking her on her starboard quarter.

Such was the extraordinary force of the blast, that the Serena heeled over till her guns touched the foaming deep. She had no power to move forward, for the blast wheeled by, and then another gust, even more violent than the first, struck her on her larboard bows ; the lightning and the thunder continuing in unabated fury. The frigate reeled under the repeated shocks, whilst amid the awful din no word could be heard.

The terrified attendants of the king came rushing upon deck, and even several of the females, frightened out of all consciousness.

The commander was standing, with his speaking-trumpet in hand, grasping the rope stretched across the deck to steady himself, when he felt his arm seized with a convulsive energy —he could not hear the words that were spoken, but a blaze of light from the still dense sky revealed the pale features of the Princess of Sorento, wrapped in her mantle, the hood torn back by the storm, and her hair streaming out in a dishevelled state.

The Serena was just then struck by a gust, even more furious than the preceding, and from a different quarter; and the sea resembled a boiling cauldron, so tossed and worried was it by the various squalls; but after this gust the whole heavens to the south-west quarter were torn widely asunder, and then the true gale burst upon them in its might and power.

Now Captain De Courcy knew what to do ; gently placing the princess upon one of the settees, lashed in their places, and begging her to have no fear, for all peril was over, the gallant frigate, dashing before the tempest like a noble racer satisfied of its triumph, De Courcy gave his orders, and these orders being carefully attended to, the frigate was brought to the wind—under her storm stay-sails.

It was broad daylight when a cry arose, " The Vesuvius dismasted ! " and all saw the brig was driving right before the gale, without a single stick standing. In three minutes she would, from the shift of the wind, run right upon them, but the frigate was instantly payed off before the wind, and the Vesuvius thus ran parallel to them. Fearing she would be lost on the coast not far off, and feeling a great affection for his old ship, De Courcy resolved to try and take her in tow. By his judicious care and skill, and being fully prepared, his vessel had suffered nothing—not even a rope had started ; the storm was driving away to the north, and a bright clear sky remained to windward, with the cheering beams of the rising sun playing on the storm-tossed water.

Edging down alongside the Vesuvius, but keeping at a safe distance, Captain De Courcy, with his speaking-trumpet, hailed the brig, and told her captain he would take her in tow, telling him to stand by and make fast the cables, and he would contrive to get on board.

Having complete control over the movements of the frigate, and being ably seconded by his officers and crew, two cables were finally got on board the Vesuvius, and then the frigate was again gradually brought to the wind. By skilful management the Vesuvius rode easily by the hausers, made fast round the stump of her foremast.

Every five minutes the king sent a message to Captain De Courcy to know how they got on, which our hero answered to his majesty's satisfaction; he also prevailed on the ladies and the Duke and Duchesse De Almanio to retire below, for the sea was getting rapidly up, and was flying over the ship like a mist; but in two hours the fury of the gale visibly lessened, and at the same time kept veering to the north-west, till, finally, the frigate could lie on her course under treble-reefed topsails, and even with the brig in tow made good way. But no sign or symptom of the gunboats or the armed zebees could be seen.

Gradually the sea fell; the sky remained without a speck; the bright sun shone forth with its glorious beams, now tempered by the refreshing north-west wind, which tempted their majesties to come on deck and breathe the fresh air, after the heat and alarms of the past night. To look at the well-arranged deck of the frigate—her spars all standing—not a rope displaced—all neat and trim, one would have supposed she had just sailed out of dock, instead of having weathered as severe a storm as ever blew, for the time it lasted.

King Ferdinand was a tolerably good sailor, being accustomed, of late years, to many trips across from Naples to Sicily.

The Vesuvius, dismasted, and in tow of the frigate, first caught his majesty's attention.

"Ah! Captain De Courcy," exclaimed his majesty, "my courtiers, and the fair dames, their spouses, must have suffered severely last night. Your old ship wanted its old commander. We must compliment you, indeed, on the skill you have displayed in keeping the ship in such exceeding good trim after such a terrible tempest; we never heard so awful a storm."

"Your majesty, I was ably seconded by my officers and crew; and if the Vesuvius has suffered, your majesty will please to recollect she had not so great a responsibility to answer for, to force her commander into minute precautions. The Vesuvius, no doubt, was caught under sail, endeavouring to keep up with the frigate, and thus lost her masts. The first burst of the storm was tremendous."

"In sooth, so it was; but cannot you manage to get the ladies from the brig, the water is getting very smooth?" demanded Ferdinand the Fourth.

"With your majesty's permission," said our hero, "we will lower the boats and render them, and those on board the Vesuvius, all the assistance in our power." •

Four hours afterwards the Serena entered the port of Palermo; but their majesties remained on board till the following morning. They were then landed in their state barge, under a royal salute from every available battery on shore or afloat.

CHAPTER XIX.

WHILST the events recorded in our last chapter were taking place, Sir Charles Wharton and family reached England, without accident or adventure. The corvette in which they had embarked having, happily for the comfort of those on board, escaped encountering an enemy's ship on the passage home.

Our heroine did not quit the land of the south without feeling a great depression of spirits. The future, as far as the feelings of her heart were concerned, looked clouded; but wishing to relieve her kind uncle's uneasiness about her somewhat delicate appearance, she exerted herself to the utmost to appear cheerful. The society of Térese Garetti was a source of exceeding comfort to her; for, acquainted with the cause of her depression, she relieved her mind much by conversing with her amiable and attached friend on the subject so dear to her heart. Sir Charles Wharton possessed a very handsome mansion in —————— square, and there Mary and her friend found every luxury and comfort that wealth and affection could procure.

Térese was in high spirits; everything was new and strange to her; her first sensations, on setting foot on English ground, were mixed and contradictory; the weather happened to be cloudy and misty, and Plymouth, under those circumstances, is deprived of its real attractions; the beauty of its scenery was hid by mists; Mount Edgecumbe was lost to the sight; but the next day was a glorious fine one; the southwest wind, and its haze and mist, had given way to its near neighbour, the north-west, and a bright clear sky, not quite so blue, Térese observed, as the Italian firmament, but still quite blue enough for contrast with the bright green fields and verdant pastures through which the baronet's carriage rolled, with its four post-horses, on its way to London. The numerous superb mansions they passed, as they travelled through Devonshire; the rich orchards, then loaded with their tempting fruits; the pretty villages, with their neat cottages hid in clusters of flowering shrubs; the roads like bowling-greens for smoothness, and the substantial comforts and cleanliness of the excellent hotels on the road, and the celerity with which they travelled, was all new and striking to the sight and thoughts of the fair Genoese.

London astounded her with its immensity; and let foreigners write and say what they please respecting our nebulous climate, and their never seeing the sun in London, it's all fudge. London is one of the healthiest cities in Europe, and enjoys as fair a proportion of sunshine as any other in the same latitude and longitude, and that is as much as we have a right to expect.

Sir Charles Wharton, with his wealth and position in society, and aristocratic birth and connections, moved in a circle of acquaintance amongst whom were many of the first nobility in the metropolis.

During his sojourn abroad he had also met, and become intimate with, several of our English nobility. Amongst those, he had become, at Nice, intimately acquainted with Lord Umfreville and his son, then a very young man. Lord Umfreville was at this time in London ; it was the close of the London season ; and shortly after Sir Charles's arrival in the metropolis, his lordship and his eldest son became frequent and friendly visitors at ———— square. Sir Charles naturally wished his niece to mix, in a moderate degree, with the world ; he did not seek to force, or at all coerce her into a matrimonial alliance, contrary to the wishes and feelings of her heart ; but he wished to wean her from an attachment he considered as perfectly hopeless. He would not have objected, certainly, to her union with Captain De Courcy, when convinced that her happiness was absolutely dependent on it. But he, knowing nothing of Captain De Courcy's private life, and believing him to be without family connection of any kind, and, as he supposed, perfectly un-English—if we may use such an expression—from long residence, intercourse, and connection with foreigners, he felt rather relieved at the termination of his niece's, or, as he firmly believed, his daughter's, intercourse with a person the world would style a fortunate adventurer.

Like all men, at a certain period of life, he looked upon a young girl's love as likely to be as evanescent as any of the other violent passions human nature is subject to, and to be easily eradicated by time and change of scene, and intercourse with the world. But good-natured, kind-hearted Sir Charles knew nothing of a young girl's heart. Anxious to let his niece see the world, as he termed London and its inhabitants, and the world to see his niece, a succession of parties and balls took place some short time after their arrival in London. Now Mary would not for worlds be so selfish, because she herself preferred seclusion, that her young friend Térese, who accompanied her to England, and was of a lively, joyous disposition, should be debarred from society, and seeing the gay sights, and enjoying the amusements the fashionable world of London afforded. She, therefore, to a certain extent, mingled in society ; went to the opera, and other places of amusement, under a distinguished chaperon.

Lady Hasarel, a widow of birth and fortune, and connected with Sir Charles Wharton by relationship, and of a kind and agreeable disposition, delightedly took charge of the beautiful Mary and her fair friend.   Miss Wharton attracted universal admiration ; her figure was graceful to a degree, and her features lovely ; but her manners and her sweet musical voice created even more attention and admiration ; though it was soon remarked she never by any chance danced at any assembly, at home or abroad ; in small and select parties, she never refused to sing, and her voice, naturally powerful and exquisitely modulated, and cultivated in a country by the first masters, and where singing is a necessity of life, she astonished and bewildered her hearers by the brilliancy, and richness, and justness of her tones.

The lively and handsome Genoese had also many admirers ; she accompanied Mary in many of her duets, and attracted much attention from her correct and well-cultivated taste.

To be invited to Sir Charles Wharton's mansion soon became an eagerly-sought-after object ; his well-known wealth might be an inducement to some of the younger sons of the aristocracy, but his niece's exquisite beauty and fascinating, modest, and retiring manner, though perfectly easy and self-possessed, was the grand attraction.

The foremost on the list to win Mary's attention was the Honourable Edward Umfreville, eldest son of Lord Umfreville. Young, handsome, and accomplished, with the advantage of having travelled over most part of the continent of Europe, and heir to wealth and title, most persons would have thought that Edward Umfreville would have a fair chance of winning Mary's love ; besides, his manners were extremely agreeable, lively, and sensible.

There was another candidate for the hand of the baronet's niece : formidable, the world would say, as far as rank and wealth weighed in the balance.   This was young Lord Eglin : he was in the Guards, and had just succeeded to the title and estates of his father.   But those who knew Mary said at once his lordship had no chance with his rival, the Honourable Edward Umfreville.   Lord Eglin was at this period six or seven and twenty, tall, well-made, and remarkably handsome ; but proud to excess, haughty, and overbearing, but with sufficient command over himself to disguise those disagreeable qualifications.

Lord Umfreville was a nobleman who had passed a considerable period of his life abroad ; he was a man of high and honourable character, somewhat proud in outward appearance, but not so in reality.   He was fondly attached to his eldest son ; his youngest was a lieutenant in the navy, and had already distinguished himself in that service ; he was then serving aboard the Danæ, twenty-gun ship, commanded by Captain Lord Proby.

The Honourable Edward Umfreville soon became passionately attached to our heroine, who, with a sigh, soon perceived this to be the case, and she regretted it; for, of all the young men she had yet met in London society, she felt a sincere esteem for Edward Umfreville.

Sir Charles was, however, rejoiced to see this attachment; he would have preferred him for a husband for his niece to any other suitor, no matter what might be his rank or wealth.

One evening, at a select party at Lady Hasarel's, Edward Umfreville was seated beside Mary, conversing agreeably on many subjects; it was a small assemblage, but the young folks were dancing in another saloon. The conversation happened to turn upon Italy.

"You must have suffered considerably during the blockade of Genoa, Miss Wharton?" observed Edward Umfreville, "for the French force within the city were reduced to terrible extremity for want of food."

"I was under the protection of a most kind friend and relative," said Mary, suppressing a sigh, "who, being wealthy, spared no pains or gold in providing us the best, at all events, that could be had; though, indeed, we lived many days, I may say weeks, without meat of any sort; but we had many luxuries in other things, purchased up at the commencement of the siege, when things were not so scarce. You have travelled a good deal through Italy, yourself, Mr. Umfreville?" added Mary, wishing to lead the conversation from Genoa.

"I was very young," answered her companion, in reply, "when my first visit to Italy was paid. My father was proceeding to travel over Dalmatia and Greece, and the Holy Land. He left me in a college at Sienna to study the continental languages."

"They speak the Italian language with a purer accent, I believe, in Sienna, than any other city in Italy?" remarked Mary.

"Yes, such is the case. My residence there, however, was at first irksome, till I found a companion greatly to my liking. He was an English lad, remarkably handsome, and of high spirit and temper. I became greatly attached to him; his name was De Courcy." At that name the young lady trembled as if struck with an ague; it was but momentarily, but her cheeks became deadly pale, such an effect had the name just pronounced upon her. She was not aware that Hugh De Courcy had resided in the college at Sienna, neither had he ever mentioned the name of Umfreville to her.

In speaking to Mary of his early life, he had merely said that, from his earliest recollection, he had been under the protection of Sir John Acton, who had spared no pains in his education; but refrained from informing her who his parents

L

were. The sudden mention, therefore, of De Courcy's name recalled the past so forcibly that she could not, at first, conquer her emotion. Edward Umfreville, at that moment, did not look up, but when he did, he was startled at seeing her still so pale ; he therefore paused, and then said, in a deeply anxious tone, with his heart's seeret in his expressive eountenance, " Good heavens ! Miss Wharton, are you ill? Is the heat too mueh for you? "

" Oh ! not at all," replied Mary, in her ealm, sweet voiee; " I am rather subject to sudden, though slight, attaeks of faintness, sinee my return to England; perhaps the effeet of ehange of elimate."

This assertion was, in point of fact, the case, but it arose from the mind, not the elimate. " Do not stir, I beg you," she continued, using her vinaigrette ; " it passes off as quickly as it eomes on."

Térese Garetti then joined them. She had observed the change in Mary's features, and her palencss ; and knowing she did sometimes feel this fainting sensation, she said, " You had better, Mary dear, for a minute or so, brcathe the fresh air from the open window."

" There is no oeeasion, Térese ; the sensation has passed." And, in truth, by a great mental effort, she quite recovered her composure, and also some portion of colour ; but, as she feared a renewal of the eonvcrsation, she detained her fair friend, and, still chatting, took a turn through the rooms to observe the danecrs.

Edward Umfreville had not the slightest idea that his mention of the name of De Courcy had caused Mary Wharton's emotion ; but he now resolved to make a bold push to obtain the objcet he cherished so deeply at heart, and this was to obtain Sir Charles Wharton's consent to address his niece, and to win her conscnt to his proposals. He had his father's approbation, but, in secret, he trembled for his success. He could not perceive, it is true, that she favoured any one, even so much as himself : and though he often remarked Lord Eglin's attention, and felt satisfied that he also admired the bcautiful girl that had so engrossed his entire thoughts, still she appeared only polite to his lordship, and even, he fancied, avoided him.

In fact, Lord Eglin had so decided an opinion cf himself, that he flattered himself that he had only to propose to be accepted. The Honourable Edward Umfreville accordingly spoke candidly to the baronet before he made any proposals to Mary. Sir Charles very warmly approved of his attentions. He wished him every sueeess, but candidly said he would leave Mary entirely to the dietates of her own heart.

Edward Umfreville was of too noble a disposition to dream

of having Mary's affections coerced. If he could induce her to return his love, he should feel himself the happiest of men ; but not for worlds would he accept her hand without her own free consent.

The following day to this conference between the baronet and Edward Umfreville, a terrible accident to the former threw his whole family into grief and mourning. Crossing the lower end of St. James's-street to the Palace, he slipped on a piece of orange peel, and, before he could recover his balance, the hind wheel of a gentleman's carriage struck him on the head, and left him senseless on the pavement. Not the slightest blame could be attached to the coachman, for so anxious was he to avoid the collision, that he turned his horses so short that the pole of the carriage he was driving snapped in the socket.

Sir Charles Wharton was conveyed home, and the first surgical assistance procured : he had received a concussion of the brain.

The distraction of Mary was overpowering. She lost all control over her mind, and repeatedly fainted. Still the doctors said he might be saved ; they were unceasing in their attentions, and after a few days the baronet rallied and recovered speech and consciousness, but the shock, it was still feared, would be fatal. Mary never left the side of his couch ; her attention and love were beyond praise .She herself firmly believed Sir Charles was her father. Father or not, she loved him with the devotion of a fond child.

The eighth or tenth day after the accident, which created the liveliest interest and attention from the baronet's friends, espe · cially in Lord Umfreville and his son, the latter appearing to suffer as much as Mary, and was almost hourly at the house, anxiously making inquiries ; and on the sixth or seventh day was admitted, by the baronet's desire, to his bedside. They remained alone for nearly half an hour, and then the young man quitted the house, with anxious and serious look. A day or two afterwards the baronet himself thought it was im- possible he could live but a few days longer ; his beloved Mary was by the side of his bed, with his hand clasped in her's.

" Mary, my beloved child," said Sir Charles, in a low voice, " we are about to part, and in this world for ever."

Mary felt choking, but with a great effort she conquered her emotion, and looking fondly and devotedly into her uncle's face, prayed that God would spare him to her yet ; " for with- out you, beloved father," and she pressed her lips to his hand, her whole frame trembling with emotion, " the world to me is a blank ! "

" Say not so, child of my heart ; say not those words. I cannot leave the world with that peace of mind I ought. I cannot turn my thoughts to God wholly and solely, for you, my idolized child, occupy them almost exclusively."

"I would leave you under the care of one who is noble and good." Mary stood in trembling silence, and the baronet continued, "Hear me, my beloved—my last moments would be blest would you consent to receive Edward Umfreville as your future husband; he is all a fond father could wish or hope for his child."

Poor Mary, she felt her heart bursting with a terrible feeling of despair, but with a heroic effort she conquered her feelings, and pressed her uncle's hand.

"Say, my child, that you consent to become Edward Umfreville's wife; let me die with the conviction that I have assured your felicity, for to leave you unprotected, and to the snares of the world, poisons my last moments."

"God give me strength," murmured the agitated girl, raising her beautiful eyes to heaven, and from which the tears ran in streams, and then, in a low, stifled voice, she said aloud, "Be it as you wish, beloved father. To afford you that peace you desire and deserve I would sacrifice, oh, how willingly, my life!"

"Bless you, God bless you, my own Mary! You remove the only bitter regret I feel in leaving this world."

The following day Edward Umfreville knelt by the side of the baronet's couch, who placed Mary's hand in that of her lover; her hand was as cold as ice. He blessed them both fervently, and then sank back exhausted. Mary was carried from the chamber in a swoon.

CHAPTER XX.

WHEN we least expect it, the mercy of a divine and all-seeing Providence is extended towards us. Sir Charles Wharton sank back, as we stated in our last chapter, totally exhausted, and perfectly persuaded that his last hour was come. In this state he lay for many many hours, merely breathing, his medical attendants fully expecting that in that condition he would sink to rest. But, as they watched, a change came over the face of the sleeper, and that fearful expression that rests on the features of the dying, but which so often changes when the hand of death is laid on the doomed, into one of peace and calmness, disappeared.

The death-like expression was passing off the baronet's features, and a slight, a very slight, tinge of colour became perceptible on his lips and cheeks. Sir Benjamin Carlow started, laid his hand on the baronet's pulse, and, for an instant, a dead silence reigned in the chamber.

"Ah!" uttered the physician to the other medical attendant,

who stood at the foot of the bed, "the pulse is returning; it's feeble, but quite perceptible. We must help nature; it is now quite possible he may rally." The physician was right. The following day Sir Benjamin declared the baronet's life was safe; but Mary, poor Mary, she heard not the joyful intelligence; she lay in a high fever delirious, and nearly a fortnight elapsed before she became conscious of the presence of those about her, and of the past.

With extreme caution, on her partial recovery, was she made acquainted with her uncle's escape from the very grasp of the grim enemy. He was not then able to leave his chamber, but he was out of all danger—weak, languid, and somewhat dejected, from anxiety. But when the uncle and niece became assured of the other's safety, they began rapidly to mend.

Mary was but a shadow of her former self when at length she sought her uncle's chamber, and threw herself into his arms, weeping long and passionately. Neither spoke of the engagement entered into, it was then thought, at the death-bed of Sir Charles; each seemed to shun the mention of the name of Umfreville; and yet daily, almost hourly, did Edward Umfreville call, and with intense earnestness inquire after Mary.

Our heroine, and her devoted, loving friend Térèse Garetti, were sitting one evening, the latter end of September, in their own chamber; Mrs. Arbuthnot was indisposed and had retired to rest, her unceasing watching and care of both uncle and niece having nearly exhausted her strength.

It was an unusually cold evening, and Mary was reclining on the sofa, gazing into the cheerful fire that blazed in the grate: her beautiful features were thin, and her cheeks faded and pale, though her eyes were still lustrous, and full of deep thought. As she thus sat, with her hands clasped, her whole attitude denoted a heart ill at ease.

"Mary, dear Mary," said Térèse, laying down the book she was perusing, "you must not yield to dejection as you do; you are fretting your life away. Your uncle is strong now; say to him at once this union cannot be. It was to render his last moments easy and happy that you nobly sacrificed yourself; but now the case is different."

"No, dear Térèse," returned Mary, calmly; "it was a solemn engagement, entered into at a solemn moment, and must not be lightly broken. I will not, now that the Almighty has so mercifully spared my uncle, render his future peace troubled: his physician declares that for some time his mind must not be disturbed; it might seriously affect his head. Neither would it be treating Edward Umfreville justly or honourably. But I will tell you what I will do, when I get a little more strength,—for he deserves, if not my love, which is not mine to bestow, certainly my esteem and friendship,—I will pray to God to enable me to forget one whose image still clings to my heart with a terrible tenacity, and trust that time, and a sense of my situation and duty, will enable me to look upon my future husband with a wife's affections; but I think it but just and right that I should candidly state to Edward, that, though I give him my hand willingly, and with an earnest wish to return his affection, my love is not mine to bestow.

"Then," exclaimed Térese, with vivacity, "Mr. Umfreville will at once release you from your engagement. I think I can judge of that young man's mind and feelings. If you cannot give him your love he will not accept your hand. This confession of yours might do if the object of your affec· tion had ceased to exist; but the man you profess to love lives, and no man, if he has a particle of manly feeling in his breast, will take for a wife a woman whose heart still beats for another. No, no, dear Mary; either confess your attachment to another and break off this unhappy engagement, or marry Edward Umfreville and bury your secret in your heart."

Miss Wharton bowed her fair head upon her hands, and wept silently and sadly; for in truth she was bewildered and almost heart-broken. "My own pride, Térese," she said, after a long silence, "has caused me all this trouble. You recollect your kind father—when the circumstances occurred that acted so fatally on the mind of Hugh, causing him to think I was false in my vows to him, and he rashly and hastily sailed from Genoa, without seeking an explanation—your father said, 'Let me, dear Mary, undeceive your noble, but rash lover,' and I replied, 'No;' for my pride was roused at the mere idea that he for one moment should believe me false; I, who had given him my whole heart—with such feelings of devotion and confidence. If the whole world had said that Hugh De Courcy was false in his vows to me, I should have scorned to have listened to the slanderers. Had I subdued all my false pride, much misery would have been spared me." Mary sighed heavily. "God direct me," she continued, "for I am incapable of sound judgment! My uncle's mind is bent on this union; Mrs. Arbuthnot strongly urges me to fulfil an engagement so solemnly contracted—tells me that it is folly and a want of self-reliance to hesitate; and that to condemn myself to a life of useless repining is both sinful and wrong."

"Mrs. Arbuthnot is a good and pious woman," replied Térese; "but she can be no judge of your feelings for Captain De Courcy. She never saw him; neither did your uncle— they knew not what a gallant noble heart his was: his love for you was passionate, devoted; he was cruelly deceived, and his life horribly and treacherously attempted. In the impulse of the moment—in the maddening belief of your faithlessness to him, he gave no time to thought—he acted as his fiery nature dictated; but, mark my words," added Térese, her eyes sparkling and her manner agitated, "mark my words: if you rashly fulfil this engagement—in a manner forced upon you—every hour of your after-life will be poisoned by the bitterest reflections."

Mary could not reply. She threw her arms round her beloved friend's neck; she leant her head upon her shoulder, her bosom heaving with contending emotions, and her mind distracted between what she considered her duty and the secret wishes of her own heart.

Several days passed, at the end of which both Sir Charles Wharton and his niece were sufficiently recovered to receive their friends.

Mary wanted strength to break the dream of happiness Sir Charles Wharton seemed to indulge respecting his niece's future establishment. Her first interview with her intended husband was one of intense agony to her heart. She found it impossible to utter a word, or reply to his most kind and affectionate inquiries, though both Mrs. Arbuthnot and Térese were present. She could not control her feelings; blinded by his ardent love, Edward Umfreville only saw in her excessive agitation and utter prostration the effects of the severe shock her nerves had received. Trusting, therefore, that a short time would restore her to her usual health, he solaced himself with the thoughts of the happiness that awaited him in the future, in his union with one to whom he was so tenderly attached.

Sir Charles Wharton, though free from immediate danger, was very far from being perfectly restored to health; his physician advised a change of scene, and a mild climate for the winter; he therefore intended proposing to his future nephew-in-law a residence in the Island of Sicily, either Palermo or Messina, for the winter, immediately after his marriage with his niece. But it was very evident to the affectionate heart of Térese that Mary would require a change of more than climate, and that before long, or her health would most materially suffer; for the struggle that was taking place in her heart, from a wish to make her uncle happy, was undermining her constitution.

One morning, as Sir Charles was reading the paper, he suddenly let it slip from his hand, exclaiming, with considerable agitation, "God bless my soul! this is—— " but with an effort he recovered himself, took up the paper, and, with a smile, said, "I am afraid, ladies, I startled you; Mary, my love, you

look paler even than usual; but do not be alarmed. It was
only a paragraph that surprised me; I daresay we shall have
peace with France shortly. Bonaparte is now, as Consul for
life, the actual ruler of the entire kingdom of France." The
baronet shortly after retired to his study, earrying the paper
with him.

Now the baronet's manner, and the anxious expression of
his countenance, as he looked at his niece, struck both Mary
and Térese; whether Mrs. Arbuthnot perceived it or not, the
two girls could not say; but they both resolved in their own
minds to get a peep at the *Times* of that day. In general they
never looked at the news, but this morning, on reaching her
own room, Mary sent her maid, Phœbe, to procure a paper—
which was soon obtained.

Miss Wharton took the *Times* with a strange feeling: an
unaccountable presentiment had taken complete possession of
her mind, and for several moments she was quite incapable
of distinguishing the lines.

Térese was almost as anxious as herself, for the kind-hearted
Genoese was resolved, some way or other, to break off what
she called a most ill-omened match. She did not deny but that
the Honourable Edward Umfreville was a most amiable young
man, and a most desirable union in point of station and
fortune; "but what signifies station or fortune," argued
Térese, "when they are coupled with a lacerated heart?"

Térese was not so romantic as to suppose that Mary was
going to die for love; no such idea entered her head, or Mary's
either; on the contrary, she felt satisfied that her friend would
make an exemplary and attentive wife; but she was convinced
she never would be a happy one; her thoughts would be for
ever on the past; there would ever be a struggle going on in
her breast, a desire to repress and banish recollection, and a
feeling of self-reproach that her efforts would be fruitless.

They now turned over the pages of the *Times* with a nervous
anxiety; to Mary the lines seemed to run one into the other,
till at length her eyes rested on the heading of a long article,
and then she read, with a palpitating heart, the words, "Arrival
in Plymouth of the splendid Neapolitan frigate, Serena, commanded by Captain Count De Courcy," The paper fell from
her hand, whilst she leaned back in her chair, her eyes closed,
and looking so like the statue of despair, that Térese was
startled.

"My dear Mary, this is altogether madness. You are not
bound to continue this engagement: be candid, see Mr.
Umfreville; state to him, as you once said you would, your
feelings and your affection for another; tell him the engagement you entered into was to insure peace and tranquillity to
your uncle's last moments."

" I am quite willing to do so, dear Térese," replied Mary Wharton, " the more so, as no word of love has ever passed between me and Edward; and he is well aware I never encouraged his attentions; on the contrary, when I perceived how they tended, I did all in my power to check a closer intimacy; he will do me justice in that, I am sure; and the occasion of our engagement was so sudden and so overpoweringly painful, I had no power to utter a word; indeed, thinking my uncle dying, and being certainly convinced I was his child, I became a passive actor in a scene that wrung my heart with anguish. But now that I think my uncle stronger, and more able to bear what will be a great disappointment to him, I will first speak candidly to him, and then to Mr. Umfreville himself."

" Now, my beloved Mary," exclaimed Térese, her eyes sparkling with joy, " you are about to act with proper judgment, and not rashly rush into a union that would surely plunge both you and Mr. Umfreville into a life of disappointment and perhaps misery; and now," continued her affectionate friend, " let us see what further this paragraph says, for assuredly Captain De Courcy, or rather Count de Courcy, I perceive, has come to England for the express purpose of explaining away his strange departure from Genoa."

" Dear Térese," returned Mary, sadly, " I must not appear to the world, or rather to those who know me intimately, to be acting from caprice or inconsistency It is known amongst our acquaintances and connections that I am engaged to Mr. Edward Umfreville. Would it not look unfeminine and unmaidenly were I to cast off a gentleman to whom I willingly engaged myself, and then permit the attentions of another? for I cannot of course give explanations of my conduct and of the past to all. Therefore I should, doubtless, be accused of fickleness, or perhaps a harsher interpretation put upon my conduct."

" Come, come, Mary," interrupted the sanguine Térese, " you must not be imagining and conjuring up difficulties and surmises. You cannot compel the world to think as you wish; therefore let people amuse themselves with ideas, like everything else in 'questa mundo,' it will only live its hour. Give me the paper, and let me see what further there is in this paragraph. She then read aloud as follows :—" The Serena frigate brings the Marquis De Policastra, as envoy extraordinary from the court of Naples to our gracious Majesty. The Serena, on her passage from Gibraltar, after a very sanguinary contest, captured a fine French frigate, the Revolutionaire, the particulars of which we cannot at present give. On board the French frigate was Lieutenant Umfreville, a prisoner, who had been picked up at sea, in a crazy boat, with a young midshipman and one seaman. Lieutenant Umfreville is the younger son of Lord Umfreville, of Langford Castle, Hampshire, and was second lieutenant of the Danæ, twenty-gun ship, commanded by Captain Lord Proby. To this ship there is a melancholy story attached, but which we are not at present at liberty to detail, as most likely it will be the subject of a court-martial. Captain Count De Courcy is, we believe, an Irishman, who from the age of thirteen or fourteen has been in the service of his Majesty King Ferdinand of Naples; his distinguished gallantry, and several very brilliant exploits performed during the present war, and besides, successful expeditions against the Barbary corsairs, has obtained him his present title and high command, though scarcely five-and-twenty. *On dit*, that on the Count De Courcy s return to Naples he is to receive the ——." Térese paused, and her cheek flushed with excitement and indignation.

"What is there more, cara?" said Mary, who was listening with rapt and delighted attention, her heart beating with a feeling of pride and joy at her former lover's glory. "Why do you pause?"

"Oh! I will read it to you, dear Mary," said Térese, "for I do not believe such nonsense. These newspaper editors can never be satisfied unless they wind up a paragraph with some flourish of their own, by way of a finale. '*On dit*,' says the writer of this article, 'that the Count De Courcy is to receive, on his return to Naples, the hand of the Princess of Sorento, a lady connected by ties of blood with the Royal family of Naples. She is said to be exceedingly lovely, a widow, and only two-and-twenty.'"

"I have not the slightest belief," answered Mary Wharton, "in such reports. I think too highly of Hugh De Courcy to credit anything of the kind; but I feel exceeding surprise how such information, partly substantiated by fact, found its way into circulation. The Princess of Sorento, you may remember, is the lady he rescued from the grasp of the Barbary corsairs. Lieutenant Baracco was with him at the time, and he told us she was a woman of great beauty, and that her gratitude to Captain De Courcy was very great."

"Oh, yes, I remember Lieutenant Baracco telling me that, and also his insinuating at the time that the princess would have been not at all loth to change her gratitude into love."

"That, perhaps, might have been the case," returned Mary, with the slightest shade of colour tinging her pale cheek, "but I must have stronger proof of De Courcy's fickleness of heart than a newspaper paragraph. How singular, dear Térese, that he should, in so strange a manner, release the brother of Mr. Umfreville from captivity! At all events, whatever may be Hugh De Courcy's intention in coming to England, whether he comes, only compelled by duty, to obey the commands of his sovereign, or from a wish to clear up the mystery of the past, I cannot say, but I now see it is clearly my duty not to deceive Edward Umfreville into the belief that in obeying the wishes of my dear uncle I am following the dictates of my own heart."

CHAPTER XXI.

It was Miss Wharton's intention to speak to her uncle the following day, when just as the family were sitting down to breakfast a note was handed to the baronet, in the hand-writing of Lord Umfreville's son. Sir Charles opened the note, and then, with an exclamation of, "God bless my soul, how sudden !" laid it down much affected.

"What is the matter, dear uncle?" inquired Mary, in an agitated voice, for latterly she had become exceedingly nervous.

"Why, my old friend, Lord Umfreville, has been alarm-iugly attacked by the gout, flying to his head, with strong inflammatory symptoms; his son writes to say he has left London on the instant, with Sir Benjamin Carlow, and that he fears by the intelligence he received from Southampton, where his lordship is, that there is but little hope of his father's recovery."

"Good Heaven! this is a very sudden calamity," exclaimed Mary, with emotion; for besides her kind feelings towards his lordship, who always appeared to treat her with especial attention, and even affection, she felt that this was not the moment to talk of breaking off an engagement with the son; and that now, most likely, De Courcy would hear of her engagement, and that without knowing anything of the cir-cumstances that had led to it. What would his fiery nature think, when this intelligence reached his ear? what would he think of her love for him, but as a passing impression? There was a great deal of agony in this thought, to her affec-tionate and guileless heart.

"His lordship," observed Mrs. Arbuthnot, "I think I heard you say, Sir Charles, is subject to hereditary gout?"

"Yes," returned Sir Charles, "he suffered slightly from it when a young man; and that induced him to travel much and take great exercise—latterly he has not done so; he is a very large man, as you know, and of late years has grown very stout. I greatly fear this attack will have a fatal termination. Edward, my dear Mary, begs me to apologize to you for leaving without seeing you; but the intelligence was too alarming to allow him making any delay."

Mary's cheeks flushed as she looked down; but with an

effort she collected sufficient firmness to say, "I wish, dear uncle, to speak with you a few minutes in the library."

"My beloved Mary," said Sir Charles, after a short pause, and without any change of manner, "I anticipate what you would say to me, and I thought it was likely to come to this. Before such true, kind, and loving friends, who know all the circumstances of the past, and also how very, very dear you are to me, there is no need of reservation.

"Like a true and noble-hearted child, when you considered we were about to part for ever, you sacrificed the fond affections of your heart to soothe my last moments. My beloved, I did not then think this love—I see your cheek flushes—do not be ashamed of it."

"Oh, no, uncle!" interrupted his niece, though the tears fell from her eyes, "I am proud of it—for, believe me, I would not have bestowed my affections on an unworthy object."

"Of that I am satisfied," said Sir Charles; "but I was saying, I did not think this love had such deep root in your heart; and knowing that Edward Umfreville possessed every qualification to make a woman happy, I thought I should be securing your future felicity by a union with him. But latterly my eyes have been opened; I see, plainly enough, the ravages that a forced consent to my wishes is making in your health, and determined, a few days back, to speak to you on the subject; particularly when I discovered, from a conversation I had with Edward, he seemed to fear that though he had gained your consent to become his wife, you still withheld your love; and asked me, earnestly, had you formed any attachment to another when abroad. I answered him candidly, that you had. He pressed my hand, considerably moved and agitated, and as he left me he said, 'We have both been too hard on poor Mary. In a day or two I will speak to her myself. On that interview my destiny depends;' and he left me."

Mary was leaning her head upon Térese's shoulder, weeping freely, for she felt, do what she would, she must be the cause of suffering to others; and her gentle, affectionate heart was grieved.

"At this present moment," continued Sir Charles, "it would be cruel to add to Edward Umfreville's uneasiness—he will himself return to the subject of our last conversation; then leave it to me, dear Mary, to set things right. There is another matter, my love, I wish to speak to you upon," continued Sir Charles, "and that is, that captain—I perceive they give him the title of count—that Captain De Courcy is now in England."

"I knew it, dear uncle," said Mary Wharton; "I read his arrival in the paper."

"I thought as much," returned her uncle, with an affectionate smile; "I roused your curiosity the other morning, and I suppose you were resolved to gratify it; so like your sex!"

"Nay, Sir Charles," said Mrs. Arbuthnot, with a smile, "I must defend my sex—do not imagine curiosity a feeling only existing in the female breast."

"Take care, Sir Charles," exclaimed Térese, her gay smile returning, seeing that affairs were likely to turn out happily for her beloved friend; "take care, or you will have a hornet's nest about your ears, if you attempt to maintain your opinion."

"Then, fair Térese, I surrender at discretion; but you must know that the Neapolitan envoy has arrived in London, and taken up his abode at the —— hotel, which has been fitted up for him and his attendants. Captain De Courcy is still in Plymouth, I heard yesterday; I believe he has received some wounds, but not dangerous ones, in a most furious, and, I am sorry to say, very sanguinary contest with the French frigate. Young Umfreville is with him; if he has not as yet heard of his father's illness. There is some sad story about his ship; but I have not heard the particulars. A mutiny, I believe; all I know is, that the ship is lost. Now the best thing we can all do, after I have had an interview with Edward, is to leave England and go to Palermo, and pass some time there; it will be the best place for all parties. What do you say, Mary—indeed what say you all? You know, Térese, your father promised, when we made up our minds and let him know our plans, that he would join us at Palermo."

"Oh, let us go to Sicily by all means," exclaimed the little party assembled round the breakfast-table.

"It will," said Mrs. Arbuthnot, "restore you and dear Mary to perfect health."

Two or three days after this conversation, intelligence reached Sir Charles that Lord Umfreville had ceased to exist. This event plunged the whole family into affliction, for they all greatly esteemed his lordship. Both his sons were by their father's couch; he was perfectly sensible for a few hours before death. Besides this distressing intelligence, Mary and Térese were secretly uneasy; for it was known to them that Captain Count De Courcy was in London, and had been presented at court by the Earl of ——. The London journals also spoke of his very distinguished appearance, his handsome and prepossessing countenance; but for so young and so fortunate a commander, remarkably serious and reserved.

"He has heard of my engagement," said Mary, with a sigh; "and his proud nature is naturally roused, and he refrains from any communication."

"Then Sir Charles ought to communicate with him," said Térese.

"Oh, certainly not," exclaimed Mary; "that, dearest, would not be correct. Recollect, I am still under an engagement, which, till dissolved, must be considered sacred. Our reconciliation must be a work of time."

"Well, pardon me," returned Térese, with vivacity, "I was born half an Italian, and I suppose have half an Italian's nature; I confess I could not exist and be playing at cross purposes with the man I love, and the man that loves me. Heigho! do you know, Mary, it's very strange, but I was never in love? and I am positively twenty-two next birthday, and you are not eighteen."

"Hush! dear Térese, hush!" interrupted Mary, with more colour in her cheeks than for several weeks previously, "do not boast, your turn will come by-and-bye, when least expected."

Whilst this conversation was taking place in Sir Charles Wharton's mansion, another was being carried on in a well-known club-room in St. James's-street.

"Who is this much-talked-of Captain Count de Courcy?" said young Lord Eglin, to an officer in an infantry regiment with whom he was conversing and lounging against the window frame, twisting his moustache, and gazing at the dames passing by in order to enter St. James's Park.

"How the deuce should I know?" returned Captain Manby · "uncommon handsome fellow! by Jove! half the women are raving about him already."

"A proud, upstart adventurer, most likely!" returned his lordship sarcastically.

"Why the deuce do you call him an adventurer?" exclaimed Captain Manby, looking surprised, "because he bears your family name? for now I remember, your mother was a De Courcy."

"That's precisely the reason I think him an adventurer; there is no male branch of the Irish De Courcy living; and he calls himself an Irishman. My mother was one of two sisters: they were the last of the Irish De Courcys."

"Well, I am a very poor hand, your lordship knows," said Captain Manby, "for remembering."

"But I do not want you to remember," said his lordship, petulantly; and then, with a sneer, added, "you remember, I daresay, that your grandfather was breeches' maker to the Duke of ——."

Captain Manby, though he coloured highly, laughed; he was Lord Eglin's toady, and could not afford to do anything else than laugh, no matter what his lordship said.

"I heard a curious story lately," said Captain Manby, wishing to forget his grandfather.

"What is it?" inquired Lord Eglin, "any scandal? for I have been out of town lately."

"No, there's no scandal in it," returned the captain; "you know the fair lady to whom your cousin Lord Unfreville is engaged."

"Oh yes," remarked his lordship, with an angry curl of the lip, "Miss Wharton; the girl is handsome enough, but as capricious as the weather, which, by-the-bye, is cursedly annoying. I had but two fair days during the past fortnight; worst shooting I ever had—but what of Miss Wharton—has she jilted my cousin Edward? I suspected something of the sort would happen; for, upon my soul, I never could see much love in her manner to him; I positively thought I had the best chance if I could have brought myself to the point; but go on, let me hear your story, and then I will have a game of billiards with you; I beat you the odd rubber yesterday, and you are in my debt a cool hundred."

"You play too good a game, my lord," said the captain, with a peculiar look back at a gentleman standing near them; "I cannot give you those odds again."

"Let us have your story, and I will play you even, for the same sum," observed Lord Eglin.

"Well," replied Captain Manby, making a sign behind his back, which the gentleman near them evidently understood, for he at once left the room. "It is now said, in certain circles, that this handsome Count de Courcy is come to England to look after his runaway lady-love, and that this run-away fair one is the much-admired and beautiful Miss Wharton."

"The deuce! is that the report?" cried Lord Eglin. "Where on earth did you pick that up?"

"At the —— billiard rooms, a fortnight ago," answered the captain: "there was a foreigner—a Neapolitan, I think—playing there, and an uncommon game he plays, and stakes his money freely."

"And wins, I dare say?" remarked his lordship.

"Yes; he bagged a couple of hundred from Sir George Temple."

"How came this foreigner," inquired Lord Eglin, "to speak of such a circumstance in a billiard-room, and that a public one?"

"Why, though the —— billiard rooms are public, they are frequented, as you know, both by noblemen, gentlemen, and foreigners; and the stakes played there are high. You know Sir George Temple is one of the very best players, and this Italian gave him five in fifty, for a hundred a-game, and beat him; and I know he kept back his game."

" ' I'll back you against any man in London,' exclaimed Sir George.

" ' I'd back myself,' said the Italian, ' two to one, against any one in England, except Captain Count De Courcy.'

" ' Ha !' exclaimed Sir George, ' I have met this gallant Captain de Courcy ; and is he a billiard-player ?'

" ' He owes his fortune to it,' returned this Italian; ' he is a favourite, and some say, and I believe it is a fact, that he is the son of the Neapolitan Minister Acton. He applied for the command of the frigate that brought the Neapolitan envoy to England ; the niece of a wealthy English baronet, to whom he had been betrothed abroad, gave him the slip, and he has followed her. Wharton, I think, was the name.'

" Whilst the Italian was telling this strange story, several gentlemen present gathered round ; but immediately after the Italian left the rooms."

" ' Well, upon my soul,' exclaimed young Ponsonby, who was present, " I think that Italian has been telling an abominable lie ! I do not believe one word of his story. I met this Count De Courcy at the Marchioness de ———'s assembly, the other night ; he is one of the finest-looking young men I ever saw, and a most perfect gentleman ; besides, his exploits in the Neapolitan navy are well known ; and as to any girl, and of all persons, the elegant and accomplished Miss Wharton, jilting him, it's a farce. Does any one know that man who has just left the room ?'

" ' I have seen him here several times, remarked one or two gentlemen present, ' but know nothing of him.'

" ' If I see him again,' remarked Lord Ponsonby's son, ' as a friend of Lord Umfreville's, I will know who he is, and his motive for spreading such a story.'

" Now this scandal," added Captain Manby, " has got wind, and crept into the higher circles, for there chanced to be many young men of family in ——— rooms that night."

" I think the tale very probable," said Lord Eglin, " I shall meet this Captain de Courcy at the Earl of ———'s, who in- vites the Neapolitan envoy and his suite after to-morrow. I will take an opportunity of asking him to what family of the De Courcys he belongs." His lordship and his friend then proceeded to the club billiard rooms, and when his lordship left, they remained debtor to Captain Manby's friend £400 ; he having backed the worthy captain every game ; his lord- ship won the two first games ; but afterwards, when the bets were doubled, the captain won, and always by what appeared to be a fluke, that is a chance stroke, and not played for.

" You have monstrous luck, Manby," remarked his lordship.

" Uncommon run," returned his companion, " almost every

second stroke a fluke ; I should have no chance with you, my lord, but for luck."

CHAPTER XXII.

To bring our story and our characters clearly and distinctly before our readers, we must retrace our steps to the fair city of Palermo, previous to the departure of our hero for England.

Ferdinand the Fourth of Naples, after his arrival in that city, felt so pleased with the care, conduct, and skill of the commander of the frigate Serena, that he created him a Count of the Neapolitan Kingdom of the Two Sicilies.

De Courcy would just as willingly have remained captain of the Serena, without the title; but his majesty, not content with the title alone, bestowed upon him and his heirs a small but beautiful estate on the island, near Catania, belonging to the crown. Our hero felt, certainly, exceeding gratitude to his majesty, and expressed his sentiments for the munificence of the king upon the proper occasion. Being anxious, beyond measure, to proceed to England—Mary Wharton being never absent from his thoughts—for the letter given him by Sir John had fully convinced him that not one iota of his love for Mary was lost, he therefore longed to reach England, to throw himself at her feet and implore her forgiveness ; at the same time explain to her how he had been misled, and induced to behave with so much apparent mystery and precipitation.

De Courcy had to await the arrival of Sir John and the Marquis de Policastra, the envoy from Naples, as it soon became to be hinted in Palermo that a formidable and danger-ous conspiracy against the king and Royal family existed in Naples ; but the entire body of conspirators, except a very few, were secured—and shortly after several executions took place, and the names of some of the members of the Caraccioli Society were made public, and the astonishment that ensued was great.

Our hero, meanwhile, frequently met the Princess of Sorento in the parties and fêtes that followed the king's arrival in Palermo ; and it was observed by many that the spirits of the once gay princess had greatly diminished ; that she had become subject to fits of abstraction, and even de-pression.

To the Count De Courcy her manner was uniformly kind, and even tender. Being anything but a vain man, it was im-possible for our hero not to perceive her preference for his society, and the pleasure it gave her.

The mansion the Princess of Sorento owned and inhabited in Palermo was situated in the Obruzza, which may be styled one of the suburbs of the city, and certainly one of the loveliest

M

spots in the whole valley. The fine remains of old Moorish fortresses or castles, still in excellent preservation, called Kriba and Zisa, adding to the romance and beauty of the locality. The princess's residence was one of the handsomest in the Obruzza; the gardens were of great extent, and many of those beautiful and magnificent trees, the date-palm, flourished luxuriantly in them. No expense was spared in decorating those gardens; for the Obruzza had been the favourite residence of the princess's husband, and after his death his rules were never neglected; almost all the tropical plants flourished in those gardens, and the varieties of the cacti were numerous and gorgeous—the fuchsia grew beneath the camphor and the gum-tree; the sweet heliotrope, and the lovely Floxilia bloomed amid a luxuriant verdure. To this retreat, and its beautiful grounds, the princess collected a very select party. Our hero was one of the invited; the following day Sir John Acton and the Marquis de Polieastra were expected.

We do not intend to delay our readers with a description of this assemblage, chiefly held in the gardens of the mansion, which were brilliantly and tastefully illuminated with devices in parti-coloured lamps.

It was a real Italian night, the air so soft and balmy, breathing in that happy clime the very essence of love. Amidst the luxuriance of nature, and the most delicious odour from the rare plants and flowers, the cavalieros and their fair dames wandered in happy forgetfulness of everything but the enjoyment of the hour.

The princess herself had never looked more lovely than on that night. She was walking gently along a most beautiful avenue, covered with the rich deep crimson blossoms of the oleander, amid which peeped here and there the pretty coloured lamps that lighted the gay party in their walks. She was leaning on the arm of Captain de Courcy, and for some moments neither spoke, finding themselves pursuing a walk free from a single intruder. The princess raising her beautiful eyes from the walk, suddenly looked up into the serious, handsome features of her visitor; there was a sadness in her look, as her eyes met those of our hero, that pained him, and at length she said, "Captain De Courcy, it grieves me to say, you have a bitter, and I fear me, a most unrelenting enemy."

"We can seldom pass through life, princess, without some trial; mine has been a fortunate career, having many friends, and kind, generous ones. I can afford to have one enemy."

"Still, that one enemy," continued the princess, seriously, "may poison the cup. When you first returned from the siege of Genoa, I received, as I think I mentioned, an anonymous letter, narrating some particulars of what had occurred to you in Genoa."

"I remember, princess, since then I have had reason to believe that the letter you mentioned was written by one whom I then esteemed as a friend. His name is now known as a traitor to his king, and I may say, that I feel satisfied that the writer of the letter you mention was Guiseppe Baracco, whom you may remember was first lieutenant of the Vesuvius, at the time we had the good fortune to rescue you and the Prince de —— from the corsairs."

The princess suppressed a sigh, saying, "I grieve to hear you say so, as you must feel the cruel deception practised upon you. Where is this Baracco now?"

"That I cannot possibly guess, princess," answered our hero, then briefly relating to her the manner in which Baracco had escaped.

The princess seemed deeply interested; there was a pause of a moment, as De Courcy concluded—and then she said, "This Baracco is, without doubt, the mortal enemy I warned you of just now, and it is very clear that he either watches you himself, or he has agents and spies that do."

"Yesterday," she continued, in a low voice, "I received this letter." She was taking one from her vest, when she chanced to raise her eyes, with a wild shriek, so fearful and so piercing, that it rang through the whole garden, she threw her arms wildly round De Courcy's neck, and the same instant the gleam of a steel poniard passed before his eyes, entered the shoulder of the princess, who, with a low moan, and a shudder that shook her whole frame, became insensible.

De Courcy could only see the hand, for the blow was struck over his own shoulder, and evidently intended for his heart; with the princess's arms clasped round his neck, he was incapable of other exertion than to seize the wrist of his opponent with his left hand, and with a powerful wrench to tear the dagger from his grasp; he then saw the figure of a man dash through the thick flowery shrubs and disappear; by this time he was surrounded with crowds of alarmed and horror-struck guests.

"Search the gardens for the assassin!" exclaimed the greatly shocked De Courcy; lifting the insensible form of the princess, who was bleeding profusely, in his arms, he carried her to the house, ordering the physician to be instantly sent for; the confounded cavalieros rushed with drawn swords through the gardens, whilst the ladies followed to the house, in a state of intense alarm, wonder, and confusion; fortunately there was a physician present, belonging to the king's household, and he instantly hastened to the princess.

De Courcy, trembling with agitation and fear of its being a fatal wound, delivering the still insensible form of the princess to the care of her distracted women and the physician, hurried into the garden, and met the different gentlemen returning from a fruitless search.

" Good God! Captain De Courcy," exclaimed the Marquis de Panigi, " how has this terrible event occurred? Have you any idea of the cause, or who is the assassin?"

" I may suspect, marquis," answered De Courcy, " who the assassin is : but the blow was intended for me, and by a sudden movement of the princess, the villain struck her."

" Who do you suspect to be the assassin?" cried several voices.

" As I may be wrong, gentlemen, it may be as well for the present to let the supposed culprit's name remain unknown."

Never was a pleasure-party so abruptly and terribly interrupted. The princess was greatly loved by all, especially by the poorer classes of Palermo.

De Courcy did not quit the house; he waited to see or hear from the two physicians, and remained in a saloon, labouring under an overpowering sensation of mental distress. As he paced the chamber, with agitated steps, one of the princess's ladies entered ; she was very pale, but still her manner gave him relief.

" She has recovered her senses, count," returned the lady, " and I thank the Madonna. The physicians say, by an extraordinary chance, or rather we should say interposition of Providence, the steel was diverted from a mortal part by a diamond zone, which the dagger struck against."

" Thank God!" returned De Courcy, fervently.

" The princess's first words were for you, count," said the signora, in a significant tone. " She demanded, in a faint voice, if you had escaped."

De Courcy was troubled, and much moved; but, mastering his emotion, he begged the lady to state to the princess, when able to bear conversation, his deep and lasting gratitude, and his earnest prayer for her recovery.

The lady then retired, and De Courcy, in a frame of mind not easily described, returned to Palermo.

This occurrence created a most universal feeling of detestation against the villain who had attempted the assassination of the princess, as it was first thought amongst the people of Palermo. Mounted sbirri, and sbirri on foot, hunted every hole and corner of the country and suburbs, the country was traversed, every suspicious-looking personage examined, large rewards offered, nothing was neglected. The queen herself drove over in the morning to the princess's villa, and the king instantly sent for De Courcy, to hear the true account from himself.

King Ferdinand listened attentively, and when our hero concluded, said in his short manner, "Well, count, please the saints, she will recover. You have our consent to offer your hand to the princess." De Courcy coloured to the temples "it s the least you can do," continued his majesty, "and it will be expected."

Our hero muttered something about honour and deep gratitude, not very plainly intelligible to the king, for his majesty immediately said, and perhaps his voice was, or De Courcy thought it a little sharp. "You do not hesitate, Count De Courcy, in offering your hand to the fairest lady in our dominions, and one also connected with ourselves?"

"Certainly not, your majesty," returned De Courcy, with difficulty suppressing a sigh of bitter regret, for the Rubicon was passed; he must for ever lose his majesty's favour; the king was tenacious to a degree of contradiction to his wishes; added to that, deep gratitude to the princess. His knowledge of her affection for him left him so moved and agitated by conflicting feelings, that he became scarcely conscious of what he said, so that he left his majesty's presence, who graciously gave him his hand to kiss with the full persuasion that it was his undoubted intention, the moment the princess was sufficiently recovered, to throw himself at her feet, and solicit her hand.

Bewildered and stupified by the strange rapidity in which events followed each other, and which seemed, do what he would, to throw him into situations contrary to the real feelings of his heart. That he felt deep gratitude to the princess he could not deny; that he esteemed and admired her was also true; but his love and devotion was for another. No one could accuse him of paying either marked or particular attention to the princess; so at least he thought; and no doubt in his heart he was sincere, but others did not think so.

The next day Sir John Acton arrived from Naples; the Marquis de Policastra was as yet on a mission in Calabria, but would, in the course of a week, be in Palermo. The princess was pronounced out of danger, but her confinement would be long. Our hero was for a long time in conversation with King Ferdinand's minister.

"You look gloomy and miserable, Hugh," remarked Sir John, "and you near the top step of the ladder, and not five-and-twenty. I hoped to have congratulated you, after my interview with the king, instead of which, you appear as if sentence of death had been passed upon you."

"Being acquainted with the state of my feelings, and my devotion for another," replied De Courcy, gravely, "would, I should think, account sufficiently for my dejection of look and spirits."

"I think," said Sir John, "that if, instead of permitting your mind to dwell upon and nourish a feeling that may be, after all, an *ignis fatuus*, you were to return the affections of a woman who devotedly and nobly threw herself between you and an assassin's knife, and who is one of the loveliest in Italy, you would show your gratitude and good sense at the same time. The king and queen now fully expect you to offer yourself to the princess; to draw back would be a folly. Had you spoken candidly to the king when he addressed you on the subject, you might have had a chance of still retaining his favour; to draw back now would be to mar your fortune in his majesty's service for ever."

"My dear Sir John," replied De Courcy, almost sternly, "do you for a moment suppose I was actuated in what I said or did by a fear of losing rank, station, or fortune? If you did, permit me to correct your error. I would have resigned all favours I ever received at his majesty's hands, without a sigh of regret, sooner than enter into an engagement repugnant to my feelings. No; I was actuated in what I did say by a deep feeling of gratitude towards a woman who freely staked life to shield me, knowing at the same time that that woman did so from love; I am not vain, neither am I afraid that you will think me so; so let this subject rest; you may depend I will do what I conceive it my duty to do."

"I am not offended, Hugh," said the minister, holding out his hand, "though you speak somewhat harshly to me; for you know right well I have loved you from a child, and have no other wish than for your welfare. I have a feeling, a kind of presentiment, that my career at the Neapolitan court draws to a close. I do not regret it; I covet a life of repose after one of excitement and agitation. I intend purchasing an estate in this beautiful island; so that when the time comes, I may find a port, as we sailors say, to cast anchor in, and ride out the tide of life, free from the storms of the political world."

De Courcy pressed Sir John's hand warmly, saying, "Excuse my hasty words, dear sir. You know not how troubled this late event has made me."

"I have no doubt of it, Hugh; it is all that villain Baracco's work, I am satisfied; he has baffled every attempt I made to entrap him; I thought he must have left the kingdom. Do you suppose it was he himself who struck the blow?"

"No, I should say no;" answered our hero; "the wrist I grasped was a thin, wiry one, with not half the bone and sinew of Baracco, who is a large, strong man, and the dagger is little better than a butcher's knife."

"Ah! per bacco, there is no want of hired assassins in this island; those rascally tanners would murder any one for half a ducat. You must be careful, especially at night; but in a day or so you will be off; this villain's designs will be frustrated. By-the-bye, I have changed my mind respecting the packet I gave you. When you reach England, should any circumstance occur that you consider your knowledge of ascertaining who are beneficial to you, open it, and act as you think fit. I am ready to come forward to substantiate facts, if necessary."

CHAPTER XXIII.

THE Serena was to sail in a day or two. The Marquis de Policastra had arrived, and all things were ready for the voyage to England.

The Princess de Sorento had partially recovered, and was now able to see a few friends.

De Courcy was unremitting in his inquiries and attention; his remarkable seriousness and avoidance of all society, and confining himself entirely on board his ship, excited considerable curiosity and much remark; but De Courcy cared little about being a subject of conversation to the gay courtiers of King Ferdinand's court. He waited for an interview with the princess with intense anxiety. At length, the very day before he was to sail for England, a message from the princess caused the blood to rush to his heart with a painful violence; he was quite aware that Queen Caroline had already spoken to the princess upon the subject of their union, and that, in fact, every one in and about the court looked upon the matter of a matrimonial alliance between him and the princess as an affair entirely settled.

With a palpitating heart De Courcy entered the saloon, where the princess, seated on an ottoman, and propped with cushions, was waiting to receive him. It was evening, and a soft, subdued light entered through the closed blinds. Clarina Obruzza was still very pale, and a good deal reduced in person.

Hugh De Courcy took the fair hand held out to him, with considerable emotion, and carried it to his lips; if not with a lover's warmth, at all events with a profound feeling of admiration and gratitude—for he was deeply affected—perceiving the princess must have suffered greatly, and for him; he saw, also, that she was agitated, and that her hand trembled in his; and that a faint colour came to her cheek. Taking a chair, De Courcy sat down beside the lady, almost as agitated as herself. Clarina Obruzza first broke the silence that followed De Courcy's warm and affectionate words, expressive of his grief at his having been the cause of so much suffering, and how deep and lasting his gratitude and admiration would be for her noble sacrifice of self in saving him.

"It would be useless, Hugh de Courcy," said the princess, in a low and agitated voice, "for me now to deny the motive of my conduct; a young and timid girl would shrink from such an avowal, but I make it, for this reason, that we meet now for the last time."

"Clarina," exclaimed De Courcy, in a voice of real emotion, "why those words?"

"Because, Hugh De Courcy, I would again, if not save your life, save you from wrecking your future felicity from a feeling of gratitude. Do not interrupt me; I do not blame you; but listen to me. I am not ignorant of what passed between you and King Ferdinand, and that he, in a measure, commanded you to offer me your hand."

"Nay, Clarina," interposed our hero, "on my soul such was not the case. If I have not thrown myself at your feet, and sued as a lover might be proud to sue for this fair hand, it is because——"

"You had no heart to bestow," interrupted the princess, calmly, but in a low, touching voice.

"Not, Clarina," said De Courcy, "a sole and undivided heart, such as the Princess de Sorento had a right to expect; but, nevertheless, believe me," and he took her thin, wasted, but still very lovely hand in his, "you should never have to complain of my devotion and earnest affection—a life devoted to your happiness."

"No, no, no, Hugh!" said the princess, with difficulty suppressing the tears that bespoke how much she suffered, and how sincere her love was; "no, this must not be—hear my reasons. When you returned from Genoa, I heard of your love affair in that city, and as I was led to believe a mere passing fancy for a pretty face—but I know differently now. You gave your love to a young and accomplished maiden of your own northern clime; I know also that treachery and deceit, and an attempt on your life, drove you from her, who loved you well. You believed her false, whilst she was true and devoted; and that now, having discovered your error, and the treachery of a false villain, you ardently long to repair your error, and throw yourself at her feet and renew your engagement. Is not this the true state of your heart?"

"Clarina, such was the state of my mind," replied our hero, in a serious tone, "previous to your generous and noble act; but now——"

The princess shook her head, and with a faint, a very faint, smile, one more of anguish than aught else, said, "Say no more, De Courcy, on this painful subject. I sent for you on purpose to tell you not to be uneasy at the king's displeasure; leave him to me to manage. From Lady Acton I have learned all I now know. She knows your feelings; and she well knew I should never feel happy with a divided heart; therefore go to England, and bestow on her who deserves your love that affection that is hers by right; and if ever we should meet again, let us meet as friends; for, believe me, you have not one more sincere than Clarina Obruzza." As she said those words she touched a silver bell upon the table, and two of her ladies immediately entered the room.

De Courcy, with a flushed cheek, rose from his seat, for he perceived clearly enough that the princess had summoned her ladies in order to end a somewhat painful scene; he therefore took the hand held out to him, kissed it reverentially, and hoping that she would shortly be restored to perfect health, quitted the chamber with a disturbed and troubled mind.

The day after this interview the Serena sailed for Malta and England. Nothing of moment occurred during the voyage to Malta, which place had the day before surrendered to the British. Leaving the despatches he carried with the English Admiral, the Serena continued her voyage.

De Courcy, on first leaving Palermo, felt exceedingly depressed, and continued so till, on reaching Malta, the excitement and the bustle attending the surrender of the place, and the animating sight the place itself presented, roused his energies; and, exerting himself, he strove to render the rest of the voyage more agreeable to the Marquis de Policastra, and the gentlemen accompanying him. His orders were to avoid, if possible, an encounter with the enemy; therefore, after passing Gibraltar a most careful watch was kept, day and night, whilst a succession of north-easterly gales, towards the middle of September, kept the Serena beating to windward along the Spanish coast. One morning, just at daylight, in a thick mist, they came close up with a fine seventy-four gun ship, of whose vicinity they were not aware till within musket-shot, when the stranger immediately showed the tri-colour flag. Captain De Courcy at once hoisted the same flag, and edged away from his dangerous neighbour, for it was blowing fresh, and the fog lifting. The stranger immediately hoisted the private signal, and this not being answered, she bore up after the Serena, discharging her bow-guns at the same time. The Serena then hoisted Neapolitan colours, returning the fire with her heavy stern-guns, which knocked the fore-top-gallant mast of the seventy-four over the side; this so enraged the Frenchman, that yawing intending to treat his puny antagonist to a broadside, but De Courcy, suspecting the object, baffled the enemy, and hoisting every stitch of canvas rapidly increased his distance, aided by the fog, which, fortunately, lasted; and, altering his course, lost sight of his opponent altogether.

Two days afterwards, with a light wind at north-west, the Serena discovered a sail right a-head crossing their course; the stranger observed them also, and hauling his wind, awaited their approach.

"What do you think she is, count?" said the Marquis de Policastra, who was walking the deck, as our hero stood regarding the stranger through his glass.

"A large frigate, marquis," replied De Courcy; "and whether British or French, it will be difficult, in this light wind, to avoid her."

"It appears a much larger vessel than' the Serena," observed the marquis: "however, count, if you cannot avoid her, you must, I suppose, fight her;" adding, with a smile, "I fancy the last alternative will be the most agreeable to you."

"There is not much disgrace," returned our hero, "in running away from a seventy-four; but this stranger is a pretty good match if he be French, of which I feel sure he is; he brings a good breeze with him, and we are nearly becalmed."

Every one became on the alert, on board the Serena; the crew, consisting of fighting men, and not accustomed, when in the old Vesuvius, to run away; and the idea of a contest with the stranger was joyful news, every man flying to his post with alacrity.

"You had better go below, my Lord Marquis," said De Courcy, addressing the Neapolitan envoy. "Your life is too important to be risked; and the enemy is, I perceive, a heavily armed frigate of more than forty guns."

"Oh, no," returned the marquis, very quietly, "if we are to fight, I am not going to run away, count, I assure you. I never saw a naval engagement, and I am curious. Ha! there goes the stranger's bunting, a splendid craft indeed!" The strange vessel, now within two musket-shots, hoisted the revolutionary flag, took in his royals, and made every preparation for a contest, if necessary. The Serena was equally prepared, and both vessels having now a fine working breeze, and both having their national flag flying, prepared for a determined contest.

The French vessel was a forty-four-gun frigate, and with her full complement of men—as it afterwards appeared—with much heavier metal than the Serena.

The Neapolitan frigate was on the larboard tack, with the wind from the north-north-west. The French ship passed within one hundred yards to windward of the Serena, and both ships exchanged broadsides; the French commander hailing the Neapolitan to surrender, upon which the Serena's crew gave a hearty cheer of derision.

The Revolutionaire, for that was the French ship's name, tacked, whilst the Serena bore up, each ship contriving to fire as her guns bore.

The Serena having paid off and got before the wind, brought her larboard broadside to bear; the Revolutionaire then put her helm a starboard, and sheered off. A furious cannonade was then maintained on both sides; the yard-arms nearly locking, until the Revolutionaire, ranging a-head, crossed the Serena's bows. So murderous and well-directed was the fire of the Serena's guns, that the deck of the French vessel was slippery with blood, and sixteen of her crew lay dead and dying, and numbers wounded besides.

On the deck of the Serena five men were killed and thirteen wounded, Hugh De Courcy himself slightly, in two places; his second lieutenant severely, was carried below; the Marquis de Policastra was also wounded slightly in the arm, but still insisted on remaining on deck, feeling the greatest enthusiasm.

As the French ship paid off, the Serena, with her starboard guns, poured in a raking fire, which was badly returned, wounding, however, a young midshipman and the first lieutenant, and cutting the main sheet. De Courcy, watching his opportunity, and having the men prepared, ran right on board the enemy, and getting locked together, he sprang on the deck, followed by his eager and determined crew. As they did so, the main and mizen mast of the Revolutionaire fell fore and aft, whilst the crew firing beneath the sails, they caught fire. During this terrible scene, De Courcy leapt in upon the enemy's quarter-deck, the Captain of the Revolutionaire firing his pistol, the ball of which broke his left arm near the elbow, but the next moment De Courcy's sword passed through his body; when a scene of furious contention ensued, in the midst of which a young man, an Englishman, a lad, and a sailor, also English, rushed to the side of De Courcy, supplying themselves with weapons from the deck, and, with a cheer, joined in the fight. They were prisoners, and had just contrived to escape from below, after a contest of twenty minutes, fierce and bloody for the time, the captain and first lieutenant being slain, and several of the other officers *hors de combat*, the ship surrendered, and all hands united in extinguishing the flames.

De Courcy, besides having his left arm broken, was wounded in several places by cutlass-pikes. The enemy, besides their captain, first lieutenant, and third, slain, had one hundred and seven wounded—some severely, some dangerously. After some difficulty the fire was subdued, and the vessels separated, immediately after the fore-mast of the Revolutionaire went over the side.

This contest was one of the most determined on both sides;

as De Courcy ascertained, afterwards, that Captain Jean Bon Audri vowed he would take the Serena, or perish.

De Courcy recollected that Captain Jean Bon Audri had been formerly captain of the Sans Culotte corvette, of twenty-two guns, which he captured the year before, off the Neapolitan coast near Gaeta, after a severe contest in the Vesuvius brig. It was blowing a gale at the time, and the French captain, after a contest of thirty-five minutes, ran the corvette ashore under a French battery of four guns, then he and his crew deserted her. Our hero, nevertheless, boarded her under a heavy fire from the battery, and destroyed her. The loss on board the Revolutionaire was exceedingly severe.

After his arm was set, and his wounds dressed, our hero recollected the young man and his companion who so gallantly joined in the fight ; and making inquiries he soon found them. The young man was suffering from a severe contusion. Perceiving at once that he was a gentleman and a sailor, De Courcy insisted on having him conveyed to his cabin ; requesting. at the same time, to know his name.

" Thank you, thank you," said the stranger, " you are very kind, my name is Umfreville—Lieutenant Umfreville."

" What!" exclaimed our hero in great surprise, "son of Lord Umfreville and brother to my old college friend ? "

The stranger looked exceedingly surprised, but replied, " Such is the case ; and I pray you extend your kindness to the young lad and the sailor with me—the former is a midshipman ; we all belonged to the unfortunate Danæ.

De Courcy accordingly had Lieutenant Umfreville, and the young midshipman, who was unhurt, established in comfortable berths, and the sailor with them taken care of.

With the wreck of the masts and spars, jury-masts were rigged the following day upon the Revolutionaire, and with his prize De Dourcy shaped his course for Plymouth, where he safely arrived.

During the voyage he received from Lieutenant Umfreville, to whom he communicated the particulars of his intimacy and friendship with his brother, the following account of the loss of the Danæ.

The Danæ was a twenty-gun ship, commanded by Captain Lord Proby.

" We were watching the French fleet in Brest," said Lieutenant Umfreville," and had just returned from joining in the chase of the Pallas, which vessel was captured by the Lorri, Captain Newman ; we had unfortunately on board the Danæ some of the men who had mutinied at the Nore ; the worst amongst them was a man named Jackson; he was one of the captains of the fore-top ; this fellow was Parker's secretary in the Nore Mutiny. It was about ten o'clock at night, and I believe most of the officers were in bed, except Lord Proby, a marine officer, the master, and myself; I was sitting in my berth, when I heard a desperate scuffle overhead; I started up, and as I entered the cabin where Lord Proby was, the marine officer rushed down the stairs, saying, ' The crew have mutinied and cut down the master, and thrown him down the main-hatchway, they have battened down the grating, and placed over it the boats filled with shot.'*

" Lord Proby made a rush, all present following, to get up the after-hatchway, but we found this guarded by more than thirty men; one of the ruffians made a cut at Lord Proby, striking him on the head. I had a loaded pistol in my hand, which I instantly fired at the man, and he fell; we were forced back, however, and by this time we found that about thirty or more of the trustworthy portion of the crew had joined us. After a strict search we gathered about a dozen cutlasses, a few muskets, and half a dozen pistols.

" ' Our only hope,' said our commander, ' is that the rascals will be forced to keep to sea:' thus the night passed without attempting anything, our numbers being too few to succeed against the mutineers; but towards morning one of the men contrived to hear from a comrade above, that the wind had changed, and that the mutineers were running the vessel under a French battery; and, in fact, shortly after we found that they had brought the ship to an anchor. An hour afterwards we heard a great bustle on deck, and presently a voice hailed us below, saying, in French, that we were under the guns of Fort Conquite, and that the French corvette, Columba, of sixteen guns, was alongside; whilst a detachment of soldiers was on board the Danæ. The same voice then demanded, ' To whom do you surrender?' After a moment's hesitation, Lord Proby said, ' To the French nation; not to mutineers.' Thus we were delivered over by those mutineer scoundrels as prisoners: we were then in company of the corvette, got under weigh, and steered for Brest. Before Lord Proby surrendered he had thrown from the cabin window, filled with lead, the box containing the private signals. On arriving at Brest, we were treated as mutineers, and all marched to Dina Prison.† On the way, during the darkness of the evening, before reaching the prison, I communicated with Midshipman Brown, and the seaman next him, a plan of escape, in which we succeeded; and after considerable privation and some sufferings, we made the coast, and seized a small miserable fishing-boat, with a sail and one oar; we had a few biscuits, a jar of water, and that's all; these we got out of a chase mare aground, near the boat, her crew being up at a village, within half a mile of the beach.

* Fact.   † James's Naval History.

In this boat we put to sea, fully expecting, or at least hoping, to be picked up by some of our cruisers, off Brest, and the adjacent coast. But a breeze of wind blew us off the shore; and for five days we endured a good deal of privation. We had just consumed our last biscuit—water we had none—the previous day, when we were picked up by the Revolutionaire. Instead of receiving kindness, although enemies, we met with remarkably harsh treatment, and were confined below, in a miserable dark hole, and ill fed. Hearing the firing when you attacked the frigate, we managed to free ourselves, and get upon deck.''

During the voyage our hero and Lieutenant Umfreville became extremely intimate. On reaching Plymouth, the Marquis de Policastra and suite proceeded to London, but Captain De Courcy and his young friend remained for a few days, their wounds, being yet unhealed, rendering them unfit for much exertion.

CHAPTER XXIV

It may be supposed that it was not without a feeling of excitement and anxiety that Hugh De Courcy set foot upon the shores of England. An ardent desire to learn whether Mary Wharton had reached England in safety—a voyage run in a vessel of war from the shores of the Mediterranean to Great Britain, was, during the period of the war, one of considerable peril—the chances of meeting an enemy being very great. This intelligence he had no means of ascertaining till he reached London ; meanwhile Mr. Umfreville had written to his father and brother, and also reported himself at the Admiralty ; for in a few days the state of the wound in his leg would enable him to bear the journey. By the return of post, he received a letter from his brother Edward. The two friends were sitting in a chamber in the Royal Hotel, Plymouth, they had just finished their breakfast, when it was brought in. Our hero still carried his left arm in a sling, but intended leaving Plymouth the following day.

"I must go directly," exclaimed Lieutenant Umfreville, pausing, in the reading of his letter.

" Nothing serious the matter, I trust?" inquired De Courcy, laying down the newspaper.

"Yes, indeed," returned the young man, "my brother has just received intelligence of my dear father having an attack of gout—he fears a very severe one—and wishes me to hasten to our family place, where my father is, as soon as possible. I will leave in an hour."

"I will accompany you as far as our roads lie together," said De Courcy, " and sincerely trust that this attack will pass off. I have heard from your brother that gout is heredi-tary with your father. and that he suffered even when a very young man; therefore these attacks are not generally so alarming to those so afflicted as to others."

"I trust in God that such may be the case!" returned the young man, rising; "poor Edward, too, was on the point of marriage with a most lovely and amiable girl, the daughter of a Sir Charles Wharton—but such is life!" and the young sailor left the room, and having his back to his friend, did not perceive that his words had turned him into a statue of stone—so rigid, so immovable, and so deadly pale had he become.

"Merciful God!" exclaimed De Courcy, "is this, then, the end of all my hopes?" For several moments he remained; disappointment, agony, and, we fear, fierce passion struggling for mastery, his hand pressed to his forehead. Nearly twenty minutes elapsed without his moving from the spot on which he stood; then taking his hand from his forehead, his features became composed and serious, somewhat paler, but retaining no longer the agonized expression of the preceding few minutes; he then passed on to his chamber to prepare for his departure for London, having previously arranged every thing requisite with respect to his ship and his prize, the Revolutionaire.

Quitting Plymouth in a chaise and four. a considerable crowd having assembled without the hotel, chiefly nautical men and sailors, for De Courcy had excited considerable admiration and curiosity at Plymouth; every attention and respect being paid him by the authorities, besides being called upon by the most influential persons in the town and neigh-bourhood. Hundreds had flocked on board the Neapolitan frigate; her size, the beauty of her build, and the fight she had sustained with her powerful antagonist. had created a feeling of exceeding curiosity. Numbers of men-of-wars' men were in the crowd assembled in the square before the hotel-door, and a succession of hearty British cheers greeted our hero's appearance. De Courcy's fine figure, young and handsome features, increased the enthusiasm a brave action always excites in the mind of a British tar. Thus his kind reception and the hearty demonstration on his departure raised the cloud from his brow; and for a time he strove to shake off the fearful depression he felt.

The friends continued their journey to Bath together, there they separated; Mr. Umfreville proceeding into Hampshire, De Courcy to London. The Marquis de Policastra wished him to take up his abode with him, but as he desired, while in England, to remain in as much seclusion as possible, he took private apartments for himself in St. James's-street. The

cruel disappointment he experienced respecting Mary
Wharton completely banished every other thought or feeling;
though he found it quite impossible to seclude himself as
much as he proposed. He had to undergo a presentation at
court, and then many of the nobility and gentry called and
invited the young commander to their houses.

The Marquis de Policastra was a gay and amiable nobleman, and one who delighted in society; and as a most accomplished politician, and the mission he was intrusted with
being a most important one, he was taken great notice of by
the court and the ministers in power.

At this period commenced the Northern confederacy against
England. Russia, though the ally of England, took offence
at the attack made by British ships upon the Danish frigate,
Frerja. Paul, the Russian Czar, showed his displeasure by
sequestering all British property in his dominions. The
capture of Malta increased the Czar's anger. Then Sweden
and Prussia assumed a menacing attitude, therefore, what
with this confederacy and her war with France, England had
quite enough on her hands.

As the purport of the Neapolitan envoy's mission to England has nothing to do with our story, we shall merely say
that the English government most willingly acceded to the
request of his Majesty of the Two Sicilies; and in less than
a month the Marquis de Policastra expected to sail from
Plymouth, in the Serena, on his return to Naples.

About this time De Courcy received a letter from his old
school-fellow, then become Lord Umfreville, announcing his
father's death. " I wish much to see you, Hugh," said his
lordship, in his letter, " for during my father's last moments,
when his recollection was perfectly restored—it lasted, alas!
for a very short time—amongst other expressions he made use
of the following remarkable words: ' I wish you, my beloved
Edward, to communicate with Sir John Acton, Prime Minister
of Ferdinand of Naples, and also with your old school companion at the college of Sienna,'—here he paused from
weakness, and alas! the fleeting of the spirit, for after a
moment he pressed my hand, and looking with fond affection at me and my brother, who knelt beside me, he said, in
low, emphatic voice, ' Do your duty, let no consideration blind
you. Adieu, my beloved children !'—the next moment he was
no more. I have no heart or mind to comment now on
those remarkable words; but it is evident to me that you
are in some strange way implicated in my father's last request
—however, in a week or so we shall meet, please God. Till
then, dear friend, farewell !

" UMFREVILLE."

"This is very strange !" continued De Courcy, and he

instantly thought of the packet of papers sealed up and given him by Sir John Acton. His first impulse was, as he had his old protector's permission, to open and inspect the documents; but on second thought, he determined to wait till after his meeting with Lord Umfreville, or do so in his presence. He had frequently heard Miss Wharton's name mentioned in the saloons of the noblemen he visited—he heard mention of her exceeding loveliness, her grace of person, and her retiring and serious manners. Her engagement to Edward Umfreville was also spoken of and commented upon.

The evening on which he received Lord Umfreville's letter he was invited to a select musical soirée at the Countess de Ponzoni's, an Italian by birth, but married to an English gentleman of good family and very large fortune. At this party De Courcy was introduced by the countess to Lady Hasarel, with whom he entered into conversation. Our hero was somewhat surprised at this introduction, as the party were invited chiefly to hear the exquisite singing and playing of the then celebrated Madame ———, and a few other carefully selected public performers.

We have stated in our previous pages that Lady Hasarel had chaperoned Miss Wharton, and that it was under her protection she had made her first appearance in English society, and that her ladyship was a woman of exceedingly elegant appearance and most pleasing fascinating manners. At first the conversation turned upon the performance of Madame———, and then upon music in general, of which science De Courcy himself was passionately fond. Therefore he became insensibly interested in the conversation which at first he pursued listlessly.

"With all Madame de ———'s power, flexibility, and compass of tone," said Lady Hasarel, "I have a young friend whose voice, in my opinion, surpasses hers. I wish you could hear her; she does not mix much in society, and latterly scarcely at all; but of all the voices I ever heard, hers is the most touching and sweet. She has nearly as much power as Madame de ———, though she never exercises it; but her manner, expression, with her exquisite tones, captivate and carry you away irresistibly."

With difficulty De Courcy checked a heavy sigh, as with a very serious, if not sad expression of countenance, he asked, "Who, your ladyship, is this dangerous syren?"

"You may truly say syren, count," answered Lady Hasarel, "if she exerted her powers of fascination to ensnare, but such is far from the case. She has passed great part of her young life in Italy. I wonder you have not heard, since your arrival, of my fair friend, who is the niece of Sir Charles Wharton."

N

De Courcy expected this name would be pronounced; and he remarked, though his voice slightly faltered, " I have heard of Miss Wharton, and that she is engaged to a very old friend of mine, Lord Umfreville."

De Courcy thought it strange that Lady Hasarel evinced no surprise at his mentioning Lord Umfreville as an old friend, but merely remarked, " Yes, Miss Wharton is engaged to the young Lord Umfreville—but now I think of it, count," continued Lady Hasarel, "you were, I understand, at the bombardment of Genoa, with Lord Keith, and, no doubt. remained there some time after the surrender of the city."

" Such was the case, my lady," replied our hero, his thoughts reverting, with the rapidity of light, to that eventful period.

"So was Miss Wharton," remarked Lady Hasarel, fixing her gaze upon De Courcy's thoughtful features. " She was there the whole time; but fortunately being under the protection of a wealthy and kind friend, escaped the miseries the less fortunate portion of the inhabitants suffered. I really must make you two acquainted; it will be interesting to you both to talk over the occurrences of that certainly eventful period."

De Courcy would not for worlds meet Mary Wharton, still he could not but express himself honoured by such an introduction.

" My young friend's engagement with the present Lord Umfreville," observed Lady Hasarel, after pausing a few moments to listen to an aria, played and sung by one of the dilettante present, " took place under rather melancholy circumstances."

" Indeed!" exclaimed De Courcy, with a start, "how so, Lady Hasarel?"

" Her uncle, Sir Charles Wharton, was knocked down in the street by a carriage, and incurred congestion of the brain. His physicians gave him over, and on, as he thought his deathbed, he implored his niece to make his last moments happy, by consenting to become the wife of the Honourable Edward Umfreville, whose father was then alive. Miss Wharton is devotedly attached to her uncle, and thinking him dying she consented."

" My God!" he exclaimed, in a voice of such deep anguish, that two ladies, passing at the moment, started and paused; De Courcy coloured to the temples, and rose up; the ladies passed on, and Lady Hasarel, also rising, said, " I hope count, I shall have the pleasure of seeing you at my house; I assure you it will give me great pleasure."

" You are very good, my lady," returned De Courcy, " and I shall certainly avail myself of your kindness."

This conversation with Lady Hasarel struck De Courcy as very singular, and raised in his breast many strange and conflicting thoughts, whilst there was a predominant feeling of relief afforded to his mind; he now understood the whole affair clearly. Mary had sacrificed her own feelings to ensure her uncle's peace of mind, in his last moments; then he argued that such a sacrifice was no longer needed. Sir 'Charles was alive and well, and why should she fulfil an engagement repugnant to the promptings of her heart? Doubt whispered in his ear—but is the engagement repugnant? is she not satisfied to let the betrothment be consummated? Lady Hasarel must, he thought, know something of Miss Wharton's previous history; the manner in which she commenced the conversation, and the entire absence of surprise at his very perceptible emotion at the time, satisfied him he was right in his conjecture. Whilst passing across a room where a few elderly persons were engaged in playing whist, De Courcy beheld the Countess de Ponzoni coming from an adjoining saloon, with a young and graceful-looking girl, possessing a decidedly foreign air, both in look and manner. As they came nearer the latter raised her eyes from the carpet, and looked towards De Courcy, who beheld her with a start of intense surprise: all the blood in his body seemed to fly to his head; for in that young girl he beheld Térese Garetti.

With a smile of real delight and pleasure the kind-hearted Italian stepped eagerly forward, holding out her fair hand, her eyes sparkling with pleasurable emotion, whilst De Courcy took that offered hand and carried it to his lips, with a feeling of pleasure indescribable. "I see," said the countess, with a very meaning smile, "that there is no need, Count De Courcy, to introduce to you my fair cousin, and countrywoman; I would have brought you together sooner, but Térese is only just returned from an early party; and now, count, I confide her to your care till supper."

"In truth, countess," replied the delighted sailor, "this fair lady has so completely taken me by surprise, never dreaming of so delightful a meeting, that I am like one bewildered. I almost doubted the evidence of my senses when I first saw her."

"Well, I now leave you to recover them," remarked the countess; "no doubt you will have a great deal to say to each other; for I assure you Térese has been most anxious for this meeting;" so saying, the countess smilingly left them to themselves.

If you wish it, dear reader, you can be alone in a crowd; so it was with Hugh De Courcy and the fair Genoese. Perfectly heedless of the various parties they passed and repassed, the musical part of the soirée having ceased, the two young people conversed earnestly in Térese's own soft liquid language.

"I cannot, Térese," observed our hero, "express to you my
amazement in seeing you in England."

"Do you not remember," returned the Genoese maiden,
"how often I have expressed a wish to set foot upon the soil
where first my mother drew her breath? When Sir Charles
Wharton and Mrs. Arbuthnot arrived in Genoa, to take our
dear Mary home, I came with them. There, do not sigh and
look so desponding," continued the lively Italian, "or else
these good folks here will set us down as lovers."

"Have I not enough to make me sigh, Térese?" inquired
De Courcy, leading his companion to a seat.

"No, not at all," returned Térese, with a cheerful, hope-in-
spiring smile. "Ha! there is supper announced, let us be mere
mortals for half an hour ; after that, we can begin at the beginning, for I have no end of things to tell and questions to ask."

"Which I will reply to faithfully, if you will only answer
me one very short one—Have I hope?"

"Esperanza should always be your motto," replied Térese ;
and then they entered the supper-rooms ; De Courcy with a
countenance so changed from his usual expression, that those
accustomed to meet him in society at once said, "This fair
Italian has thawed the ice."

CHAPTER XXV.

WHEN our hero retired from the saloons of the Countess de
Ponzoni, he entered his apartments in St. James's-street a
very altered man indeed. Hope had revived in his breast,
despair and its attendant pangs had fled. From the kind-
hearted Térese he had learned all the particulars and occurrences that had taken place from the period of his departure
from Genoa, to the arrival of Miss Wharton in England, as
well as her subsequent engagement to Edward Umfreville ;
and his beloved Mary was fully exculpated in his eyes, and
become ten thousand times more loveable than ever. Still
the engagement remained unbroken, owing to Lord Umfreville's death ; though Mary was firmly resolved never to fulfil
the contract entered into. Térese considered that it would
not be either prudent or decorous for our hero to resume his
intercourse with Mary whilst in England. Sir Charles
himself felt the necessity of breaking off the engagement,
seeing that the mental struggle Mary endured was undermining her constitution completely ; and he also felt certain
that Lord Umfreville's noble disposition would be shocked at
receiving the hand of a woman he certainly most fondly
loved, without having created an interest in her heart.

Térese explained how she came to be with the Countess de
Ponzoni, who was a cousin of her father's. She was staying

for a week with her, whilst Sir Charles and his niece visited an estate the baronet had purchased lately in Hampshire. De Courcy, on his side, gave Térese a clear and circumstantial account of the deception practised upon him, spoke of all he had suffered from having acted with such precipitancy; and the agony he had endured when first he had heard of Mary's engagement with his old college friend. He then spoke of the conversation he had had with Lady Hasarel. " Surely,'' he observed, " she must have some idea of my former ac-quaintance with Miss Wharton ? "

" To tell you the truth," replied Térese, with a smile, " I am the cause of that very conversation. Lady Hasarel is one of the kindest of women; she chaperoned Mary and myself into the gay world of London. Mary's manners, her beauty, and accomplishments, created universal wonder and admira-tion—but Lady Hasarel was surprised at her reserve ; her refusing to dance, and evident wish for seclusion. Her lady-ship often remarked to me, ' There must be some previous attachment that creates this strange, retiring manner in one so beautiful and so fascinating.' I did not deny this ; but of course refrained from giving names, till we heard of your arrival in England. I guessed at once what you would suffer should you hear of Mary's engagement, and hear it you surely would; and as Mary was resolved not to fulfil this contract of marriage, I felt an exceeding desire to let you know how she came to enter into such an engagement.

" So in confidence I told Lady Hasarel, who goes every-where, and who would be sure to meet you in society; and she said, if she could get introduced to you, she would be sure to enlighten you on the subject. She had, however, no oppor-tunity till to-night; therefore, as soon as she knew you were in the rooms, she got the countess to introduce her to you." ᴾ

So engaged were the fair Genoese and our hero with mutual communications, that they were quite unconscious that they were remarked by most persons in the countess's saloons, and it became very shortly hinted amongst the gay world, that the handsome Count De Courcy and the fair Genoese were be-trothed lovers ; but, as usual in those cases, this report did not reach the ears of the party interested; and indeed if it had, neither would have troubled themselves about it.

On the night that the musical soirée took place at the mansion of the Countess Ponzoni, we must request our readers to enter with us one of those large and lofty houses at the back of Leicester-square. This part of the metropolis is by no means a respectable or reputable place of abode, even now, but fifty years ago it was worse, or fully equal to St. Giles's for the variety and vagabondism of its inhabitants. In a large and scantily-furnished chamber of this house, at a huge, clumsy oak-table, sat five individuals. In a corner of the room, shut off by a ragged, dirty curtain, from the view of those in it, on a straw mattress lay a young girl about eighteen years of age: two or three other mattresses were in another corner of the room, covered with remarkably soiled quilts. At the lower end of the table three persons were seated, whose appearance, &c., denoted them to be Italian strolling musicians—two barrel-organs stood against the wall, with a hurdy-gurdy and a chained monkey. These men had nothing remarkable about them ; they were quite similar in look, dress, and bearing to the same professional gentlemen we see now traversing our streets and distracting our ears " with horrible sounds." They were eating their supper, which consisted of bread, onions, red herring, and bad beer. At the upper end of the table, which was very long, sat two other individuals; this end of the table approached very near to the bed, protected from view by the tattered and dirty curtain ; and as these two persons conversed earnestly, in a low voice, and in Italian, the end of the curtain was drawn gently on one side, and the light of the oil lamp burning on the table fell upon the very pretty features of a young girl within, who appeared by the expression of her features to be intently listening to the conversation of the two persons who sat with their backs to her domicile. These individuals were strong men, in the prime of life ; further description of person is unnecessary, as both have already been described. One was Lieutenant Baracco, the other Campobello, the Lazzaroni ; the latter's half-naked, but picturesque attire, was laid aside ; he was very shabbily dressed, in the same common dress as the Italian organ-grinders. He looked thin and haggard, unshaved and savage. We take up their conversation in the middle, for they had been conversing some time before we called our readers' attention to them.

" Then we can go back at once ? " said the ci-devant Lazzaroni ; " this life, in this cursed climate, is killing."

" Yes," returned Baracco, " we can return : the French are now masters of all Italy. But have you so little of the Italian left in you as to leave him who has baulked our fortunes and driven us into this Babylon of a city, in the pride of his prosperity ? "

" What can we do ? " growled the Lazzaroni ; " he is out of my reach, here ; for you can't use your knife with any chance of escape. They would hang you like a dog. He has a charmed life, I'll swear to it; not even the Malochia affects him. You failed to strike him at Palermo, and struck a woman instead; he's charmed, I tell you."

" Stuff and nonsense ! " uttered Baracco, fiercely ; " you're a weak fool to believe in such mummery. The man I employed to strike him down in Palermo, at the Princess's fête, aimed at home and well; but who was to imagine that a love-sick woman would sacrifice herself to save him?"

"Then, again," retorted Campobello, "how did he find out that there were fifty men entered on board his ship sworn to take his life? I tell you he has a charmed life."

"Try a pistol-ball within an inch of his head, and you will find out the inefficacy of the charm that protects his life."

"Easy to talk, by St. Januarius," said the Lazzaroni. "Who's to get within an inch of his head, and have a chance of escape? I want to go back to Naples. I was a cursed fool to leave the country; but I listened to your persuasions."

"You are ungrateful," exclaimed Baracco, fiercely. "Did I not, at great personal risk, save your life, when I found out, by this De Courcy's manner, on board the Serena, that we were discovered? Did I not give you money sufficient to effect your escape, and pay you and your daughter's passage to England?"

"I allow all that," answered the Lazzaroni; "but would it not have been better to have escaped into any part of Italy, where the French were, than into this infernal country, where one is expected to work like a dog to earn a mouthful of bread?"

"There was no time for choice," returned Baracco; "the English brig was on the point of sailing: an hour's delay would have placed you in the power of Acton, who would have had you executed in twenty-four hours. Our conspiracy was blown—some traitor betrayed us."

"Then why did not you," growled the Italian, "embark in the same ship, if the danger was so great?"

"Because," returned Baracco, savagely, "my love of revenge was stronger than my love of life. I had more means at hand of disguising myself than you had. You were the man they most wished to secure—for they feared your comrades. I got into a boat, dressed as a sailor, and went to Palermo with the determination of taking my enemy's life. He has baulked me in everything; superseded me; deprived me of the king's favour—he, a mere boy, and because he happened to triumph where I failed. From that time I resolved to be revenged. I might have killed him, it is true, long before, in the confusion of boarding an enemy's ship; but that would have been a poor revenge. I wished a deeper one than the mere loss of life. I trusted to poison his existence; to baulk his schemes; make him wretched—and I did so; but another sought his life in Genoa; I left that to chance, but he escaped that also. I remained hid in Palermo a few days, and then entered as a common sailor on board a Sicilian barque bound for London, which was to sail in a few days. In the meantime I heard

that this minion of Fortune was the accepted lover of the
Princess of Sorento. Thus, despite all my efforts, he was still
Fortune's favourite. Maddened by envy at his success, and my
own outcast state, I resolved to have him assassinated at a
fête at the Princess of Sorento's—I need not tell you how easy
it is to find a stiletto in Palermo—but again I failed ; and so
desperate was the pursuit after the assassin, that I was too
glad the vessel I was in sailed the following night. Whether
they have secured the man I bribed to strike the blow or not I
cannot say—neither do I care. We must now, however, back
to Naples; by this time King Ferdinand is driven from his
kingdom, and we shall undoubtedly regain our former station.
You, at the head of your brethren, may strike a blow that will
place you in a position you failed to attain, owing to this same
De Courcy; and all I require of you now is, to revenge us
both before we leave this country. I will supply you with
funds, for I have picked up a goodly sum by my skill at
play."

"All this is very well," replied Campobello, "and I am just
as anxious for revenge as you are. It was that fool of a girl of
mine who shrieked, seeing me about to strike this Englishman
with my knife, on the night of the fête in Naples—and that
shriek caused him to turn suddenly round, by which means he
avoided the blow ; but for that he would not require our assistance now to rid him of life—but how is he to be got at, that is
with safety to ourselves ? Let me see my way, and I am
willing enough."

"But what the dence did this daughter of yours shriek for ?"
demanded Baracco. "She ought to be well accustomed to see
knives drawn ?"

"Well, per bacco, who can say ; the girl declares she could
not help it. She got frightened at seeing me run such a risk
in the public streets. In my passion I struck her to the
ground ; however, she's useful to me. She's handsome, plays
the tambourine, and dances well ; and picks up enough in the
streets, with one of those organ-men, to whom I hire her, to
keep me alive in this horrid climate ; for as to work, I would
rather die than do that."

"Well, listen now, and I will inform you how you may get
at our enemy without any risk to yourself. But first, let me
tell you, the vessel that will take us to Messina sails in ten
days ; I will arrange for you and your daughter's passage.
You must not, however, remain an hour more than you can
help in Messina; get a passage to Naples at once, which will
be in the hands of the French long before you reach it."

"But, hark you, Signor Baracco," interrupted the Lazzaroni, "you need not take a berth for the girl ; I do not intend
taking her back to Naples. I'm offered a good sum for her by

my comrade here, and I'll take it. She will be in my way; and she'll do well enough here."

"I think you are right. You will get rid of a burden, and also, I suspect, a spy on your actions."

"Ah! by St. Januarius, if I thought that," exclaimed Campobello, savagely, turning round and gazing earnestly at the ragged curtain, but the head was drawn in, and not a sound was to be heard, "I would cut her throat. She is no child of mine, as far as that goes. I was offered fifty ducats, by a woman, one night, in the streets of Naples, if I would take the child and rear it; it was then two years old. By St. Januarius, I thought that as good a night's work as ever fell to my lot; it costs us nothing, signor, you know, to rear our children. So I took the child and the fifty ducats, and never thought more of the affair. I gave her the run of the streets, and called her my daughter; but do you know, she turned out a strange girl."

"How so?" demanded Guiseppe Baracco, looking a little surprised.

"Why, you see, when the woman gave me the child, the only question I asked her was, 'Has the child a name?' 'Call her Magdalene, if you like,' said the female, and she walked off, quite coolly; so I called her Magdalene. As she grew up she took queer freaks in her head, avoided the other children, took to holes and corners by herself. When nine or ten years old, she got herself taught to read and write by the nuns of Santa Catarina, who take in the children of the poor, to make singers of them, if they have good voices. Magdalene had a first-rate voice, and was very pretty; the nuns liked her, and taught her to sing, and to play on the organ, and to do many things. I did not find it all out for a long time—not till she was fourteen or fifteen, when they wanted her to leave me, and then I threatened to break every bone in her carcase if she ever went to the convent again."

"All this may be very true and curious," interrupted Guiseppe Baracco, "but it has nothing to do with what we have on hand?"

"Yes, but it may be of consequence to me," returned Campobello, "and I will tell you how. When Magdalene was about four years old I made acquaintance with a sbirri, who frequently came amongst us to hunt for certain characters, to whom we often gave shelter; for you know we possess some queer hiding-places in Naples. This man came one day to me. 'Antonio,' says he to me,' 'did you ever meet or see a woman calling herself Magdalene Caracci amongst you?' The name of Magdalene struck me, so I inquired, 'What is she, a thief?' 'Well,' replied the sbirri, 'you may call her a thief if you like. She stole a child some two years ago from an English Milor, and it is known she was in Naples with the child.'"

"What the devil kind of a story are you trumping up now?" interrupted Baracco, impatiently, "I cannot stay here all night listening to what does not concern me ;" and, rising from his seat, he added, "I will be here to-morrow night at eleven o'clock, and if you intend to do this job, say so; if not I leave you to your own resources. I will show you to-morrow night where it may be accomplished safely, and with a certainty of success. Our enemy lives in a house in St. James's-street, No. 7 ; if you watch you can see him go out every day, but to-morrow I will make my plan clear to you."

"Benissimo," answered Campobello, "I will hear your plan to-morrow night, but I think you might have listened patiently to what I had to say. Perhaps there is money to be had now I am in England, for this girl is the child stolen by Magdalene Caracci, I am sure. Now, if I had a knowledge of the language——"

"Per bacco, sell her, as you said, to your comrade—is not that making money by her? There, take a light, and let me out of this house."

CHAPTER XXVI.

HUGH DE COURCY was at breakfast the morning following the conversation related in our last chapter, held in a chamber in a house at the back of Leicester-square, between Guiseppe Baracco and Campobello, the Lazzaroni, when his attendant William entered the room, saying, in a hesitating tone, "There's a very strange girl below, sir; she insists upon seeing you, sir. I told her if she was begging I would give give her something, for she is an Italian, sir. But she began to cry, pushed back the shilling I offered her, and declared she would not go till she had seen you."

De Courcy looked up in surprise. "What is she like, William, and how old is she ?"

"A very young girl, sir—eighteen or nineteen, perhaps—she's very handsome, and dressed like a player, sir ; one of the street-organ singers."

"Very curious," muttered our hero ; "however, show her into the parlour, and I will go down and see what she wants."

William retired, and shortly after his master descended from the breakfast-room, and, opening the parlour-door, entered. Standing in the middle of the room was the young girl, with her hands clasped, and her large, dark, and certainly very beautiful eyes, fixed with eagerness in their expression on the door. The moment she beheld De Courcy she darted forward, fell upon her knees, and shaking back the long ringlets of splendid hair that fell over her features, she exclaimed in Italian, "Oh, signor, signor! will you save a poor girl from ruin who once saved your life, and who is come to do so again?"

De Courcy was amazed. He recognized at once the beautiful face that gazed up into his with an expression of such intense anxiety that he was greatly moved.

"Campobello's daughter, and in England?" exclaimed De Courcy, raising her, and making her sit down; "this is indeed surprising."

The Italian kept her hands over her features for several moments, sobbing audibly.

"Do not give way to such grief, my poor girl," continued our hero, kindly, "I owe you too much not to afford you all the protection in my power. Only let me know how you came to be in England, and what I can do for you, and how you discovered my residence."

Magdalene was greatly agitated; she trembled violently, and grew exceedingly pale, but recovering, reassured by the kind tone and words of De Courcy, she answered, "I fear, signor, you will think me bold and rash to intrude upon you; but indeed, indeed," and she clasped her hands tightly together, "my purpose is to warn you against the designs of a man calling himself Baracco, and an Italian Lazzaroni named Campobello."

"Baracco!" repeated De Courcy, with a start of exceeding surprise, "Guiseppe Baracco in England, and your father also?"

"Oh, no, signor, thanks to the blessed Madonna, he is not my father."

"Indeed!" said our hero, surprised, "how is that? but pray tell me how you came to England, and why you are in company with Guiseppe Baracco."

"We did not come in company with him, signor," and she proceeded to relate how she and the Lazzaroni, Campobello, came in a ship to London, and how the Lazzaroni met some of his countrymen, and made her play and sing in the streets to support him, till they met the Signor Baracco, he having also fled to England. She then described their lodging-house at the back of Leicester-square, and all the misery and wretchedness she had endured in being subject to the loose, brutal treatment of the Italian street musician. "I have carried this dagger about me, signor," continued the poor girl, trembling, as she showed De Courcy a small poniard she kept concealed under her bodice, "and I vowed I would kill myself if anyone touched me. Ah, Madonna, what I have suffered! but now, thanks to the Virgin, I know I am not

that savage Campobello's child, and I will work till I die to
earn a livelihood free from insult!"

"My poor girl," exclaimed De Courcy, greatly surprised at
the manner and language of the Italian girl, so widely different
from what he expected, "you shall not be exposed again to
such a life; I will take care of that. Now tell me all you
heard these men Campobello and Guiseppe Baracco say."

"I was lying awake, signor," answered the girl, "fretting
my heart sick at the life I was forced to lead—for I cannot
speak one word of English—when the Signor Baracco came
into the room, and he and Campobello sat down, out of
hearing of the other men, close by the ragged curtain that hid
me. I could not at first hear what they said—neither, indeed,
did I care—till I heard your name mentioned ; then I looked
cautiously out, and perceiving they had their backs to me, I
listened intently. Signor Baracco was persuading Campobello to assassinate you before they left England, to return to
Naples. Campobello was afraid to do so, in this country:
then I heard Signor Baracco say he had tried to have you
assassinated in Palermo, but that some princess was stabbed
instead of you. Campobello then said he was going to sell me
to the brutal organ-player to whom he hired me by the day ;
for that I was not his child. 'How is that?' inquired Signor
Baracco. 'Why, you see,' answered Campobello, 'one night,
in the streets a woman offered me fifty ducats if I would
take a child, two, or perhaps three years old, and rear it. It
was too good an offer to refuse; so I took the child, and the
woman gave me the fifty ducats. I asked her what the child's
name was, and she said, Magdalene——"

At that name De Courcy started; a strange feeling of
increased interest came over him; and, with much kindness of
manner, he said, "Was there no other name, my good girl,
attached to Magdalene?"

"No, signor," replied the girl, venturing to raise her fine
eyes to our hero's face with a look of surprise; "but Campobello said, about two years after he had taken the care of me,
one of the Neapolitan sbirri, who knew him, came to ask him
if a woman who stole a child from a rich Milor Inglese, in
Genoa——"

"Good God!" exclaimed De Courcy, "what is this you
say? you fill my mind with vague surmises and amazement.
Occurrences flash into my memory which may turn out of most
material consequence to you. Pray tell me more of this
woman who stole the child. Did you hear her name?"

"Yes, signor;" returned the girl, greatly agitated, "yes ;
the sbirri said her name was Magdalene Caracci."

"My God, how strange!" murmured De Courcy, and then
he demanded, aloud, "What more?"

" Only signor," answered the Italian, that Campobello said he was certain I was the child who had been stolen by Magdalene Caracci."

De Courcy was bewildered : if such were the case, the poor, ill-used, cruelly-treated girl before him was the daughter of Sir Charles Wharton.

" My poor child," he observed, "what you tell me fills my mind with the most profound astonishment; that woman, Magdalene Caracci, has been sought after for years by a gentleman I know, who lost his only daughter in the way you say. Be this as it may, you shall never want a protector. The Almighty, in a strange way, inexplicable to us, has perhaps given a clue to a mystery long sought to be cleared up. I must secure the person of Campobello ; but first, I will place you under the care of a most kind person, the mistress of this house. She is a widow, and has two daughters."

" But, signor, recollect," interrupted the girl, anxiously, " recollect your life will be attempted. Oh, Madonna ! if——"

" Nay, Magdalene, I trouble little about the machinations of two Italians in such a country as this. What you have just told me is of vital importance, not only to yourself, but to me also. I will not lose one moment. Stay you here, whilst I go and speak with Mrs, Mason."

Magdalene, with the tears flowing from her eyes, caught his hand, and, despite his efforts, pressed it passionately to her lips, and then sat down, hiding her face.

The young man, in his heart, pitied the poor deserted girl, and blessed that Providence which had caused her to overhear the despicable villain who so wantonly desired to barter away both body and soul. With the kindness and affection of a brother—for he almost felt satisfied she was either the lost child or niece of Sir Charles Wharton—our hero soothed the wounded spirit of the excited Magdalene, and leaving her more calm and re-assured, left the room ; and, proceeding along the hall, tapped at the door of the back parlour. On being told to come in, he turned the handle, and entered. His landlady, Mrs. Mason, and her youngest daughter, were taking breakfast ; they jumped up, with a look of surprise, anxious to know what their handsome and distinguished lodger could require at that rather early hour.

"Pray do not disturb yourself, Mrs. Mason," said the young man ; " pray both of you sit down ; and allow me to sit also," he added, taking a chair himself. " I have a favour to request of you, Mrs. Mason, which, if you grant, will greatly oblige me."

"Anything I can do, Captain De Courcy, to oblige," replied Mrs. Mason, eagerly, "you may depend on my doing."

"Thank you, Mrs. Mason," returned our hero; "I felt sure you would."

"There is a young girl, an Italian," pursued De Courcy, "concerning whose safety and welfare I am exceedingly anxious. I cannot explain circumstances at present to your satisfaction; all I can say is, that I believe her to be the child of an English gentleman of fortune, stolen in her infancy; but, till I can learn more, it is my intention to place her under the care of Sir Charles Wharton and his daughter."

Mrs. Mason's serious countenance changed at once, and she immediately said, "Dear me, how very strange, count! but I shall be most happy to take charge of her; where is the young lady?"

"She is in your front parlour, Mrs. Mason; but you must not be surprised at seeing her dressed in a somewhat theatrical style; in fact, the unfortunate girl has been forced to earn her existence as a street-dancer or tambourine-player."

"Dear me," exclaimed both mother and daughter, looking at each other; but as Mrs. Mason was in reality an excellent and very respectable woman, and having the most profound respect for a lodger who paid her six guineas a week for her house, and who was visited by the nobility, she at once added, "I have the utmost reliance on your word, Count De Courcy; therefore you may depend I will show this poor girl every kindness."

"I feel obliged, Mrs. Mason, by you acceding to my request; it will only be for a few days—till Sir Charles Wharton returns to town. She must on no account go outside the house, or she may again be entrapped."

Taking out his purse, he put a ten-pound note on the table, requesting Mrs. Mason to purchase a few articles of proper attire becoming a young lady.

"The worst of it is," said our hero, "she does not speak one word of English."

"That is awkward, count," observed Mrs. Mason; "but your attendant, Mr. Atkins, speaks Italian."

"True, William can do so after a fashion," replied the gentleman; "quite enough, at all events, for a few days."

Mrs. Mason then accompanied her lodger to the parlour. Poor Magdalene rose up, her cheeks crimson with shame; and as she looked at her short dress and tawdry attire, her eyes filled with tears as they met the surprised glance of Mrs. Mason, who exclaimed,—

"Bless me, what a beautiful girl! but what a dress—poor thing!" Then, taking her by the hand, she addressed to her many kind words, but which, of course, were unintelligible to Magdalene. De Courcy, however, repeated them to her, and the look and manner of Mrs. Mason reassured the young girl, who, after a few words with our hero, begging him to be on his guard, for his two enemies would surely watch for an opportunity to injure him, she followed our hero's landlady into her own part of the house.

De Courcy then returned to his own room, and, throwing himself into a chair, began to reflect on this strange and unexpected meeting with Magdalene, and to devise the manner in which he should communicate with Sir Charles Wharton. All of a sudden he recollected Térese Garetti, who was at Lady Hasarel's, and, jumping up, he rang the bell ; and on William making his appearance, he desired him to pay every attention to the Italian girl left under Mrs. Mason's care, and to notice, also, with particular attention, any street musicians —Italians—should he see any come about the house, and keep a keen eye upon them.

William promised to observe with the strictest attention his master's request, and left the room, his mind filled with an intense curiosity concerning the Italian girl thus strangely introduced into the house, and about whom his master was so particular.

CHAPTER XXVII.

FINISHING his toilette, Hugh De Courcy took his hat, left his lodgings, and proceeded up St. James's-street. As he came out a man, having the features and manner of a foreigner, who was standing under a doorway on the opposite side of the street, came forward, and looked keenly up the street after our hero, muttering some words to himself with a very savage expression of countenance. This man, in years about four or five-and-thirty, had a remarkably repulsive countenance, was about the middle height, strongly built, and shabbily dressed. Casting a look over at the handsome house De Courcy had left, he walked up the street into Piccadilly, and then, proceeding at a rapid pace, turned down Oxenden-street, and approached another Italian, with a barrel-organ, having a number of little figures dancing to a most irregular tune on its front, and holding a long string, to the end of which was attached a monkey, who, with wonderful agility, climbed up the spouts to the windows, with a little can in his paw, soliciting a few coppers for his master.

The man came up to the organ-grinder, who, however, kept turning away at his instrument with increased vigour, " I've tracked the girl," said he, to his comrade, "Campobello was right : she has overheard what he and that comrade of his were saying last night, for she has got into No. 7, St. James's-street. Curse the slut ! " he added, savagely; "if I have to set the house on fire I will have her out of it ! "

"Don't be rash, Jacomo, don't be rash," returned the owner of the monkey, who just then descended from a drawing-room window, with the sum of three-halfpence in his tin can.

"You are not in Italy, amico; recollect that. Go to Campobello, at the corner of Oxford-street; he is waiting for you. But don't be rash; we'll nab her yet. She's worth the money you agreed to give for her. Una Bella regazza, sensa dubia," and, changing the tune, he ground away at "Partant pour la Syrie."

The man called Jacomo ground his teeth, instead of an organ, with rage, and continued his way to Oxford-street. Under an archway, within a few doors of the corner, stood the Lazzaroni Campobello. This man, who was, a month or two back, so strong, powerful, and audacious—proud of his rule over more than five thousand of his brethren, who, at his beck, were ready to commit the most fearful excesses—accustomed from childhood to bask in the sun, or lie lazily in the shade, the "Dolce fa niente" of a Lazzaroni's life, roused into life only on holidays and festâs, and then only to decorate his scanty attire with a few gaudy ribbons, saunter through the gay Toledo, and gratify his appetite, and that of his female companion, with bread and jam, over which stewed snails were spread, that delectable mess washed down with aqua gelata, and then, when fatigued, stretch himself beneath a colonnade or portico of a palace, or the sheltered side of a church wall—and thus through life from the cradle to the grave—this man, Campobello, was now gaunt, and thin, and bony; his attire, never intended for him, fitted him badly; his face was unshaven, and his long lank black hair was hanging down on his shoulders. There was a look of savage misery about the man very remarkable.

Jacomo, the Italian who was to purchase Magdalene, walked up to Campobello, and both retired deeper into the lane.

"Well, have you tracked the ——— girl?" inquired the Lazzaroni, with a fierce oath.

"Yes," returned Jacomo, "I tracked her. I was afraid to seize her in the street in broad day, but I stuck close to her heels. She went right to No. 7, St. James's-street, and there she staid. I saw that tall, handsome man you call the Count De Courcy afterwards come out from the house; but no signs of the girl."

"Curse him! what can he keep the girl for?" cried Campobello. "I'll fire the house this night, and have her out."

"So I said," remarked Jacomo, "but Manzani laughed at me."

"Let him laugh," fiercely returned Campobello, "he's a coward. We will fire the house to-night, and in the confusion seize upon her, or stop that meddling, cursed Englishman. She's a handsome girl; perhaps he's struck with her."

"Then he shall know the length of my knife," interrupted Jacomo, with a frightful grimace; "but how is it possible to fire such a house as that, and in such a street?"

"Easy enough," replied Campobello, "if you have but the spirit to attempt it; the streets are poorly lighted, * only a few old, lazy, sleepy watchmen guard the houses during the night. I'll try it, if I burn the whole street; ah! if I could burn the whole city—they are heretics—it would be a good job."

Jacomo grinned savagely; he was desperately enamoured of Magdalene, and thought, if left with him, and her supposed father gone out of the country, he could force the wretched girl to be worse than his slave.

All the fierce passions of the Italian were roused: knowing nothing of De Courcy or of Magdalene, he at once supposed that the intentions of our hero in detaining her were evil.

"But how is it possible," he inquired, "to set a house on fire without getting into it?"

"Easy enough," answered Campobello, whom misery and savage revenge made reckless of life; "bore a hole with a large gimlet in the street door, put a thin tin tube through it, pour a subtle spirit I know of through the tube, and then set fire to it by a long thin lighted wax cord."

"But the spirit will run over the hall," said Jacomo.

"So much the better; the more it spreads the greater the chance of the house catching fire; it's sure to [form a pool somewhere; besides, I have tried the plan before now—it won't fail."

"It will take time to bore the hole," observed Jacomo, "and the watchman——"

"Tut, man, one will watch; such projects much depend on luck; the hour must be a late one. It will be a glorious revenge."

"Where is your comrade of last night?" asked Jacomo, who, as he began to cool, also began to get frightened, and to reflect how, if it was possible to escape detection after such a crime, he could ever detain the girl, who would be sure to betray him.

"You are hesitating," said Campobello, with a look of scorn and savage ferocity.

"Why, you see, you intend to fly the country in a day or two——"

"There, that's enough," fiercely interrupted the Lazzaroni, "I will not league with a cowardly fool like you. Curse the girl! let her take her chance:" and without another word he walked out of the lane.

He had scarcely got into the street when two police-officers seized him by the collar, saying, "You are an Italian; no

* No gas at this period.

O

resistance ; you are our prisoner.   Campobello was livid with rage.

" There's another rascal down the lane," said William Atkins, the Count De Courcy's attendant ; " I saw two of them go into the court."

A handcuff was in two minutes slipped over Campobello's wrists ; a crowd, as usual, had collected ; and two more police-officers came up, and then the first ran down the lane and captured Jacomo, who had no means of retreat, and who was too cowardly to attempt a rush through the crowd. The Italians were conveyed to Bow-street, and locked up till the appearance of the Count De Courcy ; awaiting which, we will account to our readers for the sudden capture of the Italians.

William Atkins, the personal attendant of the Count De Courcy, was an extremely shrewd, clever valet, and one who had his wits about him. Well aware that, whilst residing in Naples, his master's life had been attempted on the night of the fête, by the Lazzaroni Campobello, whose person was well known to him, and having his curiosity greatly raised by the appearance of Magdalene, and his master's great interest in her, as well as the precise instructions he had received, he resolved to keep a keen eye upon any Italian musician loitering about the street near the house ; at once setting it down in his own mind that some fresh attempt was about to be made on the count's life.

William was looking out of the window as his master left the house, and his quick glance detected the figure of the man opposite gazing after him.

" That's an Italian," muttered William ; " I'll watch that fellow : " so bolting down stairs, he seized his hat, and was rushing out, when Mrs. Mason called from the parlour-door, " Mr. Atkins, please come here one moment."

William, with his head full of the Italian, fancied himself in Italy ; so he answered hastily, " Saluto, saluto, signora ;" and off he bolted.

" Bless me," said Mrs. Mason to her daughter, " what's that he said ? he has gone off like a madman."

William, on getting into the street, caught sight of the Italian going towards Piccadilly, and followed him : the man turned to the right, and William was about to turn also, when he perceived his master standing at the corner of the Bath Hotel, talking to a police-officer : he ran to him, and told him that he was following a very suspicious-looking Italian, who had been evidently watching the house in St. James's-street.

" Then do you go with my attendant," said De Courcy, addressing the police-officer, " and see where the fellow goes ; you may thus stumble on this Campobello."

"Very good, sir," replied the police-officer, who was in plain clothes.

"Try and regain sight of the Italian; never mind me. I will keep you in sight," said the policeman, addressing William.

"By Jove, I'm afraid I have lost him!" cried William, hastening along Piccadilly. But just as he came up to Oxenden-street, he heard the grinding of the organ, and looking down the street, he perceived the very man he had lost talking to the man with the organ and the monkey; presently the same man came up the street again, and proceeded, as the reader knows, towards Oxford-street. William easily kept him in sight, till he came to the archway, where stood Campobello.

One look into the remarkable countenance of Campobello was sufficient for William—he remembered him on the instant; and he gazed eagerly round for the policeman. On the opposite side of the street he beheld him with another, also in plain clothes; at a sign, they at once crossed over, and the policeman said, "All right; they are in a net, they cannot escape:" and thus they were both captured.

In the meantime De Courcy had stopped, on his way to Lady Hasarel's, to speak to the police-officer he had met, and explain to him his wish to secure the person of the Italian Campobello, who lodged in a certain house at the back of Leicester-square.

"I know the house, sir," said the police-officer; "Italian street-musicians lodge there."

Our hero was just describing the person of Campobello, when his valet, William, came up.

After the departure of the police-officer, De Courcy proceeded to Belgrave-square, and knocking at Lady Hasarel's, was at once shown by the servant into the drawing-room, where he was immediately joined by Térese Garetti.

The truly kind-hearted Italian was rejoiced to see him. "I gave orders," she observed, "in case you called, that you should be shown up-stairs, for her ladyship has gone to Windsor, but will be back to-morrow : I was wishing to see you, to tell you that Sir Charles Wharton and your ladye-love arrived late last night, and that I go home—I call being with Mary, home—to-morrow."

"I am rejoiced, Térese," observed De Courcy, who felt the affection of, and was received by the fair Genoese as a brother: "I am rejoiced at Sir Charles's arrival, for a most singular and extraordinary circumstance occurred this morning, which will require my immediate communication with him."

"Good gracious!" exclaimed Terese, with some anxiety,

though she readily surmised, by our hero's countenance, that nothing serious or of evil importance had occurred.

De Courcy at once explained what had happened, and his great desire to let Sir Charles Wharton know all about it, in case they succeeded in securing the person of Campobello.

" What an extraordinary occurrence! " cried Térese ; " the unfortunate girl, poor soul, what she must have suffered! If you will accompany me, I will go at once and bring her here. She must be the baronet's niece or daughter ; what a perplexing mystery ! "

" I think, till we communicate with Sir Charles," returned our hero, pleased to see so much kindness of heart and carelessness of the strict rules of English society in Térese's words and manners, so very different from that to which she was accustomed, " we had better leave Magdalene with my good-natured landlady, Mrs. Mason."

" Well, on second thoughts, I also think so ; then our best plan will be to write to Sir Charles a short note, and appoint a meeting at your residence."

After a moment's consideration, De Courcy agreed to this method of introduction. So Térese sat down and wrote the note, briefly stating particulars, and requesting Sir Charles to send back word by the messenger what hour would be convenient to him to meet Captain De Courcy. A domestic was then summoned, and the letter despatched.

" Now, do tell me, Captain De Courcy," exclaimed Térese, " for I am, as you may well suppose, dying with curiosity, what kind of girl this poor Magdalene is : for whether or not she turns out niece or daughter of Sir Charles Wharton, she must be taken care of, and not be forced again into the frightful position from which she is now, thank goodness! snatched."

" You are a kind, generous girl," replied De Courcy, warmly, " and I trust, when you surrender that good heart into the keeping, of some happy lover, he may, as assuredly he will, appreciate the treasure he will get."

Térese laughed gaily, saying, as she shook her head, " Do you want me, count, to make myself miserable ? I am quite heart-whole now—free as air ; and really, to judge by the effect the little god Cupid has had upon some very intimate friends of mine, I should prefer dying an old maid."

A domestic here entered the room, to inform our hero that his attendant, Mr. Atkins, wished particularly to see him.

" Oh, let him come up," entreated Térese ; " I know he must have something to tell you about those Italian musicians."

William soon made his appearance. " I see by your coun-

tenance, William, that you have been successful in some measure," said De Courcy.

" Yes, sir," replied the valet, with a very self-satisfied look;
" we have laid hands on the very man you wished to secure :
we have the Lazzaroni Campobello in custody."

" You are a clever fellow, William," observed De Courcy,
highly pleased : " what have you done with him ? "

" Lodged him comfortably, sir, with his comrade, in Bow-
street. You will have to go there, sir, before three o'clock—so
the police-officer bade me inform you."

Just then a carriage drew up to the door, and a loud aristocratic summons announced a visitor of importance. Térese,
casting a glance out of the window, exclaimed, " Ah ! this is
the baronet's carriage ; he is come himself. I thought he
would."

De Courcy felt a slight degree of agitation at the prospect
of meeting with his beloved Mary's uncle : but there was little
time for thought, for the door opened and Sir Charles Wharton
entered the room, with a hasty step and a somewhat eager,
agitated manner : without any hesitation, and with a warmth
and vivacity highly gratifying to our hero, he held out his
hand, saying, " I need no introduction to Count De Courcy ;
and believe me," continued the baronet, " I take your hand
with the feelings and affection of a father."

De Courcy's cheek flushed with excitement and pleasure as
he warmly returned the pressure of the baronet's hand, saying,
he felt more than he could express at the kindness of Sir
Charles, whom he could not meet as a stranger, for he had
long looked forward to the period of their acquaintance with
exceeding pleasure.

" My fair friend here," said Sir Charles, taking Térese's
hand and kissing it with all the gallantry of the old school,
" will, I know, excuse our forgetfulness of her presence; but
now let me. I pray you, hear more fully of this strange meeting with, perhaps, my long-lost daughter or niece, and what
steps you think we ought to take in this affair. Mary is
warmly interested, and anxious beyond measure."

At the name of Mary, De Courcy felt an emotion of exceeding pleasure. Sir Charles spoke with so much warmth, and in
so affectionate a tone, that it removed from our hero's mind
any cause of restraint or reserve in his conversation with the
baronet. He talked to him as if he had known him for
months ; and the baronet himself, strongly prepossessed in
his favour, and struck with his fine noble figure and handsome
features, already felt proud of his beloved Mary's choice.

" Our best plan," observed our hero, after some further
explanations respecting Campobello and his own meeting with
Magdalene, which put the baronet more *au fait* to the matter

in hand—"our best plan will be to work on the fears of this ruffian Campobello. I have, in reality, no charge against either of those men now in custody, without bringing forward Magdalene and making things public. His attempting my life in a foreign country can only be dealt with in the place where the act was attempted. Therefore I will threaten him by avowing my intention of conveying him on board my ship, on a charge of murder, and taking him to Naples, where he is sure to be tried and executed as a conspirator; but that, if he is willing to declare all he knows about Magdalene, and tell the truth, he and his comrade shall be set free, and Campobello himself receive a sum of money to enable him to live or seek an employment."

"I agree with you," returned Sir Charles; "that is our only plan of proceeding. Sir William ——, the chief magistrate at the Bow-street office, is my particular friend, and he, I am confident, will aid our views. It is now two o'clock; so let us proceed at once to Bow-street."

Taking leave of Térese, the baronet promising that he would take upon himself at once the care of Magdalene, no matter whether the result of their interview with Campobello was satisfactory or not, as there would always remain in his mind a conviction that this poor deserted girl was the missing child of his brother—the child whose fate he had felt such anxiety about, and had so vainly sought.

Entering the baronet's carriage they drove at once to Bow-street. On the way, Sir Charles remarked, " I am quite aware, Count De Courcy, of your affection for my dear child or niece, as the case may be ; of the mutual agreement between you when in Genoa, and of the strange way in which your engagement was broken off.

" Nay, my dear sir," continued the baronet, kindly, and laying his hand affectionately on that of our hero's, seeing that he was about to offer some explanation ; "we will drop the past now, and let us talk only of the future. You are aware how my poor Mary, to render my last moments easy—for recollect, I could not know that you and Mary would ever meet again—to render my mind easy, she sacrificed her feelings, and permitted herself to be contracted in marriage to the present Lord Umfreville. This contract still exists in name : for the sudden demise of the late lord interrupted for the time all intercourse between Mary and her intended husband. Lord Umfreville is a nobleman of the highest honour and integrity : he will, and does, admit that Mary was always averse, or even pained, by his attention ; and that she continually and most scrupulously avoided receiving the marked assiduities of any gentleman. Still you will admit that, for Mary's sake, who feels acutely her painful situation, no public or marked intercourse should take place between you in England, so as to attract observation and lead to remarks. It is supposed, amongst our friends and acquaintances, that Mary is to give her hand to Lord Umfreville; and, strange to say, it is the talk of the fashionable world that you, on your return to Italy, are to be united to the Princess of Sorento, who is allied to the royal family of Naples."

"My dear sir," interrupted De Courcy, with his cheeks flushed, and considerably excited, "you may believe me, such is not the case: by a strange coincidence in the history of Mary and myself, I was nearly, from accidental circumstances, and a misunderstanding of King Ferdinand, actually from gratitude—for the princess saved my life, risking her own at the same time—about to offer her my hand. The princess was aware, however, of my devoted affection for Miss Wharton, and in an interview I had with her the day before my departure for England, she released me from all obligation in fulfilling the king's wishes, stating, at the same time, with a noble generosity, that she could not think of accepting the hand of a man whose heart was devoted to another."

"How very extraordinary!" said Sir Charles, musingly; "your destinies seem so strangely similar; but how could this report have gone abroad of your intended marriage with the princess?—not that dear Mary ever bestowed a thought upon the subject—she gave no credit to it."

"She has a noble, generous, confiding heart," replied De Courcy, with deep emotion; "and if I am permitted ever to call her mine, a life's devotion will but feebly repay her confiding love and atone for my unworthiness——."

"No, Hugh, no," said the baronet, most affectionately; "you see I am becoming fatherly in my address; do not wrong yourself. You were hasty, but——. Ah, here we are!" the carriage stopped, and the conversation ceased.

CHAPTER XXVIII.

In a strong room in the police-office, in Bow-street, were locked up Campobello the Lazzaroni, and Jacomo Lorodi the organ-grinder. They were not handcuffed, for there was no fear of their effecting an escape out of the place in which they were confined.

"I wish I had cut that girl's throat seven years ago," said Campobello, savagely, as he paced the narrow limits of his cell; "here's a cursed mess she has got us into!"

"You into," retorted Jacomo, spitefully, "you may say. By St. Nicholas, I can't see what charge they can have against me! I offered to buy the girl of you, and, corpo de Juda! what's that to any one? I earn my bread honestly."

" Oh, very!" returned the Lazzaroni, with an oath ; "perhaps passing bad coin is termed an honest employment in
this country."

Jacomo looked savage as he said, "That's all the thanks
I get for showing you the way to earn a few shillings without
work. You will peach upon me, I suppose ; if you do, I'll
swear you proposed to fire St. James's-street."

"Villain! who proposed it first?" exclaimed Campobello,
in a rage, catching his comrade by the throat. The organ-
grinder cried out " Murder!" for Campobello was a powerful
and reckless villain : the door was unlocked, and in ran two
policemen.

" Well, you are a nice pair!" said one of the policemen,
" measuring each other's throats. Are you afraid our hemp
collars won't fit your Italian necks? Come, we must handcuff you if there's any more of this row."

Campobello did not understand a word of the polite speech
of the policeman ; Jacomo did ; he was now excited, and cried
fiercely, in his broken English, " What for I keep here? what
I do, lock up with this man to murder me?"

"Oh, don't be alarmed," replied the policeman, " console
yourself; if he does murder you he'll swing for it. But come
along with me," added the policeman to Jacomo, "there's a
gentleman wants to speak with your tall comrade. You can
go about your business, if you like ; we don't want you."

" What for you take me, then, like a thief? I no stole
nothing; I'll have de compensation," said Jacomo, getting on
the high horse.

"Oh, you will, will you?" exclaimed the policeman with a
very ominous laugh; "blow me if that ain't a swell!" and,
whispering a few words in the Italian's ear, a greenish hue
coloured his skin—pale he could not turn, but he looked
quite cooled, and slunk after the laughing policeman like
a cur.

He had hardly departed before Hugh De Courcy entered
the cell, and the policeman closed the door, leaving our hero
and the surprised Campobello together. The very first
thought of the Lazzaroni was to rush upon De Courcy and
choke him. A second look at the powerful, graceful, and
healthy man before him satisfied him that he would be a
child in his grasp. So, leaning against the wall with his arms
folded across his breast, and his bushy, wild eyebrows bent in
a dark frown, he waited till the man he now noted with the
ferocity of a wild beast should speak to him.

De Courcy looked calmly at the Lazzaroni for several
moments without uttering a word; his tall, gaunt form was
greatly reduced—he was almost emaciated ; his colour cada-
verous; he was killing himself with his savage, furious, and

bloodthirsty thoughts and reflections; they left him no rest by day or night.

"I am come here," said Hugh De Courcy, breaking the silence, "not for the purpose of punishing you for your dastardly attempt upon my life in Naples, nor for your scheme, concocted with that madman Baracco, of again attempting to assassinate me. I care nothing about your plans and projects so long as they are confined to myself. I will forgive you all, restore you to freedom, and provide you with sufficient means to maintain yourself till you find employment."

"And do you think I'll work?" interrupted the Lazzaroni, with a savage, hoarse laugh.

"That's as you please," returned De Courcy, calmly, "I shall not require your services. The question now is, whether you prefer being taken to Naples on board a man-of-war, to be tried by the laws of your country as a traitor and assassin, or to answer me, on your oath, the few questions I shall ask you concerning the poor girl Magdalene, whom you have acknowledged not to be your child."

"Maladetta, cursed be her name!" said the ruffian, in a burst of passion, "do your worst; I defy you! Sooner than gratify you in any one thing you desire, I would undergo the worst torture the imbecile Ferdinand could inflict. You have my answer; so spare your trouble, and let me breathe, for I choke in the same atmosphere with you."

"You are a miserable villain," returned De Courcy, "without one particle of human feeling in your wretched carcase. You have chosen your own doom—so let it be. I do not believe it is in your power to enlighten me on the subject I require, therefore I leave you to the bitterness of your own thoughts and reflections."

"Curse you!" muttered the hardened wretch, stamping with fury on the floor. "Oh, that I had my former strength! but even now," he added, working himself into a frenzy of passion, "I will strangle you or die;" and with a sudden spring he threw himself upon De Courcy, encircling him with his long arms, and, like a maniac, endeavouring to use his teeth. Disgusted and incensed, Hugh De Courcy grasped the wretch by the throat, tore him from his hold, and exerting his whole strength, hurled him back upon the floor with such force that he lay stunned. The noise brought two of the police-officers into the room, startled when they beheld our hero, with his face flushed with excitement, his coat torn from his arm, and Campobello lying stunned upon the floor.

"Good God, sir! has the villain assaulted you?"

"He was mad enough to do so," replied our hero, "and in self-defence I was forced to be rough with him."

The policeman lifted up the man just as he was opening his

eyes, when De Courcy left the room, and proceeded to the private chamber where he had left the baronet with Sir William ———.

"Good gracious!" exclaimed Sir Charles, "what has happened, count? has the villain attempted to assault you? Your coat is torn."

"He is a hardened wretch," answered our hero, "and it is quite impossible to get one word of information from him. Neither threats nor promises have the slightest effect upon him. I suppose, Sir William ———," he continued, "it will be necessary to procure an order from the Neapolitan ambassador for the transporting of this felon on board my ship? I will take him to Naples, and hand him over to the government; he is a man that ought not to be let loose amongst his fellow-men."

"As a foreigner, Count De Courcy, you will have to do as you say. I will take care he is carefully watched till you order his removal. He must be a most confirmed ruffian."

After some further unimportant conversation, the baronet and our hero took their leave of Sir William ———, thanking him for his courtesy and attention.

"This is a disappointment, Hugh," observed Sir Charles, as soon as the carriage drove off, the coachman being desired to proceed to No. 7, St. James's-street.

"In some respects it is, Sir Charles," returned De Courcy, "still I do not think the villain knows much more than Magdalene overheard."

"What kind of girl is the poor thing, reared as she has been?"

"She speaks remarkably well, and with great propriety," answered De Courcy; "in fact, her language and manner surprised me. My landlady remarked she was very handsome, though rather dark-complexioned—a brunette; but that may arise from her constant exposure in a warm climate; her eyes are beautiful, and reminded me forcibly of Miss Wharton's."

The baronet sighed. "I wish to God, Hugh, that I was relieved from this distressing mystery respecting this girl and my darling Mary; at all events, I must take Magdalene home with me; Mary is most anxious that she should be left under her care; she is very sanguine about their relationship. I feel myself a most pressing desire to see the poor girl."

"I think, Sir Charles, you will be even more surprised than you expect."

"But what do you intend to do respecting this Signor Baracco, who appears to me a much more dangerous man to have for an enemy than that Lazzaroni Campobello?"

"Not in such a country as England," was De Courcy's

reply ; " his machinations and schemes, and vows of vengeance, are not worth attending to."

" Do not be so confiding in our laws and in our regulations as to individual safety in this great overgrown metropolis," said the baronet ; " for gold you can procure the services of as bad a class of villains as in any other city in Europe ; and I am quite convinced as great crimes are committed in London as in any city on the continent : therefore, I pray you, be on your guard, and be not too confiding."

The carriage drew up at De Courcy's residence, and both gentlemen entered the house, and proceeded to our hero's drawing-room ; the latter desiring his valet to give his compliments to Mrs. Mason, and, if not disturbing her, he would wish to see her, and the young girl entrusted to her care.

William soon returned with the information " that Mrs. Mason was in the front parlour with the young person he mentioned."

William looked so mystified that both his master and Sir Charles observed it.

" You look bewildered, William," said the former ; " what has astonished you ? "

" Lord, sir, you will be quite as astonished as I am, when you see the young——." William seemed puzzled for a time, which his master perceiving, said, with a smile,—

" Why, what has happened to the young girl, that so surprises you, William ? "

" Why, sir, she's as fair as a lily, and this morning she was quite brown ; and besides, Mrs. Mason has dressed her in her daughter's best garments, and for the life of me, sir, I can't believe it's the same person, except for the eyes."

Sir Charles looked at De Courcy, remarking, with considerable emotion, " we are right in our conjectures ; let us go down."

" My dear Sir Charles, let me go first and speak to her ; the presence of a stranger, under the circumstances, might embarrass and unnerve her, for she is excitable to a degree."

" I think you are right, Hugh ; I am just as excitable myself. So do you go, and explain things to her, but not before Mrs. Mason ; let us keep this matter for a while to ourselves ; let her think you have procured in me a protector for the poor girl, in the hopes of finding out who she really is."

" I will do so, Sir Charles, it is decidedly the best plan : " so saying, Hugh De Courcy descended to the parlour.

On throwing open the door and advancing into the room, our hero stood positively bewildered, unable to believe the evidence of his sight. Mrs. Mason rose from the sofa on which she was sitting beside Magdalene : the poor girl herself made an effort to rise, but, quite overpowered by her feelings, which seemed completely to master her, she sank back on the sofa, and burst into tears.

That Hugh De Courcy should be surprised was no wonder. It was not possible for any human being to recognize in the fair and beautiful girl, apparelled so neatly and handsomely, with her luxuriant dark hair dressed and arranged after the mode of the English maidens,—the dingy, tawdry, theatrically-attired girl, with hair gathered behind, uncombed and neglected, —there was nothing left but the large, liquid, dark eyes to recall the Lazzaroni girl, Magdalene. But that which struck De Courcy with the astonishment he evinced, was the striking likeness of Magdalene to Mary Wharton—it was impossible not to see it; it was too evident, in features, eyes, look: for the instant, De Courcy could almost have vowed he beheld his own Mary.

"You are astonished, count," said Mrs. Mason, looking quite pleased at her own handiwork; "I am amazed myself; the poor girl's skin was stained, and it's not half off yet. Oh! I am quite sure she was stolen from some high family; though I cannot understand a word she says; but she is so loving and so grateful, I have taken quite a fancy to her."

"In truth, I am astonished, Mrs. Mason," said our hero, sitting down beside Magdalene, who made an effort to rise to her feet, blushing and trembling with excitement at her novel situation; but De Courcy took her hand and gently reseated her, speaking to her in her own language, entreating her not to be so agitated and excitable, "for," continued De Courcy, "I have procured for you a kind, generous, and noble protector, in whose beautiful daughter you will find a sister."

The hand De Courcy held trembled like an aspen leaf.

Mrs. Mason very judiciously left the room: she certainly could not understand what the young couple were saying, therefore she felt herself " de trop."

"Ah, signor!" cried Magdalene, "how can I ever show my gratitude to you for releasing me from a life of degradation— to which I submitted solely because I thought it my duty to support a father? and, God help me! not speaking a word of the language, frightened by threats and ill-usage, I did that which was killing me, seeing no way of escaping."

"My poor girl," said De Courcy, "you have suffered much indeed, but all that is now over—and it is quite possible you may yet be restored to your natural guardians. In Sir Charles Wharton, who now undertakes to protect you, you may find a relative."

Magdalene started, and clasping her hands, exclaimed, "Ah, Madonna, can that blessing be possible?" and snatching up De Courcy's hand, she kissed it, and covered it with her tears

"You must conquer this emotion, Magdalene," observed our hero, affectionately; "you surprise me altogether; where have you learned the language you use, and your manner?"

Magdalene's cheeks were crimson. "Another time I will tell you everything, signor; but do not think, I pray you, that all my time was passed in the streets of Naples. Ah, no; the Madonna raised up to me a protector even there, and saved both soul and body." The girl raised her eyes to heaven, her hands clasped, and her lips moving in a prayer of thankfulness, whilst De Courcy, as he gazed upon her, thought that, excepting Mary's, he had never beheld so beautiful and so sweet a countenance.

"I will now, Magdalene," said our hero, "introduce your generous protector to you, and he will take you to his house, and there you will see his kind-hearted and beautiful daughter, whom you will love as a sister—for she is as good and pure as she is lovely."

Magdalene raised her liquid eyes to De Courcy's features; her cheek was pale, and for the first time her voice was steady and calm, as she said, "And this beautiful young lady, signor, you speak of; she is very dear to you, is she not?"

De Courcy answered, calmly and seriously, "She is dearer to me than life itself."

"Then I will love her with my whole heart and soul, and give my life, if necessary, to make her happy," said Magdalene, passionately, and then her eyes were cast down, and bent fixedly upon the carpet.

De Courcy rose from the sofa, looking grave and disturbed; and saying, "I will go for Sir Charles Wharton," left the room.

CHAPTER XXIX.

"Now tell me, dear Magdalene," said Mary Wharton, to the young ci-devant Lazzaroni girl, "the events of your young life; we have the entire evening to ourselves. Mrs. Arbuthnot and Térese Garetti have gone to spend the evening at Lady Hasarel's, and Sir Charles is at a grand banquet at the Marquis de Policastra's, with the Count De Courcy."

A week or more had passed since the introduction of Magdalene to the mansion of Sir Charles Wharton, and in that short time the fair stranger had gained all hearts by her unaffected sweetness of temper and disposition, her beauty, and the retiring diffidence and modesty of her deportment. Sir Charles, from the very first interview, was firmly persuaded Magdalene was his niece; nothing could shake his belief in Mary being his own child. Magdalene's striking likeness to Mary, in features and person, was too remarkable to be the

mere effect of chance. Mary felt already a sister's affection
for her cousin, as she called her in private; and after a day or
two's companionship, made Magdalene fully acquainted with
the strange circumstances of her own life, and the mystification of the kind Sir Charles Wharton with respect to her birth.

Mary, who expected to behold a wild, untaught, Lazzaroni,
was astounded when she beheld a young and beautiful girl,
with quiet, serious, and well-sustained manners, diffident and
timid, excitable, and yet retiring; loving and affectionate in
manner, and speaking the Italian without a particle of the
Neapolitan patois dialect. Her likeness to herself she at once
perceived—the very tones of her voice struck her forcibly : as
to Térese, she was in raptures—showed Magdalene every
attention and kindness; in fact, if her relationship to Sir
Charles had been fully confirmed, she could not have been
shown greater affection or attention.

And Magdalene evinced that she appreciated all the kindness she received: to Mary she seemed to devote herself
heart and soul; she studied her very look, strove by every act
to win her love and confidence, spoke to her unceasingly of
Hugh De Courcy, of his love and devotion to her, of his noble
nature and generous heart—how grand and graceful his figure,
and how calm and graceful the expression of his features. This
all sank into Mary's devoted heart, and she learned very soon to
love the gentle Magdalene. One thing pained Sir Charles
much, and this was Magdalene's firm faith in the Catholic
Church, its rites and its mysteries. Sir Charles was far, very
far, from being a bigoted Protestant; still it pained him to
think that his niece should be of a different persuasion to his
daughter.

The name of Magdalene, he had been satisfied, was not the
one by which she was christened. Mrs. Hudson, Mrs.
Wharton's nurse, said her child was christened Mary; so that
niece and daughter were both Mary. To satisfy himself, he
wrote to a correspondent in Hamburg to find out from him the
date of his brother's child's birth, and the name she was
christened by. One only event occurred during the ten days
from the introduction of Magdalene to the mansion of the
baronet and the opening of this chapter worthy of notice, and
that was the escape of Campobello the Lazzaroni. He was
sent to Plymouth, in charge of two police-officers ; was
securely handcuffed, and, as the men declared, as well watched
as any convict ever was; and yet he escaped from the jail of
Exeter, where he was lodged for the night, with another
prisoner, confined in the same cell, and neither one nor the
other could be traced up to that time; their escape created
exceeding excitement amongst the jail officials, as it was one
of the most daring and successful on record.

We now turn to fair Mary Wharton and Magdalene, seated before a cheerful fire, in the handsome drawing-room of Sir Charles's mansion.

" What I have to tell you of myself dear Mary," said Magdalene, in reply to Mary's request, " is merely a recital of a few simple events in a monotonous life; but it will do away with your surprise at finding me what you kindly call so well instructed, and with manners different from what you expected to see in a poor Lazzaroni girl, exposed to a life of terrible degradation and sin, and from which Providence was benignantly pleased to rescue her. It will show you, also, how and where I first beheld the noble and generous Count De Courcy, but for whom I should long since have ceased to exist."

Mary looked surprised, exclaiming, "Did Hugh save your life? You must have been very young at that time, or he surely would have remembered one so attractive and beautiful. In times past," and Mary sighed, " he used to tell me all the incidents of his life, and yet he never mentioned saving a young girl's life."

Magdalene's eyes drooped, and for a moment she remained silent and abstracted. Mary gazed into her sweet pensive features, in the expression of which there was a something that struck her forcibly, for she started and turned pale, and her hand trembled as she laid it on Magdalene's. The latter looked up, and the eyes of the two girls met; Magdalene's filled with tears: involuntarily they threw their arms round each other's necks, and for several moments neither spoke. Then Magdalene, looking up, kissed Mary's cheek, and with a cheerful, bright smile, said—"Do not be angry, dear, kind Mary, at Magdalene's presumption, in having once dared to feel an affection for the noble De Courcy. It has passed away and for ever from my heart, and henceforth I look upon him as your own, and feel for him the devotion and affection of a sister. Perhaps to allow even that is a presumption in one situated as I am; but, alas! we do not always possess the power to rule and govern our feelings or our affections."

More and more surprised at the manner, language, and feelings of Magdalene, Mary could only press her to her own soft, kind heart, and whisper, " Dear Magdalene, how different might have been your fate, had——"

" Hush now, Mary carissime, say no more on that subject; let it rest, and for ever; let me tell you my little story—you will understand all then.

" You have never been to Naples, dear Mary, and though I daresay you have often heard talk of the Lazzaroni of that city, yet you must have a very faint idea of that strange and extraordinary race—who are born, live and die, without bestowing a thought upon the morrow. I must have been nearly six

years old at the time I recollect myself running about the
streets and quays of Naples, with, I may fairly say, as small an
amount of clothing as could well be dispensed with. I can
remember, perfectly well, the kind of life I then led, with
dozens of other children. Our parents troubled little about
us; but left us to pick up as much food as was necessary to
support life, how and where we could. I know our chief place
of resort for the purposes of satisfying our appetites was the
quay, where multitudes of people assemble in the summer
time ; indeed you may say it is perpetual summer in Naples,
so mild and so soft are the breezes of winter. On the quay a
scene of perpetual eating and drinking takes place ; roasting
and boiling is always going on; every twenty or thirty paces
you meet little stalls, where water-melons are sold. Upon the
paring of these water-melons, thrown away by the purchaser,
we chiefly lived in summer and autumn ; besides, we gathered
up ears of the golden maize, and roasted them on the charcoal
fires of some good-natured stall-keeper. Then we picked shell-
fish, snails, and innumerable other commodities, on which we
existed : when satisfied we lay in the shade, and listened to the
street-players, or enjoyed the antics of the numerous mounte-
banks that congregated in this well-frequented locality; and
when evening came we congregated in groups, huddled together, and slept away the hours of the night, to begin again
the same life with the rising sun."

"Good gracious!" interrupted Mary, surprised, "where
were your parents ; did you never return to your home ?"

"Home!" said Magdalene, with a look of bitter recollection ; a " Lazzaroni has no home ; the streets of Naples and
the colonnades of its three hundred churches are the only
homes of the houseless, worthless, vicious, outcast Lazzaroni.
As a child of six years old I knew nothing of their lives ; for.
of course, my only thought then was to find food. Sometimes
my father Campobello—for such I considered him—would come
and take me from amongst the children, and look at me keenly
and inquiringly. I was much fairer than any of the other
children I played, eat, and slept with. 'Come, Magdalene,'
he would say, you are getting pretty ; you shall have a gay
ribbon, and I'll take you to a festa,' and he would do so; himself decorated with a few gaudy ribbons, and the females with
him dressed out for that day in some gaudy colours, thrown off
the following day ; and then, half starved and half naked, they
lay listlessly in the shade. or basked in the sun till a new festa
roused them from their fearful indolence. I was, perhaps,
nearly seven when I began to feel a strong repugnance to the
life I led, and a disgust of my companions. which rapidly
increased, till at length I used to hide from them. One day,
a nun belonging to the nunnery of the Annonciada found me

sleeping under the porch of the public chapel attached to the
nunnery. She roused me, and taking me by the arm, examined
me carefully. ' Whose little girl are you ? ' inquired the nun.
" Antonio Campobello's," I answered.
" ' What ! ' exclaimed the nun, with an air of surprise, ' you
the child of that turbulent and brutal Lazzaroni—impossible !
you are so fair. Will you come with me, child ?' she continued, ' we take in young maidens in our convent, and teach
them the word of God and instruct them.'
" Oh ! " I exclaimed, with tears in my eyes, " will you take
me ? I hate the life I lead ; I would be good if I could."
" Poor child, come then with me,' said the nun ; ' but though
it is not right to hide anything from your parents, still you
must not say you are taught by the nuns of the Annonciada, to
your father, or he would never let you come near us. The
child of a Lazzaroni never enters our walls ; but I know not
how it is—you interest me ; I cannot believe that you are one of
that fearful race.' Not to weary you, dear Mary, with minute
details, I will hurry over my narrative. For two years I continued attending the school of the convent, always particularly
noticed and cared for by the good nun Sister Agata. As I was
made acquainted with many things, and taught prayers, and the
necessity of religious worship, the greater became my horror
of the life I was forced to lead : I completely shunned all my
former companions, and sought out a secret recess for myself
to sleep in. Luckily, my supposed father was occupied with
schemes of his own ; he was not like the other Lazzaroni in
some things ; he would never work, it is true, but he was of a
bold turbulent character, and gained a complete mastery over
the great body of Lazzaroni. I never heard of my mother,
though I always observed a tall, handsome, fierce-mannered
female with my father ; but she never noticed me, and had
several children of her own. I happened to have, as the nun
Agata said, ' a very sweet voice.'
" When nine years old I was noticed by the abbess, and
shortly after I was taken into her presence. To this generous,
noble-minded woman, once a lady of rank, I owe the deepest
gratitude. She took a most extraordinary liking to me ; I
was with her constantly ; she would talk to me for an hour at
a time. She had me instructed in music, and I frequently
sang in the chapel of the convent with other well-instructed
girls. I could read and write, and, oh, how eagerly I sought
for knowledge you cannot think ! When I was about eleven
years of age the abbess wished to take me away entirely from
the degraded life I led : I was tall, and no longer fit to be
sleeping alone under colonnades or porches. I felt as if there
was a spirit within me that raised me above my condition.

P

When, unfortunately for me, my father discovered my mode of life and my visits to the convent, he tore from my back the few articles of decent clothing I had had given me, and threatened, uttering the most fearful imprecations, if ever I entered the walls of the Annonciada again: he carried or forced me to follow him to the cave beneath the Riviera, where he lived with the tall female I had so often seen with him. This horrid woman treated me like a brute, stripped my arms and neck, and washed me all over with a liquid that changed the colour of my skin to a darker hue than even that of the Lazzaroni girls. For three or four weeks I suffered terribly, when, for some crime committed by Campobello, he was forced to fly Naples. I was then again left to myself; I dare not go to the convent, for I was watched; but one evening the good nun Agata gave me a paper, telling me to read it, and do as it bade me. I waited till daylight, and then read, 'Do not come any more to the convent, we are forbidden to receive the children of the Lazzaroni; go to No. 7, Strada Lucia, and ask to see the Signora Canino. She will know who you are, and will be kind to you, for she is my sister.'

" 'Dear, good Sister Agata, how kind,' I exclaimed, ' to think of me at all!' At first I felt ashamed as I looked at my bronzed skin, my scanty attire, my short red petticoat. I blushed to think of going before a stranger. But, gaining courage, I went to a well and washed my face and arms, but the stain remained the same. I was not frightened, for I guessed it would not come off without some chemical process or liquid. So, making myself look as well as I could, I proceeded to St. Lucia, which is close to the splendid mansions on the Riviera : strange contrast to all this beauty and splendour, the huts of the fishermen, scooped out like caves from the hard rock, dwellings without windows or doors, rise up before the princely mansions of the wealthy. How often have I sat at night amid the rocks below the Riviera, when the moon stood high in the heavens, gazing in a dreamy stupefaction upon the glorious scene before me, the smoke of Mount Vesuvius tinged by the rays of the bright moon, as it ascended undisturbed by a breath of air; from the open windows of the villas lights gleamed out upon the vine-covered terraces; countless numbers of fishing skiffs covered the waters of the glorious bay, some with bright fires in their sterns, to attract the great fishes and lobsters that rise to the light and are caught: for hours I would gaze on this scene, till sleep stole over my weary eyelids : my life was a dream—alas ! I dream now," and Magdalene's eyes became suffused with tears.

" Dear Magdalene, why give way to those excitable feelings? Strive to forget the past, trust in the love of those whom Providence has raised up to be your protectors : recollect time and unforeseen circumstances may even more speedily than we imagine remove the obscurity that clouds our births."

" I do not deserve, dear Mary," answered Magdalene, with a sigh, " the love and kindness shown me ; I am not sufficiently grateful for so great a blessing, but please God, I will yet prove more worthy. But to continue my narrative, requesting your pardon for those outbreaks of temper. Alas ! Mary, I have been more sorely tried than you can dream of."

CHAPTER XXX.

" I PROCEEDED," continued Magdalene, " to Strada Santa Lucia, and stopped before No. 7; it was a very handsome house and a private one. This made me more timid—I feared the scorn of the servants—but as I stood, fearful of ringing the bell, the door partly opened, and, oh joy ! I beheld the mild, pensive countenance of Sister Agata: with a smile she beckoned me to come in ; I did so with a joyful heart, for I should not now have to face the Signora Canino alone.

" 'Bless me, Magdalene,' cried Sister Agata, looking at me with intense surprise, ' what have you done to make yourself this colour ?'

" ' My father,' I replied, ' ordered some woman he lives with to stain my skin, because I was fairer than his other children.'

" ' The wretch !' returned sister Agata; ' but perhaps it would have been for the better ; however, come with me, the colour of the skin makes no difference when the heart is uncorrupted—the skin can be cleansed.'

" The nun took me up stairs, through an exceedingly well-furnished house, everything looking so orderly and neat. She then opened a door, which led into a very handsomely-furnished saloon, with beautiful costly plants in the verandah, and a folding-door leading into a bed-chamber. In a large, well-cushioned, high chair, on wheels, reclined a lady. She turned the chair half round as we entered the room, and I beheld her face. A sweet and interesting face it was, pale, very pale, with the dark hair pushed back from the high white forehead ; the lady was dressed in mourning, and did not appear more than two or three and thirty.

" ' Ah,' said the Signora Canino, gazing at me, earnestly, ' is this your young favourite, sister ? I thought you said she was very fair, but she's pretty enough, notwithstanding. Come near, my child, for it has pleased God to afflict me with the loss of the use of my limbs,'

" ' Ah, my God !' I exclaimed, touched to the heart, to see one so young and beautiful, for beautiful she was, and her good heart spoke in her eyes, which were lovely.

"The Signora Canino kissed me, saying, 'I am sure you have a feeling heart, and are a good girl, or my dear, kind Agata would not be so deeply anxious about you. But this is a stained skin, sister,' continued the signora, pushing back my hair, which was extremely abundant.

"'Yes, sister,' replied the nun, 'they have stained her skin with walnut juice, I suppose, but it will come off with repeated washings with vinegar or some other acid. I will leave you now, sister, as my hour is expired;' so kissing the signora, and then me, affectionately, and telling me never to forget my prayers, and to always remember that there is another world to reward us for our trials in this, if they are borne with pious resignation, she returned to her convent.

"Well, dear Mary, for several reasons, I will speak briefly of the next three years, the memory of that beloved lady, the Signora Canino, still remains engraven on my heart in lines never to be erased. She is now a saint in glory. Peace to her ashes! During those three years I remained entirely with the Signora Canino. She was unmarried, of good family, and had a comfortable annuity, was highly accomplished, a splendid musician, and passionately fond of music. She enjoyed tolerable health, but her limbs were paralysed from a terrible fall when only two and twenty years of age. Still she was exceedingly cheerful, could amuse herself at the piano or harp; but reading for any length of time affected her in a strange way: she kept two female domestics, but saw no person save and except her sister Agata, and they were fondly attached to each other.

"I was at once domiciled in the house of the signora, and soon learned to love her dearly. I was handsomely attired, and my complexion restored to its natural hue. The signora delighted in teaching me music and every accomplishment she was herself mistress of; she wished to render me capable of taking the situation of a governess or companion. I loved music dearly, and was, the signora said, a most apt scholar. She had a choice library, and she selected the works she wished me to read to her. Ah, Mary dear, how calm, quiet, and peaceable were those days! I slept in a little bed beside my generous and beloved protectress; and I knew, after a time, she loved me fondly. She did not sleep much at night, and I so managed that I was always awake to get her anything she required, and talk to her, and soothe her when she suffered pain, which was very frequently. We drove out in a large covered carriage twice a week, and into this vehicle she was carried chair and all. When two or three miles from Naples, the chair was lifted out, and placed where a fine view could be had, and then I took plenty of exercise. I never went into the streets of Naples, for Sister Agata, who visited us once every week for one hour, told me my father was come back, and was grown a great popular leader of the Lazzaroni, and that she was sure that there would be a revolution in Naples.

" I was just approaching my sixteenth birthday, as far as I could judge, when my beloved protectress was struck with a mortal distemper, and one fearfully rapid in its progress. It was only then that I understood the signora had a brother; and, most melancholy to relate, at this trying moment dear sister Agata was absent, having been sent with four other nuns to Gaeta, to the nunnery of the Annunciate in that town, where a terrible fever prevailed. This brother, the Signor Tomasse Canino, held a situation under government; he was, as I afterwards discovered, a bad, vicious man, who in early life cruelly ill-used his sisters, but was forced by the will of their father to allow them a very handsome annuity out of the estates, or give them a sum of 15,000 ducats as their marriage portion.

"Agata Canino became a nun; Angelena Canino, my beloved protectress, was to have married a gentleman of good family, and of prepossessing manners and exterior, when the unfortunate fall from her horse, over a steep bank of more than sixty feet, crushed her lower limbs past all recovery. Her intended husband would have fulfilled his engagement, but the Signora Canino would not listen to his earnest entreaties.

" The sisters never communicated with, or spoke of, their brother, on account of his unnatural conduct to them after their father's death. Seizing the whole property, and refusing them the possession provided them by their parent's will, it was not till after much suffering, and a long lawsuit, that they gained their cause.

"On the third day of the Signora Canino's illness, she became extremely anxious for the notary, and one of the domestics was sent for one; but before he arrived, to my consternation she became speechless, and so continued till she died. Never shall I forget that terrible hour; it was night, I was kneeling by the side of the couch, bedewing with my tears the hand of my loved protectress, when I felt a grasp upon my shoulder, and a harsh voice said, ' Get up, Ragazza, let us see who you are.'

" I started up, hearing this strange, harsh voice, and gazed bewildered at the speaker; he was a man of middle height, a broad, massive, heavy man—oh, and what a forbidding countenance! with great mustachios and whiskers.

" ' Well, girl,' he again said, ' why don't you speak? Who are you?'

"I knew not what to say; I was so nervous from the watching of the three last nights, the shock of the signora's death, and the absence of Sister Agata.

" ' That is the little girl my mistress took in from the streets,

from charity,' said the former atten ant of the Signora Canino,
who had always resented my introduction to the signora.

" ' Ah, corpo de Bacco ! a charity-girl from the streets—probably a Lazzaroni. By my faith,' added this brute, ' to the
streets you must return, my beauty. Have you anything in
your pockets belonging to my sister ? If you have, turn them
out. I am no patronizer of little street scamps.'   -

" Good Heaven ! " exclaimed Mary Wharton, taking Magdalene's hand in hers, " what a savage, unnatural brute ; oh,
what you must have suffered, Magdalene ! "

" Alas ! dear Mary, I can scarcely describe to you my agony
and my shame ; for in those eventful three years I had become,
as you may suppose, a changed being. Oh, Madonna ! when
I thought of being turned into the streets without home or
shelter, and after three years' delicate care and luxuries—for
luxuries they were to me—and had rendered me quite unfit
to brave the reverses of a Lazzaroni's life. I had no money,
for I never required it. I might have put my hand on a considerable sum, always in the house, and from which I usually
paid household expenses and tradesmen's bills ; but I required
none myself. To return to this terrible, heartless man.

" ' Well,' said he, seeing me standing, stupefied and bewildered,—' Well, what do you see in me—do you think me
such a soft fool as my sister ? Come, take yourself out of
this house ; it's mine, and all that's in it.'

" ' Ah, signor ! ' said I, clasping my hands, ' in the name of
the blessed Madonna, permit me to accompany my beloved
and generous protectress to the grave——'

" Permit you, fiercely exclaimed this wretch,—' permit you
to rob me, you mean ——— Begone out of the house,
or I'll drive you forth, and give you over to the sbirri as a
vagrant little wretch. What brought you here at all ? '

" The blood rushed to my cheeks and temples; I felt my
veins, as it were, bursting ; whilst the woman, Maria, stood
gazing at me with a malicious, spiteful look. I rushed to the
bed in an agony of passion, and kissed, for the last time, the
lips so often pressed with warm affection to mine, and casting
on the heartless wretch, who was going to seize me by the arm,
to turn me out, a look of bitter scorn and contempt, I said,
' Miserable wretch, the day will come when you will yet be on
the bed of death, without a hand to close your eyes or moisten
your lips ; remember ! ' and, so saying, scarcely conscious of
what I said or did. I ran down stairs, seized a shawl, and
rushed out into the streets of Naples. I could hear the
wretch above crying out, ' Curse her, she has the malochia—I
feel it ! ' I could hear him stamp upon the floor with frantic
rage.

" ' Oh, Madonna, Madonna ! ' I repeated to myself, ' do not

abandon me.' At the farther end of the street was a shrine, lighted in honour of the Virgin Mother. I threw myself on my knees—the bitter tears were scalding my cheeks, as they ran unheeded on the pavement; I threw back the shawl that covered my bare head, and as I did so a grasp was laid on my arm, and I was raised up like a child, while a terrible voice rang in my ear, first uttering a fearful malediction—'Ah, wretch, have I found you at last?'

"I raised my eyes—I was fainting; but before I became insensible I beheld my father, Antonio Campobello."

"My poor, poor Magdalene," cried Mary, her eyes suffused with tears, "how terrible was your situation!"

"Yes, Mary," returned the poor girl, her sweet features wearing a look of such pious resignation, that any one, gazing at her then, would have said she was even more lovely than her companion: "when I recovered my recollection—for I had fainted—I found myself lying upon a bundle of straw; stripped of my clothes, and the scanty covering of a Lazzaroni girl substituted in their place. Standing near the place where I lay was the same tall, fierce-looking female I had seen before with my father, holding a can of some kind of liquid; she had just been washing me all over with it, and tying up my hair in the Lazzaroni fashion.

"'Oh,' said this woman, 'you are coming to yourself, are you? So you wanted to run from your race, and become a dainty damsel, with fine clothes. You had better take care and not try that game again, or Antonio will cripple you, mind that!' and she looked like a fiend as she turned away. I perceived I was in one of the caves of the Riviera. I thought my heart would break; but there's no use, dear Mary, in prolonging my narrative; I have shown you how I became as you now see me: the next year and a half of my life is too horrible to dwell upon.

"This terrible woman, the wife of Campobello—if wife you can call the degrading compact that joined them—took me out in a fishing-boat to bait hooks, and assist her and her eldest son, who did do some work sometimes. We were upset in a squall, running for the quay, one evening: I was just sinking, and was uttering my last prayer, when a powerful arm grasped me, held me up, and carried me ashore. I was saved from drowning by Captain De Courcy, who then commanded the Vesuvius brig. Though life was hateful, I felt too young to die, and hope still lingered in my heart that Providence would snatch me from my terrible doom. Besides saving my life, this generous, noble-minded man left a sum of money for my use.

"I saw Captain De Courcy several times, for he was often pointed out to me as he went to his boat, but he had no recollection of me. He sailed shortly after for Genoa : time rolled on, I saw no mode of escape : I was terribly watched. I overheard many conferences between my father and some strangers, in the cave at night; and I soon learned that he had become a conspirator. I pass on till the return of Captain De Courcy to Naples. I overheard a plan between several of the Lazzaroni and my father, to assassinate Captain De Courcy, under the colonnades of the church of Gesu Novo, as he returned from the Palace Reale, on the night of a particular festa, that of Piedi Grotto. I knew not what to do to save him, but I watched the manœuvres of my father that night, and discovered that he intended to surround Mr. De Courcy, with the girls and women singing and dancing, and as if to extort money, and then to stab him.

" My shriek—for you have told me how he related the event to you in Genoa—my shriek saved him, and for which I received a blow in the neck that nearly killed me. Afterwards I contrived to discover the conspiracy of entering fifty determined revolutionists on board his ship, with the hope of taking his life and seizing the vessel; the first lieutenant, Baracco, being a conspirator. I was enabled, only by hiding all night, and watching closely, to warn Captain De Courcy of this conspiracy against him.

" The discovery of Lieutenant Baracco being a conspirator, I suppose, led to the flight and arrest of the others. In the dead of the night my father forced me to follow him ; he put off in a fishing-boat, and with me was put on board a vessel sailing for England. Thus, dear Mary, you have a brief outline of my life. I have suppressed much, for it would only pain your gentle heart to hear of my terrible sufferings and privations for eighteen months. It was not till seven months after her death that I heard that dear, kind-hearted sister Agata died of the pestilence at Gaeta ; for many a long day I mourned over her loss, for I had daily expected to see her, and to her I trusted to escape from the frightful life I endured in Naples.'

CHAPTER XXXI.

DESPATCHES for the Marquis de Policastra had arrived in London, via Hamburg. For certain reasons it had been determined by the court of Naples that the marquis was to remain in England till recalled ; whilst the Serena frigate was to return to Palermo as soon as possible. This intelligence and orders were received by our hero with surprise and some vexation, as it hurried his movements. He was extremely anxious to see Lord Umfreville, and accordingly wrote to him, that he should be obliged to leave London in eight or ten days, and that he would, if his lordship could not leave Hampshire, visit him there. But Lord Umfreville arrived in London the very day he wrote the letter, and immediately waited on the Count De Courcy.

The two friends met, after so many years' separation, with a cordiality unimpaired. Lord Umfreville looked very pale, and in his manner was depressed. After some conversation on the rather sudden death of the late lord, and how deeply he deplored the loss of the best of fathers, his lordship said, "Before, my dear Hugh, we begin to talk of other matters, let me set your heart at rest upon one subject, which I know is of more consequence to you than all others—I mean respecting my engagement with Miss Wharton. I now know all; and when I learned the particulars, I immediately wrote to Sir Charles and to Miss Wharton, breaking off all engagements between us. Your beautiful Mary is an angel. I can now understand her evident reluctance to receive even common attention from the numerous admirers her beauty and sweet retiring manners attracted; but being quite ignorant of her previous engagement to you—though I perceived she only received my attentions as a particular friend of her uncle's—I was led on by the hope that time would alter her feelings towards me; therefore, when Sir Charles Wharton, then supposed dying, placed her hand within mine, I vowed to study every wish of hers through life, and earn the love I hoped one day to gain. The delusion is dissipated: I understand the past; and believe me, Hugh, in my heart I wish you every felicity with one calculated to render the man whom she blesses with her hand the happiest of human beings."

"My dear Edward," cried our hero, considerably moved by the straightforward, noble conduct of Lord Umfreville, "I did not interrupt you, or make any remark till you had said what you wished; but. believe me, I have suffered a great deal on this subject; not alone, I assure you, on my account. but for the pain I foresaw I had inflicted on you. It is I who am to blame throughout in this affair; my hasty, passionate temper, caused me to act with insane precipitation. You say you know the particulars; but you cannot be aware how basely I was betrayed."

"You shall tell me another time, dear friend," observed his lordship; "I know you were sorely tried; but now let us turn to another subject, distressing and perplexing to me to a painful degree. I wrote you shortly after my lamented father's death, and made you acquainted with the remarkable words he made use of when dying. Now it is very evident that there exists some connection relative to this mystery between you, my father, and Sir John Acton, the minister of King Ferdinand. Whatever it is I should wish to know it. I intend proceeding to Palermo, and will, if you permit me, accompany you in your ship."

" You delight me," exclaimed our hero, eagerly; " there is scarcely anything would give me greater pleasure. But, perhaps, I have it in my power to throw some light on this matter; I say perhaps, for the contents of the papers I now intend examining are quite strange to me. These papers were given to me by Sir John Acton, previous to leaving Naples, to open and examine their contents on reaching England. They are to reveal the secret of my birth, and prove my rights to my father's name, whatever that was. Your father and Sir John Acton were extremely intimate, and I am led to believe, from some expressions Sir John made use of in parting, that I shall find a relative in you, my dear and old companion."

" Good God! I thought so myself," said Lord Umfreville, considerably agitated, "from my father's words ; but let us, dear Hugh, examine those papers : strange ideas float through my brain, and recollections of many things, unheeded at the time, now recur foreibly."

" We will do so at once," replied De Courcy.

This conversation took place in our hero's chambers, and, proceeding to a very handsome desk, he opened it and took out the carefully-sealed packet. Breaking the seals, and unfolding the outward cover, the young men perceived that the packet contained several folds of paper. Lord Umfreville drew near to the table, anxiously watching his friend's proceedings. There were six separate documents and several papers enclosed ; on the top was a letter directed to Hugh de Umfreville. Our hero dropped the letter, and looked into the face of his friend, with a troubled expression. Lord de Umfreville was pale, but his features wore a calm, serious expression.

" Go on, dear friend, go on," he said ; " I am quite prepared to see in you the real Lord Hugh de Umfreville."

" No," replied our hero, firmly, " that must not be, if even it were the case ; 'tis bad enough to probe the heart of a true friend in one sense, without robbing him of title and station. No, let all be unknown :" and gathering up the papers, with a somewhat passionate gesture, he would most likely have thrown them into the fire, had not Lord de Umfreville caught him by the arm.

" Your impetuosity, dear Hugh, once before nearly sacrificed your happiness ; give not way to an impulse that too often leads to regret ; listen to me. By the side of my dying father's couch I solemnly vowed to do that which was right, and as God hears us, and has registered my vow, and as I hope for peace here on earth and hereafter in heaven, so will I keep my vow."

There was a solemnity and a deep feeling in the tone and look of the young man, as he spoke, that touched our hero's heart forcibly.

"Would that I had never sought to know my name!" he bitterly exclaimed; "that of De Courcy was a noble one, and has not been disgraced by me. I covet neither titles nor wealth; I desired to give her I loved a name she would have a right to hold, and her children, if God blessed us with them, to inherit after us; false pride, for one title is as good as another."

"No, Hugh," rejoined his friend, "you argue falsely. I do not deny but that one appellation is as good as another, when upheld with honour and integrity; but no man has a right to cast away his name and birthright from a false feeling. Be calm and just: read that letter to the end, and let us understand our relative positions. I may lose my title and property, but I should retain my self-esteem, which now I could never do if I knew, or suspected, that I held that which I was not entitled to possess."

Our hero looked exceedingly uneasy and disturbed, but taking up the letter of Sir John Acton, he read aloud as follows :—

"'My dear Hugh,—If I followed the dictates of my own heart, I would leave you in ignorance of who you are, and who were your parents, and most probably remaining in ignorance of the past would most conduce to your happiness; but circumstances have occurred that have induced me to change my mind. Your father and I were bosom friends; in memory of him who was so cruelly treated, I did my duty towards you as if I had been your father. At this time I refrain from giving you any of my reasons for acting as I have done, and simply confine myself to making you acquainted with facts, and enclosing a few vouchers and certificates of your father's marriage and your birth; being ready at any time to come forward and swear to the truth of what I now state, and also to produce witnesses if required. Your grandfather was the Lord Hugh de Umfreville, of Grena, county of Kerry, and Umfreville Castle, Hampshire, and various other estates in England. He had one son by his first wife. This son became Roman Catholic, and his father disinherited him; married again and had another son, to whom he bequeathed all his estates.'"

"There, my dear friend," interrupted Lord Umfreville, "your protector, Sir John Acton is quite wrong; but go on, I will explain afterwards."

Our hero continued, "'This son by his second wife died before he became of age; consequently, the title and estates went, by right of succession, to Lord de Umfreville's younger

brother, **Edward** de Umfreville—the present lord, whose
eldest son was your companion in the college at Sienna.
There is also a younger son, in the naval service of Great
Britain. Now with respect to your father, before he was disinherited he was devotedly attached to a Miss De Courcy,
eldest daughter of the oldest baronet in Ireland, and an exceedingly wealthy land-holder in the county of Cork and Kerry.

"'On your father becoming a Roman Catholic, and his
father, Lord de Umfreville disinheriting him, Sir Egbert De
Courcy, a stern Protestant, and a great persecutor of the
Catholics of that day—a period when they were cruelly
oppressed—instantly forbade his daughter seeing her former
lover; nevertheless, your sire carried her off. Of their after
unhappy, deserted condition, I know nothing further than that
your mother died in giving you birth, and your father, two
years after, struggling to the last to maintain the liberty of
the Catholic subjects of Ireland from their oppressing Protestant brethren, and the cruel laws then existing against them.

"'I have already told you how, on returning to Ireland, I
made it my business to find out all this, and to trace you, for
I had discovered that my poor friend left an only son. Now
to the Umfreville property and title you thus see you can
never succeed, as your father was disinherited, being a
Catholic, and besides your grandfather executed deeds purposely to cut your father or his heirs off from all chance of
succession. But it strikes me, from what I heard from the
present Lord Umfreville, whom I made acquainted with your
existence—for he was quite ignorant of it——.'"

"Ah, my God!" interrupted Lord Umfreville, in a tone of
anguish, "now I understand my poor father's anxiety. Ah!
who is perfect? but proceed, I pray you, dear friend; pardon
these interruptions."

"'That the fortune of your mother is unquestionably yours.
She was of age when she married your father, and her fortune
was £40,000, which was unjustly added to her sister's portion
when she married Lord Eglin, whose son now enjoys that
large property—for your mother inherited this £40,000 from
her grandfather. This intelligence was my chief inducement
for altering my intention of your inspecting the contents of
this packet when you pleased, to doing so on reaching
England. With the enclosed documents, any highly respectable lawyer will tell you what chance you have of
recovering this property of your mother's. I have said
sufficient now on this subject. May God direct you as to the
best course to pursue! you have my hearty wishes for your
success, and my blessing.

"'Ever your affectionate friend,   John Acton.
"'Naples, May 29th, 1801.'"

Our hero laid down the letter, and rested his head on his hand in a very thoughtful mood.

"Now listen to me, Hugh," said Lord Umfreville, as we shall still suppose him to be, to avoid confusion: "I remarked to you, as you read that letter, that Sir John Acton was incorrect in his view of the past, but quite right as to your birth, &c. I will explain my words. Your grandfather, Hugh de Umfreville, did marry again, but the son he had by his second wife died the day of his birth—another and another, strange to say, died the same way; the last nearly cost the mother her life. Indeed, from the effects of that confinement she never entirely recovered, and only survived her aged husband eighteen months. Whether Lord de Umfreville was struck with remorse or not I cannot say; but the deeds disinheriting his only son, then dead, were never found, but it was supposed, and such was the case, no doubt, that he destroyed them. My grandfather therefore came into possession of title and estates, as next in succession; for it appears either you were not supposed to be in existence, or were not thought of at all. Lord Eglin certainly married your mother's sister; he was then a very poor nobleman, but with the immense property he inherited in right of his wife, he purchased back the forfeited estates of his grandfather, which his son the present Lord Eglin holds. Now, after the lapse of so many years, it's a question whether your claims to your mother's property would be recognized."

"My dear friend," interrupted our hero, "I never intend to try the case. I have not the slightest wish or ambition to disturb the succession of any man inheriting property in direct descent, without any fraud on his part; therefore, as I have quite sufficient for my wants, and I know Mary will inherit more than sufficient for her and any children she may have, I sincerely hope, and I implore you to do so, to let things remain as they are."

Lord Umfreville shook his head with a serious smile, saying, "Your romantic ideas, Hugh, would suit the wild age when the name of De Courcy was the war-cry of a valiant race. You must assert your claims; if you despise a title, so do I, especially when I am aware I am holding one unjustly. Your succession to title and estates I will not dream of disputing, for no doubt these documents here are clear and convincing. My poor father's words prove to me he was aware of the fact, and I am also satisfied he was, just before he died, investigating papers and deeds preparatory to the renunciation of the property and title. But do not imagine that I shall be left without sufficient means for a gentleman's support. I shall be quite rich enough My grandfather's property was very considerable before he inherited the title and estates of his brother, and he had, besides, a very large fortune with his wife. My mother, also, was an heiress. She was a De Vere; so that you see I shall remain wealthy still. My younger brother embraced the naval profession from choice and love of the sea, but is handsomely provided for out of his mother's marriage portion."

Hugh De Courcy was nevertheless extremely hurt and troubled. Could he have imagined for a moment that his opening, the packet, and investigating the mystery of his birth, would disinherit his friend, he would never have attempted to satisfy a very natural feeling, that of knowing whose son he was.

From his knowledge of Lord Umfreville's character, he felt quite satisfied that once convinced of his having no right to the title and estates of Umfreville, persuasion would never induce him to retain them.

These thoughts passed rapidly through our hero's brain. Therefore, looking up with a saddened expression of countenance, he said, laying his hand upon his friend's, " This is a severe trial on both sides, for I feel so satisfied respecting your opinions of me and my feelings that I may venture to speak as I do, without fear of being thought visionary in my ideas, and of your so asserting. Will you, then, dear friend—should the law pronounce my claims strictly just and well-founded—will you ease my mind by dividing those estates equally? If you refuse me you disparage our friendship, and render the succession one of melancholy regret."

" Be it as you wish, Hugh," returned Lord Umfreville, clasping his friend's hand and pressing it warmly, " on this promise, that if I die childless the estates return to either you or your heirs."

De Courcy, with a pleased smile, assented, saying, " I prophesy, dear Edward, that will not be the case. But I have another request to make, and that is, that you will still keep to your promise of accompanying me to Palermo."

" Willingly; for I wish to leave England for a time. Now let us look over these documents, and to-morrow place them in the hands of the most eminent lawyer of the day, Sir Edward D——."

The two friends then calmly turned over the papers, and after their perusal both felt satisfied that there would be no difficulty whatever in De Courcy proving his rights, especially as there would be no difficulty made on the side of the party most interested in opposing his claims.

CHAPTER XXXII.

AFTER the two friends parted, De Courcy—as it was already late—dressed, to keep an appointment he had made to be present at a party given by the Earl of S——. It was a very select assembly; the Marquis de Policastra was there, and several distinguished foreigners from the several European courts, also the great statesman and prime minister of George III., William Pitt. At this period the nation entertained great hopes of peace, and Pitt agreed that the experiment should be tried under Mr. Addington's auspices. Our hero was anxious to meet this great and talented minister, and behold him in a kind of domestic circle.

" You are probably disappointed, De Courcy," observed the Marquis de Policastra, " like myself, in the appearance and manner of England's great minister; but when you hear him speak, in five minutes you lose sight altogether of his insignificant figure and somewhat disagreeable countenance; and in five minutes more, you would say he was a handsome man. You will have an opportunity by-and-bye. When do you think you will sail for Palermo? "

" In six or eight days at furthest," returned our hero. " Pray can you tell me who is that young man in the uniform of the Guards, talking to that very distinguished-looking lady? "

" Oh, yes; he is a young man of high rank, connected with the fair dame our hostess, and cousin to your old friend Lieutenant Umfreville—that is young Lord Eglin; he seems to regard you with a very marked expression of countenance."

" It is for that very reason I wished to know his name. This is no place to make explanations in, my dear marquis, but you will be surprised to hear that I have discovered all the particulars concerning my birth, and I find that I shall have to change my name."

" St. Nicholas!" returned the marquis, " I am glad of it in some respects, for every man naturally enough likes to know who his father is, or was, though he may not be so very curious about his mother; at all events you will never be called by a better name than the one you have added such laurels to."

Seeing Lady Hasarel and the Signora Garetti at a distance, De Courcy at once left the marquis, who began conversing earnestly with Mr. Addington upon the all-engrossing subject of peace with France. Our hero was soon walking through the magnificent saloons with the fair Genoese leaning on his arm.

"I was sure you would be here," she remarked, "and so was Lady Hasarel, and I wished so very much to see you, for I suppose you have not seen Sir Charles to-day?"

"No, my fair friend, nor yesterday; but I am equally delighted to see you, for very strange things have occurred. But first tell me how are dear Mary and Magdalene?"

"Dear Mary is very well considering all she has gone through lately," returned Térese; "her mind, however, has been greatly relieved by the very handsome and generous conduct of Lord Umfreville; his letters to both Mary and Sir Charles do honour to his head."

"He is a noble fellow, and it grieves and pains me more than I can tell you to inflict upon him at the same time two of the heaviest afflictions a man can bear."

"What do you mean, Signor De Courcy?" inquired Térese, looking surprised; "let us sit down here; I have a good deal to say, for we shall not meet again until we meet in Palermo; so Mary has arranged."

"Well," observed De Courcy, with a sigh of regret, "perhaps she is right, considering the peculiar circumstances under which she acts; but why do you say this is the last time you and I must meet?"

"Because," returned Térese, "we leave London the day after to-morrow, for Sir Charles's beautiful place in Devon, and thence to embark in the ―――― frigate for Palermo. You sail in a short time, do you not?"

"Yes; in ten days at furthest," returned De Courcy, thoughtfully. "Lord Umfreville goes with me to Palermo."

"Indeed!" observed Térese; but the name of De Courcy, pronounced rather loud, close beside them, caused both to turn round in the direction from whence came the voices, when they observed two gentlemen leaning against the pillars of a recess, conversing earnestly. One was Lord Eglin, the other was unknown to them; but the sentence they both heard caused not only surprise, but brought the blood into De Courcy's cheek.

"I know of no Irishman," said Lord Eglin, in a calm tone, "that has a right to the name of De Courcy. My father-in-law was the last male bearing that appellation; consequently, any one assuming that name, and calling himself an Irishman, must be either an adventurer or an impostor."

Térese Garetti looked anxiously into our hero's features: they were flushed and excited. Well aware of his impetuous temper, she rose up, and putting her arm within his, said, "Let us seek Lady Hasarel."

He complied, and, as he moved on, fixed his eyes for an instant on Lord Eglin.

"Ha!" said his lordship, with a very meaning smile, to his

friend Captain Manby, "my arrow hit the mark ; this gallant count looked conscious."

"Yes, by my faith," returned the captain; "not only conscious, but remarkably inclined to notice your words not in the gentlest manner, to judge by the fierce glance that shot from his dark eyes. That very handsome foreign girl on his arm I hear is his intended."

"Then you have just heard a false rumour," said Lord Eglin, sharply, "I have more authentic information. I have found out how the wind lies with this fortunate adventurer from that Italian signor who plays such a splendid game of billiards. It cost me, however, a hundred or two to get my information. This Italian billiard-player, whose name nobody seems to know, told me that this De Courcy is a natural son of Acton's, the Neapolitan prime minister, who, being a pet of Queen Caroline's, pushed this son of his on the service, and actually, when little better than a boy, put him in command of a fine eighteen-gun brig—taking care, however, to give him for first lieutenant a steady, skilful officer, much older, and who had seen good service."

"But how the deuce," observed Captain Manby, "did this Italian pick up his intelligence?"

"By Jove ! he told me in confidence that he was second lieutenant on board the same ship with De Courcy, and was in Genoa with him, and that in that city he first met with Miss Wharton, who had been, he said, previously in love with a Genoese count, whom she jilted, and permitted this De Courcy to replace him; but he, catching her inclined to favour this Genoese count again, picked a quarrel with him, and, assisted by two of his crew, actually killed the unfortunate count."

"And do you believe this strange story?" inquired Captain Manby, considerably amazed.

"Do I believe it?" returned Lord Eglin, "certainly I do ; for no sooner does this De Courcy appear in England than the match between my cousin, Lord Umfreville, and Miss Wharton is suddenly broken off."

"*Diable!* as our continental neighbours exclaim," uttered Captain Manby, "what can the girl mean ? Is not Lord Edward Umfreville, with title, fortune, and a handsome person, a better match than any Irish adventurer with a foreign title and a few paltry exploits tacked to his name ? "

"By Jove ! as to that," returned Lord Eglin, "who can account for the love of women? they are as capricious as the wind."

"Still, my lord," continued Captain Manby, "I think, by uttering the words you did, and which Captain De Courcy evidently heard, you may bring upon yourself a very trouble-

Q

some customer. It strikes me that you will hear from this Count De Courcy again."

"That's precisely what I wish to do," said Lord Eglin. "You do not suppose that an English nobleman will fight a duel with a man without a name; and I tell you it's impossible his name can be De Courcy, and he by birth an Irishman. There are family reasons, besides, that require investigation into the reason why this man assumes the name of my mother's family."

"But how did you hear of the engagement," asked Captain Manby, "being broken off between Lord Umfreville and Miss Wharton?"

"From Lady Hasarel, not an hour ago. She asked me had I seen my cousin since his return to town. I said 'No.'"

"'Then you do not know,' went on her ladyship, 'that your cousin, Lord Umfreville's engagement with the beautiful Miss Wharton is at an end?'

"I was not surprised, in consequence of what I had heard from the Italian."

"'And who is the happy man now, your ladyship?' I inquired, with a smile.

"'You know but little of Miss Wharton, my lord,' said her ladyship, very stiffly, and rather haughtily, 'or you would not speak as you do. You ought to know that Miss Wharton contracted that engagement with your cousin merely to render her uncle's last moments peaceable—for he much desired that union to take place, as he did not wish to leave his niece unprotected; and besides esteeming his present lordship, he was a very old and attached friend of the late lord. Lord de Umfreville, with the feelings of a man of high honour, finding that Miss Wharton merely accepted him in a moment of poignant distress, thinking her uncle dying, at once released my fair friend from her engagement.'

"'I beg pardon, your ladyship,' said I, with a smile, 'rumour assigns another reason. This gallant Irish adventurer, called De Courcy, they say, had a prior claim to the lady's affections.' Lady Hasarel looked annoyed, and even chagrined, so with a low bow I left her to her reflections."

"Faith, all this is very curious," remarked Captain Manby; "all I know is that Miss Wharton is a most lovely girl, and will inherit a noble fortune; but here comes the Count De Courcy again with the Neapolitan envoy, the Marquis de Policastra. I wonder does he intend to notice your very offensive speech, which he evidently heard."

"He is quite welcome to do so," returned Lord Eglin, carelessly.

The saloon Lord Eglin and his companion were in was little frequented, the company being in the other spacious apartments. Count De Courcy approached Lord Eglin, looking calm and unconcerned, and stopping close beside him, looked him a moment in the face, and then said, " My lord, I would wish to say a few words to you in private; the next room is the earl's library, will you favour me with your company there?"

"Well, really sir," returned his lordship, with a sneer, "as I have neither the pleasure nor honour of your acquaintance, I cannot see the necessity of adapting myself to your humour."

"Nevertheless, my lord," returned our hero, quite coolly, "as you made remarkably free with the name I at present assume, and attached to me the very uncoveted names of adventurer and impostor, I cannot let that pass without some explanation; therefore, as it would be ill-timed to engage in controversy in the hearing of others, I invite you to a private room, with the earl's permission, having made him acquainted with my intention of requesting a private interview with you. It is a thing that cannot be postponed."

" Oh, as you please," returned Lord Eglin, with a laugh, and taking the arm of Captain Manby, he added, " Come, let us gratify this gentleman in his whim."

So saying, the four gentlemen passed down the saloon, and the Marquis de Policastra opening a door, admitted them into the library of the earl, which was well lighted.

Lord Eglin threw himself into a chair, and with easy nonchalance, said, " Now, sir, will you be kind enough to open the proceedings, as the lawyers say, for we have not much time before supper."

" I shall not detain your lordship very long," replied De Courcy. " I chanced to hear — probably you intended I should—that you considered me an impostor and an adventurer, without any claim to the name of De Courcy. Did you not make a remark to that gentleman beside you to that effect?"

" I never deny what I once say," returned Lord Eglin, with a supercilious air, " and what I said I think."

" Then, my lord," returned De Courcy, " let me tell you you took not only a most ungentlemanly, but cowardly, mode of expressing your opinion, in a room where there were several people within hearing; and your remarks were distinctly audible to the lady with whom I was conversing."

"Well, sir," interrupted Lord Eglin, rising with a flush on his face, " if you have brought me in here for the purpose of insulting me, you have so far gained your end; but if you think I will condescend to fight a man of whom I know nothing, and who has assumed a name I know he has no earthly right to, you are mistaken."

"No, my lord," replied De Courcy, somewhat sadly ; "I did
not bring you here to insult you, or to force you to fight me :
it is sad enough when friends fall out, and take to the pistol
to decide their too-often imaginary grievances : but when two
men, the children of two sisters——"

"What do you mean, sir count?" exclaimed Lord Eglin,
with a start, his features betokening great agitation, "you do
not surely presume to say your mother was a De Courcy?"

"I presume to say, my lord, that my father, William De
Umfreville, married Eglantine De Courcy, the eldest daughter
of Sir Philip De Courcy ; and that, in point of fact, I am entitled
to call myself Hugh Lord De Umfreville."

Captain Manby started back, with a low whistle of profound
astonishment, whilst Lord Eglin, in a voice of intense passion,
exclaimed, "And do you think, clever adventurer as you are,
that you will find me such a fool as to believe this trumped-up
romance? You must think me very credulous, count, indeed."

"Believe or not, as you please," returned our hero, a little
excited, "but this I tell you, you will be forced to believe it ;
and now, having stated so much to you, I offer you a fair
choice : your lawyer is at liberty to examine my claims to the
title and estates of the late Lord De Umfreville, and the property of my mother, Eglantine De Courcy : if, after that, you
refuse to make me an ample apology for the excessive rudeness
of your remarks to this gentleman, your companion—remarks
heard by several other persons in the room also—I have
therefore been forced to explain what I have now stated to
you to the Earl of ————, therefore, deeply as I regret
proceeding to hostile measures with a relative, still, my honour
as a gentleman requires that alternative."

"It is a vile conspiracy," said Lord Eglin, passionately,
"and I warn you that I never will submit to your claims,
preposterous and impossible as I know they must be ; therefore, though you may deceive others, you will not me ; and as
to an apology, the only one you will ever receive from me
will be from the muzzle of a pistol. I maintain what I said,
and will repeat it if your memory fails you." So saying, with a
violent gesture, and throwing from him the chair he rested his
hand on whilst speaking, he passed rapidly out of the library,
leaving his friend Captain Manby perfectly bewildered and
abashed.

"A remarkably intemperate and ungovernable young man
is this Lord Eglin," observed the Marquis de Policastra ; "I
cannot understand such ill-feeling and gross ungracious language from a British peer. You have no alternative, amico,"
continued the marquis, taking the arm of the vexed De Courcy :
"though I know you detest duelling, you must still conform
to the usages of society, as it is now constituted."

" I really cannot understand so much bitterness," remarked our hero, " from a man I never met or exchanged a word with. As to those absurd stories you tell me about—such as my being my kind-hearted protector's natural son, and all the other rumours afloat in the social world—I fancy that this Guiseppe Baracco, who is concealed, as I told you before, somewhere in London, has managed to set them afloat."

" I wish the police could lay hands upon him," cried the marquis; " he's a dangerous man, and very likely to get back to Naples and join the revolutionary party. That other villain, Campobello, has also contrived to escape ; however, that is of little consequence now, though he might have done much mischief at Naples at one time. In my opinion, the best thing you can now do is to assert your claims at once to the Umfreville peerage, which will put a stop to all the absurd scandals afloat."

On re-entering the crowded saloons they found the company on the move to the supper-rooms; so, seeking the Signora Garetti, our hero proceeded with her to the magnificent supper saloon, where every delicacy of the season was laid out in profusion, and with exquisite taste.

" How did you manage, signor count, with that proud and haughty young noble ? " demanded Térese, anxiously; " he was one of Mary's most assiduous admirers at one time ; but her distant manner and evident dislike to his attentions roused his pride, and then he ceased persecuting her. I felt very uneasy whilst you were away."

" After supper, Térese, I will tell you a strange story, which you have not yet heard hinted, and which I wish you to impart to Mary, though I know it will pain her generous and loving heart."

" Then why," inquired Térese, seriously, " make her acquainted with it ? "

" Because, my fair friend, it is unavoidable, as it will be publicly known in a few days, and I should wish her to hear the truth before you all leave England."

" But you have not told me what that Lord Eglin said : he apologized, of course."

" Hush ! we have too many listeners now, Térese ; you will not retire immediately after supper, I hope ? "

" In half an hour, most likely," returned the Genoese maiden ; " Lady Hasarel rarely stays supper when she goes abroad. She remained this evening expressly to please me. By-the-bye, I do not see Lord Eglin anywhere ? "

" Very likely he has retired, " returned our hero, looking down the long line of supper-table.

This most social of all meals, though by no means the most healthy, passed over, and then our hero and Térese Garetti sought an opportunity for a few moments' conversation, during which he made the fair Genoese acquainted with his interview with Lord de Umfreville, and the disclosures made in consequence of the contents of the packets.

Térese was amazed beyond measure. Much as she esteemed our hero, and delighted as she was in her heart at his restoration to his birthright, still, knowing the amiable nature and kind feelings of Lord de Umfreville, she judged by her own feelings what he must suffer,—disappointed in the choice of the heart, and suddenly deprived of both titles and esates.

"I see, Térese," remarked De Courcy, "that you feel for my noble friend almost as keenly as myself, as I told him : had I known, or could I have imagined the result of opening the packet given me by Sir John Acton, I should never have dreamed of gratifying my curiosity ; for ambition had no hand in my desire of knowing who I was : it was to give Mary a name that could not be disputed, that urged me to the inquiry."

" Yours was a very natural wish, count, and no human being could blame you—it was your duty, painful as I know it must be ; but I rejoice, and so will dear Mary, when she hears that you will divide the estates, and that your friendship is still as great as ever."

The approach of Lady Hasarel put an end to the conversation ; so, escorting both ladies to their carriages, and promising to call on her ladyship the next day, Hugh De Courcy shortly after retired with the Marquis of Policastra.

CHAPTER XXXIII.

THE introduction of Magdalene into the family of Sir Charles Wharton became a source of infinite pleasure and happiness to Mary, and interest to Térese Garetti ; there was something so soft and endearing in the manners and actions of Magdalene that it was impossible not to love and admire her. With a quick and sensitive disposition, and a natural aptitude to learn, she had acquired, during her residence with the accomplished Signora Canino, double the amount of information she might otherwise, in the ordinary course of education, have attained. She surprised even the talented Mary Wharton with her power of voice, her skill and judgment, and her perfect execution in music. Once this science' has been acquired, it is not to be forgotten ; the eighteen months of wretchedness she had endured after her loss of the kind-hearted signora neither broke her spirit nor robbed her of that elegance of manners almost inherent to Magdalene, who was naturally graceful and easy, and in the three years of seclusion with the Signora Canino she had read much, and profited by

what she had perused : even her very early life had been pu-
rified and redeemed by her intercourse with sister Agata and
the lady abbess of the Annonciada; so that when restored
to a state of society she was calculated to shine in, she soon
forgot the miseries, and sorrows, and degradation she had
endured.

Sir Charles Wharton was proud of this acquisition to his
family circle. "Now," said the kind-hearted baronet, "I am
sure, at all events, of having under my roof my daughter and
my niece, though perhaps there may be a doubt as to which is
which."

The baronet had received an answer from his correspondent
in Hamburg, who wrote back word that Mr. Edward Wharton's little girl was born in the year 1783, and was baptized by
the name of Mary Elizabeth, in the church in Hamburg.
The date and name corresponded with the baronet's conceived
opinion ; Magdalene, by her own account, made herself out to
be about eighteen, which assertion corresponded with the date
of Mr. Edward Wharton's little girl's birth. The baronet,
therefore, expressed a wish that she should be called Elizabeth, and that the foreign name of Magdalene should be
dropped. Respecting her religious principles, neither Sir
Charles nor Mary troubled themselves, nor made the slightest
effort to turn her thoughts from her own mode of worship.
Elizabeth, as we shall henceforth call her, was so good and so
pious, and regular in her devotion, and so free from super-
stition or prejudice, that the baronet soon began to reconcile
himself to have a Catholic niece. She was to be called Elizabeth Wharton, introduced everywhere as such ; and as all the
household of Sir Charles were old and attached domestics,
they obeyed the order without making their unexpected inmate
the subject of gossip or wonder—loving the new comer too well
not to gladly welcome her to their master's home.

The family were all busy preparing for their departure, first
to Broomsgrove, the baronet's place in Devonshire, and then
to Plymouth, there to embark for Palermo.

Sir Charles resolved to take with him but four tried and
faithful domestics, and Phœbe, Mary's own especial attendant ;
other attendants could be procured when they had fixed upon
a residence in Sicily. The morning following the brilliant
assembly at the Earl of S——'s, Térese Garetti astounded the
whole family during breakfast, by relating circumstantially the
whole of her conversation the preceding night with the Count
De Courcy.

Sir Charles Wharton fell back in his chair as if electrified.
Mary turned pale and looked bewildered, whilst Elizabeth's
eyes sparkled with delight; for Térese spoke in Italian purposely. Elizabeth, who knew nothing of Edward De Umfre-

ville, only thought of the delight De Courcy must feel at discovering who his parents were, and also at finding himself of such distinguished rank.

" God bless my soul," cried Sir Charles Wharton, " what a romance! Poor Edward, what a blow this must be to him! Upon my life, if I had my choice, I would rather remain a De Courcy."

Elizabeth looked surprised, saying to Mary, :" How is this? you do not seem to rejoice in this good fortune of my generous deliverer."

" Because, dear girl," answered Mary, " it deprives a very amiable and noble-minded gentleman of a position in society he was reared in, and always led to imagine he was entitled to : when I explain to you our intercourse with this gentleman, you will cease to wonder at me. Dear Hugh deserves his rank and wealth, but I know his heart so well, that I am sure his accession to this title and property pains him; the man he deprives of these advantages has been his early and dearly loved friend."

" Well," observed Sir Charles, " I really am so puzzled and surprised, that my wits are rambling. I must go and see Hugh this morning, and bid him farewell for a time. What shall I say from you, Mary? I know he does not expect you to congratulate him, and yet it seems deuced hard, that in regaining his rights, and taking his own name, the name of his forefathers, he is to be left without one kind wish or congratulation from those to whom he is so dear."

" My dear uncle," replied Mary, with a bright flush upon her cheek, " there is no fear of that; Hugh knows our hearts as well as we do his. You may tell him all here wish him every happiness on regaining a name he has so long earnestly wished to obtain : it was the dream of his youth—the ardent desire of his manhood."

Sir Charles Wharton left the three fair girls conversing, and entering his carriage preceded to visit our hero. He found De Courcy and Lord Umfreville together. The worthy baronet was rejoiced at seeing them such fast friends, despite the unfortunate occurrence that had taken place—one friend depriving the other of his inheritance.

" I rejoice to hear, Edward," said Sir Charles, " that you accompany Hugh to Palermo, and I trust that what has passed will not interrupt the friendship and intercourse of our families."

" I should be grieved to the heart, indeed, Sir Charles, should that blow become the penalty of loving without being loved : no, I trust that Miss Wharton will always look upon me as a sincere and devoted friend. I was going this morning to visit you all, but a very unpleasant event took place last night at the Earl of S——'s."

" Bless me," said the baronet, " what has happened?"

Hugh De Courcy related his overhearing the words of Lord Eglin, and his after-conversation with him, adding, " and this morning his lordship, determining to be still the aggressor, Captain Manby has waited upon me to request a settlement of our dispute, as he calls it, by trying to shoot each other to-morrow morning at six o'clock."

" God bless my soul!" exclaimed Sir Charles, greatly distressed, " what outrageous, uncalled-for conduct : but you are not surely going to gratify this hot-headed youth in his un-christian-like proposal."

" What is to be done, my dear Sir Charles?" said De Courcy, with a smile; " I have no intention of shooting at him, I assure you; still I must gratify his insane desire to have a shot at me. His cousin here has tried all possible arguments to turn him from his purpose in vain. What,' he exclaimed, ' because you tamely submit to be deprived of title and fortune by a —— adventurer, do you think I will follow in the same train? No, by ——, I will shoot him as sure as my name is Eglin!' What can you do with a man using such language as that?"

" But, good God! you are not going to stand and be shot at like a rook?" remonstrated the baronet, looking startled; " this man, I am told, is a dead shot—his skill is notorious. You have no right to cast away your life in this mad manner."

" You are quite right, Sir Charles," observed Lord de Umfreville, seriously; " to me this is a very painful affair. If any man could refuse the challenge, Hugh might fairly do so; his name is associated with so many gallant actions that he need never fear a shade of reproach being cast upon him for not meeting his antagonist, and that antagonist his own cousin."

" I do not know that, dear friend," returned De Courcy, " people are very insincere in judging such cases as this : if you are determined to brave the world's opinion, it's another thing, but, believe me, as human nature is now governed, the man who refuses to meet a challenge, would, no matter what his previous character, run a very great chance of losing his position in society : besides, I am told, and Edward here is quite aware of it, so intemperate and vindictive is Lord Eglin, that he would never rest till he publicly insulted me and forced me to use means to repel his hostility. I should greatly dislike : therefore I am fully determined to give him this meeting. If he should not be content with vindicating his honour, as he calls it, or rather as Captain Manby called it, by firing a shot at me, why I will not then answer for my own temper."

" But zounds, Hugh," exclaimed the baronet, with considerable vivacity and anxiety, " if he shoots you the first shot, to the deuce with all your romantic ideas!"

De Courcy smiled, saying, " My dear sir, I have often seen men who could split a wand at twenty yards miss their man at eight paces. It is not a gallery-practised shot that is most to be feared. Let this young nobleman have his way, he may learn wisdom by it."

" Well, all this is bad logic," said the old baronet; " I trust the world will improve, and that a day may come when men will become too sensible to do such things ; but as it stands, if men really receive insults and are provoked into duelling, in Heaven's name, if they go out to fight, let them fight, and not stand like rooks, to be picked down without a struggle."

De Courcy gradually calmed down the excitable feelings of the baronet, and by degrees brought him to talk on other subjects.

The letter of Sir John Acton was read to him, and then he looked carefully over the documents in the packet, which the two friends were going to place in the hands of the eminent lawyer, Sir Everard Hope.

" Yes," observed Sir Charles, thoughtfully, after perusing them all, there is nothing wanting but to prove identity, and that is very simple. Now it strikes me that this bitter hostility and conduct of Lord Eglin arises partly from his knowledge that he holds in his possession the now very large fortune of your mother, Eglantine De Courcy, afterwards De Umfreville. She, it appears, inherited £40,000 from her grandfather, which your father, my dear Hugh, never received, though fully entitled to. Sir Egbert De Courcy died, as well as I now recollect, suddenly and without a will ; so that your father, had he lived, would have been entitled to the half, certainly, of the great estates left by him ; instead of which, Lord Eglin's father, one of the most extravagant noblemen in Europe, probably, inherited the whole, and his son soon after him. Now Lord Eglin's mother is still living, and she must know all this, and that she unjustly inherited her sister's property. The present Lord Eglin, therefore, sees clearly that if you prove yourself entitled to the Umfreville title, you will also become entitled to the division of Sir Egbert De Courcy's estates, besides the £40,000 left your mother by her grandfather; and as the present Lord Eglin inherited a very impoverished property in comparison to what it ought to have been, he dreads your claims, which would sweep away three parts of his estates."

" But, my dear sir, I never intended to disturb his succession ; Lord de Umfreville stated as much this morning to him, to endeavour to get him to be reconciled, and, as relations, settle matters amicably; but he scornfully scoffed at my pretensions, and refused all terms of reconciliation."

" Then, in Heaven's name, let him bide the consequences," cried Sir Charles.

" Such must be the case," said our hero; "these documents and papers will immediately be delivered over to Sir Everard. But when do you depart, Sir Charles?"

"After to-morrow for Broomsgrove," replied the baronet: " on the 25th we leave Plymouth for Palermo in the —— frigate."

" You cannot make the voyage under a braver, more skilful, and kind-hearted commander than Captain Friend," remarked our hero: "I was very intimate with him during the blockade of Genoa: pray remember me to him."

Sir Charles thought for a moment, and then said, looking the young man steadily in the face, " Will you both sup with me to-night and bid us farewell: who knows," added the kind-hearted baronet, in a tone with a touch of saduess in it, " who knows how and when we may meet again?"

There was a bright colour for a moment in the pale cheek of Lord de Umfreville, but, suddenly looking up, with a cheerful smile, he said, " With the greatest pleasure, Sir Charles; and I am sure I can answer for Hugh. Can I not, dear friend?"

"You have a noble heart, Edward," returned De Courcy, grasping his hand.

The baronet looked delighted; observing, "Edward, you have not seen Hugh's fair *protégée*, Magdalene, henceforth to be called Elizabeth; on my honour it is difficult to distinguish her from Mary, when they are dressed alike. I will now leave you, still trusting something may turn up to prevent this very objectionable meeting to-morrow; at all events, I shall say nothing about it at home."

This proposed meeting again with Miss Wharton, to Lord de Umfreville, was in many respects painful. Still it was a trial he determined to go through; for connected in such firm ties of friendship with De Courcy, it was his firm purpose to witness their happiness without a feeling of envy, and, if possible, without regret: he made no doubt but that time, which softens all afflictions, and enables us to bear the ills that flesh is heir to, would have its effect with him; for he looked forward with delight to his intercourse with De Courcy, who promised, the moment he could do so with honour, to retire from the service of the Neapolitan king, and make his home in England.

To Hugh De Courcy, the thoughts of seeing his beloved Mary, before leaving England, was rapture—it was more than he had expected; and so occupied was his mind with his visit, that the disagreeable event that was to take place on the morrow was only recalled to his thought by a visit from the Baron de Molina, a Neapolitan gentleman, who had accompanied the Marquis de Policastra to England; this gentleman was to be the Count De Courcy's second.

Having arranged with the Baron all the preliminaries for the following morning, and leaving everything entirely to his discretion, when he took his leave, the two friends set out for the lawyer's house in —————— square. Sir Everard Hope was at home; and the two young men were shown into the private study, where he almost immediately joined them.

Sir Everard Hope was very well known to Lord de Umfreville, and the lawyer received the son of his old friend, the late lord, with earnest politeness.   Lord de Umfreville introduced the Count De Courcy, saying, "My dear Sir Everard, you will be surprised no doubt at the object of our visit."

"Whatever may be the cause, my lord, that has procured me the honour of this visit, I congratulate myself upon it," replied the lawyer, with a facetious, pleasant smile.

"We have come to consult you, Sir Everard," continued Lord de Umfreville, "upon a very singular freak of Dame Fortune.   I find I must surrender my title and estates."

"Surrender your title and estates!" repeated the lawyer, with a start, and with an accent of surprise; "you surely joke, my lord?"

"No, my dear sir, not now; this is past a joke; though believe me, in surrendering both title and estates, it is a consoling reflection that they go to a near and very dear friend indeed: permit me to introduce you to the real Lord de Umfreville, in the person of the Count De Courcy."

Sir Everard Hope was so completely overwhelmed with astonishment that he remained leaning back in his chair, gazing at the two young men, as if in a dream.

"God bless my soul!" he exclaimed, at length, passing his hand across his brow, "you bewilder me, my lord; how is this possible?   Your noble father inherited the title and estates from his father in direct descent, you——"

"Yes, my dear sir," interrupted Lord de Umfreville, "there you are quite correct; but my grandfather inherited the property from his brother. who was supposed to die without heirs: now suppose the elder brother left a grandson, would not that grandson be the actual heir?"

"Unquestionably," returned the lawyer, "but——"

"Well, not to mystify you, my dear sir, the fact is this; the Count De Courcy is the grandson of the elder brother; and these papers," our hero laid the packet on the table as his friend spoke, "will put you *au fait* to the whole matter: as they will require your careful perusal, Sir Everard Hope, we will not ask you to examine them now; whatever advice you give my friend here will adopt; but there is one thing I wish to observe, and that is, I am so thoroughly satisfied of the Count's rights that not the slightest opposition will be offered by me."

" Well, gentlemen," said the lawyer, still considerably surprised, "those papers shall have my most earnest attention, and if at this time to-morrow you will honour me with a visit, you shall hear my strict and unbiased opinion."

" Thank you, Sir Everard," returned De Courcy, "and afterwards, if you will favour me with your attention, and you find I am entitled to the titles and estates in question, I will, when the law decides the case, explain to you how I wish to proceed in this affair."

" I feel proud, Count De Courcy, of your confidence." answered the lawyer, "and believe me, my lord," he added, turning to our hero's friend, "I grieve deeply at this unexpected stroke of fortune; but, as well as I remember, your grandfather's personal property was considerable, and of this you hold possession."

" Oh, my dear sir," returned Lord de Umfreville, cheerfully, "as far as fortune goes I shall do very well; and as to titles, I would rather lose a dozen than such a friend as this;" and he laid his hand affectionately on De Courcy's shoulder.

Shaking the lawyer by the hand, the friends departed.

CHAPTER XXXIV

THE fashionable resort of duellists at the period of our story, when duels were as frequent as a shift of wind, was at a place not a mile from Blackheath. It was the month of September; therefore it was broad daylight as two carriages made their appearance, approaching this ground. Six persons alighted from the carriages, and walked in separate groups of three to the ground selected. These six persons consisted of the combatants, their seconds, and two surgeons, each gentleman taking his own.

Lord Eglin, attired in a military undress frock, looked well and unconcerned: Hugh De Courcy was in plain clothes; his demeanour calm, collected, but serious. Lord Eglin's second was his sworn follower, Captain Manby, a gentleman well accustomed to such encounters. The domestics of each having deposited the duelling cases of pistols, retired with the carriages to some short distance.

Hugh De Courcy, as he stood, waiting for the preliminaries to be settled by the seconds, felt not one particle of animosity or ill-feeling towards his antagonist, but would most willingly have shaken hands, and buried in oblivion the cause of their quarrel altogether.

Lord Eglin, to judge by the stern expression of his features, showed anything but an amiable or placable disposition.

De Courcy's thoughts, notwithstanding the affair in which he was about to become an actor, were fixed upon Mary

Wharton whom he had met the preceding evening, when all the past was forgotten in a moment by two hearts so fondly attached. Lord de Umfreville's manner and conduct in that meeting was admirable : he approached Mary with the kindness and affection of an attached brother, and immediately won her from all restraint or reserve, rendering her faithful heart truly happy during the evening. At supper he conversed a great deal with Elizabeth ; he seemed forcibly struck with her likeness to Mary, and evinced unusual interest in his manner and in his conversation with her.

Elizabeth herself having been made acquainted with Lord de Umfreville's noble conduct, and his determined relinquishment of title and fortune the moment he discovered his friend was entitled to them, regarded his lordship with a pleasing feeling.

Knowing the particulars of her early history, Lord de Umfreville was perfectly astonished at the beauty, the intelligence, and the charming manner of Elizabeth.

Thus the evening passed away, to De Courcy one of the happiest of his life—to De Umfreville, with far less painful feelings than he could have anticipated.

Sir Charles Wharton's kind heart exulted in having, as he called it, achieved a triumph ; he was greatly attached to Lord de Umfreville, and in heart cherished a secret wish that Elizabeth might in time replace the void Mary had made in his heart.

With recollections of the past night's happiness filling his mind and thoughts, De Courcy stood waiting to be summoned to take his part in a contest repugnant to him in every sense. All being ready, Baron Molina placed our hero at his appointed post, handed him his weapon, and pressing his hand as they parted, said, " When I drop my glove, fire—it is the signal agreed upon."

De Courcy nodded his head, and stood calmly regarding his antagonist, who took his place ten paces distant.

The two seconds then retired a few paces, and Baron Molina held the glove aloft, and seeing both gentlemen attentive, dropped it. Instantly Lord Eglin's pistol was raised and fired. His opponent felt the ball graze his shoulder very slightly, and, raising his pistol, fired in the air.

With a scoffing laugh, Lord Eglin immediately exclaimed, " As I thought : but that is a stale trick : I demand another shot."

" My lord, answered De Courcy, " between relations, such a contest as this is disgraceful ; if you will be satisfied, I am ; I feel no animosity to you whatever.

" My case is different, sir," returned his lordship; and turning to his second, he said, speaking harshly, " I demand, as I have a right, a second shot; that is child's play, I did not come here for such foolery."

Our hero was vexed and irritated, and stepped back to his position with a flush of anger on his cheek. Captain Manby observed it, as well as the fierce flash from his dark eyes. " Be steady, my lord, this time ; " he whispered to Lord Eglin; " before, you were a shade too high."

Baron Molina, with a rather unceremonious oath, and a look of anger at Lord Eglin, observed to De Courcy, " You had better, count, not waste powder and ball, or else we may not meet, and get curt thanks."

De Courcy made no reply, but the moment the glove fell he fired ; Lord Eglin staggered, dropped his pistol, and sank down.

De Courcy was hit at the same time, but it was only a flesh-wound, and caused neither pain nor uneasiness : he advanced towards his lordship, saying to Baron Molina, " He is not much hurt, I took care of that; it is the pain that caused him to stagger and fall." As they advanced, Lord Eglin regained his feet, supported by his surgeon and Captain Manby: his right wrist had been broken by the ball from De Courcy's pistol, and the agony of the wound had occasioned faintness.

" You are bleeding, count," observed Baron Molina anxiously ; " are you hit ? "

" Very slightly, indeed," returned our hero ; and stripping off his coat, as his surgeon approached, it was perceived that the ball had narrowly escaped doing serious injury : as it was, it was a mere flesh-wound, and a slight bandage stopped the flow of blood. After this had been placed on, he advanced towards Lord Eglin, not wishing to quit the ground without an attempt at reconciliation: but pale, suffering, and exhausted as he was, his lordship stoutly refused even to exchange words with his antagonist, saying, in a bitter tone of resentment, " that the time would come when he might expect to meet him again; but as to reconciliation, that would never take place."

" His lordship is a stern and unforgiving antagonist," observed Baron Molina, " and yet he may thank his stars that he is not now a dead man, which he would have been, had you felt the same spirit as animated him."

" It is very strange, baron," returned our hero, " but things must now take their course; I cannot be expected to feel for a man who so openly expresses and evinces so decided a hostility for me."

The several parties then entered their carriages and returned to town, where De Courcy found Lord de Umfreville anxiously awaiting him. For many reasons it would not have been prudent for him to have been in the late encounter : he shook his friend's hand warmly, saying, "Indeed, indeed, Hugh, I have suffered great anxiety. Knowing Lord Eglin's character and his skill as a duellist, and being aware you would reserve your fire, I trembled for the consequence."

" Well, I confess," replied De Courcy, "that it was not altogether without risk that I stood before his lordship's pistol: he was perfectly cool and apparently collected, whilst his aim was steady: he hit me twice: probably over-anxiety prevented him from killing me the first shot. It was no use standing tamely to be killed, so the second time I disarmed him by an ugly wound ; I had no alternative ; and I fear it will be a long time before he will regain the perfect use of his right hand."

" He is a man," said Lord de Umfreville, " I never could like, neither is he liked by his brother-officers—quarrelsome and capricious in temper, dissipated and extravagant to excess, and evincing a vindictiveness of feeling when thwarted or obstructed in any individual pursuit; so that though his rank and fortune procure him followers amongst his own class, he has few real friends. My lamented father could never bear him ; you know he married his father's sister."

" Then, supposing he never marries, or has no heirs male, who succeeds to the Eglin title ? "

" Why, I believe I am the only male representative of the family, excepting yourself: his mother is your aunt, and his father was my uncle."

De Courcy, though he did not complain, felt the wound in the side painful, and requiring rest; therefore, stretching himself on the sofa, he left Lord de Umfreville to proceed on his visit to Sir Everard Hope, alone.

His lordship had scarcely departed before Sir Charles Wharton drove up to the door: his anxiety had been so intense all the morning that his family had perceived that something unusual preyed upon his mind, and Mary, whose sweet features spoke of renewed hope, and a mind at peace, had noticed the fidgety, uneasy manner of her uncle, and his loss of appetite.

Térese Garetti at once suspected something, knowing what had occurred at the Earl of S——'s, and her conjectures approached something very near to the truth.

When Sir Charles, immediately after breakfast, ordered his chariot as soon as possible, and shortly after drove off without a word of explanation, Mary looked startled, and said, " Dear Térese, can you imagine what has disturbed my uncle this morning? he seemed quite abstracted and uneasy at breakfast ; and now he has gone off without a word, and we are to leave town at three o'clock."

" Some business he very likely forgot yesterday," observed

Mrs. Arbuthnot rising: " come, Elizabeth, we must go on with our packing."

Mary and Térese were left alone, and the former looked into the latter's thoughtful countenance, saying, " I see by the expression of your face, Térese, that you suspect, partly at least, the cause of my uncle's uneasiness, for uneasy he certainly was; I know you have an idea what disturbed him."

" Indeed, dear Mary, I can only conjecture, and you know it would be very foolish to fret ourselves conjecturing."

" Still I have become alarmed, for I am satisfied my uncle's uneasiness has something to do with Hugh. Now do tell me, cara, what you suspect?—anything but suspense."

" I can only suspect, dear Mary, that a quarrel may have arisen between De Courcy and that disagreeable man, Lord Eglin. You know I told you what occurred at the Earl of S——'s. Men are hot and impetuous, and a quarrel may have arisen out of their interview in the earl's library."

Mary's cheek betrayed her feelings, but she conquered her emotion, saying, " No doubt such is the case, and our uncle knew of it, and has hurried off to hear the result. Now God forbid that either should fall; of all things in this world I hold in most abhorrence, is a duel; and that Hugh, who has faced death undauntedly in many a terrible form, should think of—— "

" Come, come, dear Mary," interrupted Térese, throwing her arms round her cousin's neck and kissing her fondly, as she saw tears she could not restrain trembling on her eyelids, " you, who always blamed Hugh for looking at the gloomy side of the picture, arc now conjuring up a phantasmagoria of your own. Let us go and employ ourselves, and get our little trifles ready; depend on it, you will have no cause to mourn over any misfortune to your lover."

Mary exerted herself, and strove to drive away the anxious thoughts that would, despite her endeavours, occupy her mind; still her car was ready to catch at every sound. She knew Sir Charles must be back soon, for post-horses were ordered at three o'clock. It was past one, however, before the baronet's chariot returned : Mary heard his step on the stairs, and with a heart beating with anxiety, she hurried down to meet him. The first glance she caught of her uncle's fine, open, cheerful features showed her that he, at all events, had quite lost the look of uneasiness his face wore in the morning.

" Ha, Mary, I see," exclaimed the baronet, throwing himself into a chair—" I see you have had an inkling of what was going on ; but, thank God, this detestable affair has ended without any fatal result."

" Then there was a duel, dear uncle ? " said Mary, anxiously.

"Ha," remarked the baronet, "so you had a suspicion of this affair? Well it is over, and no great harm done, thank God! but if ever there was a frippery, quarrelsome, vindictive fellow living, it is Lord Eglin—he has now got something to keep him quiet for a while at all events."

"Good heavens!" exclaimed Mary, with a shudder, "then Lord Eglin has been wounded, and Hugh——"

"Oh, nothing the matter with him, only a mere scratch ; though he was deuced near paying dearly for his generous forbearance."

Mary sighed ; she thought what might have been the consequence had Lord Eglin succeeded in his vindictive intention. Térese entered the room, and Sir Charles gave them both a full account of the duel, which shocked both girls exceedingly. Sir Charles then told them that he had driven over to Sir Everard Hope, as he was anxious, before leaving town, to hear his opinion of the papers left with him for his examination.

The baronet said he found Lord de Umfreville there. Sir Everard declared that there was not the slightest doubt respecting the authenticity of the papers, neither would there be any difficulty in establishing the Count De Courcy's claims. Some little time would be necessary, of course ; and the lawyer also gave it as his opinion, that Lord Eglin would dispute every inch of the ground, as the Count De Courcy's claim involved a considerable amount of his property. It would be necessary to send to Ireland for several vouchers, and also get answers to one or two important questions which it was necessary Sir John Acton should give on oath.

Sir Everard was to proceed as he thought fit; but in the meantime the parties engaged in the suit were to remain as at present, till the Count De Courcy found it convenient to retire from the Neapolitan service, and return to England.

CHAPTER XXXV.

On the 1st of October the Dauntless frigate sailed from Plymouth, en route for Gibraltar, Malta, and Palermo, having on board Sir Charles Wharton, his family and domestics. Captain Friend had at one time received great kindness from the baronet, who had released him from great pecuniary embarrassment; whilst through his friendship his family were made comfortable, and himself enabled to follow his naval career. Captain Friend took the only opportunity he had of showing his gratitude, and finding Sir Charles and family were proceeding to Palermo, offered the baronet the entire use of his chief cabins for himself and family : this was extremely acceptable to Sir Charles, who had hesitated at embarking in a merchant vessel.

The weather happened to be remarkably fine, and the wind fair. The presence of three such beautiful girls on the quarter-deck of the Dauntless created quite a sensation; even the young midshipmen made themselves as smart as possible. The first two days out of Plymouth nothing could exceed the beauty of the weather. Sir Charles Wharton and family were treated with the most generous attention by Captain Friend. He had an excellent band on board—some of the performers, it is true, were amateurs: two or three of the officers were first-rate musicians, and several very pleasant evenings were spent in listening to the band, whilst the ladies walked the quarter-deck: all were seasoned sailors, so that that pest of a sea life, sickness, was no drawback to their enjoyment.

"I see, Captain Friend," observed Sir Charles, "that you have some foreign sailors amongst your crew."

"Not exactly amongst my crew," replied Captain Friend; "but I have given a passage to Palermo to nearly a dozen Neapolitan seamen, who served, they tell me, with Nelson, at the time he was in Naples. One, a very superior man in language and manner, says he was quarter-master in a ship with the unfortunate Prince Caraccioli, and that, for murmuring at his horrid fate, he and his companions were forced to fly, and shipped themselves on board a British ship for England. Now all that affair is forgotten, at least so he hopes, and he wishes to return to his native land. I very willingly allowed the whole batch to work their passage."

The sixth day there was an appearance of a change in the weather, and when the wind shifted on the seventh day, the hoisting of a heavy weight out of the hold caused a number of seamen to assemble at the hauling tackle; Térese, Garetti, and Elizabeth happened to be standing near the railing, looking at the work, when suddenly Térese felt her arm grasped forcibly by Elizabeth, who fell back a pace or two, and on looking up into her face, she perceived she was as pale as death.

"Santa Marie! Elizabeth, what ails you; not sea-sick, surely?"

"No, no," whispered Elizabeth, pulling the Genoese away; "do you know who is on board this ship?"

"No, Madonna; not the least idea. Who did you see?"

"Hush! not a word," returned Elizabeth! "let him remain undiscovered—wretch as he is. I would not like to have him seized and manacled."

"But who is he, dear Elizabeth? You quite startle me; not that any dozen men, let them be ever so bad, could hurt you here. Who did you see?"

"Campobello, the Lazzarone," whispered Elizabeth; "there was no mistaking him; though he has cropped his long hair

R 2

and shaved his face quite clean, and is dressed like a common sailor."

"Madonna, you amaze me!" cried Térese ; "do point him out to me "

" Oh, Saint Marie forbid!" Elizabeth replied; "the sight of his terrible eyes terrifies me. As he was going along with the rope. I caught his look all of a sudden fixed upon me. I thought that it had the fabulous power of the rattle-snake, or that he possessed the malochia. I could not stir till he passed on, and then, as you know, I trembled."

" Horrid wretch ! why not tell the captain?" said Térese; " why leave him free—though of course he cannot harm you."

" Better leave him alone till, at all events, we approach Palermo," observed Elizabeth.

" Well," answered Térese, thoughtfully, " I heard Captain Friend tell Sir Charles he had several Italians on board, to whom he had allowed a free passage. Now it is not at all improbable, if you are right respecting Campobello, but that Lieutenant Baracco may be here also. I should know him, I am sure, let him disguise himself as he may. It is very strange how they managed to escape all pursuit. As to that deceitful villain, Baracco, who twice attempted the Count De Courcy's life, he ought, if he is on board, to be arrested ; for he is a traitor, besides an assassin. But, dear Elizabeth, we had better say nothing about this discovery of yours to Mary; they can do no harm here, though, as you say, they ought to be secured before we land in Palermo, for there they might plot mischief."

This discovery of Elizabeth s made her very thoughtful, and reluctant to go on deck. The next two days, however. the wind blew hard and direct against them, and whilst making for the Spanish coast near the bay of Cadiz, under double-reefed topsails, three ships were discovered, under close canvas, standing out on the opposite tack. As Captain Friend's directions were to avoid encountering the enemy whilst he had despatches on board, he tacked ship, and stood out on the same board.

The foremost ship sailed well, purposely retarding the progress of the Dauntless. Captain Friend allowed the stranger to approach so as to make her out clearly. On a nearer approach. he discovered her to be a beautiful frigate, but certainly not English ; he then tried his speed with every sail set, but still. without an additional canvas to those she commenced the chase with, she came rapidly up. After an-other steady survey through his glass, Captain Friend recog-nized her for the Neapolitan frigate Serena. This was a pleasing surprise to the captain, who immediately ordered his main top-sails to be thrown aback to await the coming up of the Serena. At the same time, the news that the Serena was close up with them found its way to the cabin, and sent a glow to the cheek of Mary, and an increased palpitation of the heart. Our heroine was soon on deck, leaning on the arm of the pleased Sir Charles, and accompanied by the whole family.

" What a beautiful sight, and what a noble ship ! " exclaimed Mary, with a feeling of pride that her gallant lover commanded her.

" Yes," replied Captain Friend, with an admiring glance at the Neapolitan frigate, " I never saw a more beautiful specimen of naval architecture ; wonderful, that people who can build such ships cannot find sailors to man them ! "

"And yet, Captain Friend," said Mary, almost proudly " the Serena and the Vesuvius, both Neapolitan ships, have performed brilliant actions."

" Undoubtedly, Miss Wharton," returned the Captain, " but who took them into action ? who taught the sailors their sea-manship, and gave impetus to their courage by self-example " As fine a fellow, Miss Wharton, as ever trod the deck of a ship, and an Englishman to boot."

"I beg your pardon." interrupted Sir Charles, with a sly look at Mary, whose cheeks vied with the roses ; " Captain De Courcy is an Irishman."

"All the same, my dear sir," returned the captain ; " an Irishman has the honour of old England as much at heart as any Englishman living ; and we have found, at a pinch, more than once in our army and navy, that no braver or better soldiers or sailors ever existed than Irishmen. The day. I trust, is not far distant when national prejudice will cease, and that the bulk of Englishmen will judge fairly of their past friends, and not take as a picture of an Irish gentleman the absurd caricatures exhibited on our stage as a specimen of a genuine Irishman ;* but, by Jove ! there goes the gun and the colours, which all this time I have forgotten."

Ten minutes more and the graceful Serena was alongside the Dauntless lying-to, and, in a few minutes more, her six-oared gig was pulling alongside, with Hugh De Courcy and his friend, Lord de Umfreville, in her ; next moment they were on deck. Mutual congratulations took place between all parties. Our hero pressed the hand of his beautiful Mary with a feeling scarcely possible to describe ; all were rejoiced to see Lord de Umfreville, who looked well, and was in exceeding good spirits.

Captain Friend, as he warmly shook hands with his old acquaintance, De Courcy, said, " But how, in the name of wonder, did you come up with us ? When did you leave Plymouth ? "

* Captain Friend speaks fifty-six years ago.

"Two days after you, Captain Friend; but it appears you kept a more westerly course, and had contrary winds. We ran along the Spanish coast with a fine steady breeze all the way; had a short brush with a French corvette and three very smart privateers. We sank one of the privateers, and whilst capturing the two fine merchant ships which you just see away in-shore, the corvette, with the loss of her mizen and fore-top mast, got into ————. so putting a prize crew into each of the brigs, I continued working up for Gibraltar, till I got a glimpse of you; at first I thought you were a French frigate, but was very much rejoiced to find friends instead of an enemy."

"Ah, by Jove!" laughed Captain Friend, "I see, count, how the wind lies; I fancy, only that my fair guests are on board, you would as willingly have discovered me to be a French cruiser as not, eh?"

Whilst the party on the quarter-deck were enjoying this unexpected and happy meeting, two persons right in the bows of the Dauntless were conversing earnestly, and with rather a startled look. They were attired as sailors, and their faces were much disguised by being clean shaved, and their hair cropped close; but a keen eye, and one who knew them well, would, after a moment, detect in one the features of Guiseppe Baracco, and in the other those of Antonio Campobello. They had watched the approach of the Serena with intense uneasiness, for Guiseppe Baracco knew her well, and a feeling of overpowering bitterness pervaded his heart; he cursed fortune, his own existence, and the luck, as he called it, of Hugh De Courcy; cursed him in his heart as the destroyer of his fame and fortune. Strange delusion! that this man, well educated, with good mental powers, with skill and talent sufficient to raise his own fortunes, and yet who never for a moment imputed his failure in not rising to fame and opulence to his own invidious conduct. No, with a prejudiced, envious eye, he laid his downfall to our hero's preponderating good fortune, which had blasted his. Yet such was very far from being the case, for Hugh De Courcy's interest, had he followed his advice and wishes, would have placed him in the very position he had intrigued so unworthily to gain, and for which he had committed himself as a traitor to his king and a false friend to the man who really esteemed him. Blinded by his hate, he leagued with a common, uneducated, vindictive ruffian, to gain his ends, no matter by what means: even if he himself failed, so that he poisoned the cup of happiness to De Courcy, he felt satisfied.

When they beheld the boat with our hero and Lord de Umfreville pull up alongside, their uneasiness increased. Baracco almost despaired; a terrible resolve was taken, and his hand nervously grasped a loaded pistol he always had concealed about his person. Both retired to the very farthest part of the frigate, and leaning over the bow conversed in a low voice.

"Do you think, Antonio, that the girl will betray you? if, as you say, she positively recognized you."

"Maladetta, yes, she recognized me well enough," returned the ruffian, with a terrible expression of countenance, "but she will not betray me; she has a soft heart, that girl. It was a cursed, unlucky affair, her overhearing us that night, for till then she firmly believed I was her father—that ruined all, my power over her was gone."

"But who is the girl? She's so like that other with the English baronet, whom they both call uncle, it is so strange; then look at her manner and carriage, she would pass in the drawing-room of a duchess."

"Corpo de Diavola! did not I tell you she resided several years of her life with a first-rate educated woman; besides which she was quick, and she picked up lots of information from an old fool of a nun."

"All that's very well," returned Baracco, musingly, "but whose child is she? Come, don't think I'm the dupe of that story of yours, of a female giving you some fifty ducats in the streets of Naples to take care of her. Tell the truth. We may make something of it; you cannot get out of——"

"Hush!" interrupted Campobello, "come down below, and I'll tell you all about her; but curse me if I do not have my revenge on her yet!"

"There are more than twenty turbulent spirits on board this ship," said Baracco, as they descended the ladder; "they were mutineers and pardoned, but a spark would set them in a flame again."

"Watch an opportunity," replied the Lazzarone, with a laugh of savage enthusiasm, "and burn this infernal ship. I can't stand work of this kind."

"You are a fool or a madman!" observed Baracco, rather startled, "but take it coolly. Something may turn up between this and Palermo."

In the meantime our hero, after passing a few happy hours with those on board the Dauntless, returned to his own ship; Captain Friend delightedly agreeing to keep company the remainder of the way with the Serena to Palermo, providing De Courcy would remain for twenty-four hours in Gibraltar. To this proposition our hero was too happy to agree; and the following morning both ships anchored off the mole, in that stronghold of Great Britain.

A very pleasant day and evening were passed by the whole party from the Dauntless, with our hero, at the hospitable mansion of the Governor. De Courcy's two prizes came in the following morning; they were fine brigs, and richly laden from the foreign colonies of France.

The news had just reached Gibraltar that Buonaparte had, through the intrigues of his brother Lucien, with the famous Godoy, the Prince of Peace, induced Spain to declare war against Portugal; and that the court of Madrid had agreed to make over to France, either by sale or hire, six sail of the line lying in the port of Cadiz.* These ships were to be manned by French sailors, and then, in conjunction with a Spanish force, enter the Tagus and sack Lisbon. The only vessel-of-war at this time at anchor at Gibraltar was the fourteen-gun sloop Calpé, commanded by the Honourable George Lawrence Dundas.

Our hero brought intelligence to Gibraltar that the British squadron was off Cadiz. Accordingly the captain of the Calpé despatched his lieutenant in a boat to the fleet, with intelligence that the fleet of Monsieur Lenois were seen off the rock.

Our hero would very much have liked to have remained and joined the British fleet, but his orders were to get to Palermo with all possible despatch; therefore the Serena and the Dauntless both sailed the following morning, much to the regret of the Governor and Captain Dundas. The Serena had to shorten sail considerably, in order to keep company with the Dauntless; but the second day a sudden and dense fog shut them out from each other's sight; it was night also, and the Serena, two hours before the fog set in, had increased her canvas, and stood away to the northward to examine several suspicious sails in that direction. During the night the wind veered into the south-west, the fog increasing; Captain Friend stood on his course, thinking the fog would lift with the dawn, but instead of that it increased, and the wind suddenly shifted into the northward, blowing exceedingly hard. For two days the vessel continued working along the Barbary coast, and, to judge by the soundings, at no very great distance. The weather continued singularly foggy, considering the point the wind was in; the sea was at times very heavy, with rainy and squally weather; so that for the two days after parting company with the Serena, none of the ladies had appeared upon deck. Sir Charles Wharton went up now and then to see how they got on, but the thick haze and squalls of rain and wind soon drove him down again to the cabin. Though confined below, and the motion of the ship violent at times, none of the party, excepting Mrs. Arbuthnot, suffered at all from sea-sickness. Mary became uneasy at their losing sight of the Serena; she

* We beg to state that we may be wrong by a few months as to the exact period of this transaction.—AUTHOR

felt as if nothing could happen to them as long as her lover's ship kept them in sight. The third night was still intensely thick, but the sea moderate, the wind shifting more into the west, and towards midnight into the south-west. Captain Friend was rejoiced at this change of wind, as it enabled him to keep off the coast, which he felt satisfied he was rather near to. About two o'clock in the morning—Captain Friend had retired to rest about one—the first lieutenant, a very skilful and steady officer, was on deck; it was blowing fresh, but steadily, the ship under her full top-sails, going about eight knots an hour, when the man on the look-out cried out, in an alarmed and startled tone, "Breakers under the ship's bows!" and the next moment the frigate struck with tremendous violence; at the same time her foremast went by the board, right over her bows. In an instant a scene of terrific confusion and alarm ensued, the entire crew hurrying up from below half dressed, and bewildered by the suddenness of the catastrophe.

When the ship struck, Sir Charles Wharton and all his family were asleep; but the fearful shock of a craft going nearly eight knots an hour through the water, coming all at once upon a reef* of hard rock, was terrible. With a wild cry, Mary and Elizabeth, who slept in the same cabin, found themselves thrown violently against the sides of their berth, and the swinging lamp knocked against the deck, was smashed to pieces and the light extinguished, whilst the crash of the falling mast added to their bewilderment and terror; then came the flapping of canvas, the rattling of blocks, the creaking of the guns, and the groans of the bulkheads, as the ship heaved at first to the shock of the sea, then crashed down upon the rocks, with that horrible sound so terrible to the ears of a seaman.

"Ah, my God, Elizabeth," exclaimed Mary, "we are ashore upon the rocks! Heaven help us! we are lost; and this darkness is terrible."

"Be of good heart, dear Mary," answered Elizabeth, preparing to dress herself as well as she could in the dark; "this is a large ship, and will not go to pieces easily; dress yourself, dearest."

Whilst she spoke there was a knock at the door of their cabin, and the voice of Sir Charles called out anxiously to them, demanding if they were hurt.

"No, dear uncle," exclaimed Mary, "but we are in the dark; how is Térese and Mrs. Arbuthnot?"

"Do not be alarmed, dear girls," said Sir Charles, "there

---

* On this reef our talented and lamented nautical writer, Captain Marryatt, lost his son, a lieutenant on board, we forget the name of the frigate, which struck on this reef.

is no one hurt; but we are aground on a reef. I will give you a light."

In a moment or two he returned with a light and Mary's attendant, Phœbe, who slept in the cabin occupied by Térese and Mrs. Arbuthnot. " Oh, my God, Miss, is not this frightful? " the poor girl was shaking all over.

" Dress yourself quickly, girls," said Sir Charles, " and come out into the cabin; perhaps we shall have to take to the boats."

Mary shuddered, but she and Elizabeth quickly dressed themselves. The frigate seemed wedged, for she only rolled slightly from side to side, but they could hear the shocks of the seas as they broke against her side and burst over her decks. Over their heads there appeared a terrible commotion—stamping of feet, the rattling of chains, loud voices commanding, and at times fierce oaths and imprecations from several turbulent and violent hands.

Mary and Elizabeth were soon in the cabin, where Térese and Mrs. Arbuthnot joined them; the girls threw themselves into each other's arms, kissing each other affectionately, and protesting they would thus perish or live together. Sir Charles did all he could to encourage them; he said he had no fear if the crew remained true to their officers ; as the weather was not so very rough, he would go see what was doing, and bade them have heart and trust in Providence. Presently a wild uproar was heard on deck, and then hurried footsteps rushed down the cabin stairs ; and Sir Charles, Captain Friend, and the first lieutenant, a gentleman of the name of Scott, entered the cabin.

" Wrap yourselves in your mantles," exclaimed all the gentlemen at once, so hurried and eager were they to save the females ; " but keep up your nerve ; we must leave the ship, there is not a moment to lose."

" Merciful God ! " exclaimed Mrs. Arbuthnot, " the ship is on fire !" As she spoke a bright red flame lighted up the cabin from the skylight above.

" Then God only can help us," said Mary, in a low voice to Elizabeth, to whom she clung; " but let us not despair."

" No, beloved Mary," said Elizabeth, firmly ; " in almost worse perils—for there are worse perils than death—I have never despaired."

Assisted by the gentlemen, the females, showing wonderful courage, gained the deck. What a scene presented itself ; the fore part of the ship was in flames, the bright blaze shooting up in spiral wreaths, whilst volumes of dense smoke blew over the deck ; luckily the ship lay with her stern partly to the strong breeze blowing, so that the flame did not make as rapid progress aft as they would have done, had the wind blown the other way. The sea all around them was a sheet of foam tinged with red by the flames. No land, not even a bare rock was to be seen; the boats were all safely launched, the marines and steady seamen keeping guard, but some package of gunpowder or other combustible at this moment took fire and exploded, and from that instant all control was lost, and a scene of the most terrible and horrible confusion ensued. In vain officers commanded; a wild rush was made for the boats; men were trampled under foot; the marines, steady to the last, even fired their muskets to repel the furious crowd.

In this appalling uproar, Mary, who was clinging to Elizabeth, and supported by Sir Charles, was suddenly seized by the waist; the baronet was thrown down, and Mary and Elizabeth were borne rapidly on, their mantles over their heads stifling their shrieks; presently they felt themselves lifted over the side, and then those that bore them fell forward, but were caught by others below. The two girls still retained their senses, but they were nearly stifled; they knew not what to think, but they felt they were seated in a boat, and then a voice said, "Maladetta, now be quick; cut the rope, we are all clear!"

"Oh, Madonna," mentally exclaimed Elizabeth, "that voice!" the language was Italian, and the voice was Campobello's.

As the boat shot from the side, the guns, heated by the flames, exploded, and the loud roar of the cannon close over their heads was so horrible that Mary, half fainting, made an effort to free herself from the mantle. A strong hand, however, held her round the waist, and another kept the mantle fast. She could judge that the boat laboured through a heavy sea, for she felt the cold splash of the wave as it flew over them; but suddenly there was a loud and fearful explosion; the sea appeared to rock under them, and the boat trembled from stem to stern.

"Ha, Saint Nicholas!" exclaimed a voice close to Mary's ear, "that's the last of her." Our heroine knew the voice, and she shuddered with horror and astonishment, for it was that of Guiseppe Baracco.

"Now, signora, you may look about you," exclaimed the same voice, and the hoods of the mantles were drawn back, and the hands that held them were withdrawn.

CHAPTER XXXVI.

FOR several moments neither of the poor girls could distinguish any object, for the fog was still dense upon the water; but recovering themselves, and instinctively grasping each other's hands, they perceived that they were in a very large boat with eleven men, and that Guiseppe Baracco was steering, and six men pulling. Mary had never seen Campobello, therefore she knew not whether he was there or not; but Elizabeth, with a shudder, recognized him, even in that dull light.

"Merciful Heaven!" whispered Mary, the tears nearly blinding her, "what has become of our dear uncle and all the unfortunate persons in that doomed ship—dear, dear Térese, and Mrs. Arbuthnot, and our poor servants? Ah, my God! I trust they got into boats."

"Now, my lads, ship the mast," exclaimed Guiseppe Baracco, breaking the silence, "and hoist the sail; we managed this matter cleverly."

"St, Januarius assisted us," said one of the men; "but Campobello fired the hold famously."

Mary and Elizabeth uttered a cry of horror. "Then it was that wretch who set fire to the unfortunate ship," whispered Mary.

The fact was, when the ship struck, the Italians congregated together; Guiseppe Baracco, a skilful and cool seaman, at once planned the seizing of a boat, putting some provisions into her, and stealing away; the craftiness of some of the frigate's crew, intending to steal a boat themselves, aided their design. But the fiendish malice of Campobello was not satisfied; he contrived to fire the forecastle, and then, as the flames burst forth, he pointed out to Baracco the females on the quarter-deck, and proposed, in the confusion, to seize them. Baracco's thirst for vengeance, even in that terrible scene, against De Courcy, revived, and he resolved to attempt the seizure of Mary. The explosion of a small quantity of powder created the panic described, and in the dismay of the moment the Italians made a rush and carried off the girls. With immense risk and perseverance they made their way through the surf round the frigate, pulling in a different direction to any of the other boats. What their ulterior object might be they had not yet determined. Hoisting their sail, the boat flew before the wind, whilst Guiseppe Baracco steered.

To describe the agony of mind, the anguish and suffering of the two maidens, would be impossible. Soaked by the seas breaking over the reef, at the mercy of such a ruffian as Campobello, and a man so unprincipled as Guiseppe Baracco, their situation was too horrible to think of.

"Surely, surely," whispered Elizabeth, into Mary's ear, "some of the frigate's boats will come near us; if this fog clears off with the daylight we shall be seen."

"Ah, Elizabeth," replied Mary, "I feel sick at heart; I shall have no strength to contend against this cruel misfortune."

"Yes, yes, carissima," returned Elizabeth, "the Madonna

will give us strength; these wicked wretches will be punished yet. Courage, Heaven is above still!"

It was past two o'clock in the morning when the unfortunate Dauntless struck on the reef; from the striking to the final explosion two hours may have elapsed, therefore about an hour after leaving the fatal spot daylight struggled through the fog; the wind was a steady breeze, and the sea tolerably smooth, though a heavy ground-swell existed—running from north to south. Anxiously and fearfully did the wretched girls watch the increasing daylight.

Summoning all her natural courage and firmness, Mary Wharton, fixing her eyes upon Guiseppe Baracco's face, said, "How is it, Signor Baracco, that you have thus forcibly torn us from our protectors, and exposed us, who never injured you, to this cruel suffering?"

Guiseppe Baracco looked into the pale, beautiful face of the speaker for a moment without answering; there was an expression of fierce satisfaction on his strongly marked features as he let his penetrating glance rest upon Miss Wharton.

"I have not exposed you, signora," he replied, speaking calmly, "to any more suffering than you would otherwise have had to endure. As to the rest, and why I have acted thus, it is to plant one thorn in the breast of him who has plunged many into mine; in fact, madame, revenge is my motive."

"And is such a revenge," asked Mary, with a look of scorn, and her cheek flushing from excitement, "worthy of a brave man? It is only the coward and the renegade who aims to gain his ends by an outrage on a sex that cannot resist him."

"He who seeks revenge, and feels the canker in his heart, little heeds the means, signora," returned Baracco, bitterly. "De Courcy will feel this blow deeper and more acutely than fifty poniards in his heart."

"Coward!" exclaimed Mary, passionately, "you have not gained your ends yet."

"We shall see, madame," returned Baracco, with a sneer.

Mary threw the hood over her face and wept in silence.

Campobello, in the meantime, moved from his seat, and threw himself beside the terrified Elizabeth, who shrank with loathing from his touch nearer to Mary.

"So," said the villain, in a low voice, "you thought to sacrifice your father to gratify your love of finery and fine houses; you wanted to be pampered, did you?"

"Wretch!" exclaimed Elizabeth, trembling and clinging to Mary, who threw her arm round her, gazing at the same time with a look of disgust at Campobello, "you are not my father; your own lips confessed it, and my heart always told me such was the case."

"Corpo de Domonic!" laughed the wretch with his mocking
tone, "so your little heart told you you were not a Lazzarone
—well, perhaps so; since you won't be my daughter you shall
be my wife after the Lazzaroni fashion—will that please
you?" and he laughed with a hideous mockery.

Such horror did the villain's words create, that Elizabeth
instantly felt a wish to cast herself into the sea; but at that
moment two of the men in the bow of the boat called out, in
a tone of alarm, "A large ship right ahead!" and the next
moment they were alongside a vessel of war, and a scene of
intense confusion took place in the boat. The ship was lying-
to, and in the fog they had run right against her before the
alteration of the helm could avert the catastrophe. The
boat's bows were stoved in, and the two girls, bewildered and
confounded, were thrown from their seats into the bottom,
whilst curses and imprecations burst from the terrified Italians'
lips. Immediately ropes were thrown over the side of the
man-of-war, and grapnels made fast to keep the boat from
sinking, whilst several men belonging to the frigate instantly
tendered assistance, and a young officer, who observed the
females, slung himself over the side into the boat. She was
fast filling with water, but, raising them up, and struck with
their beauty and appearance, he called for assistance and the
ladder to be lowered over the side. In a few minutes more
the rescued girls stood upon the deck of the Minerva, thirty-
eight gun frigate, commanded by Captain Jules Epron.

Guiseppe Baracco in the meantime having also, with the
rest of the Italians, gained the deck, was surrounded by a
crowd of gazers, who however kept back as Captain Epron
and one or two officers came up, all astonished at the appearance of the two pale and frightened young ladies.

Guiseppe Baracco stood for a moment bewildered, biting
his lips with intense vexation and disappointment, knowing
his position was critical, and one difficult to extricate himself
from.

Captain Jules Epron approached, and politely raising his
hat, for the style of attire and manner of the two maidens at
once satisfied him that his strange visitors were of the higher
class of society.

"May I request to know, mademoiselles," said the Captain,
"how you come to be in so distressing a situation, in an open
boat, and so far from a European shore: I fear some disaster
at sea."

Before Mary or Elizabeth could find words to reply, Guiseppe Baracco stepped up, saying, "Captain Epron, I suppose
you scarcely recollect me in this disguise; you may remember,
however, Lieutenant Baracco, of the Vesuvius, Neapolitan
brig."

"*Ha, parbleu!* how is this then, lieutenant, I see you and these ladies in this plight? but I must not keep them standing thus. Pray follow me, mademoiselles; I have already several ladies on board, and I am sure they will gladly receive you and attend to your wants. You are English, if I mistake not?"

A dark shade passed over Baracco's face as Captain Epron; a very handsome and gallant officer, of some six and thirty years, politely assisted Mary and Elizabeth along the deck of the ship.

Mary now felt safe, notwithstanding she was on board a French ship, and in answer to Captain Epron's question she replied, "Yes, monsieur, we are English, and were wrecked last night in the Dauntless frigate on some reef. The vessel exploded shortly after, having been set on fire." Mary paused, for she thought Elizabeth might still feel some shadow of doubt respecting Campobello's being her father.

"*Mon Dieu!* mademoiselle!" exclaimed Captain Epron, "that was a terrible disaster. What became of the officers and crew—the captain probably your father?"

"No, monsieur." returned Mary, "our uncle, Sir Charles Wharton, was a guest of the captain. We were proceeding to Palermo when the vessel struck. In the confusion we were forcibly seized by Lieutenant Baracco and those men, and cruelly torn from our friends and forced into the boat; and, God help us! but for your unexpected presence we know not what might have been our fate."

"Ah, *parbleu!* this is serious," exclaimed the Captain, with emphasis; and, turning to his lieutenant, he said, "Secure all those men that came up from the boat. I will examine them presently." As they advanced along the quarter-deck three ladies, wrapped in fur mantles, ascended the cabin stairs.

Mary and Elizabeth, at the sight o' persons of their own sex, felt an emotion of exceeding relief; but as they came closer, and Elizabeth looked into their features, she started back, and, catching Mary by the arm, exclaimed, rather loud, "Ah, Madonna! the Princess of Sorento!"

Captain Epron caught the words, and gazing into the beautiful but pale features of Elizabeth, said, "Then Madame Obruzza is known to you?"

Mary was so completely astounded and bewildered at thus meeting face to face the woman whose courage, devotion, and love had saved her lover's life, that she remained rooted to the deck, incapable of moving or uttering a word, her eyes fixed intently upon the unquestionably lovely features and fine person of Clarina Obruzza.

Can we attempt to account for the feelings and sensations
we sometimes experience as we gaze into some peculiar face.
The Princess de Sorento paused within a few feet of Mary
Wharton and Elizabeth, and saw both were young, beautiful,
and singularly interesting; though hurriedly attired, and a
night passed in suffering of mind and body had paled the cheek
and left the eyes languid, and with an expression of distress
in them, yet the princess could not take her gaze from Mary's
face. She knew at a glance that they were English, and a
strange feeling crept over her as their eyes met; her own cheek
grew pale, why—for her life she could not say; but involuntarily stepping forward, she said, in a low, sweet voice, which
trembled a little, "You are——" she paused; and our heroine
replied with exceeding emotion, "Mary Wharton."

"I knew it," exclaimed the princess, exceedingly moved,
and throwing her arms round Mary's neck, she kissed her
most affectionately, saying; "My poor girl, what has brought
you into this sad state? but come with me, this is no place to
keep you standing in,"

To describe Mary's feelings at this affectionate and sisterly
greeting from one she could least have expected it from
would be scarcely possible, so confused and mingled were her
thoughts; she, however, returned the princess's kindness by a
look of admiration and gratitude, and pressing her hand with
much emotion, followed her and her ladies into the cabin of
the Minerva, Captain Epron saying, "I rejoice, mademoiselle, to see that you are amongst those who will alleviate
your distress. If this fog clears, which I think it will shortly,
we may be able to afford help to others, who doubtless escaped
from the wreck in the boats of the frigate."

Captain Epron then ordered the men taken on board from
the boat to be brought before him. All the Captain knew of
Guiseppe Baracco was, that he was the first lieutenant of the
Vesuvius, and that he was a revolutionary conspirator in
Naples; he also, some time back, encountered the Vesuvius,
when commanded by Captain De Courcy, and failed in capturing the brig after five and twenty minutes' sharp contest off
Gaeta—in which he lost several men and his fore-top mast; the
Vesuvius, by skilful manœuvring and a shift of wind, getting away from her formidable antagonist. This escape of
the Vesuvius, and her captain daring to resist for a moment
a frigate of thirty-six guns, and finally escaping, annoyed
Captain Epron very much at the time, but he inwardly gave
due credit to his spirited antagonist.

The Minerva was one of the frigates lying at Gaeta at
the time the king and royal family sailed in the Serena for
Palermo; and Lieutenant Baracco, as one of the conspirators,

visited the Minerva secretly, and had a few minutes' conversation with Captain Epron on the possibility of surprising and capturing the royal family.

We may at all times use, confer with, and even highly reward traitors ; but we believe they are, no matter how high-sounding their objects and projects, always looked upon with disgust. Captain Epron was a gallant man, and although an enthusiastic revolutionist, he did not consider himself a conspirator ; he was fighting for the liberty of his country—cruelly ill-governed and oppressed—but Baracco was a conspirator against his king, and, eager for self-aggrandizement, was willing to admit a foreign power to rule over his native land. Captain Epron therefore did not receive Guiseppe Baracco with any cordial feeling, especially after the charge brought against him by his fair guests.

Baracco looked sullen and indignant as he and the rest of the men were brought before Captain Epron and his officers by a guard of marines.

" May I ask the reason why I am thus treated ? " he demanded fiercely, the moment he was brought before the French commander.

" Certainly," replied Captain Epron, calmly. " These young ladies say, ' that they were passengers or guests on board the Dauntless frigate, which struck upon a reef last night, and was set on fire, and that you, Lieutenant Baracco, —for one of the young ladies especially named you,— forcibly seized them and carried them off from their natural protectors.' "

" That's one side of the story," exclaimed Baracco, with a sneer, " but the fact is this : I was forced to work my passage to Palermo in the Dauntless, having, as you doubtless know, been forced to fly from Naples on the discovery of the Caraccioli conspiracy. This man here," pointing to the Lazzarone, " is Campobello, who was to have raised the population in Naples, as we agreed, in favour of the French Revolution—he also fled to England, and with him his daughter; she contrived to escape from him when there, and got introduced, in some way, by imposture of course, into the family of Sir Charles Wharton."

Captain Epron looked exceedingly incredulous, but Guiseppe Baracco continued : " In the terrible confusion on the deck of the British frigate, the men having got at the spirits, and disregarding their officers' orders, began rioting and destroying everything ; thus the ship caught fire, I suppose. We naturally, being all Italians, sought to escape, and seized a boat for ourselves ; and Campobello, eager to recover his daughter, seized her, and Miss Wharton clinging to her with fright, and we, having no time to lose, carried both into the boat to save

S

their lives; and for doing this, we have been put under arrest by your orders."

"Well, *parbleu!*" observed Captain Epron, with a smile, "yours is a very strange and somewhat improbable story. Signor Baracco, as relates to one of those young ladies being that man's daughter. It is ridiculous to think it."

"Then you doubt my word, Captain Epron?" cried Baracco, with a fierce gesture of defiance; "recollect, you have no authority over me; I and thousands of others have declared for the revolution, and have tendered submission to France; and we were acknowledged and afforded protection—I therefore protest against this arbitrary treatment on your part."

"Well, *parbleu!*" returned the Frenchman, "you may argue that matter with the committee when we get to Toulon, where I am bound in company with the Sylphide corvette, which I suspect is close at hand; but as these young ladies seem well known to a lady of rank, on board my ship, formerly styled the Princess of Sorento——"

"What!" exclaimed Guiseppe Baracco, starting back, and turning pale, and looking very disturbed,—"what, the Princess of Sorento on board this ship?"

"Even so—you seem knocked all of a heap. However, as I do not want to be harsh, or adopt severe measures, till better informed, you are all at liberty to remain at large; but as you, Lieutenant Baracco, are gravely accused of carrying off by force one of those young ladies from her uncle's protection, I must insist upon your not intruding into her presence; whilst under my protection she shall have every attention paid to her, and when I hear further particulars from her I shall know how to act;" so saying, Captain Epron made a sign to the marines, who withdrew, whilst he himself turned away from the furious and disappointed Italian.

"That's not a very likely story that Neapolitan has just told us," remarked Captain Epron, to his first lieutenant. "Who could believe that either of those beautiful girls was the daughter of such a ruffian as that Italian Lazzarone? I have heard of this fellow before now."

"They are a piratical-looking set of ruffians," returned the lieutenant; "there is some mystery in this affair of the English frigate; if she struck last night upon a reef, we cannot be far off the coast; there is no reef marked on the charts from Cape Bona to Algiers."

"No," returned the captain, "not on the charts; but I have heard of a dangerous sunken shoal off the coast, some-where between the two places you mention. I wish this fog would lift; for I think those heavy northerly gales have driven us farther in than we suppose."

CHAPTER XXXVII.

In the meantime the Princess of Sorento conducted the bewil dered yet gratified Mary and her cousin to the cabin of the Minerva, where they found three ladies—one a distinguished-looking, elderly dame—but they almost immediately retired into private cabins, leaving the princess alone with the cousins. The former just touched a bell, and the steward of the ship entering the saloon, she requested that breakfast might be served as soon as possible, for it was yet early.

"You must, my dear girls," said Clarina Obruzza—Mary and Elizabeth having laid aside their soaked mantles—"you must have suffered terribly all night; and after such a horrible occurrence as a ship on fire. One of my attendants brought me word, some time since, that a boat, with several persons and two young girls had come alongside, their ship having been destroyed by fire during the night. I went upon deck, thinking I might be of use, little dreaming I should at length meet with one I had so often heard of, and so earnestly wished to see."

Mary felt her cheeks burn; but she saw so much of kindness, and even affection, in the princess's look and manner, that her restraint almost immediately vanished, and she warmly returned the fair Clarina thanks for her graceful attention to her and her cousin.

"Before I ask or answer any particular question," said the princess, "you must take some refreshment, and afterwards some repose. I can then supply you with everything you may require."

"Alas! princess," said Mary, "our chief distress is caused by the lamentable state of uncertainty we remain in with respect to the fate of our beloved uncle, and other persons most dear to us, whom we left escaping from the burning frigate."

"They, no doubt," said the princess, "managed to get into the other boats. But, here is breakfast; come with me; a little addition to your toilette," she added, with a smile, "will refresh you."

Summoning one of her female attendants, they all retired from the cabin. In half an hour afterwards a very charming party were assembled round the breakfast-table of the princess; amongst the company was Captain Epron, who looked with astonishment at the two fair girls seated near the princess.

"*Parbleu !*" thought the French commander, "that rascal, Campobello, must have the most monstrous assurance to think of calling one of those lovely girls his daughter."

Though both Mary and Elizabeth looked sad, heavy, and

dispirited, yet the efforts of the princess and the attentions of her attendants had remedied, in some degree, the defective and hurried toilette of the night before.

"Pray, Captain Epron," asked the princess, "is this fog going to last out the month? it has already been our constant visitor for nine days."

"Nearly so, indeed, madame," said the captain; "but I think we shall have a change; there will be a new moon to-night, and the wind is veering into the north-west. Pray, mademoiselle," he continued, turning to Mary, "what time did your ship strike last night?"

"I think I heard my uncle say about two o'clock this morning," returned Mary.

"Poor child," said the Countess de Morlaix, the distinguished-looking, elderly lady, a Frenchwoman by birth, and an emigrant, "what you must have suffered!"

"I thought I heard you say, mademoiselle," said the captain, "that the frigate was set on fire; did her crew mutiny?"

Mary looked at Elizabeth, who was conversing in a low voice with a very pleasing lady next her, but Elizabeth, raising her eyes, said, speaking steadily, "That she feared the frigate had been set on fire by one of the men who was in the boat with them, as she overheard the others applaud one of their comrades for doing so."

"*Parbleu!* then I was very wrong," said the captain, "to let those rascals loose about the ship; I will have them carefully watched. As to the frigate," continued the captain, "she would, had she not been set on fire, have most likely got off the reef, for there was not much wind, and very little sea on."

Mary was then induced, by some further questions of the captain, to give a full and clear account of their disaster. She stated also how they had lost sight of the Serena, the Neapolitan frigate, commanded by Captain De Courcy, though she was conscious that her voice faltered a little as she pronounced her lover's name.

"Ha!" said Captain Epron, with much vivacity, "the Serena is a noble frigate. I understand her brave and gallant commander is an old antagonist of mine, and I strongly suspect he is not far off; in this light weather, the boats of the Dauntless will either make for the African Coast, or be picked up by some British cruisers—the Mediterranean is full of them. I kept this course partly to avoid meeting any between Malta and Bona, but the northerly gales drove us to the southward of Bona—at least I think so; but this singularly prolonged foggy weather has baffled all observation."

Shortly after the captain withdrew, and the princess persuaded the two girls to lie down for two or three hours.

On the departure of the Serena for England, and the complete restoration of the princess to health, after her fortunate escape from assassination, King Ferdinand of Naples became extremely pressing with her respecting her forming a matrimonial connection. The King insisted she should, for political reasons, marry the Duke de ———. Clarina steadily refused, and finally so exasperated the King, and then the Queen, that her situation in the court became extremely unpleasant, so much so, that the princess, although Naples was the focus of revolution, embarked for that city, without even taking leave of their majesties. She had resolved never to marry an old man, and in that resolve she placed the king's wishes at nothing, and the sovereign was allowed to discover the very determined character of the young lady he had hitherto moulded to his will.

She retired to her pretty villa in the suburbs of Castella-mare, which is seated on the sea-shore.

Time passed pleasantly and cheerfully. Clarina had the good sense to endeavour to forget a man whose affections she could never hope to win—to banish Hugh De Courcy from her recollection was out of the question, but she resolved she would never think of him in any other light than that of a sincere friend. She often thought she should like to see this fair English girl who had so entwined herself round his heart. She fancied she would know her at once if she stood before her,—for she had her description by heart ; but Clarina never expected to behold her successful rival.

In the meantime the city of Naples became more and more disturbed as the revolutionary army was advancing ; and finally Naples once more belonged to France. The princess, however, was not at all disturbed in her residence during the first occupation of the city by the French, or in the proceedings immediately afterwards ; but in course of time the French commissioners became grasping and avaricious. The princess found out that her property in Naples was coveted, and that, like the unfortunate Prince Caraccioli, she was expected to declare herself a revolutionist, and devote her fortune and interest to uphold the republic. Not wishing or liking to trust herself any longer in a country more convulsed even than France itself, which, under the First Consul, was rapidly returning to order and good government, she resolved to proceed into France, and to Paris ; encouraged in this resolution by the Countess de Morlaix, who had great expectations of recovering her husband's estates under the new order of things. Once this idea entered the princess's head, she followed it up ; and being introduced to the nephew of the countess, Captain Jules Epron, who was ordered to Toulon with despatches, she accepted the offer of his frigate to take her and the countess and their suites to Toulon. On embarking in the Minerva, Captain Epron was forced to run through the straits of Messina, owing to the reported appearance of an English squadron seen off Gaeta; northerly gales drove him towards Cape Bona, and the dense fogs that ensued induced him and the Sylphide corvette, his consort, to lie-to till the fogs cleared away, knowing that English cruisers were likely to be met with in those seas; thus it chanced that Mary and Elizabeth were saved from cruel suffering by coming upon the frigate unawares.

The cousins found themselves much refreshed from the repose and quiet of the three hours they were left to themselves.

"We shall be carried to France, dear Mary," observed Elizabeth. "What will become of us there?"

"Oh," returned Mary, "if I was only sure of our dear uncle and other dear friends' safety, I should not fret about our own situation. The Princess of Sorento has a kind and noble heart, and what a lovely, superior woman she is! How did dear Hugh resist such fascinations of manner?"

"Because he had your sweet face engraven too strongly on his heart," replied Elizabeth.

"But he knew this charming princess before he had seen me."

"Ah, well, Madonna," said Elizabeth, with a slight sigh, "I suppose the object of our hearts' choice is marked out for us, and we cannot resist our destiny; but the princess is lovely enough to turn any man's heart. I have often gazed at her in Naples, as she drove of an evening past the windows of the Signora Canino's house, with wonder and admiration."

A slight tap at the door announced the princess.

"Well, ladies, how do you feel now—did you sleep?" kindly questioned Clarina Obruzza; "you look, at all events, refreshed."

"So indeed we are, dear madame," answered Mary, "and feel in our hearts deep gratitude for your kindness."

"Ah!" said the princess, "if women will not feel for one another, who will? I wish to have a long chat with you both. This audacious Lieutenant Baracco has made the most absurd statement to Captain Epron, but which he totally discredits."

Elizabeth felt that she must have been the subject of conversation, and her cheek paled when she thought of the wretch Campobello, and his probable assertion that she was his daughter.

Having accompanied the princess into her private cabin, they sat down, whilst Clarina Obruzza in the kindest manner begged her guests to make her fully acquainted with all the particulars regarding themselves.

"Oh, Madonna!" exclaimed the princess, in the greatest astonishment, as Mary related that part of her early history having reference to Magdalene Caracei. " Do you know who this mysterious Magdalene is? I have scarce a doubt upon the subject. She is my aunt."

"Your aunt!" cried both girls in utter astonishment. " Good Heavens! Does she still live?"

"Yes," returned the princess, seriously, "she does; and is now the wife of a Calabrese noble, but who is looked upon by the French as a brigand, as he has armed the entire peasantry in the mountains of the Crati, and wages a war of terrible extermination against the invaders of his country."

Mary and Elizabeth were bewildered; but the princess, now much more interested, begged the former to finish her narrative; afterwards she would explain to her why she considered her aunt to be the mysterious Magdalene Caracei.

Whilst the princess is listening to Mary's narrative, we will, in our next chapter, beg our readers to accompany us on board the Serena frigate.

CHAPTER XXXVIII.

PREVIOUS to the setting in of the foggy weather, which delayed the Dauntless in her voyage, the Serena frigate, as we before stated, bore away to the northward to reconnoitre some strange sails seen in that direction; they turned out, however, to be only British ships-of-war making for Gibraltar. After exchanging signals, the Serena made all sail to rejoin the Dauntless, by that time out of sight; then followed the heavy gales from the north and north-east, and afterwards dense fogs set in. During these fogs the Serena was kept under easy canvas, working at times to windward and then continuing her course, with a favourable breeze.

" I fear," remarked Hugh De Courcy to Lord de Umfreville, "that we shall not see any more of the Dauntless till we make our port. About two o'clock in the morning he was roused by the officer of the watch stating that he heard the firing of several guns at a considerable distance; they were heavy guns too.

" In what direction?" demanded De Courcy, leaping out of bed and dressing himself.

"Away west and by south, sir," replied the officer. " I should say the firing was quite ten miles off."

" Very odd!" remarked De Courcy, as he ascended the deck; " perhaps some vessel on shore."

As he looked in the direction pointed out, the fog so thick as to render objects fifty yards off imperceptible, he beheld a strange gleam of light through the mist, and immediately followed a dull booming sound, and then naught was heard but the night wind, as it whistled through the rigging.

"By Jove, that's a very strange sound!" exclaimed De Courcy to his lieutenant, "an explosion, I fear. Could any ship, I wonder, have caught fire and exploded? hearing these guns first, and then that gleam of light, and dull sound, looks like it."

"Brace round the yards and keep the ship away to the south-west," he continued, addressing the officer of the watch. "I wish to Heaven this fog would lift! Let a gun be fired, also, at intervals between ten and fifteen minutes."

The topsails were accordingly braced round and the sails filled, and gradually the frigate paid off, and was steered in the direction from whence came the sound of the firing. A careful look-out was kept, though indeed the fog rendered such precautions almost negative. The wind blew a fresh breeze, but with little sea. The first gun brought Lord de Umfreville on deck.

"Did you think we had stumbled on an enemy?" said our hero, joining his friend; "I am sorry to have disturbed you." He then stated his reason for firing.

"I trust nothing has occurred to the Dauntless," remarked his lordship, anxiously. "She ought to be in our neighbourhood if she kept on in the course agreed upon."

"So I think," returned our hero. "Lieutenant Biaggi tells me the guns were, he thinks, fired by some ship in distress, and about ten or twelve miles distant. When I have run eight or nine miles I will keep burning blue lights."

Under single-reefed topsails, with no other sail set, the Serena soon ran the distance, firing a gun every quarter of an hour. She was then hove to, and blue lights burned. About five o'clock in the morning, just as dawn was expected to make, and one of the blue lights had expired, a loud hail was heard to the westward of the frigate, at some distance.

"By Heavens, that's an Englishman's hail!" exclaimed De Courcy, eagerly; "fire another gun, and keep the lights burning."

"Ay, ay, sir," returned an old quartermaster, an Englishman, who had long sailed with De Courcy, and was a favourite, "that hail came from English lungs, and no mistake."

All on board were now eagerly looking over the sides, when again the hail, and a hearty one, was heard, and then two dark objects were seen looming through the fog, which proved to be boats full of people. In a few minutes the first boat, containing more than thirty persons, and pulled by six oars, was nearly up with the ship, when De Courcy, with a bound, rushed to the side, exclaiming to Lord de Umfreville, "My God! the long-boat of the Dauntless." His lordship hurried after his friend, whilst the rope-ladders were lowered over the side.

Hugh De Courcy could scarcely command himself; he felt sick, giddy, and confounded; for by the strong glare of the blue light he beheld, in the stern-sheets of the boat, Sir Charles Wharton, Térese Garetti, and Mrs. Arbuthnot; but she whose form he eagerly sought, and without whom existence appeared a blank, was nowhere to be discovered; the other boat, the cutter, now came up, but the females in her were Sir Charles's domestics. "Good God! Sir Charles," exclaimed our hero to the baronet, as he gained the deck, "where is Mary—where is Elizabeth?"

The baronet looked heart-broken, and Térese and Mrs. Arbuthnot paralysed; still Térese spoke, as Sir Charles had grasped the hand of De Courcy, and wrung it with a feeling of despair.

"Dear Hugh," she exclaimed, "do not look so despairing. Mary and Elizabeth were both saved, but they are in another boat. They were carried off by those wretches Baracco and Campobello."

De Courcy and Lord de Umfreville were utterly confounded. Baracco and Campobello on board the Dauntless, and able to carry off Mary and Elizabeth from the decks of a British frigate, appeared so incredible. Sir Charles, recovering himself a little, said,—

"Such is the case, Hugh; but if this fog clears up, they cannot get away from your pursuit. Surely there is another boat yet; she cannot be far from here. Captain Friend and his officers are in her. They said they would keep near the shoal where the Dauntless struck, and finally blew up, and hoping in the daylight to save some of the ill-fated crew, who were, he supposed, clinging to portions of the wreck."

All hands aboard the Serena were, by this time, upon deck. De Courcy ordered out his own boats, and a crew into each; daylight was making rapidly, and the fog slightly decreasing.

Accompanying Sir Charles, who looked haggard and fearfully dejected, and the females into the cabin, where some wine and cordials were placed on the table by the steward, our hero learned the particulars of the loss of the Dauntless, whilst Térese explained how Elizabeth had recognized Campobello. Térese herself, too late, and in the horror of the moment, whilst each expected the ship to blow up, had recognized Guiseppe Baracco rushing across the deck; the next instant a terrible pressure of the frightened crew separated them all, and it was only by almost superhuman exertion that Captain Friend and his officers got the females safely into the long-boat.

About an hour or two after pulling away from the burning ship they first heard the Serena's gun, they then changed their direction, and kept, as they heard each gun, in that direction till they beheld the blue light through the fog.

De Courcy for a moment almost gave way to despair; but
seeing the baronet looking to him for relief, and for exertion,
he roused himself from his apathy and despondency, and,
with Lord de Umfreville, hurried upon deck, and manning
four boats, despatched them under careful officers, in the direction of the reef, which the petty officers of the Dauntless
said was about four or five miles to the south-west of where
the Serena lay.

De Courcy and his companion consulted together, each
giving his opinion as to the direction it was likely that Guiseppe Baracco might take with his captives. Some of the men
in the cutter declared they had seen one of the boats of the
Dauntless, with two females in it, and several men pull off
from the burning wreck dead before the wind. This De
Courcy thought not improbable ; it was possible, as the wind
then was, to make the coast of Sicily ; but what Baracco's
purpose in taking off the two girls could be, they could not
possibly conjecture, unless, as Lord de Umfreville suggested,
they had been carried off from motives of vengeance, without
any fixed plan.

Till the fog cleared up, of which there now appeared every
symptom, the wind shifting at the same time into the north-
west, the Serena was left lying-to, till the return of the boats.

At the expiration of three hours the boats returned, with
the Captain of the Dauntless, in his own boat; between them,
they had saved nearly thirty poor fellows, clinging to pieces of
timber, and large masses of the unfortunate frigate.

Captain Friend, as he grasped our hero's hand, seemed
dreadfully depressed. " This is a terrible blow, De Courcy," he
exclaimed ; " a fine ship lost to the service, and, worse still,
many poor fellows have gone to their last home ! The reef on
which the Dauntless was lost is not marked down on any
chart I have : still, had she not caught fire from some fatal
negligence, she might have been got off;—but what is this I
hear about Miss Wharton and her cousin ? surely those Italian
rascals have not carried them off except to save their lives.
Where could they expect to reach ? for if they attempted to
land on the Barbary shore, they would be seized and carried
up the country ; therefore most likely they will keep the sea.
See, the fog lifts and disperses rapidly ! "

The order to make sail sent the men up the rigging, and
soon the Serena, under full canvas, was standing away dead
before the wind, her own boats hoisted in, the others in tow,
with a steersman in each. Men were sent aloft to keep a
careful look-out, for the fog was clearing rapidly away, and
already the coast of Barbary was looming in the distance.

Sir Charles, restless and miserable, could not be persuaded
to take repose ; he came upon deck, and, like the rest,

anxiously scanned the horizon. About three o'clock in the day the sky became tolerably free from mist, and the sun shone out cheerfully over the rippling waters of the Mediterranean. They could now distinctly see the outline of Cape Bona, on the Barbary coast, distant about eighteen miles. "Sail away to the south-west!" exclaimed the look-out aloft; but no boat was to be seen, far as the eye could scan the waters.

Another sail in the same direction was then seen, and the second lieutenant, ascending the rigging, declared them to be vessels of war, steering a northerly course.

"It's very possible," exclaimed our hero, addressing Sir Charles, "that the boat we are looking for might have reached those ships this morning, and the crew, doubtless, have been forced to give an account of themselves."

"In God's name, then, dear Hugh," said the anxious baronet, "give chase! it is possible we may catch them, unless they have made for the land."

"No, my dear sir, I do not think there is any fear of that; they would be too much afraid of the piratical natives of this coast to do so; much more likely to make for Sicily; and those vessels lay right in their course."

The cutter and gig of the Dauntless were now hoisted on board, and the launch and other boats cast adrift; a cloud of sail was set on the Serena, so that in less than an hour they made out the two vessels, one a very fine first-class frigate, the other a corvette of eighteen guns.

"Those are French ships," observed De Courcy, after a steady survey. The Serena was then four miles off; half an hour more and the leading ship, the frigate, hauled her wind and hoisted English colours.

"This will not do," said De Courcy to Captain Friend and Lord de Umfreville, who were standing beside him; "I know the frigate, it is the Minerva; the corvette I do not know. The commander of the frigate is as gallant a man as ever breathed. I escaped from him once in the Vesuvius brig, favoured by the wind and a few lucky shots."

They were now within two miles, and Lieutenant Biaggi, who was in the mizen cross-trees with his glass, said he was certain he saw females on the quarter-deck of the frigate. Hugh De Courcy's heart beat quicker as he heard the words of the lieutenant, and, running up the shrouds, took a steady gaze at the frigate. The white robes of two or three females, amidst several officers on the quarter-deck of the Minerva, caught his sight, but as he kept his glass upon them they disappeared, descending, he supposed, into the cabin. The corvette was, perhaps, two miles to leeward of the Minerva; both ships were under top-gallant sails and royals, but the

Minerva at once furled her royals and brailed her courses, showing evident symptoms of preparing for action if need be ; and down came the English colours, the tri-colour replacing them.

De Courcy still held on, hoisting no colours, till he came within speaking distance, when Captain Epron immediately hailed the Serena, demanding whether De Courcy acknowledged the Republican Government of Naples or the King of the Two Sicilies.

" King Ferdinand ! " exclaimed De Courcy, standing on the carriage of a carronade, and raising his hat.   This salute the Frenchman returned, whilst our hero, as the two vessels ran parallel to each other, and not sixty yards asunder, hailed the Minerva, demanding of Captain Epron if he had seen a boat with two females and several Italians in her, within the last twelve hours.   Before the captain could reply, a white scarf was waved from the quarter-deck of the French vessel.

" Thank God, my child is safe ! " exclaimed Sir Charles, beholding the signal.

Captain Epron then waved his hat, exclaiming, " All safe, they are here ! " and he jumped down from the gun-carriage.

De Courcy, with a feeling of relief, though mingled with regret, ordered the sailing-master to stay ship, whilst the Minerva wore round on her heel.

An intense anxiety prevailed on the decks of both ships : all knew there would be a terrible contest, for the commanders of both were men celebrated for their chivalry and their gallantry—both young and eager for glory.   Both commanders were too chivalrous to fire a single shot before both were ready to begin the action.   The females had to be put in a place of security from shot.

" You must, Sir Charles, and you, Edward," said De Courcy, turning to Lord de Umfreville, " take charge of the ladies and females in the hold of the ship ; it's the safest place."

" Good God! and must you fight ? " exclaimed Sir Charles, dismayed ; " surely there is no need of so unnecessary a proceeding ; think of Mary and Elizabeth."

" My dear sir," replied De Courcy, somewhat sadly, for his natural high spirit and ardour was damped, knowing what Mary would suffer when the first shot should reach her ear, " I must do my duty, whatever may be my fate ; there will be no fear for dear Mary's life ; my antagonist is a gallant gentleman, and will secure your nieces from danger of shot ; and now let me beg of you to retire."

Sir Charles was much cast down and very miserable, but knowing he should only be in the way, he wrung our hero's hand and retired.   Lord de Umfreville would on no account quit the deck.

"I shall attempt to carry the Minerva by boarding, observed De Courcy to Captain Friend, who joined him.

" I side with you there," replied the English captain ; "but that corvette will be an ugly addition; I see she is working up fast to have a hand in the pie ; the French frigate is a very fine ship, though you evidently outsail her."

" Oh yes," returned De Courcy, " I can do that easily."

The females and Sir Charles were placed in the securest position in the ship; Térese, though rejoiced in her heart at the safety of her two cousins, could not but tremble at the thought of the coming engagement.

" Oh, count!" exclaimed the poor girl, with much emotion, " is there no way of avoiding this horrible fight; why should two brave men thus try to destroy each other?"

" To uphold the cause of royalty against revolution and anarchy, and the honour of our flag; but fear nothing, I have a noble, brave crew, and, please God, before many hours are over you shall embrace your friends."

The drums on board both ships just then beat to quarters.

It was near six o'clock in the evening before the action commenced, the vessels steering south-east, nearly before the wind ; the action then became very animated on both sides, the crews of each ship being under perfect control, and remarkable for their superior discipline.

An early attempt of the Serena to board was, however, frustrated by the skilful and judicious management of the helm of the Minerva ; shortly after this, the Sylphide corvette, which by this time had stationed itself on the Serena's starboard bow, taking advantage of a sudden shift of wind, was enabled to gall the latter considerably, but suddenly bearing away, the Serena poured a destructive and well-aimed broadside into the Sylphide, which brought down the fore-top mast and cross jack-yard, which relieved the enemy from interference for awhile. As yet not a man had been killed, and but few hit on board the Serena; the sails and rigging of both ships showed, however, the effects of their well-directed fire.

Edging still closer to his antagonist, De Courcy poured in so incessant a discharge of grape and canister, and round shot, that the Minerva's stays, backstays, shrouds, tacks, sheets, halyards, and small spars were shot away, and finally. by the fall of her main top-mast, though his own fore-mast came down at the same time, he was enabled to run her on board. Twice, with a hearty cheer, the boarders of the Serena were gallantly repulsed. Just at this moment the Sylphide, finding the two frigates locked together, and fighting fiercely, gallantly ran right alongside the Serena, firing a heavy discharge of musketry into her decks.

De Courcy then resolved to board the Minerva, at the head

of his boarders, leaving to Captain Friend, Lord de Umfreville, and the English crew, to drive back the Sylphide.

The crew of the Minerva, inspired by the gallantry of her commander, and cheered by the triumphant shouts of the crew of the corvette, who fancied they had the Serena between two fires, stood bravely, but they found out their mistake when alongside, for the height of the frigate above them so baffled their skill, that they wished to disentangle themselves; but the Serena's crew made them fast by lashing their fore-yard to their mizen-shrouds.

In the meantime De Courcy beat back the Minerva, and springing on to her decks at the head of his men, a most furious hand-to-hand fight took place. None of the great guns were now used; but in the tops of the French ship numbers of marksmen were placed, who kept up a destructive discharge from their muskets.

A loud cheer, that the corvette had surrendered, redoubled the ardour of the Serena's boarders; but the crew and officers of the Minerva fought with a desperate determination, Captain Epron himself leading them on with a resolve to fall or conquer.

The contest had lasted above two hours, and it was quite dark, but numerous battle-lanterns and other lights threw a strange glare over the furious combatants.

De Courcy was struggling to gain the quarter-deck, where Captain Epron and several of his officers were disputing every inch, for the Serena's men, relieved from the contest with the Sylphide, were swarming over the side and down the rigging on to the deck of the Minerva. Lieutenant Biaggi, with a picked crew, ran up the rigging to dislodge the men in the tops, whilst Lord de Umfreville fought his way to the side of De Courcy, inspired by the fierceness of the contention. The fore part of the French frigate was, however, won, but the captain, and chief officers, and the *élite* of the crew, still held the after part of the ship, and showed no symptoms of yielding. De Courcy had received several cutlass wounds, when seeing his friend borne down by a rush of the enemy, and a tall, powerful man about to thrust a pike into him, he turned, and with a blow of his sword severed the pike-handle, whilst the man, with the impetus of his course, came full against him and bore him down. Lord de Umfreville struggled to his legs, but the butt of a musket struck him again senseless to the deck. As our hero was springing to his feet, having with a blow of his sword, in the face of the Frenchman, freed himself from his grasp, two men, with savage fury, rushed upon him, a strong glare of a battle-lantern fell on the face of the foremost sailor, who held a pistol in his hand.

At once our hero recognized Guiseppe Baracco, who, with

a fierce oath, thrust the pistol against De Courcy's head, but before the trigger was pulled the cutlass of young Pamfilé. third lieutenant of the Serena, was driven into his body to the hilt; the trigger was pulled, in the agony of death; but the second of time thus gained saved De Courcy, the muzzle of the pistol slipped aside, and, excepting a slight scratch on the side of the head, he was unhurt.

But even this brief stoppage in De Courcy's onward career inspired fresh hopes in the crew of the Minerva, and, with a hearty cheer, they drove back the Serena's men to their own vessel, many supposing their commander slain; but his voice reassured them, and again they gained ground, till De Courcy and Captain Epron, their uniforms cut and hacked, their hats lost, and their faces covered with blood and perspiration, met.

"Yield, Captain Epron, and save further carnage, I pray you," said De Courcy, "the ship is ours!"

"Not while I live," returned the French commander, bleeding from several wounds, and his left arm hanging useless by his side.

Their swords crossed, and Captain Epron was driven back; again he rallied, aided by his second lieutenant and a brave few, but De Courcy caught his sword-arm in his grasp, and wrenched, by his superior strength, the weapon from his hand, whilst Lieutenant Pamfilé hauled down the tri-colour, and the men of the Serena, joined by the English crew of the Dauntless frigate, who had carried the fore-deck of the Minerva, gave three tremendous cheers; the remaining officers, &c., then surrendered.

Captain Epron, after De Courcy had released his grasp, staggered back, leaning against the wheel, faint and exhausted, and bleeding profusely from several wounds.

"I regret, Captain Epron," said our hero, approaching him, "to see you so much hurt; pray let me assist you to the cabin, to receive assistance from your surgeon."

"Your usual good fortune, Captain De Courcy, sticks to you still," replied the Frenchman, bitterly; "I would rather have died than yielded this ship."

"All that man could do, Captain Epron, you have done— we cannot control fate," answered De Courcy, kindly; "if we have conquered, it has been a dearly-won fight, I strongly suspect."

CHAPTER XXXIX.

DE COURCY was right; it was a dearly-won hand-to-hand contest; but he remained master of a noble frigate and a very handsome corvette; the latter, lying so low beneath the frigate, became so terribly exposed to the Serena's heavy guns,

that had the commander not surrendered, the vessel would
have been instantly sunk. Seventeen of the Serena's crew
were slain, and of the Dauntless upwards of thirty severely
wounded, and fifty with wounds of various sorts. Captain
Friend and his first lieutenant both severely hurt, and Lord
de Umfreville, besides several cuts and thrusts, had received
a severe contusion on the head. De Courcy himself was
wounded in several places, but not of sufficient consequence
to prevent his attending to his friends and the duties of his
ship.

Besides Captain Epron wounded, his second and third
lieutenants were slain ; several petty offices and seven and
twenty of the crew killed, and nearly ninety wounded. A
severer fight, for the time it lasted, is not on record, if we
except the gallant action between the British ship Neander,
fifty-gun frigate, and the Généreux, French seventy-four, or
rather eighty-gun ship,

It may be supposed that De Courcy's first impulse, after
issuing orders to separate the three ships, and other necessary instructions quite useless detailing to our readers, was
to inquire after his beloved Mary and her cousin. He had,
however, first seen Lord de Umfreville carried to a berth and
a surgeon in attendance ; Captain Epron was also taken
below, for he was quite overcome from loss of blood.

Having washed away the effects of the contest, De Courcy
proceeded to descend into the cabin of the Minerva, where
Sir Charles Wharton was to follow, and where, he understood
from the steward of the frigate, the ladies then were. With
a palpitating heart he entered the principal saloon, but fell
back startled, for he perceived it was tenanted by no less than
half a dozen ladies. Somewhat surprised, he nevertheless
advanced, supposing that Captain Epron's wife and family
were on board. Pushing open the door he entered, and the
very first person his gaze rested upon was the Princess of
Sorento. De Courcy remained rooted to the floor, though the
eyes of his beloved Mary (who, pale as death and trembling,
was reclining back upon a sofa) were fixed upon him.

" Princess, can this be possible ? " exclaimed De Courcy,
with a flush over his fine features, and saluting the beautiful
but very pale Clarina Obruzza with studied courtesy.

" You have made us all look like ghosts, Count De Courcy,"
answered the princess, with a slight tremor in her voice ; " but
here is a fair countrywoman of yours, who has trembled, I
am sure, as much for your safety as her own—indeed a great
deal more. We were shut up in a very disagreeable place, I
assure you, and every shot made us cling to each other like
frightened sheep.

Mary looked into her lover's face and held out her hand,

and, in a voice that trembled with contending emotions, said,
"And my dear uncle, and Térese, and Mrs. Arbuthnot, I
trust they are safe?"

"Safe and well," returned our hero, pressing the hand
offered him to his lips, respectfully, but gazing in Mary's eyes,
which were suffused with tears, with a look far more eloquent
than words.

In some degree this meeting was painful to several of the
party, particularly to Mary; but the entrance of Sir Charles
Wharton, followed by Térese Garetti, also looking pale, haggard, and frightened, was a relief to all. Mary started up,
and threw herself into the delighted baronet's arms. The
worthy, kind-hearted Sir Charles could not utter a word, as
he again and again embraced his two nieces. De Courcy, in
the meantime, stood conversing with the princess, and explaining to her and the Countess de Morlaix the result of the
action. They were both grieved on hearing that Captain
Epron was so severely hurt.

"You are vulnerable only in one point," said the princess,
in a low voice, as the countess turned to address one of the
other ladies; "let me congratulate you," she added, with a
sweet, kind look and manner, "in having gained so priceless a
heart as Mary Wharton's. I shall always remember her, and
the few hours passed with her, with a feeling of relief and sincere pleasure."

De Courcy looked his gratitude, for his heart was too full of
joy and thankfulness to say what he felt.

"I suppose," observed the princess, changing the subject, it
being a relief to herself, "you will proceed with your prizes to
Palermo?"

"Unless, princess," returned De Courcy, "it is your wish
to go elsewhere."

"No," she said, after a moment's thought, "I will return to
Palermo, and make my peace with their majesties. I doubt it
was a rash act my going to France; besides, I may be of
service to Sir Charles Wharton. You look surprised, but I
know all Mary's history, and it turns out that the mysterious
Magdalene Caracci is my aunt."

"How extraordinary!" exclaimed De Courcy, amazed by
such an assertion.

"However," added the princess, "this is no time to talk of
these things. Do you wish us to move from this ship into the
Serena, or can we stay here?"

"You will be more at home here, princess," replied our
hero, "till we reach Malta; we will then arrange differently.
I have to land Captain Friend, his officers, and crew, on that
island. Captain Epron will proceed with us to Palermo; he
is too ill to be moved, and I wish to restore him and his

T

officers to their country; he is a brave and gallant man, and,
I hear, is sadly vexed at the Sylphide joining in the contest
after his signals not to engage."

" Madonna !" cried the princess, surprised, " then you had to
engage the two ships?"

" The Sylphide, I may say, gave herself up," returned De
Courcy; " she rashly ran alongside, forgetting our power to
sink her; she lay low in the water, and thus was forced to
surrender or be sunk."

The conversation became general, and shortly after Sir
Charles and our hero withdrew, leaving Térese with her two
cousins.

De Courcy returned to the Serena, giving the command of
the Minerva to his first lieutenant, and a prize crew. The
Sylphide made sail under the charge of Lieutenant Pamfilé,
after the sad duty of disposing of the dead had been fulfilled.

The crew of the Serena were busy repairing damages and
getting up a new fore-top mast, and replacing sails that were
cut to pieces. On the decks of the Minerva and Sylphide the
same busy work was going on.

After his slight cutlass wounds had been dressed De Courcy
proceeded to the cabin where lay Lord de Umfreville. He
was rejoiced to see that he was considerably better, the stunning blow on the head that he received being his worst hurt.
Our hero told him of the death of Guiseppe Baracco, by the
hand of Lieutenant Pamfilé, and that Campobello was lying
dangerously wounded by the thrust of a pike on board the
Minerva.

" Those villains have met their desert," said his lordship.
" I hope you found the Miss Whartons safe and uninjured?"

" Quite so, dear Edward, and most anxious concerning
your hurts. With this breeze we shall be in Malta to-morrow;
a day or two of repose is all you will have to undergo, thank
God!"

" Yes," returned his lordship, "we have much to be thank-
ful for; Captain Epron made a gallant defence, and I rejoiced
at hearing that, though severely wounded, he is not dangerously so."

The next day, by noon, the three ships were at anchor in the
harbour of Valetta.

Though still suffering from his wound, Captain Friend and
his officers and crew embarked the week after, and in the court-
martial that afterwards ensued, he and his officers were honourably acquitted of the loss of their ship.

The tenth day after arriving in Malta, the Serena again
sailed with the prizes for Palermo. Captain Epron was just
able to leave his couch as the three ships entered the harbour

of Palermo. During the voyage the princess and suite, with Mary Wharton and her cousins, occupied the entire cabins of the Serena, and many pleasant and social hours were passed by our hero in the society of his beloved Mary : the restraint she at first felt in the presence of the princess wore off, so amiable and affectionate was the whole manner and bearing of the beautiful Clarina. It was also observed by our hero with sincere gratification that Lord de Umfreville, who was rapidly recovering, seemed to feel peculiar pleasure in the society of Elizabeth; her strong resemblance to Mary first attracted him; her sweet retiring manners, charming voice, and singularly cultivated taste first surprised and then charmed him.

The arrival of the Serena, with the Minerva frigate and the Sylphide, excited quite a sensation at the court of King Ferdinand. De Courcy again became the lion of that volatile court; there was no end of the favours showered upon him by the Queen and the ladies of her court ; but our hero's whole thoughts were centred upon Mary. Sir Charles Wharton rented a charming villa close beside the Princess of Sorento's, in the Obruzza, where the family at once removed. The princess, after some little manœuvring, and a very well-acted penitence, obtained her pardon from King Ferdinand, and once more made her appearance at court.

Campobello, the Lazzarone, still suffering from his wounds, was handed over to the authorities, to be dealt with as a traitor and assassin.

Sir John and Lady Acton received our hero with their usual kindness and interest in his affairs; they listened to his adventures with attention and great sympathy, and expressed a wish to be introduced to Lord de Umfreville, who was equally anxious to see Sir John, for from him he expected to hear many particulars explained which were still rather obscure.

The revolutionary party were in full possession of Naples, and the war raged in great fury in Calabria.

As soon as Captain Epron was sufficiently recovered, he and his officers and crew embarked in a neutral vessel for Toulon, taking a friendly leave of our hero, who supplied them with every requisite in money and necessaries they required.

One evening, when the whole family party were assembled in the mansion of the princess, she gave Sir Charles, as she had promised, the history of her aunt's life, as far as she was acquainted with it, and which our readers will peruse in our next chapter.

CHAPTER XL.

" On the banks of the river Crati, and at the foot of the Ap-
pennines, stood the castle of Crotono ; I say stood," continued
the princess, " because in the terrible earthquake that occurred
eighteen years ago the castle was levelled to its very founda-
tions, and the greater part of that lovely, romantic country
devastated. Many towns and villages were uprooted and
destroyed, and above thirty thousand persons perished. The
castle of Crotono and an immense tract of country belonged to
my mother's father, the Baron Malfi de Crotono.

" My grandfather, on the mother's side, had two daughters,
but no son, which disappointment soured his temper and disposition : for he was proud to excess of his ancient name and
race. His daughters were reared in great seclusion, though no
pains were spared to render them accomplished ; they lost
their mother early, which was a great misfortune. I often
heard my mother say, in after years, the sisters were both
beautiful. I never saw my aunt ; but my mother has told me
she was very lovely, and gifted with a rare and extraordinary
voice. There were but sixteen months between the two
sisters. Clarina, my mother, was just eighteeen, and Magdalene, her sister, something more than sixteen, when, from
political reasons, the Baron Crotono, who was connected with
the royal family of Naples by relationship, set out with his
two daughters for that city, to the infinite joy of Magdalene,
who was of a terribly wild and ungovernable spirit, and who
detested the solitude of the castle of Crotono.

" Scarcely three months had passed in Naples when my
aunt suddenly disappeared : no possible trace could be obtained
of her ; but as the first singer of the royal opera disappeared at
the same time, strange surmises were formed. This man, by
name Cambria, was remarkable for the beauty of his features,
as well as for the exquisite tones of his voice ; and Magdalene
often expressed herself enraptured with his person and his
voice. Be this as it may, both disappeared at the same time.
My grandfather was furious ; he offered great rewards for any
trace of the fugitive, but in vain. Shortly after this event, my
mother married the Duke de Obruzza, one of the highest
noblemen in the kingdom, and my grandfather retired to his
castle of Crotono.

" I was scarcely four years old when the terrible earthquakes
occurred that destroyed the castle, and the whole of my grandfather's property became a wilderness ; he himself and his
whole household perished amid the ruins of the castle.

" During succeeding years naught was heard of Magdalene
de Crotono but vague reports. It was whispered she was

seen and recognized with Cambria, performing as an opera-singer in Venice and other cities; but in the disturbed state of Europe at this time my mother had no means of investigating these reports. At the age of seventeen I married the amiable Prince of Sorento, and the following year I lost my beloved mother; I was only nineteen when I became a widow. Some four or five reports reached Naples, that a Count and Countess de Castagno had made their appearance in Cosenza, in Calabria, and that the countess declared herself to be the youngest daughter of the late Marquis of Crotono, and the count claimed the lands formerly possessed by her father. Before people had time to recover from their surprise at this sudden re-appearance of my aunt, Magdalene de Crotono, as Countess de Castagno, another rumour got afloat—that another Count and Countess de Castagno had appeared in Cosenza, and revealed themselves to the bishop, who acknowledged them to be the true representatives of Crotono and Castagno, and that the count had assembled his feudatory vassals and driven the impostors out.

" King Ferdinand refused to acknowledge the count and countess's claims; and the Count de Castagno soon assembled a powerful force of mountaineers and brigands and maintained his and his wife's rights. Things were in this state when the French invasion frightened the people of Naples, and especially the king; but the Count de Castagno now turned his arms against the invaders, and performed some splendid actions, which so pleased the king that he gave him up the lands, and made him a knight of the order of St. Constantine. Now you must suppose that the appearance of my aunt in Calabria, after a disappearance of so many years, created intense surprise and curiosity in the Neapolitan court, and every one became anxious to learn how the past years of her life had been spent, and how she came to be the wife of the disinherited son of the wolf of Calabria, as the old Count of Castagno was called. I myself naturally felt great curiosity; but as I never had seen my aunt, I could form no judgment. But the Cavaliero Luigi Macheroni, the signor who some years before had spread the report that he had seen my aunt in Venice with an immensely rich English gentleman, and that they travelled together as man and wife, took it into his head to travel to Cosenza, to see the Countess Castagno. He did so, and returning to Naples, told me, in confidence, that my aunt was the female he had seen in Venice with the English signor; he would swear to it. I entreated the Signor Macheroni, for the sake of the family, to say nothing of this, as he might be mistaken.

" ' Do you remember, princess,' said he, ' some years ago—though by-the-bye you were too young. but I remember it well, and it struck me forcibly at the time—there was a very large reward offered (I was then chief of the police), for the discovery of a person calling herself Magdalene Caracci, who had stolen a child, a female, from an English gentleman of rank in Genoa.'

" ' Why, Madonna,' I interrupted, ' you do not surely think because my aunt's name is Magdalene, that she and Magdalene Caracci could be one and the same? '

" ' No, princess,' returned the cavaliero, 'not because of the name ; but listen to me : as minister of police I was written to by a Signor Garetti, a merchant of Genoa, begging me to endeavour to trace this Magdalene Caracci, if possible ; he stated particularly her appearance, her age, &c. ; that he suspected her to be either a Neapolitan or a Sicilian.

" ' I sent a clever sbirri amongst the Lazzaroni, a fellow very popular amongst them ; he picked up a few particulars, the most important of which was, that a strange female had deposited a child with the Lazzarone Campobello, and given him a sum of money to take it off her hands. I got hold of this Campobello ; he did not deny the transaction, but declared the child died four days after ; he swore so positively that I was induced to believe him ; however, after three months' diligent investigation, and through the agency of the police in various cities, I discovered that a female answering to the description of Magdalene Caracci had been seen at Milan ; I heard of her again at Como, where the English gentleman she resided with died ; from Como I failed in tracing her, and from that time till I heard of the return of Magdelene Crotono to Cosenza I failed in hearing of or tracing her. Now I am convinced that your aunt, princess, is the identical Magdelene Caracci, but, of course, I refrain from further inquiries.' I thanked the Cavaliero Macheroni, and begged him, as this belief of his could lead to no good result after so many years, to refrain from speaking of it, and the talk about the Countess of Castagno expired.

" When Miss Wharton," continued the princess, " related to me the incidents connected with her birth, I at once mentioned to her my belief that my aunt, the Countess Castagno, was the mysterious Magdalene Caracci. The question now is, how to obtain accurate information on this interesting subject, for we may naturally suppose the Countess Castagno will do all she can to bury in oblivion the errors and deceptions of her early life."

The party present, consisting of Sir Charles Wharton, his nieces, Hugh De Courcy, and Lord de Umfreville, listened to the princess with profound attention ; like her, they felt persuaded that Magdalene Caracci and the Countess Castagno were the same individual ; but, nevertheless, the mystery of

Sir Charles Wharton's two nieces' birth was by no means cleared up.

"I should very much like," said the baronet, "if it were not for the war now raging in Calabria, to visit the residence of the countess, satisfy myself as to her being Magdalene Caracci, and trust to circumstances, if I recognized her, in inducing her to reveal to me the mystery of the past."

"It would be a desperate risk, Sir Charles, at present," replied the princess, " to venture into that country, where war to the knife is carried on, and where every stranger is treated as an enemy or a spy."

"Oh, do not, dear uncle, dream of going there!" cried Mary, anxiously; "any knowledge you might obtain could never increase my love, or alter yours for me and Elizabeth."

"True, my dear child," answered the baronet, "it could not; but yet there is a longing at the heart we cannot control. Love you both more than I do I could not; yet I would give much to have the mystery of your births cleared up."

"I will send a messenger into Calabria," observed the princess; "it is only a day's sail from this to the Calabrian coast, and a trusty messenger, a native of Calabria, would easily make his way to Cosenza without risk, and deliver a letter. My aunt can have no object now in withholding the truth, and perhaps my persuasions would have the effect of inducing her to do so; at all events the experiment is worth the trial."

To this the baronet heartily agreed, and returned the princess thanks for the exceeding interest she evinced in his behalf. Accordingly, in a day or two, a native of Calabria was found, the letter written, and the messenger took his passage in a small vessel bound to St. Enfeemio.

Whilst waiting the return of the messenger, a British frigate arrived in Palermo, on the 26th of October, with the cheering intelligence that peace had been signed in London, on the first of that month, between England and France. This intelligence caused the greatest transport of joy in the Neapolitan court in Palermo. The fêtes and rejoicings that took place in consequence were magnificent. Queen Caroline hinted to the princess that she expected Sir Charles Wharton's nieces, of whose beauty she had heard so much, should be presented.

Sir Charles had no objection, though Elizabeth felt a natural repugnance to figure amid a court where she might possibly be recognized by some one as Campobello's daughter, the Lazzarone girl. But Mrs. Arbuthnot and Mary showed her how impossible such a contingency was. No human being could recognize in the fair and beautiful niece of Sir Charles Wharton the dark-complexioned and half-clothed Magdalene.

One of those events, quite frequent at the period of our
story in Palermo, now occurred, and created considerable
alarm to the court, and especially to the Lazzarone king. At
this time there existed in Palermo a community styled the
" Conciarotte," which made all other classes, even royalty
itself, tremble. The members were not exactly like the
Lazzaroni of Naples—neither did they resemble the Traste-
vereni of Rome—for they were far more to be dreaded. They
were held together by mysterious laws, and enjoyed privileges
and immunities which even Ferdinand himself was afraid to
interfere with. And these men, so leagued together, were
neither more nor less than the tanners or leather-dressers of
Palermo. It chanced that a sbirri had the hardihood to arrest
one of the Conciarotte and consign him to prison. That night
the tanners rose in a mass, assaulted the prison, released all
the malefactors, Campobello among the rest, and fired the
building, besides committing various other outrages. King Ferdinand the next morning shrugged his shoulders and laughed,
saying, " My worthy tanners are sometimes as troublesome as
my Lazzaroni subjects ; but say what you will—they are a
very useful body of men. Let them alone, they will be quiet
before night ; " but many an honest citizen had to regret the
horrors enacted in a few hours by those wretches. The Queen's
Italian Guards kept patrolling before the royal residence all
the night, but did not otherwise interfere.

" So that villain Campobello is once more at liberty," said
Lord de Umfreville to Hugh De Courcy. " What a government! " he added ; " troops sufficient to crush those merciless
ruffians last night, and yet not a man stirred from the ranks."

" It is deplorable," responded De Courcy ; " it was the same
with the Lazzaroni at Naples ; they, at times, terribly disturbed
the quiet of the city ; and yet the king would not permit his
loving subjects, as he called these rascals, to be punished for
their little peccadillos. Poor fellows ! ' he would say, ' they are
very harmless, and at times their spirits overpower them,
but they soon return to their peaceable life and gorging
macaroni.' "

" How did your audience with the king end this morning? "
questioned Lord de Umfreville.

" Well," returned our hero, " pretty well ; Sir John Acton
tendered my resignation, relating to his majesty my reasons
for doing so, also stating that had the war continued I would
have remained in his majesty's service."

" His majesty was gracious enough to say, ' he deeply regretted that circumstances should cause me to give up a profession in which I might shortly expect to reach the highest
rank, but of course he accepted my resignation ; and knowing
it was my wish to purchase the French corvette Sylphide, he

very graciously ordered that I should accept her as a gift from himself, and to-day I had an audience purposely to tender my thanks and gratitude."

I intended to fit up the corvette as a yacht, to take us all back in the spring, and to visit, as we have agreed, Genoa ; and to call the corvette the Dauntless, in memory of the unfortunate frigate of that name. I am picking up an English crew by degrees, out of the merchant craft, and a few old men-of-wars' men I had in the Serena. Two and twenty will be quite sufficient to take the Dauntless home.

"Young Pamfilé I got promoted to second lieutenant of the Serena, Biaggi to be first, and the command, I hear, is to be given to Captain Septimo."

"Well, all this is very satisfactory," said Lord de Umfreville, " and I congratulate you. The princess proposed an excursion after to-morrow to the famous convent of Capucins, to visit the vaults ; but Mary and Elizabeth objected, as the sight of those veiled remnants of the dead would be anything but pleasing ; and we go, instead, to the Roman castle of King Rogu."

"Very good," remarked De Courcy, " the change is for the better. Do you know, Edward, I think Mary, without intending it, is converting Elizabeth, who begins to rather doubt the efficacy of the saints, and has taken to seriously reading Mary's collection of books on religious subjects ? "

"I have observed her reading the Bible attentively myself," replied Lord de Umfreville ; " and though I am very far from a bigot, yet, as all her family connections are of the Protestant persuasion, and she has doubtless to pass her life in a Protestant country, if she leans to that belief through her own conviction, I know it would impart a great pleasure to Sir Charles, though he refrains from saying one word on the subject."

"By-the-bye, the princess's cousin, the Marquis de Caraccioli—same family, I believe, as the unfortunate prince of that name—seems greatly taken with our lovely and fascinating friend, Térese Garetti."

"I have observed his attention," said our hero, " and I think at last the fair Térese is caught in Cupid's meshes ; he is a very handsome and highly-accomplished young nobleman, and by all accounts very amiable."

The following day the Princess of Sorento was greatly shocked by the return of her messenger from Calabria with both his ears cut off close to his head. This event created a profound sensation in Palermo amongst those concerned in the miserable man's misfortune. Sir Charles was grieved, and insisted on giving the poor fellow a sufficient sum to render him comfortable for the rest of his days ; the man himself did not appear to feel the loss of his ears so much as a burning desire to be revenged on those who had deprived him of those certainly ornamental additions to the head.

The messenger gave the following account of his ill-starred journey:—He related that he reached St. Enfeemio in thirty hours, and at once crossed the country without mishap, and arrived at Cosenza; he there inquired where the Countess Costagna resided, and was told in the fortress of Nilocastra, about six leagues from Cosenza, amid the mountains.

The princess's messenger hired a mule and a guide, and set out for the fortress, through a wild and almost impassable country; he described the fortress, which description we omit at present, and, on obtaining admission, sent his letter by a domestic to the countess. Half an hour afterwards he was ordered in to the great hall, and there he beheld the countess, who looked, he said, "in a terrible rage;" he described her as a tall, grand lady, with an eye of fire, full in her person, and about forty-two years of age.

"Are you the villain," said the countess, "that brought this letter?" holding out the princess's in her hand.

"Yes, excellency," replied the messenger, bowing to the ground, and feeling rather alarmed, for the hall was filled with heavily-armed men, who stood grinning at him the whole time.

"Good," answered the countess, with a terrible smile, and, making a sign with her hand, four of the brigands, for such he said they looked like, seized hold of him.

"Thank your stars, wretch," cried the countess, "that my lord is absent, or he would hang you from the walls for daring to come hither with such a letter to me; and thus I treat it!" and, tearing it to pieces, trampled it under foot; "and now, villain, for fear you should forget your visit to the fortress of Nilocastra, and be induced to repeat it, you shall not go back without a remembrance. Cut the villain's ears off," she added, "and drive him out of this territory!" In vain the unfortunate wretch strove to throw himself at the feet of the terrible countess; he was dragged out of the hall and out of the fortress, set upon his mule, and conducted to the extremity of the valley. After descending the hill on which stood the fortress, reaching a wild and secluded spot, they threw him on the ground, and one of the brigands coolly drew out his knife, sharpened it scientifically, and, taking a small leather bag from his pouch, he very gravely observed, "Amico, we do not wish to rob you of anything; you shall have your ears as relics. Now shut your mouth, and do not be disturbing the peaceful serenity of this place by your noise," and forthwith the brigand cut off his ears, and, putting the pieces in the bag, threw it at his feet, and left him howling with rage and agony on the ground.

As soon as he could recover himself, and had staunched the blood, he mounted his mule and reached the hamlet of Legliano. He there related his doleful story; but instead of commiseration, the people of the wretched Locanda only shook their heads, saying, "He was lucky to lose only his ears!"

CHAPTER XLI.

WE have stated in our last chapter that the Princess of Sorento was greatly shocked at the cruel treatment her messenger had received at the hands of her aunt. It proved to her very clearly that the Countess de Castagno was fully determined never to identify herself with Magdalene Caracci. Still her present violent conduct was quite contrary to the opinion the princess had formed of her character, and, judging of her by her conduct during her residence with Sir Charles Wharton's lady, previous to her death, the princess was exceedingly grieved and annoyed.

De Courcy, in talking the matter over with Lord de Umfreville and Sir Charles, expressed a doubt as to whether the Countess Castagno was in reality the same person who has figured as the mysterious Magdalene Caracci.

" I have been thinking so myself, Hugh," said the baronet, " and so exceedingly curious am I respecting the identity of the two persons, that, if you are willing, I will accompany you to Calabria, and get to Cosenza, which, I hear, is a considerable town. There is peace now the French have retraced their steps, and, as strangers travelling to see the country, we may get a glimpse of this formidable countess."

" I am most willing to go, Sir Charles," answered De Courcy; " I have felt a desire to do so from the moment that poor fellow returned so barbarously mutilated; but we must be cautious, for, in war or peace, I understand they laugh at the king's authority in some parts of Calabria."

" I have no fear as to anything disagreeable occurring, or any injury to our persons," said the baronet, " but I would rather the girls knew nothing of our expedition till after we are gone. We depend on your watching over their safety, my good lord."

" Faith, it is a very hard case to be excluded from joining you," remarked Lord de Umfreville; " I should amazingly like to see the wilds of Calabria, and also the people."

" I should not like to leave the girls," observed Sir Charles, " without some male protector to accompany them in their walks: not that I think there is the slightest risk in rambling about the populous neighbourhood of Palermo. Still, they would miss us all three, so you must really turn guardian for a few days."

" Well, Sir Charles, it would be very ungallant to refuse
the post of guardian to such fair demoiselles as the three
cousins ; but the princess, depend on it, will occupy all their
time."

" Perhaps," observed the baronet, after a moment's thought,
" the best plan will be at once to tell them where we are going ;
the princess may be able to point some certain mode of seeing
this fierce countess."

In the evening—assembled in the saloon of the Princess of
Sorento, where almost every second evening was spent in conversation, with music and song to beguile the hours—though
the first week in November, there was not the slightest signs,
as far as mildness of weather went, of the approach of winter
in that delightful climate—De Courcy introduced the subject
to the princess, and stated his and Sir Charles's intention of
proceeding into Calabria.

Clarina Obruzza started, and looking into our hero's face,
said, earnestly, " You are not aware of what a country Calabria
now is ; it is swarming with disbanded and disorderly soldiers,
deserters, a starving peasantry, and whole bands of savage
brigands.   Except in the principal towns, you have no accom-
modation ; hotels there are none, and the habitations of the
poor farmers detestable."

" But all those disagreeables are mere nothings to men,"
replied De Courcy.

" No, I agree to that," said the princess, with a smile ;
" they would be inducements to you, who love difficulties ; but
worthy Sir Charles has nothing of the Knight Errant in his
nature or disposition ; and though you would have no wind-
mills, like Cervantes' hero, to contend with, yet you would
encounter too many disagreeables for an English baronet, of a
certain age, to bear."

" Oh, princess, you mistake Sir Charles ; he is full of
energy and spirit ; his early life hardened his constitution, and
I assure you he would think little of a few nights passed at
Fresco, if it ever came to that.   But, by landing at San
Giovanni, we can make a tolerably good route of it to
Cosenza."

" Benissimo," said the princess, " and when at Cosenza,
what can you do ?   The castle of the countess is buried in the
wild hills of the Cerata, a country from time immemorial infested with hordes of brigands."

" I have often heard of these brigands," observed De Courcy,
" their number, and their ferocity ; but I have always been
puzzled to think how the said brigands exist.   Calabria is
described as an impoverished country ; then who do these
brigands plunder—on what do they live ? "

" Mostly upon the produce of the chase ; game of all kinds

abounds in the forests and mountains. Though Calabria is now poor, it was once rich; the transport of merchandise through the country remains great, for you have the sea on both sides. The feudal system still exists, and many of these bands of brigands form the body-guard of the powerful barons and seignors of Calabria. Ah, Madonna Mia! you would be surprised to see the train of armed retainers a Calabrese noble entertained and supported a few years ago."

"I fancy, princess," said De Courcy, with a smile, "that they were allowed to help themselves now and then from their neighbour's stock, like our Scotch rovers of the last century."

"Something of the sort, I daresay," returned Clarina. "But if you will go this wild-goose chase to see my aunt, go in the character of hunters, and take half a score of well-equipped attendants with you: Sir Charles is not too old to love a day's sport."

"The idea is exceedingly good," said De Courcy ; "wild as Calabria is, her people are singularly hospitable."

"You can pass yourself off easily as a Sicilian signor come to enjoy a few days in the chase of the wild boar. Take young Pamfile with you; he will enjoy it in earnest. Hunt in the vicinity of the fortress of Nilocastra, get benighted, and demand hospitality; it will be granted immediately. Let Sir Charles keep in the background, or at least disguise himself well, and ten to one if the countess ever recognizes him ; if she does, I do not see that you incur much risk; for though my redoubtable aunt ventured to cut off poor Massari's ears, she will never dream of trying the same experiment upon you."

"Faith, it is to be hoped not," answered De Courcy, laughing heartily at the semi-serious comic smile of Clarina Obruzza.

"I am trying," added the princess, thoughtfully, "to make light of this journey, because I know, once you take a thing into your head, count, you will do it; and the more the peril the greater the excitement and inducement."

"Now I may fairly request to know," said Mary Wharton, seating herself next the princess, "what you are planning ; I have detected my uncle's looks, he is a very indifferent actor, and I strongly suspect you both have some project in view."

"You are quite right, dear Mary," replied De Courcy, with an affectionate look into the beautiful features of his intended. "Sir Charles intends a visit to Calabria, to endeavour to get a glimpse of the Countess de Castagno, and I intend, of course, to accompany him."

Mary looked serious, and turning to the princess, she asked. "And do you approve, dear lady, of this wild scheme?"

"Well, carissima," returned the princess, with a smile, "I

think it is always better to coincide with our lords and masters than to oppose them. What think you?"

" I will not attempt to offer advice in this case," remarked Mary, seriously, "for I know my dear uncle would not put himself to this trouble, and perhaps danger, without well considering the result. So I shall not express my opinion on the subject, only trusting that no accident of any kind will happen on the journey."

" In truth," said the princess, " I do not see very great difficulties in the way : bad roads, no inns, very indifferent living, and a wild, but romantically-picturesque country, will be the chief features of their journey. It is only an affair of six or eight days, at furthest ; before we have time to miss them they will be back."

A hunting excursion to the forests of Calabria was a very common amusement amongst the young nobles of the Neapolitan court, therefore our hero was soon equipped and furnished with every requisite.

A government despatch boat, zebec-rigged, was to convey the party to San Giovanni, and await their leisure. The corvette Sylphide, now styled the Dauntless, was undergoing great alterations in her cabins and fitting-out; she was to be rigged as a three-masted schooner, which would require a less number of hands to work her; all her guns, excepting four, were taken out and stowed in the hold; altogether she promised to make a remarkably handsome yacht. As a corvette she was overmasted and rigged, and her new fitting-out, with the masts raking considerably aft, gave her a very rakish appearance.

Our hero had an interview with Sir John Acton before his departure; he made no secret with his old and kind protector of the real object of their expedition.

"It is a somewhat wild project, Hugh," said Sir John ; "the baronet, I think, had better remain behind, and Lord de Umfreville take his place."

" But you forget, Sir John," returned our hero, "that the baronet alone could recognize this Magdalene Caracci. I never saw her."

" True," returned Queen Caroline's minister, " you are right there. Still, be careful, and on your guard; you go to a savage land, and a wild race exist about Mcastro. The Count de Castagno is reported to be a chieftain of fierce and predatory habits. There are some strange stories about him; his father was a terrible man before him, and was notorious for his tyranny.

"I remember four or five years ago," continued Sir John, " when Magdalene de Crotono, the Countess de Castagno now by right of her husband, reappeared in Cosenza, and claimed the lands of her father, which were forfeited to the crown, a commissioner was sent down to investigate her claims and to identify her person; this gentleman was well acquainted with all her family, and knew the sisters well at the time of their visit with their father to Naples. The commissioner proceeded to the town of Cosenza, where he was seized by a party of brigands, and forcibly carried to the fortress of Nilocastra, a very strong place, he says, and then, to his indignation, brought forward in the great hall of the castle. There he beheld the Count de Castagno. The commissioner indignantly and bitterly complained of the outrage committed on him, and threatened the count with the severest punishment for insulting a king's messenger."

" Tell your king from me,' said the count, with a scornful laugh, 'that he will have quite enough to do to keep his own crown, without robbing his subjects of their rightful possessions. As to investigating the claims of Magdalene de Crotono, you know that all the possessions of the Marquis de Crotona, in Calabria, were settled on his youngest daughter; his Neapolitan and Sicilian property is held by his eldest daughter, the Princess de Sorento; the Calabrese estates were unjustly claimed by the crown, because Magdalene de Crotono was accounted as one dead, and her father unjustly disinherited her. The only question therefore at issue between us is her identity.' As he said the words, he made a signal, and the doors at the further end of the hall were thrown open, and a richly-dressed lady entered; she looked exceedingly haughty and imperious, but the commissioner regarded her keenly and inquisitively, and though twenty—perhaps more—years had passed, he felt satisfied, from her general appearance, and her eyes—which were always remarkable for their beauty—and a slight scar over the left temple, the consequence of a fall from her horse when in Naples, and which occurrence he remembered well, that he beheld Magdalene de Crotono. 'Are you satisfied?' demanded the count with a sneer. 'I shall reply to no question, sir count,' answered the king's messenger, ' whilst under this illegal restraint ; release me, and meet me with this lady, in open court, at Cosenza, and I will answer you. If you will do this at once, and request my pardon for the outrage committed upon my person, I will justly and fairly investigate that lady's claims.' The count laughed, in mockery, saying, 'I hold the lands, and will keep them ; but tell your king, if he does not molest me, I will be a loyal subject, and help him in his time of need.'"

"This fierce count," observed our hero, with a smile, " seems to have had a foreshadowing of what was about to come."

"Yes," returned Sir John, "the signs of the times were

then visible; however, he dismissed the messenger, after
offering him all kinds of refreshments and courtesy, but the
Cavaliero Ottosino indignantly quitted the fortress and returned to Naples, and reported the result of his journey into
Calabria to Ferdinand the Fourth.

"The king at first looked serious, then he smiled, saying,
' Then you think, Cavaliero, that the Countess de Castagno is
the Marchese de Crotono's daughter?' ' Yes, sire, I do confidently think so—but to seize me, your majesty----' ' Yes,
yes,' interrupted the king, laughing, ' it was very wrong; we
will speak to Sir John about it.' I was well aware what a
country Calabria is, and how impossible it would be, in the
then threatened state of the kingdom, to deal with the powerful and refractory nobles of that territory, so I advised his
majesty, for the present, to let matters rest. The will of the
late Marchese de Crotono was an unjust one, for his daughter
had certainly a better right to the property than the crown.
' Well,' said the easy king, ' I think so too; and you see, the
count says he will prove a loyal subject—so let it be.'

" But in the meantime a young officer of infantry, quartered
in Cosenza, took offence at some insult the count inflicted on
him, for intruding on his territory, and marched his troop to
arrest the count. By Jove! he roused a nest of hornets; his
troop had to take to their heels—two of them were killed, and
several wounded—and the officer himself stripped of his
uniform. King Ferdinand was then really annoyed, and was
giving orders to arrest this audacious count, when the French
troops, advancing from Rome, turned the tables. Afterwards,
as the revolution marched on, and French troops invaded
Calabria, the Count Castagno became a formidable enemy to
them, and a war to the knife ensued between the count and
the French, who could never root him or his followers out of
their mountain retreat.

" King Ferdinand was so pleased at his devotion, as he
considered it, to the royal cause, that he abandoned his claim
to the lands, and the count now possesses them in right of his
wife; but this said wife has turned out a desperate virago, by
all accounts. Ambitious, haughty, and imperious, she domi-
neers over the entire country around, like a queen, and defies
all laws. Now that peace is proclaimed, things cannot remain long as they are, for the laws must be respected. Two
infantry regiments and a troop of cavalry will shortly be sent
to Cosenza—this will bring the count to his senses—during
the war it was impossible to interfere. Now you know something of your man—be cautious, and do not rashly beard the
lion in his den."

CHAPTER XLII.

THE west wind blew fresh from the bay of Palermo the happy, as the Santa Rosalia, the government despatch-boat, darted out from the mole, her lofty latine sails distended to their fullest by the fine breeze blowing, and driving her through the still waters at the rate of ten knots an hour. On board were our adventurous party, Hugh De Courcy, Sir Charles Wharton, and Lieutenant Pamfilé, with a dozen well-armed and active attendants, and six couple of splendid dogs.

It was a beautiful day; though November had commenced, there was not a cloud in the sky, and the breeze blowing off the Sicilian shore left the deep blue waters like a lake, sparkling and rippling in the bright sunshine, through which the dolphins were sporting and showing their "backs of gold."

The Santa Rosalia hugged the Sicilian shore in her course for the straits of Messina, therefore Sir Charles, to whom the scenery of that lovely coast was quite new, enjoyed it to the full.

"With this wind," observed De Courcy, addressing Sir Charles, "it will not take us more than ten or twelve hours to reach Messina. We will cast anchor there for a time, and then run across for either San Giovanni or Amato, a bay sheltered from this wind, which blows right in on the Calabrian shore."

"This is a glorious country, Hugh!" said Sir Charles; "and if it were inhabited by Englishmen——"

De Courcy laughed. "You are thinking of the riot the other night, Sir Charles, which fifty well-trained soldiers would have suppressed with ease."

"And yet those ruffians were allowed to commit such dreadful outrages," observed the baronet,—"you, who have lived amongst them so many years, must know the cause."

"A weak-minded king, my dear sir, and a pleasure-loving, inert population; a tyrannical nobility, passionately addicted to play; a profligate court; and a priest-ridden, superstitious race—an ill-governed kingdom from beginning to end. I am firmly convinced, though it is now proclaimed peace, that peace is a shallow one, and that France will possess the Neapolitan dominions before long, and King Ferdinand either become their slave or lose his crown."

"Queen Caroline is an energetic, courageous, and high-spirited woman," said Sir Charles.

"True," returned De Courcy, "but for her the king's power would be scorned; but then she mars all by the profligacy she not only permits but encourages in her court."

U

The day passed pleasantly, for every league offered some new object of romantic beauty, with Mount Etna towering above the lesser hills of the interior. After twelve hours' voyage, the Santa Rosalia anchored in the Port of Messina. As it was scarcely fifteen miles to San Giovanni, they did not weigh anchor till two hours after sunrise; the scene around them attracted all their attention—the Santa Rosalia spread her lofty sails to the same steady breeze as on the preceding day—the sea before Messina was crowded with every variety of craft; two fine English frigates off the port were preparing to pass the narrow passage, whilst numbers of merchantmen, of all nations, were under sail, taking advantage of the leading breeze, to run through a strait so terribly feared by the early navigators. The wild shores of Calabria, scarcely ten miles distant, rose before them as they scudded swiftly before the breeze, leaving the green hills and mountains which rise behind the spires and lofty towers of fair Messina in the distance.

As Messina receded from their view, the numerous towns and villages so snugly nestled amid the hills of Calabria, covered with the richest foliage, and backed by the lofty mountains of the interior, came into view.

"Yonder," said the captain of the zebec, "is the town of Reggio, in that deep bay. It forms a fine object."

Our adventurers thought so too; Sir Charles was surprised at the beauty of the shore, and its fine beeches, on which the sun's rays fell with dazzling brightness, for he had pictured to himself a wild and rugged coast, not a picture of pretty towns and hill-side villages; he had yet to behold the wilds of Calabria.

Landing at San Giovanni, a small town on the shores of a wild bay, the party hired mules and guides for Legliano, the nearest village to the Count Castagno's castle. They intended sleeping their first night in the town of Rosarno, where they understood there was a tolerable locanda; thence, to the residence of the count, the road ran through a wild romantic country, covered with forest, and full of game of all sorts: at San Giovanni the host described the interior of the country to be in a terribly disordered state, and infested with brigands, styling themselves patriots and firm supporters of Il Re Ferdinando—but, with so well-armed a party, and coming to Calabria as mere hunters and sportsmen, there was little to be apprehended from the brigands, as they could not expect much plunder, and were certain of a desperate resistance.

The Englishmen thought little about the brigands; they were all armed with rifles, pistols, *couteau de chasse*, and boar-spears.

"Well, Mr. Bernard," said William, De Courcy's valet, to Sir Charles Wharton's personal attendant, as they rode after their masters. "this is something new, is not it?" brandishing his pike with a very warlike action, which induced Mr. Bernard, who was an elderly man, and by no means of a bellicose nature, to keep a little wider apart.

"Why, yes," returned the sober and sedate attendant of the baronet, eyeing his belt with a brace of pistols in it. "It's very pretty to look at, but I sincerely trust it's all show. You, Mr. William, have had a seasoning in warlike affairs, and have heard a cannon loaded with tin canisters and grapes."

"Bless your soul, Mr. Bernard," interrupted William, with an air of importance, "they do not load cannon with tin canisters. We call the heap of balls, old iron, and other miscellaneous articles crammed into a cannon grape and canister. I assure you I have stood in a shower of such like commodities many times without winking."

"Ah!" said Mr. Bernard, "I should prefer a shower of anything else—rain for instance, that only wets your skin, the other leaves no skin at all sometimes; but who are those strange-looking gents yonder, sitting on the rock with their great, long guns on their knees?"

"Ah, by Jove!" exclaimed William, eyeing the group and grasping his pike firmly, "they are brigands, I should think, by their dress."

"I sincerely hope not," returned Mr. Bernard, "for what you call by the fine name of brigands mean thieves."

"Oh, dear no, Mr. Bernard; don't fancy that Italian brigands are like our London thieves, who ease you so gently of the contents of your pockets. They plunder in a military fashion; wear mustachios, lots of ribbons, sashes, and buttons; but, by Jove, look! there's the very picture of an Italian brigand."

The party were just then proceeding through a wild valley, the hill on one side clothed to the very summit with noble trees, and on the other a succession of magnificent rocks, piled fantastically one above the other. Over one bold projecting ledge a bright sparkling stream, on which the sun played through a vista of the wood, shot right out, and fell dashing and splashing in foam and mist over the rocks below. The apparent hunters were proceeding slowly through this romantic pass, admiring its beauty, when six or seven men, each carrying the long rifle of the Calabrian mountaineer, rose up from the rocks where they were resting themselves or basking in the bright warm sunbeams.

"Now, Sir Charles," cried our hero, to the baronet, "you will have an opportunity of seeing the Calabrian patriot or brigand, as the case may require; those are fine-looking men?"

Six athletic-looking men approached the party, saluting them with great cordiality and wishing them "a pleasant day;" and then patting the dogs on the head, inquired if they were going to hunt in the woods of La Rocea. If so they could put them on the track of a fine boar.

Those men were picturesquely and handsomely attired; the high conical, Calabrese hat, round which was passed a broad red ribbon, the ends flaunting in the breeze over their left shoulder. The upper and lower garments were of bright colours, with tags, tassels, and buttons innumerable; round the waist a fanciful sash of silk, with the long formidable knife stuck in it; their legs were protected with leather gaiters, and over the shoulder was the strap that held the large powder-horn; most of them had a profusion of long, curling, black hair, with mustachios and whiskers of luxuriant growth. Such was the attire of the Calabrian patriot, brigand, and mountaineer.

In answer to their salutations and questions De Courcy said that they did not intend halting that day, but hoped to have good sport in the forests about Legliano.

"Eh! signor, that's dangerous ground to hunt in," remarked one of the mountaineers.

"Why so?" inquired De Courcy of the man who walked beside his mule, the others sauntering by the sides of the other mules, chatting facetiously with their riders.

"Because," returned the Calabrese, "the Count de Castagno is lord over that territory, and he allows no one to hunt without his permission or the king's permit, for Ferdinando Nostro keeps the right of hunting all our forests."

"We would not have come to Calabria," replied De Courcy, "for a week's sport without the king's royal permission, which we have in proper form; otherwise we intended, in courtesy, to ask the baron's permission to hunt his woods."

"Ah, bravo, signor! may you have good sport in a fine country. We would drink your health and success if the signor was willing," and the brigand, which no doubt he was, looked up into our hero's face, with a very meaning expression,

"Oh, certainly," replied De Courcy, laughing; "perhaps this will help you to increase your good wishes for our success;" and, taking a couple of gold pieces from his purse, he threw them into the man's hat.

"Corpo de Baccho!" cried the brigand, with a pleased smile, pocketing the handsome donation, "you have a free hand as well as a strong arm : nothing is lost that is freely given."

"Riverderla, signors," and, doffing their hats, the patriots, brigands, or mountaineers, as they would separately style themselves on different occasions, dropped astern, and our party proceeded, laughing and chatting over their first meeting with a Calabrian bandit.

It was nearly sunset as the party reached their quarters for the night, and well had the princess warned them not to trust to Calabrian locandas for refreshments. One of their mules was loaded with a plentiful supply of the good things of this life ; therefore they very cheerfully put up with the want of other things.

The next day arrangements were made for a boar-hunt in the great forest, at the back of Count de Castagno's castello. Some forest guides and beaters were hired, and every preparation made for the sport ; and much the two young men enjoyed the idea of so exciting an amusement as a boar-hunt.

The people in the locanda and the peasantry of the village seemed exceedingly shy in speaking of the Count de Castagno or of his residence ; they said he was then at home, and frequently hunted himself in the forest, which abounded with game of all sorts.

The distance from the locanda to the forest was about three leagues ; to reach it our adventurers had to pass the castello, or, as the Calabrians styled it, the fortress of Nilocastra. It was built, they said, on the site of a once princely and magnificent fortress, impregnable in the middle ages, and held by a Calabrian prince, an ancestor of Mario de Castagno.

Having breakfasted early, and leaving the Macheroni, Larda, and Gioga wine untasted, which was all the refreshment the hostess could supply them with, the party set out, still mounted on their mules.

Starting from the locanda, the first league of the horse-road kept mostly ascending, and winding through a very beautiful but uncultivated country, another league, and nearly all trace of cultivation became lost: they then entered upon a tract of the most romantic and sublime scenery it was possible to behold. The mountains rose in vast ridges, peak above peak, the sides formed of jagged masses of volcanic rock : impetuous torrents descended the ravines, forming fine sheets of water in the hollows, and then again shooting over abrupt ledges, came thundering down through the gorges to find their way to the ocean.

"Eccolo !" cried one of the guides, "Il Castello Nilocastra."

They had turned the angle of an immense rock, and opened

into view a magnificent amphitheatre of hills, in the middle of
which rose a lofty mound formed of immense masses of rock,
and on this stood the fortress of the Count de Castagno.   It
was of considerable extent, but quite a modern erection,
without any attempt at imitating the ancient fortress that once
frowned on the same site.   Still, from its position, being out
of reach of cannon-shot from any of the adjacent hills, it was
a place of considerable strength, as much as from its massive
rampart walls and its height above the plain, and the extreme
difficulty of approaching it with cannon.   It had neither
moat nor drawbridge, but the steep ascent cut through the
rocks was narrow, and completely defended by two formidable
cannon.   The walls surrounding the main building, which
looked an exceedingly handsome one, were very lofty and
massive.

Our hunting party passed close along the foot of the rocky
mount, and could clearly make out the main entrance—immense gates, flanked by square towers a few feet higher than
the walls.   There was not a human being to be seen on the
walls.

" It will not be so easy, I imagine," said Sir Charles, after
a long gaze at this singularly-constructed castello, or fortified
mansion—a much more appropriate name than either castle
or fortress—"it will not be so easy to see the inside as it is
the exterior."

"I am beginning to be of your opinion, my dear sir," observed our hero, thoughtfully.

" We must follow up the Princess of Sorento's project," put
in Lieutenant Pamfilé—"stay till nightfall, and then request
the count's hospitality for the night."

"Yes," returned De Courcy, " we may try that, but we had
better send back our attendants, and only us three request admittance ; so formidable a party as we are might keep the
gates closed against us.   We could say we had lost our way,
and got separated from our guides."

Debating over various schemes, De Courcy and his companions at length arrived beneath the shades of the great
forest that extended from where they entered to within a
league of Scilla.   There they dismounted from their mules,
and, unpacking the hamper of provisions, prepared for a lunch,
previous to commencing the sports of the day, for it was yet
very early.

The forest abounded with deer, and several had been seen in
the valleys as they approached the wood, but were extremely
wild.   Whilst partaking of the refreshment laid before them
by their attendants, their guides and beaters following their
example, they were surprised by the sound of horns in the

direction of the castle of Castagno, and presently a remarkably well-tuned note on the French horn satisfied the listeners that another hunting party was approaching the forest.

"It would be very droll, Hugh," said Sir Charles, "if the count should have taken it into his head to hunt to-day, and thus anticipate our intention of visiting him; and, by Jove! here comes a numerous party of chasseurs."

De Courcy turned, laying down a cold fowl he was dissecting, and all the rest of the party did the same, and directed their attention to the new-comers.

First rode a gentleman on a strong, spirited bay steed, and by his side a lady in a very handsome and richly-decorated riding-dress, with a plume of feathers in her Spanish hat, and mounted on a very mettled Spanish palfrey. The former was a tall, powerful man, dressed in a hunting suit of dark green cloth, with a black belt round the waist, holding a *couteau de chasse* and a hunting-horn. He carried in his hand a long boar-spear, and at his back was slung a rifle : the lady also carried a light boar-spear. Some paces behind were a numerous retinue of hunters, all armed and attired like the men our party had met the previous day; they all carried guns, and several ox-goads and pikes. Some fifteen or twenty dogs were held in couples by several huntsmen, with horns slung round their necks.

All this was not, of course, seen at first sight, but we describe the strangers at once, as most convenient : behind the huntsmen three domestics in livery led three handsome horses, saddled and bridled.

De Courcy, the baronet, and Lieutenant Pamfilé, rose to their feet as the cavalcade drew up close beside them : immediately the gentleman on the bay horse threw himself off, and, approaching our three friends, politely saluted them by raising his plumed hat ; and fixing his dark eyes at once upon our hero, he said, "I presume I have the pleasure of saluting the Count De Courcy?"

Our hero, surprised, bowed, saying, "You are quite right, signor, such is my name ; but your knowledge of it surprises me."

The gentleman smiled. He was an extremely handsome man, of dark complexion, jet-black hair and moustachios, and dark, penetrating eyes—somewhat fierce in his aspect, it is true, but still he was eminently handsome, and in years not more than four or five and thirty.

"I will clear up the mystery by-and-bye, count," said the stranger ; "permit me to introduce myself and spouse. I am the Count Castagno, and this lady," leading forward the horse she was mounted upon, "my good lady countess."

Sir Charles Wharton started and changed colour as his eyes
rested on the countess, unremarked by the lady, who had hers
fixed upon De Courcy. "We are mistaken," he muttered to
himself; "there is a likeness, but I can swear this lady is not
Magdalene Caracci."

De Courcy raised his hat from his head, and saluted the
countess, who returned a gracious smile. She was in years
perhaps two or three and forty, but looked less; tall and finely
formed, her handsome hunting-dress displaying her full figure
to advantage. She sat on her horse gracefully. No one could
deny that her features were exceedingly handsome, and her
eyes dark as sloes, and brilliant, but there was a haughty air
of superiority about her look and manner that struck De
Courcy at once.

"If you and your friends will mount the horses I have
brought for you, Count De Courcy," said the Calabrese noble,
"I will explain why I intercepted your progress as we ride
along. I hope you will not refuse me, as I have promised myself the pleasure of showing you and your friends a good day's
sport in this wild country."

"You are very kind, count," replied our hero, determined
to take things as he found them, yet longing to ask the baronet
if the Countess Castagno was the Magdalene Caracci they
sought: he then introduced Sir Charles as an English gentleman, and Lieutenant Pamfilé as a brother-officer. The count
bowed; the horses were ordered up, and the party mounted. A
merry blast on the horn was blown by one of the huntsmen,
and the whole cavalcade proceeded at a slow pace into the
forest, along broad avenues leading between the noble trees.

CHAPTER XLIII.

De Courcy rode between the Count and Countess de Castagno. The Calabrese noble said, addressing our hero,—

"That you may not think it strange I should so easily have
become acquainted with your name, I must tell you that a
messenger from Palermo reached me yesterday, bearing a
letter from the Prince de Buttera, who is a near kinsman of
mine, stating that the gallant Count De Courcy, the much-
talked-of commander of the Serena frigate, and two or three
friends, were about to visit Calabria for a few days, to enjoy
the pleasures of the chase; that they would, doubtless, be in
my neighbourhood; and if so, he wished me to show them
every attention in my power. Last night I heard of your
arrival at Legliano, but it was too late to disturb you, and just
as you passed this morning I was setting out to meet you; so
count, you see, the mystery is easily cleared away."

De Courcy bowed; he was, nevertheless, greatly surprised, for he knew the Prince de Buttera very well, meeting him of course at the Neapolitan court; but why he should thus interest himself about him or his excursion to Calabria puzzled him.

"Were you ever in Calabria before this visit, count?" asked the Countess de Castagno.

"No, madame; I have often sailed along your romantic coasts, both east and west, but never landed."

"We have been sorely tried the last few years," remarked the Calabrese; "our lives have been spent hunting down our maladette invaders: the whole country is infested. Every-where you go you see marks of revolutionary France."

"The Calabrese have defended their country well," observed De Courcy, "and its chiefs and mountaineers deserve all the praise the king bestows upon them."

The count bowed; just then some of the hunters who had gone forward returned, and stated that if the count and party stationed themselves in the open glade they had just then entered they would be able to drive a whole herd of red deer past them. Accordingly dismounting, and giving their horses to their attendants, each prepared his rifle.

The red deer abound in the wild glens and forests of Ca-labria, where, before the final subjugation of that country by the French in the war of 1806 and 7, the feudal system existed in full force. The Calabrese peasant, clad in his doublet and inner vest of undressed skins, kept together by thongs of lea-ther or rough horn buttons, deep red breeches of cotton, and a hat of plaited straw, on which was usually fastened a leaden or sometimes a clay image of the Madonna, a pouch, and a knife stuck in his girdle, completing his attire; in manners and thought differing little from the peasant in the time when the barbarian soldiers of Hannibal roused them from their slothful life. These peasants in the nineteenth century felt the same devotion for their hereditary lords, and were as much his slaves as any vassals of the bygone ages, and the acts of tyranny and cruelty enacted by the Calabrian signor upon his dependents would scarcely be believed if recorded here.

Hugh De Courcy stood leaning on his rifle, and seizing an opportunity to say a word to the baronet, who troubled little about his weapon, which lay upon the ground at his feet, inquired in a low voice, "is the Countess de Castagno the Magdalene we seek?"

"No," replied Sir Charles, in a low voice; "I can swear to that."

"Strange!" thought De Courcy, "how is this?" There was no more time for words, for now came the barking of dogs, the shouting of men, and the helter-skelter of a whole herd of red deer, driven by the beaters and hunters through the open glade before them.

"Now, Count de Courcy," exclaimed the Calabrese noble, cocking his rifle, "for a trial of skill between us. There is a noble stag leading," and levelling his rifle he fired: the animal was hit, for he bent his head, but still went on at a tremendous pace: the next instant Hugh De Courcy fired, and the beast rolled over on the plain: crack went Lieutenant Pamfilé's rifle, and down went a red deer.

"Ah!" cried the Count de Castagno, "by St. Januarius, the rifle is no plaything in your hands, gentlemen. But now came wilder shouts in a different direction, shrill blasts on the horn, and bursting through the thick underwood at their back, out rushed a fierce boar, foaming at the mouth, and hotly pursued by a band of mountaineers, attired like the brigands our party had first encountered on their way to Legliano. So sudden and unexpected was the visitation of this denizen of the forest, that he came upon the party before they were ready to receive him. William Henderson and Mr. Bernard were the nearest, and as they turned round, uncertain whether to fly or stand, Mr. Bernard exclaimed, in a voice of alarm and amazement, "What a monstrous pig!" The next moment the animal dashed between his legs, carrying the astounded and horrified attendant of the baronet some twenty yards, sprawling on his back. Roars of laughter burst from every mouth: the ill-starred Mr. Bernard, however, escaped with only a rough fall, and three minutes afterwards the spears of the Count Castagno and De Courcy had finished the boar's career.

William ran to pick up his friend, and Sir Charles anxiously assisted, but Mr. Bernard was unhurt, suffering only from a fright; but internally he vowed never again to place himself in such a situation as to become the jockey of a wild boar.

Another boar was killed, after a fine-spirited run with the dogs and horses: several deer and some pheasants, and other game, were bagged, and then, towards sunset, the whole party, seemingly highly pleased, set out on their return to the castle of Nilocastra, where the count insisted they should all be entertained for the night.

They proceeded to the castle by a different road, running through a very beautiful valley: the hills were covered to their summit with the sombre pine, whilst the mountains in the background rose up against the blue vault, unsullied by a cloud.

Had it been summer the valley itself would have been rich in beauty, for there were abundance of the olive-tree, the vine, and the glossy-leaved ilex scattered in luxuriance; here the myrtle and arbutus, the date-palm and the cactus, grew in profuse luxuriance amid the ferruginous rocks that bounded the path on one side. A few hamlets were nestled amid the hills; and old crosses and ruins met the sight every hundred yards. But this pretty valley soon changed for a wilder scene, and for nearly a league the party traversed as wild and savage a glen as any in Calabria.

"There, Count De Courcy," said the Calabrese noble, to our hero, "you may hunt the lynx and the wolf, later in the season; and below this, in the valley, you will find the wild buffaloes capital sport."

"It is a wild abode to all appearance, is it not, Signor de Courcy?" asked the Countess de Castagno; "you little expected to behold such a contrast to the beautiful scenery around Napoli, and scarcely three days' journey from the capital."

"It is magnificently wild, indeed, countess," returned our hero; "you have probably become so accustomed to it that you do not feel its desolate aspect."

"It's my native land, count," returned the lady: "I was born and reared here: my father's, the Marquis de Crotono's ancient castle, at least the ruins of it, are not two leagues distant: the terrible earthquake, twenty years ago, totally destroyed it, and greatly changed the face of this part of the country."

"Were you in the country at the time of this terrible visitation?" questioned De Courcy, greatly puzzled at the mystification existing about the identity of the countess and Magdalene Caracci.

"No," returned the lady, quite calmly: "I was in Northern Italy at the time: but see, our scenery changes again—there is Nilocastra."

De Courcy looked round, and perceived that they were approaching the fortress, on its eastern side, through a very well-cultivated and rich valley, scattered over with small hamlets and isolated dwellings: he also perceived that the count had ridden somewhat in advance, and was earnestly conversing with several of the armed mountaineers: amongst them his quick eye recognized the very brigand to whom he had given the gold pieces the previous day.

"We shall be a formidable party, countess, to entertain," observed De Courcy; "I fear we are intruding on your good lord's hospitality."

"Oh, by no means, count," returned the lady, with a smile; "in Calabria, such assemblies, at certain periods, in our mansions, are very frequent, and ten times more numerous. Before the French invasion, our nobles kept almost open houses. One hundred, and often two hundred, guests sat down to table at a hunting party, and that for a week or ten days at a time: the French, in attempting to crush our ancient rights and privileges, have raised against themselves a host more formidable than they anticipated: had they entered the Calabrian territory as rulers, and respected our faith and our customs, they would have been received with open arms; for the rule of the imbecile Ferdinand was disregarded, and his libertine, reckless troops, hated for their irregularity and the excesses committed by the officers."

De Courcy acknowledged there was some truth in this: but he became more and more puzzled respecting the countess, though he fancied he saw a resemblance in her fine features and haughty mien to the Princess of Sorento.

"You know that the Princess of Sorento," observed De Courcy, after a moment's thought, "is one of the most admired ladies of the Neapolitan court. You have not seen her, I suppose, madame."

"No," answered the countess, looking steadily in De Courcy's face, "I never saw her, but I have heard a great deal of her, and lately I have received a very singular letter from her, in which it seems she wished to identify me with a certain impostor called Magdalene Caracci. She spoke so positively of this fact, and implored me so earnestly to confess crimes of which I have no cognizance of, that I lost my temper, and to prevent any more such messengers making their appearance here, and giving rise to such absurd stories, that to frighten the man, I ordered his ears to be cut off. In reality I meant it only as a menace, but it seems the men I ordered to take this fellow out of the teritories discovered him to be a spy and traitor of the French general's—one who had betrayed his country several times, and who, being afraid of the vengeance of his countrymen, had fled to Palermo. In revenge, they really, I understand, cut off his ears."

"Well, madame," remarked our hero, beginning to think that the princess and her informant, the ex-minister of police, were deceived respecting the countess and Magdalene Caracci being one and the same person, "I confess to you, that I came with my friends into this country not for the purposes of hunting, but really to discover, if possible, whether you were—pardon me if I speak candidly—the Countess de Castagno and Magdalene Caracci at the same time."

There was an angry flush over the haughty features of the Countess, and her eyes flashed fire as they met the steady, calm look of Hugh De Courcy; but after a moment she replied, quietly,—"I must know more of all this strange affair, Count De Courcy; my niece was not explicit, and I felt the insult too keenly to look calmly upon the matter. You, Count

De Courcy, are a man whose name has been widely extolled, and your character and conduct, your gallantry and exploits, spoken of even amid the hills of Calabria. The count, my husband, received a letter from the Prince Buttera, recommending you and your friends to his hospitable attention ; there was in this letter a doubt respecting your safety, and a kind of threat held out that, if anything occurred to you, we should repent it. There was no need of this—you are as safe here as in Palermo. Our characters—I mean my husband's and mine —have been cruelly misrepresented, because he bravely asserted my rights to the estates of my father, then unjustly held by King Ferdinand : but here we are, count," and, looking up, our hero perceived they were at the foot of the hill on which stood the fortress.

" You need not fear entering our abode; though, indeed," added the countess, with a smile, " from all I have heard, fear is a sensation you never felt. Some time this evening I will give you a slight sketch of my life ; it may lead you on the right track for discovering this Magdalene Caracci, who was not unknown to me in former years." Thus saying, the countess touched her spirited horse with the whip, and rode up to the side of her husband ; whilst De Courcy, a good deal surprised, and no little curious, joined Sir Charles Wharton and Lieutenant Pamfilé ; and then the whole party began ascending the mount to the castle-gates.

" We are completely out in our conjectures respecting the Countess Castagno and Magdalene Caracci, Sir Charles," said our hero to the baronet.

" Yes," answered Sir Charles, " I strongly suspect we are in a false track after all, for most assuredly this lady is not Magdalene : there is a likeness, and rather a strong one, about the eyes and brow and jet black hair ; but I am satisfied it is a mere chance resemblance : her voice, manner, appearance, and particularly her nose and mouth, are distinctly different. The Countess de Castagno has a very short upper lip and Roman nose, and a haughty expression natural to her style of features. Magdalene's nose was perfectly straight, and her upper lip rather long. She had a slight scar over the left eye—the countess has not the slightest; besides, her figure is much fuller, and more erect and masculine, and the tone of her voice different. Magdalene had a low, sweet voice : she struck me as one sprung from a low grade, but wonderfully improved by admixture with the better class of society. Magdalene's feet were rather large—the countess's, I perceived, are small and well-formed."

" It is all very strange," said De Courcy, musingly : but just then the Count Castagno rode up by his side.

"I have just heard, Count de Courcy," observed the Calabrese noble, "that Rigueaг, the French general, who had
returned from Upper Calabria, has pushed on his forces into
this province.   Now that peace has been signed between
England and France, he is resolved to crush and annihilate
us, and has eight hundred men and a strong body of cavalry
now within three leagues of this castle, whilst a corps of flying
artillery is following, most likely to reduce my stronghold,
which has so often defied them."

"And what do you intend doing against such a force,
count?" questioned De Courcy: "I should have thought the
peace of Amiens guaranteed the crown of the Two Sicilies to
King Ferdinand."

"Before to-morrow morning," said the Count Castagno,
fiercely, "there will be two thousand armed peasants amid
these hills. England has deserted our cause, and left us to
cope with the invaders as best we may; but not a man of
these merciless marauders shall escape:" and striking his
horse fiercely with his spear he forced him up to the front
gates of Nilocastra: in a few minutes the whole cavalcade
entered, and drew up in the wide court before the mansion.

We have before described Nilocastra to be not a fortress
according to the accepted term of the word, but a remarkably
handsome modern mansion in the Neapolitan style of architecture: it had no defence in itself; its strength lay in the
massive lofty walls that surrounded it, and the precipitous
nature of the rocky mount on which it stood, only accessible
by one winding ascent: the walls were flanked by low square
towers, and in embrasures in the wall were planted some very
formidable guns and wall-pieces : the greater gates were protected by two thirty-two-pounders, mounted so as to command
every winding of the road: there was no drawbridge, but the
gates were defended by a portcullis, suspended from the two
square towers, and raised by chains and a ponderous wheel.
Round the immense court before the mansion were numerous
out-offices, evidently for the use of the defenders of the place,
from which numerous domestics came out to take the horses
and receive the party.

The Count Castagno conducted his guests into the principal
hall of the building, occupying nearly the entire breadth of
the mansion, and of lofty proportions. Galleries, supported
on pillars, ran round this hall. A magnificent staircase of
marble led to the upper chambers of the mansion, and two
long and lofty saloons, almost gorgeously furnished, were
entered from the hall : from the pillars of the hall some old
time-honoured banners and armour were suspended, and
against the walls many warlike trophies of the middle ages.

At this period of our narrative we have no space for minute narration; our readers must therefore excuse us if we hurry over the details of the splendid repast prepared, and the choice wines of Calabria and Sicily that graced the board in massive crystal decanters, and poured into elaborately-worked silver goblets, many of great antiquity. A profusion of rich and massive plate decorated the table. During the repast, the count and countess did all they could to render themselves agreeable and courteous : the hauteur of the countess was completely laid aside, and both the baronet, our hero, and his lieutenant, acknowledged that the Countess Castagno was a most charming and agreeable hostess, and as a host the count also, and no way could they account for the strange reports spread to their disadvantage.

In the course of the evening, the countess, seating herself beside our hero in one of the saloons into which they retired after dinner, gave him the following brief outline of her early life, which we lay before our readers in our next chapter.

CHAPTER XLIV

WE omit that part of the countess's history related by the Princess of Sorento, to our hero, and take up the narrative from the period of her flight from Naples with the opera-singer Cambria.

" You have doubtless heard from my niece," continued the Countess, " that I fled at the age of sixteen from Naples with a public singer, named Cambria. Such was the case, but no one but myself knew that Tancred Cambria was the only son and heir of the notorious Count Tancred Castagno, one of the most terrible and ferocious of the Calabrian chieftains, and whose very name was a terror to all dwelling in Calabria Ultra.

" Even to his son and heir, his severity and tyranny were so excessive that he fled his home, when only fourteen, and wandered into Italy   It is needless relating his adventures. His father disinherited him, and left his broad lands to a distant kinsman. Blessed with a vigorous constitution, and a fine voice, young Tancred studied music and singing in Venice, under a celebrated master, who took a fancy to him, and having remarkable talents, he soon excelled. As he grew up, he followed singing as a profession, and acquired fame as the Signor Cambria. At the age of five-and-twenty he came to Naples : his father was dead, and his estates in the hands of a powerful noble

" I knew who the Signor Cambria was before I eloped, but it would only have insured my being shut up in a convent if I had revealed my attachment to my father; and as I was of a peculiar turn of mind myself, and had then a surprising voice and taste for music, we determined to travel over the continent, under the name of Caracci, after we were married. In Vienna we first met with a singer at the grand opera, of the name of Magdalene Caldivini : she was young, beautiful, and fascinating; and a strange likeness to each other, and the same Christian name, first drew us into strong intimacy : she had a slight scar over her left eye ; so had I at that time, but which has since totally disappeared. I soon discovered that though Magdalene Caldivini was a splendid singer, yet that her education was very imperfect. After a time we became so intimate that she told me her history. She confessed she knew nothing of her parents, that she had been reared in the streets of Naples, and that the only relative she ever knew was a brother, and that he was one of the Lazzaroni, by name Antonio Campobello."

An exclamation of surprise escaped De Courcy, which caused the countess to pause. Looking inquiringly at our hero, she said, " Then you know something of this Lazzarone Campobello?"

" Pardon me for interrupting you, countess," replied De Courcy ; " when you have finished your narrative, I will explain the reason of my surprise."

The countess continued :—" Magdalene told me, in speaking of herself, that the master of a strolling company of singers and players, hearing her sing a hymn one evening, before the shrine of a Madonna, tempted her, by bribes and promises, to go with him and his company. She was then but fourteen years old. Though a mere country performer at fêtes and festivals, her master was a clever musician, and took great pains with her ; and having a fine voice, and a taste for music, she improved wonderfully. I need not speak of her after-life ; at this time she was about twenty-one, perhaps less. Our intimacy continued some time. She was extremely pleasing and artful, but full of deception. She contrived to get from me a true account of who and what I was, and who my husband was. We travelled together to several cities in Northern Italy ; but at Milan she formed a connection with a rich Englishman, left the stage, and departed with him from Milan. This is the last I saw of Magdalene Caracci, but not the last I heard of her.

" Years passed over, when the stormy scenes enacting in Italy raised my husband into action, and he resolved to make an effort to recover his own estates and mine. We travelled into Calabria, but on reaching Cosenza we were astounded at hearing that the daughter of the Marquis of Crotono had returned, with her husband, the Count Castagno, to Crotono, and claimed the lands of her father; and that a commissioner was coming from Naples to investigate her claims.

" We hurried on to Cosenza, and declared who we were, to the bishop. But the French forces marched into Calabria, the whole country rose *en masse*, and a fearful war of extermination ensued. My husband declared himself to his father's vassals, and soon assembled round him a formidable force. In the meantime, the impostor Magdalene, and the pretended Count Castagno, fled. The King's commissioner ordered us to appear in Cosenza, but we had him seized and brought here. To make my likeness more forcible, I imitated a slight scar over the left eye; for this commissioner formerly knew me very well, and that I had received a mark over the eye when a girl, from a fall. The doctors said then the scar would always remain; but they were mistaken. The commissioner, I saw, though enraged at being thus treated, remembered me well enough. However, he returned to Naples, and the King gave orders to dispossess us; but we defied his power. My husband then drove out the possessors of his father's estates, and, raising almost an army, defended his possessions from the French invaders, and aided the cause of the King so successfully that his Majesty granted him the lands, and sent him the star of St. Constantine.

" What became of the impostor Magdalene Caracci and the pretended Count Castagno, I cannot say—so fearfully disturbed has this country been. Such, Count De Courcy, is a brief outline of a strange life, if you knew but all; at all events, it ought to satisfy you that I am not the Magdalene you seek. When these troubles cease, I hope yet to see my niece, the Princess of Sorento, and prove to her the falseness of her assertions."

" I pray you, countess, not to attribute to any unkind motive the assertions made by the Princess of Sorento in her letter: when I explain to you how we were induced to consider you to be the Magdalene Caracci we sought, you will cease to be surprised."

Accordingly, De Courcy related his own history, and the tale of Sir Charles Wharton's two nieces, and their connection with Magdalene Caracci.

The Countess Castagno was surprised, but, nevertheless, quite unable to clear up the mystery that enveloped the two nieces of Sir Charles Wharton.

" I suspect," she remarked, "that this lazzarone, Campobello, could throw some light upon this affair. It is, however, very evident, that my Magdalene Caracci and yours are the same person. Who the false Count Castagno could be I have no

x

idea; but it is very evident that the Englishman Magdalene formed a connection within Milan must have been the brother of Sir Charles Wharton "

Finding it perfectly useless to remain longer in Calabria, the following morning our hero and his friends, after a very cordial leave-taking from the Count and Countess of Castagno, left the fortress, and without any accident or adventure reached San Giovanni, and re-embarked for Palermo.

Sir Charles Wharton was now inclined to let things remain as they were; as it seemed quite impossible to trace Magdalene Caracci; and, as no material consequence could result in not clearing up the mystery to either of the two girls—as the baronet's large fortune was completely at his own disposal— he resolved to take no further steps in the matter.

On reaching Palermo they found the city greatly disturbed, and the people alarmed by the riotous conduct of the Conciarotte, and a revolutionary feeling gaining ground amongst the other classes of citizens. So frightened became the pusillanimous Ferdinand, that he left Palermo with his entire court, and proceeded to Messina in the Serena frigate; leaving his capital nearly at the mercy of a lawless and ferocious mob, headed by the chief elders of the Conciarotte. Sir Charles Wharton and our hero proceeded to the residence of his nieces. Lieutenant Pamfili hastened over land to Messina to join his frigate.

Mary's heart beat with a joyous feeling as she beheld her lover safe and well: she and her companions were greatly alarmed at the riots, and had longed for their friends' return. Lord De Umfreville had been unceasing in his attention and watchfulness during their absence. Most of the nobility had followed the court to Messina, but the princess still remained, and declared she would not leave on any account till Sir Charles and our hero returned from Calabria.

Sir Charles declared it was his wish to sail at once for Genoa, and get away from a country so ill governed that a mere rabble awed the court and government. Sir John Acton and family were with the King.

De Courcy was by no means sorry to hear of Sir Charles's determination to leave: he promised that the Dauntless should be ready for sea in two days: and having paid a visit to his friend, Lord De Umfreville, at his hotel, related to him the result of their visit to Calabria, and settling concerning their departure, he proceeded to the villa of the Princess of Sorento.

Clarina De Obruzza's pale cheek flushed as De Courcy entered the saloon, where she was seated at a window, gazing out listlessly upon the bright sparkling waters of the bay that lay before Palermo the Happy. She started up as she heard his step, for her thoughts were even at that moment centred upon him. Alas! the princess, with all her power of mind, could not conquer the feelings of her heart—De Courcy still occupied his place there : she could not banish his image, sleeping or waking : still she struggled with all her woman's heart, and strove only to consult his happiness, and secure for him the woman he loved.

Conquering her emotion, she held out her beautiful hand with a smile of welcome, saying, "You have returned, count, sooner than I expected; but where the heart is," she added, trying to speak cheerfully, "the body must be also."

"We had nothing, princess, to detain us a day longer," replied our hero : "we completely failed in gaining any solution of the mystery we sought to clear up : this Magdalene Caracci is still unfound,

"Madonna! you astonish me," cried the princess ; "how is that—is not my aunt the Magdalene Caracci you sought?"

"No, in truth, princess, and you will be surprised when I tell you all."

He then gave the princess a full account of their journey, and their interview with the Countess De Castagno.

"You amaze me," said Clarina, as De Courcy finished, "and yet I rejoice that my aunt, though her career has been a strange and varied one, was not capable of such wickedness as this Magdalene Caracci, who turns out to be, after all, the sister of this terrible villain, Campobello, now one of the worst leaders of the Conciarotte."

"Is that true?" exclaimed De Courcy, greatly astonished ; "it may then be possible yet to seize this ruffian : but how is it, princess, that the king has left his capital to the mercy of a few lawless rioters? Surely it is not by Sir John's advice?"

"Most certainly not," replied the princess ; "he strongly advised the king to warp the Serena frigate into the harbour, with her guns pointing towards the tanners' quarters ; to surround their abodes with the Queen's Italian Guards and the two regiments of St. Eufemio, arrest all the ringleaders, and make a terrible example of them; and, finally, destroy their murderous den, which so long has been a festering sore to Palermo. But the king, as usual, followed his weak, pusillanimous nature, and ran away from a danger instead of meeting it ; and now, Palermo is left with a weak, timid garrison, a rather mutinous population, and a licentious, formidable rabble, only waiting till their audacity has gained sufficient impetus to fill our beautiful city with riot and bloodshed."

"I fear, in that case, princess, it is not safe for you to remain any longer here. Why should you expose yourself to the risk others have fled from?"

"I wished to await your arrival," returned the princess, "and I did not like to leave your fair friends, who seem greatly frightened; but I now think our best plan will be to proceed to-morrow to Ventumara, about eighteen miles from Palermo. I possess a very charming country residence there, in which we can remain till your ship is ready for sea, for I assure you there is terrible evidence of the intentions of the rioters."

De Courcy agreed with the princess, and said he would at once speak to Sir Charles, who was himself very uneasy.

"Well then, count, let us all meet here this evening, and arrange the plan for our departure to-morrow. I confess I am not easy in my mind; these terrible Conciarotte commit such fearful acts when roused into sedition."

After some further conversation with the princess, and promising to bring Lord De Umfreville, who was a great favourite, in the evening, our hero departed, and proceeded into the city to see some of the officers of the regiments of St. Eufemio, whom he knew.

As he entered by one of the beautiful gates that led through a remarkably handsome street into the great square, called the Ottangolo, he observed great crowds of people conversing in a most excited manner. Numbers were coming out of the numerous churches; round the chapel dedicated to their favourite and patron, Saint Rosalia, a body of infantry were assembled. This chapel is extremely rich, and forms one of the many in the Cathedral. Here are deposited the relics of the saints, preserved in a large box of silver, enriched with precious stones.

De Courcy spoke to the officer on guard, who said the people were in a most excited state; that he had orders to keep guard, but not to leave his post or interfere.

"This is very extraordinary," observed our hero; "surely, even now, there are military sufficient to restore order."

"We expect two regiments from Messina to-morrow," replied the Neapolitan officer, "and two from Syracuse, which ought to be here by this time, for they were to be embarked in two gun-boats the day before yesterday, and the wind is fair. Several of the nobility are leaving the city now, retiring to the country till these riots are quelled."

"I cannot understand all this," thought De Courcy, as he pushed on through the crowded streets, on his way to the mole, and, taking a boat, went on board the Dauntless, now quite ready for sea, excepting provisions and a few trifling necessaries. He had shipped about thirty active seamen and two officers—one a Neapolitan, who had served a long time with him in the Vesuvius, and who was very desirous to accompany our hero to England: the other was a retired master, formerly in the British service, a man who in the prime of life had lost an arm, and, like many another, lay by neglected. He had come out as captain of a fine merchant ship, which the owners, for some reason or other, had sold to the Neapolitan government for a transport.

De Courcy ordered the Dauntless to be ready, in case of an emergency, to put to sea at a moment's warning : he therefore wished her to be warped to a certain spot, which he pointed out, and also desired that her two boats, with an armed crew in each, should keep within hail of the mole all night, as affairs looked alarming in the city. Having made his arrangements, desiring to be prepared, our hero returned on shore, visited and spoke to several officers of the two regiments of St. Eufemio, and to the commander of the sbirri ; which latter officer really appeared alarmed. he, accompanied by Lord De Umfreville, proceeded to the villa of the princess.

CHAPTER XLV

THE party assembled in the Villa Obruzza on the memorable night of the 17th November, consisted of the princess, Sir Charles Wharton's family, Lord de Umfreville, and Hugh De Courcy. They were about to sit down to a light, elegant supper, which the princess made a constant habit of doing about ten o'clock, when the loud report of a cannon from one of the castles commanding the harbour, startled the females of the party. Mary Wharton turned deadly pale, and clung, with a strange feeling of terrible alarm, to our hero's arm. None of the others, though they started, felt the same alarm.

"You tremble, Mary," said De Courcy, in a low voice, " why do you give way to such fear ?"

"I cannot say," replied Mary, with a sigh, " but I have felt a terrible depression ever since your departure into Calabria, and which has not decreased even now that you are with me."

Whilst yet she spoke, the sound of the alarm bells from many of the churches came full and distinct upon the ear.

" The Conciarotte are evidently abroad to-night," remarked the princess, speaking calmly. "Go, Antonio," turning to one of the startled domestics, " and discover what has caused this disturbance."

De Courcy's first impulse was to go himself and see the cause of the ringing of the bells and the firing of the cannon ; but all implored him and the other gentlemen not to leave them. "At all events," observed our hero, " let us be prepared, in case any of the stragglers should think of visiting the Obruzza."

By this time, those in the saloon had proceeded to the windows, which opened out on a beautiful balcony, over which was a handsome trellis-work, all covered with parasite plants of rare growth, and resplendent in bloom, even in the depth of winter. The Obruzza is a suburb of Palermo, and one of the most lovely spots in the Val-di-Mazara. The windows of the villa faced the bay, and standing out on the balcony, a clear view of Palermo, in the day-time, was obtainable.

As the princess stepped out on the balcony, accompanied by all in the saloon, several rockets shot up into the air, and then followed the loud boom of cannon.

" These rockets proceed from some ship near the mole, and the guns also," exclaimed De Courcy.

As he spoke, a bright fierce flame shot up into the sky, over the square of the Ottangolo ; then were heard peals of musketry, and the furious shouts and cries of an excited mob.

" This is serious," observed De Courcy, to the princess ; " I would advise, whilst there is yet time, that you and all the females retire for the night to the village of Pola ; there the rioters will not go. We will stay, and, with your armed domes- tics, guard the villa."

" I care nothing for the villa, in comparison to our own in- dividual safety. If you will all accompany me, I will at once order my horses and carriages. You could do nothing save sacrifice your life, count, by remaining, should the Concia- rotte attack the villa of the Obruzza."

" Oh, dear Hugh, do not dream of staying here," whispered Mary ; " what could you do against a mob ? "

It was too late : a tremendous shout rent the air, and the blaze of a hundred torches threw a wild glare over a terrible multitude of ruffians, who came rushing down the broad road uttering the wildest cries, and tossing their torches in the air, and shouting, "Down with the dastard nobles and their villas ;" and many other such exclamations.

Closing the windows, the terrified females retreated into the saloon, whilst De Courcy and Lord De Umfreville rushed out, to collect the frightened domestics. There were eight or ten male servants belonging to the villa, and in one wing of the mansion was a chamber, set apart by the late prince, as a kind of armoury : it was full of splendid arms, which were always kept in great order, by the especial wish and command of the princess.

" Close the great iron gates," said De Courcy, to the butler ; " collect all the men, and follow me to the armoury."

Several of the domestics were stout, hearty fellows, and devoted to the princess ; they ran and bolted and barred the gates, whilst the rioters were plundering and burning the adjacent villa, belonging to the Marquis de Montecelle, who was at Messina with the king, the domestics of which had escaped by the back door; and in ten minutes the ferocious mob were plundering and smashing costly mirrors, rare vases, statues, and pictures, each a gem, and not to be purchased for gold.

In a short time, De Courcy, Lord Edward, and all the domestics, were armed with carbines, pistols, and swords, of which there were an abundance. It was De Courcy's wish that the princess and the rest of the females should attempt to retreat through the extensive gardens at the back, and from thence into the country; but as he was proceeding to solicit them to take that step, the villa of the Marquis de Montecelle burst into a blaze, the flames shooting out in forked wreaths, and catching the trellis-work of the beautiful balconies, the whole became a sheet of flames. During this time a tremendous uproar raged in the city; peals of musketry followed in rapid succession, which shewed that the troops were, at all events, this time engaged with the Conciarotte. The gardens of the princess became, like magic, filled with a ferocious rabble, whilst an equally furious mob were assaulting the gates in front.

"Great God! De Courcy," said Lord Edward, "the women will be sacrificed."

"Make good the house," exclaimed De Courcy, in an agitated voice, but in a collected manner: "bar the doors, my men, and from the upper balconies we can pour down a steady fire upon those ruffians: they have no fire-arms, I think—only their long knives and pikes."

With a fierce shout, the mob at the back, above five hundred in number, made a rush at the doors, whilst those in the front were kept back by the great iron gates and high walls surrounding the villa. A discharge of ten carbines was poured down on the mob, killing several, and wounding others, only increasing their fury, whilst their yells and execrations were appalling. Still the doors resisted, and repeated volleys from De Courcy's stout followers began to awe the rioters, who were trampling on their own dead.

"Dash your torches through the upper windows," shouted a voice from the crowd, that made De Courcy start: it was as light as day from the flames of the adjoining villa; and pushing through the mob, he beheld a powerful man with a dozen others carrying a massive beam of timber to force the doors— it was Campobello, the Lazzarone. A loud roar from the front struck a chill to the hearts of the defenders of the villa, for it proved that the rioters had torn down the gates, and were advancing to the front door.

The princess and Sir Charles, with his nieces, pale as
death, clinging to each other, came hastily from the saloon ;
the terrified female domestics of the villa rushing here and
there in the wildest confusion.

The Princess of Sorento, though pale as death, was firm
and collected. She laid her hand on De Courcy's arm, as he
was levelling his carbine at Campobello : it was, alas ! a fatal
interruption—for De Courcy paused—" We will seek the
vaults," said the princess, " they are fire-proof ; you may be
able to defend the entrance till help, which is near, comes."

The idea was a good one ; but just as they were preparing
to descend the stairs, the doors at the back gave way with a
thundering crash ; and, with a hideous roar of triumph, in
rushed the Conciarotte, with Campobello at their head.

" Ah ! maladetta Inglese ! " shouted the ruffian, with a
terrific imprecation ; " my time is come—vengeance ! "

" Wretch ! " exclaimed De Courcy, " your time is come : "
and he levelled a pistol at the advancing lazzarone. Just as
he pulled the trigger, a long knife, hurled at him by one of
the gang, stuck in his arm, and altered his aim. The trigger
was pulled nevertheless ; but Campobello, despite the discharge of Lord Edward's pistols and the carbines of the
domestics, which all found victims amid the struggling mass
wedged between the walls, still advanced, and, drawing a
pistol from his belt, levelled it at De Courcy, who was beating
back with his sabre the ruffians who had climbed the iron balus-
trade. With a shriek, the devoted Clarina de Obruzza, who
saw the aim of the lazzarone, threw herself forward in front
of our hero, and received the ball in her priceless heart. For
an instant her eyes rested on De Courcy : that look was never
forgotten, through a long life : the same instant the princess
lay dead in his arms.

" Oh, God ! " exclaimed De Courcy, the blood rushing to
his temples with the fury and agony he felt. Resigning the
body to the horrified Lord Edward, Hugh De Courcy became
like an infuriated madman, cutting down all before him. He
reached Campobello. In vain the villain again fired another
pistol ; in vain were poignards, pikes, and knives thrust at
him. Bleeding profusely, but heedless, or not feeling his
wounds, with a blow of his sabre, a heavy dragoon weapon,
De Courcy clove the skull of Campobello to the chin. As
the brute fell, headlong, others replaced him ; but De Courcy
fought like a madman, and, struck with terror at his superhuman strength, the Conciarotte fell back, and the multitude,
wedged in the narrow pass, could barely act.

Lord De Umfreville and four of the domestics gallantly
followed : several Conciarotte lay dead upon the stairs ; when

the rush of a body of King Ferdinand's troops through the front door, led by an officer our hero knew, turned the scale, and then a terrible massacre of the Conciarotte ensued, the hall and passages being strewed with the dead and dying.

Driven from the villa, the insurgents still rallied in the gardens; but De Courcy, who seemed to have no other thought but to slay, still pursued them, aided by a body of the regiment of St. Eufemio. Repeated volleys of musketry stretched numbers on the flower-beds and parterres, while De Courcy's sabre brought down its victims at every blow, till at last, with a howl of rage, they fled in every direction.

The flames of the marquis's villa still lighted up the frightful scene; on every side lay the dying and the dead, and the severely wounded. Several soldiers were grievously hurt, four quite dead, with thrusts from knives.

At length De Courcy paused in the pursuit, and leant on his sword. He was alone, at the extremity of the garden: a heap of dead lay at his feet: the soldiers had passed on, still in pursuit, bayonetting and shooting every wretch that came in their way. The horrors committed that night equalled in atrocity those of the year 1820.

Hugh De Courcy felt as if he were dying. He had received numerous stabs all over his body; the blade of a knife was broken in his arm, and a gash across the right temple covered his face with streams of blood. For a moment he stood bewildered; the trees and plants seemed to swim before his sight, and the ground to reel under him; the dead—their grim, distorted faces, upon which the red glare of the flames played, seemed to mock him; and still he thought of but one object, and that was Clarina De Obruzza, and the last look of undying love that had glanced from her eyes as life faded away for ever.

With a groan of agony, De Courcy tried to stagger back to the villa; but his weakness, from loss of blood, overpowered him. Suddenly he felt himself grasped by the leg and pulled to the ground: he was in the grasp of a dying Conciarotte, one who had fallen by a blow from his own hand.

"Ah, holy Rosalia!" muttered the dying man, "revenge is sweet:" and his grasp was on De Courcy's throat. Our hero was powerless; he was fast relapsing into insensibility; his eyes were closing. The dying wretch had no power but with his hands. "Ah! maladetta, my knife!" he muttered; "but he's dying too: oh, Santa Rosalia! for only one stab." Groping about, he seized a comrade's knife, and rolled over to plunge it into De Courcy's throat; the point of the blade was even touching the skin, when death claimed its victim. The

grasp on the knife relaxed, and, with a half-breathed imprecation, the Conciarotte fell over his intended victim a corpse.

Whilst De Courcy was pursuing the Conciarotte with the
King's troops, a scene of indescribable agony and lamentation
took place in the villa of the unfortunate Princess of Sorento.
Mary Wharton, who, with the Princess of Sorento, had recognized the villain Campobello, and saw the muzzle of his
pistol within a yard or so of the breast of her lover, had also
started forward with a wild cry of anguish, but Térese Garetti
threw her arms round her and held her back ; but when the
princess, who was considerably nearer, received the fatal ball,
Mary rushed to her side and clasped her inanimate body in
her arms, with feelings of anguish perfectly indescribable.
Even De Courcy's perilous situation and his fierce pursuit of
the Conciarotte were forgotten, as, with clasped hands, and
eyes filled with tears, she gazed on that lovely face, which,
even in death, retained its exquisite beauty.

"My God ! my God !" murmured Mary ; "and is it thus
we part ?" and, bending her head on the body of the princess,
she sobbed as if her heart would break. Térese and Elizabeth, appalled and horrified, could say or do but little to
assuage Mary's grief, who knew that the undying love of the
princess had caused her to throw away her life, either to save
De Courcy or to perish with him ; and her first thoughts were
"Oh, that he had never seen me : that his love might have
been hers ; and, oh ! how different would have been her
fate !"

The female domestics of the princess were distracted, and
wrung their hands, and lamented in loud tones her cruel fate.
Poor Sir Charles Wharton was quite overcome, and almost
stupified.

After the princess's body had been carried into her own
chamber, Lord De Umfreville prepared to follow in the footsteps of De Courcy. He was unhurt, and only two of the
domestics had received severe wounds.

The staircase, and the hall, and the gardens, were strewed
with the dead and dying, and the steps and floor slippery with
blood.

Mary turned to Lord Edward ; she scarcely could gather
strength to speak, what with intense grief at the death of the
princess and the horrors of the night. Her voice trembled
as she said, " Permit me to accompany you, my lord ; I fear,
in my heart, Hugh is lying wounded—perhaps," she shuddered,
" dead—somewhere in the gardens ; for he was covered with
blood when he rushed down the stairs. Oh ! the horrors of
this night will never, never be forgotten."

" No, I think not," replied his lordship, sadly ; " but stay,

I pray you, where you are; you can be of no service; and, most probably, in the fury that animated him at the sight of the prineess's death, he has followed or led the troops into the eity."

" Suspense is worse than death, my lord."

" Where would you go, my child?" asked Sir Charles, taking her hand; she looked imploringly in the baronet's faee, but the words failed her.

" I will accompany you, Mary," observed Sir Charles; and all three, preeeded by two of the domesties with torches, de-seended the stairs.

Mary eovered her person and head with a mantle, and, leaning on the baronet's arm, passed shuddering through the passage strewed with the dead. At the foot of the stairease lay the powerful body of Campobello, his head nearly divided by the terrible blow of De Courcy's sword: he was a ghastly sight, and the poor girl shook all over, as if in an ague, but still her eyes eagerly scanned all round, and examined every body : the door, drawn from its hinges and bolts, lay pros-trate, and on it two more of the fierce Conciarotte, one still alive, but life ebbing fast. A smothered malediction eseaped his lips as they passed, and, shaking his clenched hand, he fell back writhing on the ground.

" Oh, my God!" murmured Mary, " he may be lying, like this miserable wreteh, bleeding to death."

" Do not eonjure up horrible faneies, my child," entreated the baronet, as they emerged into the garden, late so trim and beautiful, now trampled and torn to pieees ; costly vases demolished, statues overturned, and beds of winter flowers the resting-place of the dead. It was easy to traee the path along whieh the Coneiarotte had fled, though they spread over the garden in every direction to escape the fire of the infantry.

Thus they passed on ; possibly would have missed the body of De Courey, for the eorpse of the Conciarotte lay over him, had not the light of the toreh flashed upon his sword, lying near. With a ery of anguish, Mary darted forward and threw herself in despair by the bodies. She thought her lover dead, for he lay perfectly motionless. With elasped hands, she remained, as if turned into a statue, on her knees; she had no power to utter a word or to move; agony seemed to have paralysed her. Lord De Umfreville and the baronet, equally shoeked, drew off ths body of the Coneiarotte, and, as the former plaeed his hand on De Courcy's breast, he ex-elaimed, joyfully,—

" Thank God, he lives! he has only fainted from loss of blood."

Mary heard the words; she bent her head, and covering her face with her hands, sobbed as if her heart would break. The terrors of the night, the shocks she had received, were too much for her, she became quite hysterical.

Assistance was soon procured, and De Courcy conveyed at once to the baronet's residence, which was close by the princesss's villa, whilst Lord De Umfreville himself insisted upon proceeding to Palermo to seek a surgeon.

CHAPTER XLVI.

WE pass over a space of nearly seven months from the eventful night of the seventeenth of November, long remembered by the people of Palermo with fear and dread; and terrible as the calamity was, it led to no good result; for though several of the nobility were massacred in their mansions, their houses plundered, and many burnt, whilst hundreds of the lower orders on one side or the other, perished, yet, no steps were taken by the government to prevent a recurrence of the like atrocities, till the never-to-be-forgotten rising of the Conciarotte in 1820, when the fearful enormities they committed, and the death of several of the highest nobility, with the destruction of several streets, and even churches, roused the dormant wrath of the king, and the tanners were finally crushed, and their dens destroyed and burnt down.

Had not the gun-boats fortunately arrived in the midst of the riot, and landed the two regiments from Syracuse, with a body of the Queen's Guards, the night of the seventeenth of November might have exceeded in horrors that of 1820.

It was the latter end of May: Palermo the Happy, as the Italians styled their beloved city, was blessed again with the presence of royalty: the Val-di-Mazara never looked more lovely. A light breeze from the north curled the waters of its bay, covered with a countless number of ships and craft of all sizes; the bright sun shone on their ample canvas; the heavy trader, the gay frigate, the light felucca, with its lofty triangular sails, the speronare, and even the scampa-via, still floated and voyaged on the Neapolitan waters.

A remarkably beautiful rigged yacht, of three hundred tons, had just weighed anchor, and spreading her snow-white sails to the gentle breeze blowing, stood out from the roadstead, and shaped her course seaward. The flag of old England was waving from her peak, but no pendant fluttered in the breeze from her lofty mast-head. Catching the breeze, she glided gracefully and swiftly from the shores of Sicily. As she passed the royal frigate, the Serena, from whose standard

floated the winged horse of Napoli, the yards were manned by
the entire crew, and cheer after cheer pealed over the tranquil
waters; her officers on the quarter-deck waving their hats to
those who stood upon the after-deck of the yacht, Dauntless.
Hats and scarfs were waved in adieu, and then a salute from
the frigate's guns pealed over the waters—a farewell salute to
a loved commander, who had so often brought his crew vic-
torious out of many an unequal fight. The guns of the Dauntless returned the salute, and then all became still.

De Courcy stood upon the deck of the Dauntless, gazing
with a serious, troubled look, and a heart filled with emotion,
at] the graceful Serena : and then, as he turned and let his
glance rest upon the lovely suburb of Obruzza, his eyes became
moistened with tears. He looked exceedingly pale and worn,
for he had but just recovered from a violent, and, for a long
time, dubious struggle with the grim enemy of mankind. He
looked sad, in truth, though fair and loving Mary Wharton
stood by his side, anxiously watching every change in his
features. She herself shed tears for the memory of Clarina s
devotion, and her untimely, cruel death, pressed heavily on
her heart; it took long months, nay years, to soften the remem-
brances of that hour.

The death of the generous, talented, and beautiful Princess
of Sorento created a sensation of horror, not only in Palermo,
but at the Neapolitan court, then at Messina. Though one or
two nobles, and several gentlemen of distinction, with their
wives and families, were mercilessly butchered that night by
the miscreants, the Conciarotte, still nothing was talked of but
the death of the princess, and the hopeless state of the Count
De Courcy.

The princess was buried with almost regal pomp in the
cathedral church of Palermo. The people could scarcely have
mourned more for King Ferdinand, for the princess's charity
and noble generosity were not to be surpassed ; her wealth was
distributed to the unfortunate with princely liberality. Miss
Wharton and all the English in Palermo attended her remains
to their last resting-place, and for days and weeks afterwards
Mary remained inconsolable ; for at the same time her heart was
throbbing with deep anxiety for her lover, who was then lying,
as it was thought, in a hopeless state. After weeks of suffering, he was at length pronounced out of danger; and at the
expiration of two months could take gentle exercise in the
gardens of the villa. To the devoted and untiring care of
Mary he owed his life.

Clarina Obruzza's death weighed heavily on his heart ; for
to save him she had thrown away her precious life : sleeping
or waking, her dying look of love and devotion haunted his

mind and thoughts. But, to patient, loving Mary, he turned for consolation ; and, in her pure and devoted love, in time regained his former health and energy.

At length the family of Sir Charles Wharton prepared to return to England. De Courcy first proceeded to Messina, and had a very gracious reception from King Ferdinand and his Queen. They both expressed their deep regret at the unfortunate fate of the Princess de Sorento. The royal pair could easily perceive that our hero had suffered much, and that the event preyed deeply upon his mind. The King then bestowed upon him the order and star of St. Constantine ; he then kissed their majesties' hands, and bade them farewell.

With his kind-hearted protector, Sir John Acton, he had a long and interesting interview. The minister of Queen Caroline presented him with several important letters and documents relative to his birth : some of the letters were in his father's own handwriting. Sir John and his lady bade our hero farewell with much emotion, and De Courcy himself felt the parting exceedingly, but promised to return at some future time to visit a country that would ever be dear from memories of the past.

Having nothing further to detain them in Sicily, the whole party, as described in the beginning of this chapter, embarked on board the Dauntless yacht, and shaped their course for Genoa. The family of the Signor Garetti received them with open arms, and for several days the bitter memories of recent events were softened by the pleasure of again meeting those dear friends.

One evening, the Signor Garetti said to Sir Charles Wharton, " I have important news, my dear friend, to communicate to you : the mystery is solved at last."

" How so?" returned the baronet. slightly agitated, " have you learned anything of Magdalene Caracci?"

" Yes," returned the Signor Garetti, " the mystery is solved. Mary is positively your own child."

" God be praised!" exclaimed Sir Charles, with energy ; " you cannot, dear friend, conceive the rapture and delight this intelligence gives me. To Mary this news will be great happiness ; for although she appeared contented with the love I had for her, whether as father or uncle, still her heart longed for the truth ; but how, in the name of wonder, have you ascertained this most ardently-desired intelligence?"

" From the lips of the ill-starred Magdalene Caracci, as we call her. She actually died about two months ago in this city : I visited her in her last moments, and had a document drawn up and witnessed by two gentlemen of my acquaintance."

" Well," returned the baronet, very seriously, " so Magdalene is dead. She has caused much sorrow, some misery, and much doubt; but peace to her ashes!—what caused her death, dear friend?"

"A broken heart, I should say," replied the Signor Garetti: "deserted, robbed, and abused by her husband, for she was married, and to a worthless, vagabond adventurer. When she sent for me, I was amazed : I found her dying, and without the common necessaries of life. I need not tell you I did all I could to alleviate her sufferings, and render her last moments less painful. She willingly communicated to me all the facts relative to the abduction of your daughter, and also of your brother's child. It appears that your brother Edward was a man of the most extravagant habits and profuse expenditure ; he dissipated all his resources. In his intercourse with the equally extravagant Magdalene Caracci, he was driven to commit many disgraceful acts. Finding that a disclosure must soon take place—for he forged his brother's name to some bills and bonds—Magdalene planned the scheme to steal the child and place her own little girl in its place, when the time should come to do so. Having possession of the child, they imagined that they would have a certain power over you, when your brother's delinquencies became known to you. The plan was carried out by Magdalene with admirable but wicked dexterity.

"The fatal illness of Edward, and your sudden appearance at the villa at Como, upset all their plans, and forced her to decamp in the night. Making her way to Milan, she drew the large sum of money lodged in the bank in her own name, for Edward was completely her slave ; her power over him was extraordinary : then taking the child, she travelled, under false names into the Neapolitan kingdom. Fickle and wavering, devoted to a life of pleasure, Magdalene, when in Naples, placed the poor child with her brother Campobello the Lazzarone, giving him a sum of money to take it off her hands, but still not to lose sight of it, for the child might yet be valuable. Some time afterwards, she, whilst in Florence, formed a connection with a Neapolitan noble, handsome, needy, and profligate. Magdalene's fascinations persuaded him to marry her: they rambled through various countries, and finally the daring idea of personating the Count Crotono, whose history she was well acquainted with, and to whom she is said to bear a strong resemblance. Travelling into Calabria as the Count and Countess of Castagno, they had the audacity to take posesssion of the résidence and estates of the count, being aided by a band of brigands in their pay, the troubled state of the country, and her chance resemblance to the well-remembered daughter of the old Baron Crotono. But the unexpected appearance of the real count and countess drove the usurpers to abandon their false position.

" It is unnecessary to give you any further details of Magdalene's life : for a few years she passed a precarious existence; her husband, it seems, treated her barbarously, and finally was killed in a gambling-house in Pisa. Remorse and misery followed, and then, broken-hearted, and in a deep decline, she came to Genoa, and died."

" In truth a sad history," obesrved Sir Charles ; " but we have to thank a merciful Providence so little evil has resulted from her terrible machinations."

During the stay of the party in Genoa, the young Marchese Caracioli arrived from Napoli to claim the hand of the fair Térese Garetti, and a time was fixed for their union.

Our hero naturally inquired after the Count De Spinola, and was informed that he was alive and well, leading a wild and dissipated life in Florence.

We need not describe the parting of our hero and heroine, and Sir Charles, from the amiable family of Garetti: there were deep regrets on both sides; but promises of future intercourse softened the separation.

The Dauntless sailed for England, where she arrived, after a very pleasant voyage, remaining for a few days at Cadiz. Twelve months after their arrival in England, De Courcy, then Lord De Umfreville, received the hand of his beautiful betrothed. At the same time Edward De Umfreville became the husband of the gentle and affectionate Elizabeth Wharton, and three years afterwards succeeded to the title of his cousin, Lord Eglin, who fell in a duel with a brother officer.

THE END.